THE HANDBOOK
OF LARGE GROUP
METHODS

THE HANDBOOK OF LARGE GROUP METHODS

Creating Systemic Change in Organizations and Communities

Barbara Benedict Bunker
Billie T. Alban

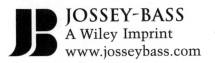

JOSSEY-BASS
A Wiley Imprint
www.josseybass.com

Published by Jossey-Bass
A Wiley Imprint
989 Market Street, San Francisco, CA 94103-1741   www.josseybass.com

AAdvantage® is a registered trademark of American Airlines. Conference Model® is a registered trademark of The Axelrod Group. Microsoft Visio® is a registered trademark of Microsoft, Inc. MindGenius® is a registered trademark of Gael Ltd., Scotland. Prozac® is a registered trademark of Eli Lilly and Company. 21st Century Town Meeting® is a registered trademark of America*Speaks*.

Limit of Liability/Disclaimer of Warranty: While the publisher and author have used their best efforts in preparing this book, they make no representations or warranties with respect to the accuracy or completeness of the contents of this book and specifically disclaim any implied warranties of merchantability or fitness for a particular purpose. No warranty may be created or extended by sales representatives or written sales materials. The advice and strategies contained herein may not be suitable for your situation. You should consult with a professional where appropriate. Neither the publisher nor author shall be liable for any loss of profit or any other commercial damages, including but not limited to special, incidental, consequential, or other damages.

Readers should be aware that Internet Web sites offered as citations and/or sources for further information may have changed or disappeared between the time this was written and when it is read.

Jossey-Bass books and products are available through most bookstores. To contact Jossey-Bass directly call our Customer Care Department within the U.S. at 800-956-7739, outside the U.S. at 317-572-3986, or fax 317-572-4002.

Jossey-Bass also publishes its books in a variety of electronic formats. Some content that appears in print may not be available in electronic books.

Library of Congress Cataloging-in-Publication Data

Bunker, Barbara Benedict.
    The handbook of large group methods: creating systemic change in organizations and communities / Barbara Benedict Bunker, Billie T. Alban.
        p. cm.-(The Jossey-Bass business & management series)
    Includes bibliographical references and index.
    ISBN-13: 978-0-7879-8143-3 (cloth)
    ISBN-10: 0-7879-8143-5 (cloth)
    1. Organizational change—Management. 2. Community organization—Management.
I. Alban, Billie, T., date. II. Title. III. Series.
    HD58.8.B857   2006
    658.4'06-dc22   2006012331

Printed in the United States of America
FIRST EDITION
HB Printing   10 9 8 7 6 5 4 3 2

CONTENTS

3 Organizations in Crisis 78

4 Working in Polarized and Politicized Environments 139

5 Working in Communities with Diverse Interest Groups 199

6 Working Cross-Culturally 246

For
Douglas R. Bunker
and for
Lynn Alban Shea and Margarita Alban

PREFACE

We believe in using stories to communicate and to enhance remembering. In our first book on the topic of Large Group Methods—*Large Group Interventions* (Bunker and Alban, 1997)—we frequently used stories from our own and others' experiences to enhance our explanations of the twelve Large Group Methods we were presenting for the first time. Many readers told us how much they enjoyed and were helped by these descriptions of real situations in search of a solution.

In this book—*The Handbook of Large Group Methods*—we answer the following questions:

- What has happened since we first created a framework for these methods?
- For what and how are they being used now?
- Have new methods emerged?
- Are the methods being changed or adapted?

We have organized this book around six challenges that organizations and communities are confronting as we move through the first decade of the 21st century. Each challenge is unique and makes special demands on the organization or community that experiences it. In each chapter, we have gathered cases that show how the challenge was responded to in a particular situation using Large Group Methods. These cases really are great stories, and we hope you enjoy reading them as much as we have enjoyed working with these authors and finding out about their work.

Here are some examples of the important issues that are addressed in the cases:

- What can a company facing bankruptcy do to engage everyone in redressing the situation?
- How does a metropolitan region composed of many interest groups develop and agree on a plan for their future?
- Can parents and their teenage children talk about often undiscussable topics like drugs, AIDS, and sex?
- How does a worldwide NGO really involve all their employees in many countries in planning the next ten years?
- Can the FAA reduce gridlock in our airways by bringing together all the stakeholder groups affected?
- How do you merge two very competitive organizations into one productive organization?

These are a few of the challenges that the cases present—but with an added benefit. We asked each author to tell the story but to end by telling us what they have learned from this experience about using Large Group Methods. These reflections will be invaluable to business and community leaders, as well as to practitioners who need to consider what methods to use or how to adapt methods to a particular situation.

Quite a bit goes on in each case. So even though we have placed a particular case in one section and under one challenge, there may be issues of special interest in cases across the various sections. To provide an easy guide for where to look, we created the section titled "The Matrix," which follows Chapter One. There we list all the contributions in the book and tell you what topics you can expect to find in each. For example, there is an article on the use of technologies (IT) in large group events in Chapter Eight, but technology is also used in interesting ways in some of the cases. For that reason, "IT Use" is a category in The Matrix, and if you want to know all the places in the book where there may be information about their use, you would consult that column of The Matrix. The same is true for the different methods like Future Search, Appreciative Inquiry, or Open Space. Cross-cultural issues are discussed in other cases, as well as the ones in the cross-cultural chapter, so The Matrix will help you locate all the pertinent data. We hope that if you have specific needs, you will find this way of referencing topics useful.

Why We Wrote This Book

We are chroniclers of the development and spread of Large Group Methods. This book documents new developments since we first described and compared twelve Large Group Methods in 1997. By 2004, we were hearing all kinds of interesting reports on the uses of Large Group Methods in communities, as well as in business, health care, and educational organizations; reports came from North America and Europe, as well as from Africa, Asia, and Central and South America.

We wanted to know more, but our networks were finite. We proposed a special issue of *The Journal of Applied Behavioral Science* (JABS) on Large Group Methods (March 2005) that we agreed to edit because that meant we could send out a "call for papers" through professional associations, as well as practitioner networks. Was as much going on as our personal contacts led us to believe? We waited with interest for the response. When the deadline for submissions came, we were excited to find that we had many more articles of good quality than there was space to publish. This confirmed our intuition that a great deal of interesting work was going on. When the JABS special issue was published, we began hearing about other exciting work and asking people to write it up. As we talked with these colleagues, we began to understand that they were using Large Group Methods to engage very significant challenges in extraordinarily imaginative ways in our society!

How This Book Is Organized

We decided to organize this book around some of the important challenges that organizations and communities face in the 21st century. More and more of our own consulting work is shaped by what our clients need to do. Why not see if we could show how these methods are being used to meet particular challenges? In each of the following chapters, we describe a challenge, then several innovative solutions that involve the use of Large Group Methods.

> *Chapter Two:* To involve all employees in important decisions in large global organizations
>
> *Chapter Three:* To enlist everyone in meeting an organizational crisis
>
> *Chapter Four:* To find areas of agreement in highly conflicted and polarized situations
>
> *Chapter Five:* To bring together diverse interest groups in the community to work toward a common goal
>
> *Chapter Six:* To work cross-culturally in organizations and communities
>
> *Chapter Seven:* To embed new and more effective ways of working in organizations and communities

In each chapter, we set the scene from our own perspective, highlighting the contributions of the cases that follow but also adding our own understanding and insight.

How to Use This Book

We suggest some specific ways to use the book in the sections that follow.

Part One: Setting the Stage

Part One provides an introduction and orientation to the book and includes Chapter One. The Matrix appears at the end of that chapter.

Chapter One: That Was Then, but This Is Now: The Past, Present, and Future of Large Group Methods. If Large Group Methods are new to you, you should probably start with Chapter One, which gives both a historical and a theoretical perspective and describes each method briefly. If you know and use these methods already, you may want to skim the first part of Chapter One and focus on the second half of the chapter, where we give a general overview of what is happening currently in this area of practice. Three methods that have been developed since our first book—Appreciative Inquiry, The World Café, and America*Speaks*—are also described in this section of the chapter.

The Matrix. At the end of Chapter One is a section titled "The Matrix," mentioned earlier, which will help you decide how you want to read the rest of the book. If you are interested in one of the six broad challenges, you will simply want to read our opening essay on the topic and the cases in that chapter. However, if you have more particular interests, you may want to find all the cases in educational or business settings. Or you may want to review all the cases using Future Search or Open Space. Some of you may want to locate all the cases that include cross-cultural issues (they are not all in the cross-cultural section); others may want to see how graphic facilitation and interactive technology ("IT Use") are incorporated in Large Group Methods. Consulting The Matrix will allow you to search the book for all the relevant information on a topic of particular interest.

Part Two: Six Challenges for the 21st Century

Each chapter begins with a description of a challenge, as well as our views on the issues the challenges create. We then show, through case examples, how Large Group Methods can be used to address each challenge. We also provide ideas about what is unique and interesting in each case. We suggest that these cases could be used with clients to give them an example of how Large Group Methods can help them with issues they are facing.

Chapter Two: Widely Dispersed Organizations and the Problem of Involvement. How do global organizations engage their employees effectively? How do you hold work meetings with a subset of the organization or community and still involve the people who cannot be present in a meaningful way?

The Cases

1. "Innovation at the BBC: Engaging an Entire Organization," by Mee-Yan Cheung-Judge and Edward H. Powley
2. "Whole System Engagement Through Collaborative Technology at World Vision," by Soren Kaplan and Ronald Fry

Chapter Three: Organizations in Crisis. Bad things can happen through negligence, but events like hurricanes, 9/11, and other catastrophic events can also hit an organization or community. How can leadership enlist, challenge, and involve employees and citizens in turnaround strategies?

The Cases

1. "Back from the Brink at American Airlines," by Beth Ganslen
2. "From Fragmentation to Coherence: An Intervention in an Academic Setting," by Rosemarie Barbeau and Nancy Aronson
3. "Creating a World-Class Manufacturer in Record Time," by Richard Lent, James Van Patten, and Tom Phair
4. "Planning Strategically for an Uncertain Future: The Boston University Dental School," by Gilbert Steil Jr. and Michele Gibbons-Carr

Chapter Four: Working in Polarized and Politicized Environments. Organizations and communities have interest groups and coalitions that intend to have their own way. Large Group Methods take a different approach to working with conflict. How does the search for common ground address conflict differently than conflict resolution methods? What do Large Group Methods bring to the very conflicted organizational issue or community debate?

The Cases

1. "Trust and Transformation: Integrating Two Florida Education Unions," by Sylvia L. James, Jack Carbone, Albert B. Blixt, and James McNeil
2. "Bringing Multiple Competing National Health Service Organizations Together," by Julie Beedon and Sophia Christie
3. "Clearing the Air: The FAA's Historic Growth Without Gridlock Conference," by Marvin Weisbord and Sandra Janoff
4. "Working with Corporate Community Tensions on Environmental Issues," by John D. Adams and Ann L. Clancy

Chapter Five: Working in Communities with Diverse Interest Groups. A growing need across the world is for people to come together and make decisions about what they want for their communities without becoming polarized and paralyzed. How do we get community groups to "sit down and reason together"? (Isaiah, Chapter 1, verse 18).

The Cases

1. "SpeakUp!: Bringing Youth, Educators, and Parents Together for Critical Conversations," by Marie T. McCormick

2. "Building Coalitions to Create a Community Planning Tool in Israel," by Tova Averbuch
3. "Taking Democracy to a Regional Scale in Hamilton County," by Steven Brigham

Chapter Six: Working Cross-Culturally. Large Group Methods are being used around the world. What adaptations need to be made when they are used in Asian, Latino, or African cultures? Since the methods are very democratic and participative, are there places where they should *not* be used? Are there rules of thumb for working with them cross-culturally?

The Cases

1. "Whole Systems Change in Mexican Organizations," by Michael R. Manning and José DelaCerda
2. "From Strategic Planning to Open Space in East Africa," by Theo Groot
3. "Training Indonesian Facilitators to Lead Community Planning for Women and Children," by Kim Martens, Rita Schweitz, and Kenoli Oleari
4. "World Religions Engage Critical Global Issues," by Ray Gordezky, Susan Dupre, and Helen Spector

Chapter Seven: Embedding New Patterns of Working. How do we sustain and implement change within our organizations? How do we embed more productive ways of working across organizational boundaries with both internal and external stakeholders?

The Cases

1. "Work Out: From Courtship to Marriage at General Electric," by Annmarie Sorrow
2. "Embedding the Core Principles at Boeing," by Richard H. Axelrod and Emily M. Axelrod
3. "Moving to the Next Level at the Canadian Institute for Health Information," by Larry E. Peterson and Rebecca Peterson
4. "After the Dance," by Glenda H. Eoyang and Kristine Quade

Part Three: Resources for Large Group Methods

The final chapter in this book (Chapter Eight) includes a variety of useful resources. Three articles are included: one about the transitions in the process of planning and implementing a large group event and strategies for running meetings, another about the use of graphic facilitation in large group events, and the final one about using interactive technology as part of the large group process:

1. "Tools for Effective Transitions Using Large Group Processes," by Thomas N. Gilmore and Deborah Bing
2. "Graphic Facilitation and Large Group Methods," by Carlotta Tyler, Lynne Valek, and Regina Rowland
3. "Using Interactive Meeting Technologies: Overcoming the Challenges of Time, Commitment, and Geographic Dispersion," by Lenny Lind, Karl Danskin, and Todd Erickson

Following these chapters, "The Reading List" suggests books that give an overview of this field, describe particular methods, or provoke deeper thinking. There is also information about each of the authors.

◆ ◆ ◆

We hope you will find within these pages good reading and many new and interesting experiences and ideas. We believe that there is always more to learn, and we hope to contribute to the ideas that help all of us work together to create better communities and organizations.

Acknowledgements

Some forty-nine people have collaborated to write the twenty-four cases and articles that enrich this book. Their work is a window on the world of Large Group Methods. Their willingness to work with us and cheerfulness even when writing multiple drafts for sometimes difficult deadlines has made bringing this book to life incredibly stimulating and fun for us. Although there is a brief bio for each author at the end of this book, their writing says much more about who they are.

We have been privileged to work with Byron Schneider and Mary Garrett for a second time as our editors from Jossey-Bass. Kathe Sweeney's editorial guidance completes this fine team. As on the first occasion, it would be hard to imagine a better experience.

Finally, our colleagueship seems not only to survive, but to be enriched by these forays into what others are thinking and doing as we frame the current environment of Large Group Methods. We both take a great deal of pleasure from doing this work together.

April 2006   Barbara Benedict Bunker
                                                               Buffalo, New York

                                                               Billie T. Alban
                                                               Bloomfield, Connecticut

THE HANDBOOK
OF LARGE GROUP
METHODS

PART ONE

SETTING THE STAGE

CHAPTER ONE

THAT WAS THEN, BUT THIS IS NOW

The Past, Present, and Future
of Large Group Methods

We opened the local paper to read in the headlines that the Federal Aviation Administration (FAA) had announced a decision to limit the number of planes using the Ft. Lauderdale Airport because of the high airport congestion and resulting delays in landings and takeoffs. This decision also involved using two secondary runways that, up to that time, had been mostly quiet. The mayor of the county was quoted as saying that the move came as a complete surprise and that the noise implications for several neighborhoods had not been considered. Activists and neighborhood spokespersons also commented negatively. In short, the FAA treated the airport and airline companies as though *they were the system*, without taking into consideration all the people whom the decision affected: neighbors and property owners, county officials, citizens concerned about ecology, and others who might be affected by the decision and thus were stakeholders.

This handbook is about methods for involving stakeholders in decisions about any system change. Certainly, had the FAA used one of the methods presented in this book and involved key stakeholders in the decision-making process, it might have taken a bit longer to present a new plan for the Ft. Lauderdale Airport. But we believe they would have been far more effective in implementing the changes they wanted to make.

The idea that change must involve the whole system has been growing in currency over the last forty years. The practice of family therapy, for example, developed as therapists got clear that treating only the child was much less effective than dealing with the whole system that participates in the illness. In the same way, organizations have often focused on individuals or groups as "the problem" when, in fact, the problem was system-created.

Not surprisingly, systems theory has been around longer than good practice. Katz and Kahn (1966) published the first edition of their seminal book on organizations as systems—*The Social Psychology of Organizations*—in 1966. To be sure, some change practitioners, particularly those whose practice is based in Gestalt theory or the Tavistock organizations-as-systems (Miller and Rice, 1967) work, have always worked with the whole system. The ability to implement these ideas, however, was limited by the lack of methods to bring all the stakeholders together to do the work of change. Until the 1980s, most problem-oriented consulting focused on individuals, interpersonal issues, group functioning (team effectiveness), and inter-unit productivity. At the same time, change processes led by top management that affected the direction of the whole organization usually occurred as a waterfall process: the plan or strategy began at the top and slowly cascaded down the organization hierarchy. By the time it reached the floor of the organization, a rather watered-down version usually remained, and much time had elapsed.

One of the most interesting breakthroughs in organizational development (OD) history occurred in the 1980s and 1990s. OD practitioners, working with systemic problems in organizations, developed methods for bringing together "the system"—all the concerned parties or "stakeholders"—in one place to make decisions about the issues facing them (Weisbord, 1987). The idea that when we are working with a systemic issue we need to draw the boundaries of the system *to include affected stakeholders* is more recent than notions of simply working with the whole system to bring about effective and sustainable change. We believe that this expansion of our understanding of how to decide what, exactly, constitutes the system developed (in consulting) simultaneously with the development of the Large Group Methods that make doing this kind of work possible.

The history of the development of these methods can be understood in three periods: (1) invention and early development (1980s to 1993), (2) adoption of the new methods (1993 to 1997), and (3) diffusion, experimentation, and the embedding of these methods (1997 to the present).

Invention and Early Development of Large Group Methods

Three precursors made the invention of Large Group Methods possible in the mid-1980s. The precursors were theory and practice developments in understanding organizational change that began in the 1950s. Large Group Methods could not have developed without these three strands, which we discuss in the next sections.

Change in Systems

The first strand was the emphasis on systems in the organizational work of Eric Trist and Fred Emery in the 1950s that developed from their study of new technology that was introduced into the British coal-mining industry. Their theory of sociotechnical systems showed how changes in technology can disrupt system functioning, even when what is being introduced is a more efficient technology. In their study, the new technology disrupted established and valued social relationships at work. The dissatisfaction caused by this disruption resulted in a loss of productivity. They proposed a theory that requires attention to the fit of the technological and the social system for the best productivity (Emery and Trist, 1960). Their work helped practitioners understand that change in one part of the system (technology improvements) can affect the rest of the system (who people work with), and this leads to unanticipated effects. Thus sustainable change requires attention to the whole system and systemic intervention.

The work of Trist and Emery in Britain was followed a decade later in the United States by the work of Katz and Kahn (1978), which we mentioned earlier. Katz and Kahn's work had a big impact on the field of organizational behavior, where their book became a standard text. Because this was a period in history when many consultants were also university professors in organizational and social psychology, the ideas were available in the practice of consulting.

Focus on the Future

The second precursor was a shift from focusing on solving organizational problems that are rooted in the past to focusing on the future and its potential. This occurred in both North America and Great Britain. In the United States, Herb

Shepard—a creative early OD practitioner—began working with individuals in the late 1960s in "life planning," that is, doing experiential exercises in which people created their own desired futures. He found that "futuring" created positive energy for change at the individual level.

About the same time, Ronald Lippitt, at the University of Michigan, noticed in his problem-solving work with organizational clients that dealing with problems drains energy. In contrast, he discovered that when you ask people to invent a future they would prefer and enjoy, energy is created in the people doing the planning. Lippitt began consulting with many cities in Michigan that were being devastated by the closing of automobile plants. He brought city stakeholders together in large group meetings—up to three thousand in one town—to create and plan their new future. The effects of this work of focusing on the future are reported in *Choosing the Future You Prefer* (Lippitt, 1980). It is interesting that this work, which, we see in retrospect, was clearly groundbreaking, was viewed by many practitioners at the time as a kind of curiosity. Those were the days of the growth of team-building and problem-solving methods, and many practitioners had practices in which this was their major business.

In the United Kingdom, emphasis on the future developed when Eric Trist ran a conference with Fred Emery, working with the merger of two aerospace engineering organizations in the early 1960s. They asked the two merging companies to consider what kind of company they wanted to become in the future. This process of searching for a desired future eventually became the Search Conference—a method that Fred and Merrelyn Emery would go on to develop further. Merrelyn Emery devoted more than thirty years of her practice in Australia to working with this method in organizations and communities, as well as at the national level (Emery and Purser, 1996).

Many Small Groups = One Large System

The third precursor was the work done by the National Training Laboratory (NTL) Institute in the 1960s in large summer laboratories at Bethel, Maine. In the community workshop and the college workshop, trainers learned to work with large groups by creating small groups within a larger framework. This created a model for working with larger groups of people, which only fully developed during the 1980s.

These early strands of work came together in the mid-1980s when, almost simultaneously, the importance of working with the whole system became focal for OD practitioners. The first clear statement of this new approach appeared when Marvin Weisbord wrote a history of thinking about organizations: *Productive Workplaces* (1987). As he reflected on what had worked and what had not worked in his own change practice, he realized that when he could "get all the stakeholders in the room," he had been able to effectively create changes that were desired and desirable. Out of the thinking expressed in this book and a dialogue with Eric Trist and Merrelyn Emery about their Search Conference work, he developed a new method that he called Future Search. One way it differed from the Search Conference was that it was intended for a larger group of seventy or more, which meant that many stakeholders could be present.

Also in the mid-1980s, Kathie Dannemiller—a student and colleague of Ron Lippitt—was asked to train Ford middle managers to be more proactive. Understanding that the Ford system did not encourage this kind of behavior and that many hours of training would probably not be successful, she refused the quite extensive contract. The stunned potential clients at Ford asked her what she might do to reach the objective. After thinking about it, she proposed that they give her five hundred managers from three levels of management for a week in an off-site location if they really wanted change. This was the birth of Real Time Strategic Change—a method that involves stakeholders in planning and implementing changes for a better organization future. Real Time Strategic Change is now called Whole-Scale Change (Dannemiller Tyson Associates, 2000). The breakthrough that occurred in this work was the large number of people who could be involved at one time so that a whole plant or organization could work on the same issue together and make decisions that would stick and could be immediately implemented.

About the same time but in a quite different structure, Harrison Owen created a new method of gathering people with passion and energy to discuss a topic in a method he called Open Space (Owen, 1997). Again, hundreds of people could participate in creating the agenda for the one- or two-day meeting and engage the topic as they wished.

These breakthrough methods not only accommodate a large number of participants, but they do not require that professional facilitators be at every discussion table; leadership roles are rotated among table participants. As a result, some participants develop new skills that they take with them to the workplace, as they learn to facilitate or act as scribe or reporter for their table group. Rotating small group leadership roles made the use of these methods much more available to communities and organizations without big budgets. The composition of the table groups is heterogeneous ("max-mix") for much of the work but also occurs in functional groups when appropriate to the task.

Adoption of the New Methods (1993–1997)

As the 1990s progressed, differences among the methods gradually became clearer. Some of the publications and activities that encouraged this development were the following. A special issue of *The Journal of Applied Behavioral Science,* edited by Bunker and Alban (1992), gathered articles by originators of several different large group interventions. They shared the idea of working with large groups of stakeholders. In addition to some of the methods already mentioned, Dick Axelrod was using a series of large group conferences to redesign work in a process he calls the Conference Model. Don Klein proposed that his 1970s SimuReal method was a systems model that could accommodate many stakeholders and was included. The Inter-Cultural Association (ICA) was using and further developing methods that they had learned in the early days of OD from OD practitioners. Although associated with individual practitioners, all these methods were being developed and refined in practice as ways of gathering stakeholders together to engage each other about issues of common concern. Interest was so intense that the special issue required five additional printings.

A typical large group meeting is held in a large open room with many five-foot (or slightly larger) round tables set up for working sessions. These are not the usual six-foot banquet tables because they need to be small enough in diameter that people can talk easily across them without shouting. A platform for the two facilitators is located in a place optimal for viewing from all the tables. Flip charts are stacked on the side walls to be available when needed. The logistics staff, usually wearing a distinctive color, circulates in their assigned sectors, bringing printed instructions and materials to the tables, as well as microphones for the periods of reports or discussions.

Beginning in 1993, two developments went hand-in-hand. First, the developers of methods wrote books on how to use their methods and spoke at national conferences; a few offered training workshops in the method. Practitioners were thirsty for this new knowledge. They wanted to understand in as much detail as possible what these methods were and how they worked. At the same time, Bunker and Alban (1997) developed and presented a framework for understanding all twelve of the original methods in training workshops and at conferences. There was so much interest that for four years (1995 to 1998), Tom Chase helped plan and sponsor a Large Group Interventions Conference in Dallas, Texas, that was attended by method originators, practitioners, companies using the methods who offered a case describing their experience, CEOs talking about what it was like to involve the whole company, and organizations that were "shopping," that is, thinking about using these methods. Mobil, for example, brought a multilevel group of fourteen people to a conference before they decided to use Real Time Strategic Change with one of their divisions. Our book and the Dallas conferences increased the diffusion of these methods. As interest grew, developers of all the methods began to both offer public workshops and publish their own books on how to use their method. As a result, more and more people became acquainted with Large Group Methods.

The differences among methods gradually became clear, as methods were adopted and used. For example, some methods are easier to learn and adopt than others. Methods with a structured flow of activities like the Search Conference or Future Search are easy to grasp. This means they are easy to try out on an unsuspecting client. In early periods of innovation, there is always a certain amount of experimentation. Ethical practitioners keep this to a minimum and do not suggest methods when the issues are not appropriate for the method. Gathering stakeholders is expensive in time and resources. It should be reserved for issues that are worthy of this kind of commitment, such as the future plans for the organization or important problems.

Some methods also take a longer time commitment to plan and implement than others. Work Design takes months, with many large and small meetings; Open Space can be set up and run with very short lead time; custom-designed methods like Real Time Strategic Change require planning with an internal design team, so they need longer lead times than structured methods. However, it is typical for all methods to have a planning group representing all aspects of the system to advise and manage the whole process.

The framework described in *Large Group Interventions* (Bunker and Alban, 1997) compares all the Large Group Methods in three categories based on outcome: (1) methods for the future, (2) methods for work design, and (3) flexible methods for whole-system participative work. For readers unfamiliar with these methods, we describe them very briefly here. For a more detailed explanation, the developers of these methods have all published detailed descriptions and, in many cases, how-to books to help people who want to use them (many can be found in "The Reading List"—a feature of Chapter Eight, which provides resources). For a comparison of these methods for those trying to decide which method to use, consult our 1997 book. This *Handbook* focuses on current practice, that is, how these methods are being used now to meet six major challenges of the 21st century. Cases illustrating the use of these methods and combinations of these methods appear in the chapters that follow.

Methods for Creating the Future Together

Five main methods are used when an organization or community wants to create a plan for moving into the future that they prefer (rather than simply responding to whatever happens). The methods are the Search Conference, Future Search, Whole-Scale Change, the ICA Strategic Planning Process, and Appreciative Inquiry (AI) (see Figure 1.1). Since AI is a newer method for future planning that has come on the scene as a Large Group Method more recently, we will describe it later in this chapter. It is also fair to say that, occasionally, Open Space and SimuReal may be used for future planning. They will be discussed under "Methods for Discussion and Decision Making," which represents more of their use.

The Search Conference

The Search Conference, developed by Fred and Merrelyn Emery (Emery and Purser, 1996), is a two-and-one-half-day conference for thirty-five to forty participants who are members of a system. Diverse groups work together in discussions that scan the current environment and understand it, examine their history as a system, assess the present situation, and agree on a future. One-third of the time of the conference is devoted to planning for actions that will allow them to realize the future they have agreed that they want. In this model, conflict is acknowledged but not dealt with at length. The emphasis is on finding what is held in common and can be agreed to by all as the basis for proceeding.

FIGURE 1.1. LARGE GROUP METHODS FOR CREATING THE FUTURE

THE SEARCH CONFERENCE
Purpose: To create a future vision
Merrelyn and Fred Emery

- Set format: Environmental scan, history, present, future
- Criteria for participants: Within system boundary
- Theory: Participative democracy
- Search for common ground
- Rationalize conflict
- No experts
- Total community discussion
- 2.5-day minimum
- 35 to 40+ participants
- Larger groups = Multisearch Conference
- 1/3 total time is action planning

FUTURE SEARCH
Purpose: To create a future vision
Weisbord and Janoff

- Set format: Past, present, future, action planning
- Stakeholder participation (no experts)
- Minimize differences
- Search for common ground
- Self-managed small groups
- 18 hours over 3 days
- 40 to 80+ participants
- Larger groups = Multisearch Conference

WHOLE-SCALE CHANGE
Purpose: To create a preferred future with systemwide action planning
Dannemiller and Jacobs

- Format custom-designed to issue
- Highly structured and organized
- Theory: Beckhard Change Model
- Common database
- 2 to 3 days + follow-up events
- Use of outside experts as appropriate
- Use of small groups and total community
- Self-managed small groups
- 100 to 2,400 participants
- Logistics competence critical
- Daily participant feedback
- Planning committee and consultants design events

ICA STRATEGIC PLANNING PROCESS
Purpose: Strategic planning

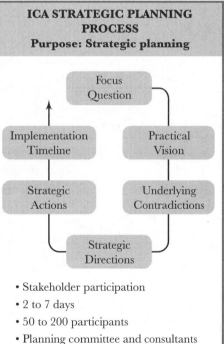

- Stakeholder participation
- 2 to 7 days
- 50 to 200 participants
- Planning committee and consultants design events

Source: Bunker and Alban, 1997.

Future Search

Future Search was developed originally by Marvin Weisbord and then refined over a number of years in collaboration with Sandra Janoff (Weisbord and Janoff, 2000). Future Search got its inspiration from the Search Conference but proceeds somewhat differently. In the first place, the activities of the table groups and general sessions begin by examining the past at three levels— personal, system, and world. Then participants create a "mind map," which is a graphic representation of the trends in the environment that are impacting organizational decisions. Stakeholder groups select a trend from this scan that they believe affects them in important ways, and they discuss what they are doing and not doing about it. Next, stakeholder groups analyze the present by talking about what they are both proud and sorry about in their current organization or community. Finally, "max-mix" groups create skits about the future they want and dramatize it for the whole group. Then, themes crossing all the skits are agreed on as the common ground on which the group can move forward into planning for actions to realize these future themes. Compared with the Search Conference, Future Search engages people more emotionally, as the activities are both rational and affecting; from thirty-five to one hundred or more people can be accommodated at a Future Search.

Whole-Scale Change

Whole-Scale Change (originally called Real Time Strategic Change), developed by Kathie Dannemiller and later with her collaborator Robert Jacobs (Jacobs, 1994), is a flexible method that can include hundreds and even thousands at an event. Unlike Future Search and the Search Conference, Whole-Scale Change custom designs the process of each event to the particular client situation. Even so, there are predicable activities that occur regularly in these events because all are based in a systems understanding of what is needed to do future planning. There must be some kind of assessment of the external environment and understanding of the past and present, as well as focus on a direction desired for the future. Whole-Scale events can include customers and suppliers, as well as expert inputs as needed. Virtually all Large Group Methods work with some kind of planning and design team ahead of the event. In this method, that group collects daily reactions during the two or three days and adjusts the design as needed.

ICA Strategic Planning Process

The ICA Strategic Planning Process (Spencer, 1989) developed originally from the work of the Ecumenical Institute of Chicago, which was greatly influenced by the NTL training and education. They have developed their own method that a network of practitioners in the United States and Canada use in community development, as well as in organizations. Planning events may go on for as long as five days in order to develop specific and implementable plans. At the beginning, the emphasis is on data collection around the issue or focal question. Then a practical vision is created that all agree on. The next step is unique to ICA, and we think it is very useful. Participants discuss the "underlying contradictions," which are those things that get in the way of moving toward the vision of the future they created. The question is: What could prevent us from realizing this vision? This surfaces the psychological resistances, as well as the real barriers. This question is pursued in depth in a search for root causes that can lead to good ideas about what to do. So the next step of action planning follows naturally: select strategic actions that will help overcome the contradictions and then make implementation plans for the whole change effort, planning how, when, who, and what will be done to move forward. ICA works with systems and their stakeholders of any size up to about two hundred.

Methods for Work Design

Work design methods originated in the sociotechnical systems thinking of Trist (1981). In our 1997 framework, there were four large group work design methods. Three methods that developed separately—the Conference Model, Whole-Scale Work Design, and Fast Cycle Full Participation—have blended with each other so as to be indistinguishable, though still are practiced by those titles. The other work design method—Participative Design—is quite different, in that it starts at the bottom of the organization and moves upward (see Figure 1.2).

The Conference Model (Axelrod and Axelrod, 2000), Whole-Scale Work Design, and Fast Cycle Full Participation Work Design are three models of work design that appeared in our original formulation, with enough difference in approach to warrant separate discussions. Since that time, the demand for

FIGURE 1.2. LARGE GROUP METHODS FOR WORK DESIGN

LARGE GROUP WORK DESIGN **The Conference Model, Whole-Scale** **Work Design, Fast Cycle Full** **Participation Work Design**	**PARTICIPATIVE DESIGN** *Fred and Merrelyn Emery*

• Integrated series of large group meetings.
• 1 to 2-day sessions
• Topics:
    Create the vision.
    Conduct environmental analysis.
    Conduct work systems analysis.
    Conduct social system analysis.
    Develop a blueprint for the new
      organization/process.
    Plan for implementation.
• Whole system communication strategy is followed between meetings.
• Small task force work adds detail to large group meeting results.
	• The process is bottom-up.
	• Organizationwide education is first step.
	• Management sets minimum critical specifications.
	• Each level coordinates and controls its own work.
	• Each unit designs its own work.
	• Six design principles are used to redesign work.
	• Multiskilling is the norm.

redesigning work has diminished, due mostly to the decrease in manufacturing in the West and off-shoring. Now client needs and requirements, more than a particular model, seem to determine the flow of the work design process. For these reasons, we have combined the three methods into one generic description. It may be, however, that with some clients a true version of the Conference Model or Whole-Scale Work Design is adopted. As far as we know, Fast Cycle Full Participation is not often practiced.

Work redesign that involves the whole system is a change that takes a number of months. It is authorized by the organization's leadership, who set the goals and clarify the boundaries and constraints. Usually, a planning or design team is then appointed to be in charge of the overall process, which occurs in a series of spaced events, often about a month apart. In these large group events, stakeholders create a preferred future, interact with relevant customers and suppliers to understand their expectations, and perform a technical analysis of the work system identifying problems that are leading to lowered efficiency or quality. Then suggestions for how to design the system so that it meets its goals and operates excellently are solicited and considered; the most promising are selected and implemented. At the same time, key support processes may need to be aligned with the new design.

Throughout this process, there is constant two-way communication with the whole system. Those who do not attend events have an opportunity to give inputs to issues being debated. The idea is to involve and keep involved as many people as possible so that when the new system "goes live" there are few surprises. As many as six thousand employees have been involved in this type of work design.

Participative Design was created by Fred and Merrelyn Emery (1993); contemporary modifications have been made by Bob Rehm (1999). Participative Design is an organizationwide process whose assumption is that the people who do the work know the most about it and are therefore the best people to decide how to get it done effectively and efficiently. This is a bottom-up approach to work design, as contrasted with a top-down approach. The work design starts literally at the bottom, or lowest level of the organizational chart. The people at this level gather for education about the six design principles they will use to redesign their work and their jobs within the "critical specifications" set by the organization's leadership. The basic principle that is operative in the redesign is that each level coordinates and controls its own work.

When the first level has completed their redesign, the next level meets to ask: "What is our work?" This is where the process gets very interesting because usually the people included at that next level up have been supervisors. But if the lowest-level people are now coordinating and controlling their own work, the question the former supervisors must address is, What is their work now? According to this method, the process proceeds up to the top of the organization. We know of only a few organizations that have completed the whole process from bottom to top, but the method can be used in well-defined sections of an organization.

Methods for Whole-Scale Participative Work

In addition to the four methods we included in our previous book (SimuReal, Open Space Technology, Work Out, and Whole-Scale), two new methods have been developed in the intervening time. We give a brief summary of the four here (see Figure 1.3). Later in this chapter we will describe the two new methods: The World Café and America*Speaks*.

FIGURE 1.3. LARGE GROUP METHODS
FOR WHOLE-SYSTEM PARTICIPATIVE WORK

SIMUREAL
Purpose: Do real-time work on current issues, test future designs, learn about system
Donald and Alan Klein

- Organization selects issue for work.
- Room arrangement reflects organization's structure.
- People act their organizational roles.
- There are periods of stop action and reflection.
- Decision process is agreed to in advance.
- 1 day
- 50 to 150 people
- Facilitator needs expertise in process consultation.

WORK OUT (General Electric)
Purpose: Problem identification and process improvement

- Improvement target selected.
- Employee cross-functional meeting held.
- 1 to 2 days
- Process: Discuss and recommend
- Senior management responds immediately.
- Champions and sponsors follow through to implementation.
- 30, 60, 90 day follow-up

OPEN SPACE TECHNOLOGY
Purpose: Discussion and exploration of system issues
Harrison Owen

- Is least structured of Large Group Methods.
- Uses divergent process.
- Large group creates agenda topics.
- Interest groups form around topics.
- Newsroom printouts allow for sharing information across interest groups.
- One facilitator lays out format and ground rules, "holds the space."
- Facilitator needs an undestanding of large group dynamics.
- 1 to 3 days

WHOLE-SCALE INTERACTIVE EVENTS
Purpose: Problem solving
Dannemiller and Jacobs

Uses same methodology as Whole-Scale in Figure 1.1.

- Flexible method with many different uses.

Source: Bunker and Alban, 1997.

SimuReal

SimuReal was created by Donald Klein in the 1970s and has subsequently been developed by Alan Klein (Klein, 1992; Klein and Klein, 2005[1]). A physical simulation of an organization or system and its players is set up in a large space. Stakeholders to the theme or focal issue are invited to participate in a one-day (or shorter) learning and action-taking event. People act in their normal roles during action periods on the selected issue or problem. During stop-action periods, a trained facilitator guides the whole system in a discussion of what happened and what everyone observed. Then they go back and work some more, followed by another stop-action discussion. After three iterations of this cycle, the whole group decides on appropriate actions to take as a result of their learning. Although invented as a problem-clarification and remediation method, SimuReal has been used to test potential organization designs and changes.

Open Space Technology

Open Space Technology (OST) or Open Space was created by Harrison Owen (1997) and is the method with what might be called a minimalist structure, as compared with others. It is a divergent process in which anything from small to very large groups of participants are invited to gather and create the agenda for discussion of whatever seems important to them around a focused topic or theme. Only one facilitator is needed to lead the process, and as long as the facilities allow, any number of people can participate.

At the beginning of the meeting, which can be from one day or less to three days or more, everyone is seated in a large circle of chairs. In the first hour the facilitator describes the reason for meeting and the norms and rules of Open Space. Then the facilitator invites people to come to the center of the circle, write the topic they want to discuss on half a newsprint sheet, sign their name, and announce their topic to the group. Then they go to a big open wall where they select a time and place, written ahead of time on sticky notes, and post their topic with time and place of discussion on the wall. This becomes the agenda for the meeting and the place where people can find out what is going on. The agenda can be added to at will, as long as the person who posts the topic agrees to show up at the appointed time and begin the discussion. Each day is divided into discussion periods of an hour, or a bit more.

The whole group gathers again in the big circle at the end of each day for "The Evening News." If there is more than one day, they begin each day's work with "The Morning News." These are brief and quite informal gatherings about whatever the participants want to say. Everyone can find out what is being said in discussion groups they do not attend by going to a different wall on which summary reports from the discussion groups are posted as they are typed out on computers in "the newsroom" by the proposers of the topic.

Most Open Space meetings also add some convergent activity such as dot voting (placing small, colored sticky dots on wall charts to show preferences), prioritizing, or some form of action planning onto this basic format in order to take what has happened in the discussions and move forward. Open Space can be used for endless types of discussions, from sensing whether an issue is really important, to getting input about important decisions that are about to be made, to creatively thinking, as a group, about new products or future services a company might offer.

Work Out

Work Out is a participative problem-solving method that was created at General Electric under the impetus of Jack Welch's leadership (Slater, 1999). A high-level sponsor authorizes the gathering of all the relevant stakeholders to a particular problem in one place for several days to address and take action on the problem. In the final afternoon, the sponsor and other managers or executives with the authority to make decisions attend and publicly authorize or veto proposals from working groups. Then over the next thirty, sixty, and ninety days, short progress reporting meetings are held. It is expected that action will be complete in ninety days and results and cost savings known. The method proved so successful internally that General Electric began offering training to its clients and suppliers. The method has been widely adopted by companies that have often used their own name for it.

Whole-Scale Interactive Events

Whole-Scale Interactive Events (Dannemiller Tyson Associates, 2000) are events that are custom-tailored for a particular engagement. An example is bringing together New York City stakeholder organizations to take action on the alarming increase in tuberculosis among the homeless people living in the city. The design for the meeting in Whole-Scale events in all three categories is created by assessing three elements: (1) level of dissatisfaction, (2) existence of a vision or goal, and (3) clarity of first steps that one can take to begin moving toward the goal. The theory is that all three factors must be correctly in place for any change to occur.

Continuing Development of Large Group Methods

During the 1990s, practitioners were learning these methods and building an experience base. Some chose to define themselves as specializing in one of these methods. Others added competence in some of the methods as they needed it in a more general practice of organizational change. Because work redesign, which developed from sociotechnical design theory, usually occurs over months and even years, there is a group of practitioners who mainly do this work. Future-planning consultants, however, often know several of the future methods. There are networks of practitioners of some methods such as Future Search and Open Space who meet online and in person to learn from each other and offer expertise to communities and nonprofits with limited budgets.

Core Characteristics of Methods

Every method has a set of underlying principles that are considered to be central. As we look across all the methods, we propose four core characteristics that we believe are accurate and essential characteristics that span all the Large Group Methods.

1. *Inclusion of stakeholders:* The first core characteristic is that the people invited to participate include those who have a stake in the issues being discussed, regardless of level or function or whether they are inside or outside the organization. For example, a business may invite customers, suppliers, even competitors as it plans for the future. In the community, this means whoever is affected, regardless of position, class, or power. A public school issue could involve everyone in the school system, including students and janitors, as well as parents, citizens, politicians, and whoever is relevant to the issue at hand.

Essentially, these are democratic methods that encourage all voices to be heard. They encourage input to decisions employees or citizens are asked to support. It is important to point out that this does not necessarily mean that five hundred stakeholders get together and make the decision. They may be the decision makers, or their input may be incorporated by an executive group that is present at the event and responsible for the organization. Both levels of decision making work well if people know in advance what the ground rules are.

Practitioners who propose these methods need to understand that not all leaders and managers want to involve stakeholders in having their say or in mutual decision making. This means that sensitive negotiation and coaching are part of contracting with executives about the use of these methods. There have been instances where practitioners, in their eagerness to help the client move into action, did not insist that the client really understand what these methods do in terms of stakeholder voice, involvement, commitment, and new ideas, and what they require in terms of leadership participation, support, and follow-up. Taking enough time to fully educate the leadership during the contracting phase of the intervention is key to realizing the true potential of these methods.

2. *Engagement of multiple perspectives through interactive activities:* Participants engage in a series of activities that explore the organization or community context and help them think more broadly than their own perspective. This strategy accomplishes several things. First, it prevents people from leaping into problem solving and taking action before the context is fully explored. Second, it exposes them interactively in small groups to a diverse group of stakeholders with very different perspectives in a process that allows everyone to participate and to be heard. This increases the amount of information available and expands participants' understanding of issues, leading to the possibility of out-of-the-box thinking.

3. *Opportunity to influence:* These structures allow people to have *voice*—to be heard—and to influence the outcomes under discussion at the meeting.

4. *Search for common ground:* A goal and the process structure of many of these methods focus attention on finding the areas of agreement—the *common ground*—that participants share. In large groups with many different stakeholders, there are bound to be differences, many of them. That is not of great concern because there is no objective to resolve all the differences.

None of these methods use conflict resolution strategies to deal with differences (Bunker, 2000). The objective in most of the methods is *to find common ground*, that is, to understand what those present and representing the system *agree on*. The assumption is that once what is agreed on is clear, it is possible to move forward from that common ground, even though differences remain.

Current Trends and New Methods

Since the publication of our book *Large Group Interventions* in 1997, a great deal has happened in the field, as more and more organizations and communities have used these methods for their own purposes. We have been particularly interested in many accounts of the spread and use of these methods worldwide; we have presented workshops on the methods described in our book in many countries. In March 2005, Robert Marshak, the acting editor of *The Journal of Applied Behavioral Science,* invited us to edit a second special issue on Large Group Methods (Bunker and Alban, 2005). This gave us the opportunity, twelve years after the publication of the first special issue, to again send out a "Call for Papers" and ask for articles that would show what has happened in the use and spread of these methods. The *Journal* invitation was an excellent way to answer our questions and find out how and where these methods are being used.

We were amazed when we received more than fifty manuscripts and descriptions of possible submissions for the *Journal.* These submissions were from six continents; we only had room for ten manuscripts! This was a further confirmation that these methods were being used globally for a variety of needs.

Diffusion: Spreading the Word

Malcolm Gladwell (2000), in his book *The Tipping Point,* describes the tipping point as the moment when ideas and products are diffused and accepted by a critical mass. After our book was published, we started offering workshops to familiarize people with the methods described in the first part of this chapter. Training workshops were a major vehicle through which the core concepts and skills were made available to consultants, leaders, and academics around the globe.

Many of the developers have published books and articles (some translated into other languages) on their particular approaches. The use of Internet technology, including listservs and Web sites and the newsletters of the developers, have also increased knowledge and connected people interested in these methods. Presentations at major conferences of organizations like the Organization Development Network and the Academy of Management, as well as at many international meetings and at organizational change training-and-degree programs like the Columbia University Program for Organization Development and Human Resource Management and the Pepperdine University and American University–NTL degree programs, have all helped with the dissemination of these concepts. Multinational corporations began to use these methods internationally to address complex organizational issues. Today there are skilled international external and internal consultants who use these methods in their work. Companies like General Electric have been strong on internal capacity building and have chosen not to rely on external consultants. They have trained their people worldwide in the use of Work Out. One of the authors remembers sitting in a restaurant in Danbury, Connecticut, hearing a young woman at the next table say, "I am leaving tomorrow for India to train our people there to run Work Outs."

The March 2005 special issue of the *Journal of Applied Behavioral Science* documents the international diffusion of Large Group Methods with articles on a joint venture between a U.S. multinational and an Indian family business, an example from IKEA in Sweden on improving their distribution system. In the same issue, Suzanne Weber writes about the diffusion of Open Space, Future Search, and mixed designs in German-speaking counties. She documents over nine hundred conferences using Large Group Methods run in Germany over the period of three years. In this book, Chapter Five focuses on the cross-cultural use of these methods, with three case examples of work going on across the globe. In other chapters, cases from Great Britain and Canada can be found.

Diffusion: Stakeholder Engagement

Another significant factor in the diffusion of Large Group Methods has been global economic and social pressure, particularly in the public, government, and nonprofit sectors. There has been growing recognition of the value and necessity of stakeholder inclusion and a growing demand from stakeholders to have a voice in important decisions that affect them. Large Group Methods have been used to address many community and public sector dilemmas where agreement among diverse stakeholders is essential for movement on important issues.

There is a growing polarization today regarding environmental issues: economic development versus ecological sustainability, water for agriculture versus water for drinking, states' rights of eminent domain versus the rights of the homeowners. There are many instances where Large Group Methods have been used effectively to bring stakeholders together to work on these polarizing issues. In developing countries, the United Nations, NGOs, and local governments have found it essential to learn how to work together, set priorities, define responsibilities, and develop action plans. This is not easy, as these agencies have different cultures, different structures, and their own priorities. We have seen a variety of Large Group Methods used to address these issues. Necessity may have been the mother of use and adoption. Environmental pressures and demands have helped with the global dispersion of Large Group Methods.

Adaptations and Innovations

There are many examples, some in this book, where a Future Search, Open Space, or other method has been used in its original form with excellent results. There are other situations in both the private and public sectors where a specific client need or constraint has resulted in combining or introducing new methods to address specific requirements. This book provides examples of some of the variations. For example, the BBC took one of the new methods (AI) and stretched the process over months. The Boston University Dental School combined a Future Search format with the introduction of scenario planning; the World Vision case used a Future Search format but added interactive technologies in order to involve 4,500 people in 100 offices worldwide.

We have also seen some of the core principles and activities of Large Group Methods used to enhance ordinary meetings. A few years ago we were at a hotel near the Denver Airport. As we passed the ballroom, we noticed a large group of people sitting at tables, six or seven to a table, busily working. We were told it was a cross-section of employees from the recently opened airport trying to find solutions to some of the baggage-handling problems. We hung around for a while, and finally at a break asked the meeting facilitators for a more detailed account of what they were doing and what method they were using. "Oh," they said, "there is something we call the Blue Book; we have combined something called Work Out with something called Future Search and a few ideas of our own to work on issues connected with the opening of the new airport." They had all of the key elements: the system in the room, an interactive process that gave people an opportunity to give their perspective, and a process to identify the issues, solve the dilemmas, and take action. (The Blue Book was *our* book, although it was never our intention that it would be used as a how-to book!)

Several weeks later we were at a large corporate headquarters and passed a conference room. We noticed twenty or so round tables; six to eight people sat around each one. We were told it was a corporate briefing. The format was presentations, discussions at the tables, and opportunities to raise questions and concerns and get responses from the leadership. We asked why they were not using an auditorium arrangement. We heard, "This works much better. People get a better understanding of the materials presented through discussion at the tables; they ask clarifying questions and give good suggestions about the issues."

"How did you come up with this way of doing things?" we asked.

They replied that one of the executives had seen this done at another company and thought it worked well!

Many churches and synagogues today, when calling a new pastor or rabbi, use some of the exercises from Future Search to clarify the kind of leadership they need for their future. They may use history timelines, a mind map on current issues affecting the faith community, and an assessment of their strengths and weaknesses. The data generated help the search committee develop a profile of the skills and experiences they need in the new leadership.

Donald Schön, in his book *Beyond the Stable State* (1971), talks about "ideas in currency." Once ideas get into circulation they spread rapidly, and the origin of these ideas is lost. Several years ago, one of the authors heard an interview with James Baker, who was secretary of state under President G.H.W. Bush in the early 1990s; he was commenting on the Israeli-Palestinian situation. Baker seemed to indicate in the interview that it might have been a mistake not to have included some of the key stakeholders at the first Camp David meeting. The assumption had been made that the two leaders spoke for their people! The idea of key stakeholder participation is an important part of many of these methods. What surprised us, however, was the use of the word *stakeholder*. We wonder if there may be fallout into the general culture of some of the basic ideas from these methods. Here are some examples:

1. The idea that stakeholders need to be involved in decision making is not a new idea, but using the word *stakeholder* connotes involvement. The word is appearing more and more frequently in the media and in business language.
2. Rotating leadership in small groups is more commonly practiced today, reserving professional facilitation for times that are expected to be more confrontational or complicated.
3. Large corporate meetings are often held today in a conference or ballroom, with participants sitting at small round tables instead of in auditorium style. The tables allow for discussion of key issues; participants have the opportunity to ask questions and give feedback to the leadership.
4. The term *finding common ground* appears frequently today, especially in situations of high divergence.

New Large Group Methods

In this section, we describe three new methods that were not included in our first book because they had not been developed. These are (1) Appreciative Inquiry Summit Meeting (see Figure 1.4), (2) The World Café (see Figure 1.5), and (3) America*Speaks* (see Figure 1.6). It is clear that these new methods are built on many of the core principles described earlier.

Appreciative Inquiry Summit Meeting

David Cooperrider, along with some of his colleagues from Case Western Reserve, originally developed AI as a data-gathering method. The data could be collected either in an organization or in a community setting.

A Unique Approach to Data Gathering. What made this approach unique was the focus on what was going on positively in the area being researched. If the issue were gender relationships in the organization, data would be collected on positive experiences that members of the organization had had with the

FIGURE 1.4. LARGE GROUP METHODS FOR CHANGING THE FUTURE: APPRECIATIVE INQUIRY SUMMIT MEETING

APPRECIATIVE INQUIRY SUMMIT MEETING
Purpose: To build the future on recognizing and expanding existing strengths
David Cooperrider

- Format similar to Future Search
- Participation not limited by number, includes stakeholders
- May be done over several days
- Four phases:
    Discovery: Interviews and storytelling surface positive strengths.
    Dream: Based on stories and interview data, group builds a desired future.
    Design: Group addresses the system changes needed to support the desired future.
    Delivery: Group plans for implementing and sustaining the change.

opposite sex. People were encouraged to tell stories about these relationships. Follow-up questions would probe the elements and interactions in these relationships that created this positive experience.

These key elements were then extrapolated, and the next issue to be addressed was, "What do we need to do in this organization to create more of these positive experiences?" This process has been used very effectively in the merger of two companies that need to create a new company culture out of two previously independent companies. Rather than one company "acquiring" the other and imposing its culture, AI holds the promise of there being a real merger, of taking the best of both old cultures and blending it into a new culture that everyone can subscribe to. In the same way, in a community setting people are often asked what they particularly appreciated about their community. They are encouraged to tell stories about their positive and affirming community experiences. The philosophical approach starts with what is already working and uses the strengths identified as building blocks for a better future. This method reframes situations in such a way that people recognize what is already present, active, and life enhancing, and then ask, "What do we need to do to create more of these experiences?"

The Meeting. As Large Group Methods developed, Cooperrider and his colleagues had the opportunity to experience several of these methods. As a result, they developed the Appreciative Inquiry Summit Meeting (Ludema, Whitney, Mohr, and Griffin, 2003), which is a four-day large group event that brings together stakeholders in the organization or community to share the data collected, hear the stories, and retain the best of the positive values and practices of the organization or community. The group then focuses on ways to augment the positive aspects of what has been identified.

Each day is a new phase: Discovery, Dream, Design, Destiny (the "4-D" process). In the Discovery phase, employees are trained to interview other employees about positive experiences in the organization and what they see as the organization's values and strengths. The task of the interviewer is to tease out the core elements that help create these positive experiences. This phase may occur as part of the AI Summit, or it may happen in advance of the meeting.

The next phase—the Dream phase—now uses Large Group Methods to bring together the system and its stakeholders to plan how to build the positive elements from the interviews into a vision of the desired future state. The best stories from the interviews may be retold at the summit meeting and the core elements presented as "future possibilities." However it is done, the group comes to some common ground about what they want to achieve in their future.

In the Design phase, participants plan actions to create and sustain the future they want. This involves examining leadership, infrastructure, policies, and systems that would support the proposed changes.

Finally, in the Destiny phase, innovation teams that volunteer to achieve specific goals after the summit ends self-organize for action.

The Focus on What Is Right. AI is one of several Large Group Methods that does not spend time trying to problem solve the present but, instead, focuses on creating a better future, once the current reality has been acknowledged. When people focus on what is wrong, they lose sight of the positive things that are happening. Then it is easy to become stuck in trying to fix what is wrong rather than focusing on the "more that could be." This method has become very popular and is often combined with other methods. We think it corrects an imbalance in how Westerners look at their world. We are trained very early in critical thinking. The more education we have, the more critical we may become. As a result, we end up looking for what is wrong, often only acknowledging what is right as an afterthought. The AI Summit Meeting corrects this imbalance by combining elements of Future Search with some form of storytelling and data sharing on positive experiences around the theme.

In this book, there is an innovative use of the AI Summit at the British Broadcasting Company (BBC), where the summit was modified and spread out, with intervals of several months between phases of the summit in order to involve the 27,000 employees at the BBC (see Cheung-Judge and Powley in Chapter Two). In the same chapter in the World Vision case (Kaplan and Fry), an AI Summit is held in Bangkok with 150 representatives of this worldwide relief agency, while 4,500 other employees in 100 offices around the globe participate before, during, and after the summit in an imaginatively structured online community.

The World Café

Another new Large Group Method is The World Café, developed by Juanita Brown. This method is being used separately or in combination with other methods (Brown and Isaacs, 2005). The World Café is a process that fosters authentic conversation and takes about two to three hours. Each World Café activity is focused around a theme that engages the invited group of stakeholders. They sit at small café-style tables, four or five people to a table, covered with "tablecloths" made of drawing paper, and are given pens or markers. Each group is given about twenty to thirty minutes to both talk about the theme and sketch their ideas on the tablecloth. After twenty minutes or so, the table host instructs them to leave one person at the table who will communicate the substance of the conversation that just occurred to the next group. Then everyone else separates and goes to a different table, and the process repeats itself.

There are at least three iterations of this process before the final groups post or report the ideas their table has developed. The entire group then engages in a town meeting discussion of what has occurred. If themes are identified, they can lead to whatever action is appropriate. This process is very useful in settings where there are factions or where people have fixed ideas and need to engage each other and hear different perspectives on the situation. The World Café method mixes people up for a different conversational experience. A focused

FIGURE 1.5. LARGE GROUP METHOD FOR DISCUSSION AND DECISION MAKING: THE WORLD CAFÉ

THE WORLD CAFÉ
Purpose: A conversational process that helps a group explore an important issue
Juanita Brown

- Overarching theme or question to be explored
- May be done in a 1/2 day to 2 or 3 days, depending on issue
- Large space set with café tables that seat 4 people, a café environment
- Tables are covered with butcher paper with markers and crayons available
- No limitation in numbers of people, more is better than too few
- Consists of a number of rounds lasting 20–30 minutes
- After each round three people move to another table, one person remains to host the arrivals from another table
- New groups share previous insights and continue exploration
- Periodic community reporting of ideas and insights
- Listening to diverse viewpoints, and suspending premature judgment is encouraged

theme that fully engages the participants is critical to a productive experience. The World Café can be used in groups as small as twelve and as large as twelve hundred.

One of the interesting aspects of The World Café is the use of café tables, creating a casual environment that is familiar in many countries: the coffee house, pub, or sidewalk café where people gather for conversation. In the March 2005 issue of *The Journal of Applied Behavioral Sciences*, there is a description of The World Café in Singapore, where its similarity to the local coffee houses facilitated in-depth conversations that might not have occurred in a more formal environment. This method has been widely used internationally from Sweden to Singapore. In this book, it is used as a way to bring citizen action groups and refinery management together for discussion about environmental issues (Adams and Clancy in Chapter Four).

America*Speaks*

During the 1990s, Caroline J. Lukensmeyer began work on a method for involving larger groups of citizens in critical policy issues that affect them. These meetings created discussion and deliberation among diverse groups of citizens. Rather than the usual panel presentations and audience questions to a panel, citizens participated in discussions at round tables (ten people per table). Lukensmeyer, after experimenting with different formats, started an organization—America*Speaks*—which is committed to participative democracy and uses this Large Group Method to give citizens voice in a new and effective way. In the late 1990s in major cities across the country, America*Speaks* held conversations on the dilemmas facing the Social Security system. A trained facilitator led each table discussion in order to ensure that people stayed on the task and no one dominated the discussion. Prior to the meeting, participants received a detailed and balanced discussion guide to increase their knowledge of the issue.

FIGURE 1.6. LARGE GROUP METHOD FOR DISCUSSION AND DECISION MAKING: AMERICA*SPEAKS*

AMERICA*SPEAKS*

Purpose: To engage community/citizen groups in a process of learning and discussion around important issues affecting these groups

Carolyn J. Lukensmeyer

- Format designed to engage the issues
- Participative democracy
- Full spectrum of stakeholders a basic requirement
- Laptop computers at each table to record discussion themes
- Key pads for voting for every participant
- Table facilitators structure discussion
- Overhead screens display discussion themes and voting tallies
- Subject matter experts on call to discussion tables
- Several hundred to 5,000 participants
- Usually one day
- Extensive prep and set up work

A unique aspect of this method (because the gatherings often involve hundreds or thousands of people) is the use of technology. Innovative software is used that allows people at the round tables to discuss a topic and input their ideas on a laptop provided to each table. The inputs from each table go to a central group that organizes and posts the themes from all the tables on large screens visible to the whole community. In addition, each participant has a keypad to vote agreement or disagreement with the recommendations presented.

America*Speaks* became highly visible in July of 2002, headlined on the front pages of many newspapers, when nearly five thousand people gathered at the Javits Center in New York City to react to proposals to redevelop Ground Zero. As a result of the input from participants, the architectural plans were changed. An interesting description of their work, along with several examples, appears in the March 2005 issue of *The Journal of Applied Behavioral Science*. In this book, Steven Brigham writes about their involvement in long-range planning for the three-state metropolitan area around Cincinnati, Hamilton County (see Chapter Five).

The Future of Large Group Methods

Large Group Methods are now part of the practice of many OD and change consultants. They may use them by their official names or modify and relabel them for their own purposes. Whatever the case, they are in widespread use. What will happen as we move further into the 21st century? Based on the work that is currently going on, we think several areas of development can be predicted. First, we expect the spread of these methods to non-Western cultures to continue. Second, we believe that the usefulness of Large Group Methods in community settings or wherever diverse interest groups must work together predicts their expanded use there. Third, the use of technology, as seen in several cases in this book, will continue to lead to innovative adaptations of these methods using technology.

Part Two of this book is organized around the six areas of great challenge in the 21st century mentioned in the Preface. We think these challenges—more than the authority of methods—are currently driving practice. Organizations these days are stretched. Communities are dealing with issues of great moment with limited resources. The issues are urgent, and stakeholders want to have a voice in the decision making. Large Group Methods make it possible to widen the circle to include more people in the movement toward effective action. To see how all this is happening, read on!

Note

1. For information about their 2005 article, "SimuReal: A Large Group Method for Organizational Change," contact A. A. Klein, & D. C. Klein at Klein Consulting, 11006 Wood Elves Way, Columbia, MD 21044, alan@klein.net.

References

Axelrod, E. M., & Axelrod, R. H. (2000). *The Conference Model.* San Francisco: Berrett-Koehler.

Brown, J., & Isaacs, D. (2005). *The World Café: Shaping our futures through conversations that matter.* San Francisco: Berrett-Koehler.

Bunker, B. B. (2000). Managing conflict through Large Group Methods. In M. Deutsch & P. T. Coleman (Eds.), *The handbook of conflict resolution: Theory and practice.* San Francisco: Jossey-Bass.

Bunker, B. B., & Alban, B. T. (Eds.). (1992). Large group interventions [Special issue]. *Journal of Applied Behavioral Science, 28*(4).

Bunker, B. B., & Alban, B. T. (1997). *Large group interventions: Engaging the whole system for rapid change.* San Francisco: Jossey-Bass.

Bunker, B. B., & Alban, B. T. (Eds.). (2005). Large group interventions [Special issue]. *Journal of Applied Behavioral Science, 41*(1).

Dannemiller Tyson Associates. (2000). *Whole-Scale Change: Unleashing the magic in organizations.* San Francisco: Berrett-Koehler.

Emery, F. E., & Trist, E. L. (1960). Socio-technical systems. In C. W. Churchman & others (Eds.), *Management sciences, models and techniques.* London: Pergamon.

Emery, M. (Ed.). (1993). *Participative design for participative democracy.* Canberra, ACT, Australia: Centre for Continuing Education, Australian National University.

Emery, M., & Purser, R. E. (1996). *The Search Conference: A powerful method for planning organizational change and community action.* San Francisco: Jossey-Bass.

Gladwell, M. (2000). *The tipping point: How little things can make a big difference.* New York: Little, Brown.

Jacobs, R. (1994). *Real Time Strategic Change.* San Francisco: Berrett-Koehler.

Katz, D. T., & Kahn, R. L. (1978). *The social psychology of organizations.* New York: Wiley.

Klein, D. (1992). Simu-Real: A simulation approach to organizational change. *Journal of Applied Behavioral Science, 28*, 566–578.

Lippitt, R. (1980). *Choosing the future you prefer.* Washington, DC: Development Publishers.

Ludema, J. D., Whitney, D., Mohr, B. J., & Griffin, T. J. (2003). *The Appreciative Inquiry Summit: A practitioner's guide for leading large-group change.* San Francisco: Berrett-Koehler.

Miller, E. J., & Rice, A. K. (1967). *Systems of organizations: Task and sentient systems and their boundary control.* London. Tavistock Publications.

Owen, H. (1997). *Open Space Technology: A user's guide* (2nd ed.). San Francisco: Berrett-Koehler.

Rehm, R. (1999). *People in charge: Creating self managing workplaces.* Stroud, Great Britain: Hawthorn.

Schön, D. (1971). *Beyond the stable state.* New York: Norton.

Slater, R. (1999). *The GE Way field book.* New York: McGraw-Hill.

Spencer, L. J. (1989). *Winning through participation.* Dubuque, IA: Kendall/Hunt.

Trist, E. L. (1981). The evolution of socio-technical systems. In A. H. Van de Ven and W. F. Joyce (Eds.), *Perspectives on organizational design and behavior.* New York: John Wiley.

Weisbord, M. R. (1987). *Productive workplaces: Organizing and managing for dignity, meaning, and community.* San Francisco: Jossey-Bass.

Weisbord, M., & Janoff, S. (2000). *Future Search: An action guide to finding common ground in organizations and communities* (2nd ed.). San Francisco: Berrett-Koehler.

THE MATRIX

Case Examples by Category

	Sector				Situation		Methods	
	Business-Industry	Nonprofit-Educational	Health Care	Community	Cross-Cultural	Conflict	Type	IT Use
Chapter 2: Geographically Dispersed								
BBC		✓					AI	✓
World Vision		✓		✓	✓		AI	✓
Chapter 3: Organizational Crisis								
American Airlines	✓						Mixed	✓
USC School of Education		✓					FS	
Chemical Plant	✓						FS + Kaisen	
BU Dental School		✓	✓				SP, FS, WD	
Chapter 4: Conflict								
Teachers Union		✓				✓	WS	
Health Service UK		✓	✓	✓		✓	WS	
FAA	✓	✓				✓	FS	
Petrochemical	✓			✓		✓	WC	
Chapter 5: Communities								
SpeakUp!		✓		✓	✓		AI, FS	
Israel		✓		✓	✓	✓	OS	✓
Hamilton County		✓		✓		✓	WS, IT	✓

Chapter 6: Cross-Cultural

Mexico		✓		FS, OS, PD ✓
Africa	✓	✓		OS
Indonesia	✓	✓	✓	FS
Parliament	✓	✓	✓	Mixed

Chapter 7: New Patterns

General Electric	✓			WO
Boeing	✓			Core Principles
Canadian Health		✓	✓	OS

KEY: AI—Appreciative Inquiry
FS—Future Search
Mixed—Combined methods
OS—Open Space
PD—Participative Design
SP—Scenario Planning
WC—The World Café
WO—Work Out
WD—Work Design

PART TWO

SIX CHALLENGES FOR THE 21st CENTURY

The six challenges represent the cutting-edge areas that organizations and communities must engage to flourish in the 21st century. When we began this book, we spread a big net: we talked with many clients and consultants who are facing important and often difficult issues that are paramount for them. In this fast-changing and flattening world, their work is a reflection of what organizations are wrestling with. This means, in our view, that organizations and communities see these issues as priorities.

Unlike our first book about Large Group Methods (1997), where the methods themselves were the focus of attention, this book represents a shift in attention from method to particular types of challenges that are critical in today's world.

What are these priorities? What challenges are important enough that organizations are willing to spend resources to gather their members to deal with them?

The heart of this book is six challenges that organizations and communities are currently giving priority as they move forward into the 21st century. In the chapters that follow, we describe each challenge and present cases that illustrate the use of Large Group Methods to address the challenge. We also include concepts and reflections from our own work and experience.

CHAPTER TWO

WIDELY DISPERSED ORGANIZATIONS AND THE PROBLEM OF INVOLVEMENT

The global economy has encouraged the development and spread of organizations that span the oceans and have offices worldwide. This is true not only in the business world but in nongovernmental organizations (NGOs) such as relief organizations and service and religious organizations that operate across borders. At the same time, people in many organizations do not feel a great sense of ownership, even though enlightened management knows that people are a great resource and wants them to feel valued and to contribute their ideas. The challenge in this world of bigger and bigger organizations that are more and more spread out is how to help people feel that they are a vital part of the whole.

We got our first taste of this issue while consulting for a Cleveland-based company that had operations in France, Great Britain, and Singapore. The company was trying to rationalize their human resources system across national borders, and they were planning their first-ever international meeting in France. The whole previous history had been to bring people into the headquarters in Cleveland for all important meetings.

They wanted to plan a meeting that (1) met specific human resource goals, (2) acknowledged and celebrated the cultural diversity that was present, and (3) had a positive impact on the rest of the organization. The first goal—the specific meeting task—is typical of most meetings. The second goal of dealing with the several cultures present and creating a meeting structure that is comfortable and productive for all is a topic we deal with in some depth in Chapter Five. The third goal—engaging the whole organization—is the focus of this chapter.

How do you hold work meetings with a subset of the organization or community and still involve the people who cannot be present in a meaningful way? The oldest answer to this question was to publish and distribute reports of what happened at the meeting to all the appropriate people. Of course, the reports usually came out weeks or months after the meeting and had lost their currency by the time they arrived.

Everyone knew this was not a good solution. Then we got the idea that "action planning" within the framework of the meeting might have an impact on how effective the follow-up was. We discovered that if you did not allow plenty of time for planning and organizing for action during the off-site meeting, not much was likely to happen. On the other hand, if you did form task forces and let people decide what commitments to the future they were willing to make, quite amazing things could happen! Large Group Methods, with a few exceptions, usually are very careful and sometimes quite innovative about planning the transfer process between what the meeting decides and how that is translated back to the organization or to others in the community (see Chapter Seven on this topic).

A core concept underlying Large Group Methods is to *get the whole system in the room.* As these methods have developed, ways have been found to involve more than just a small, representative sample of the organization or community, and the payoff for involving all the stakeholders has become more apparent. Especially after using these methods and seeing the results in commitment and energy for change, it is not surprising that organizations want to involve more and more people. In the 1980s, a gathering of five hundred Ford managers facilitated by Kathie Dannemiller was mind blowing. In the 1990s, interconnecting two thousand people in four ballrooms was an amazing accomplishment. In July 2003, almost five thousand people spent a day together at the Javits Center in New York City, as America*Speaks* led them in a participative discussion of how the World Trade Center site should be redesigned and allowed them to register and display their views for the decision makers who were present. We have learned how to engage exceptionally large groups in one place for a day or two and do it effectively.

But *what if the very large group is not all in one place? What if the project needs more than an intense day or two to develop a plan and take action?* This is the new issue that the cases in this chapter address. We believe it is a timely issue that will resonate with many readers. How do you involve the whole system in understanding, thinking, and planning for important organizational priorities when the organization is dispersed and you want as many people as possible involved? Today's organizations are located in offices around the world. But this question is just as relevant to a small company in western New York State, headquartered in Buffalo, with offices in Binghamton, Glens Falls, Elmira, and Jamestown. The issue at stake here is: When do you bring people together physically, at the cost of both time and money, or when do you use more virtual ways of involving them in the action? Your organization may be worldwide and you may have to think about time zones, or it may be regional and in one time zone, but you still have to decide when to meet face-to-face and when to communicate in other ways.

The interesting research on virtual teams that has been growing steadily since the late 1990s deals with just this issue for small task groups whose membership is dispersed. But we are talking about the *whole* organization and its stakeholders, which is another level of magnitude.

What news is there from the front lines? What have people who have dealt with this problem learned? We are delighted with the two cases presented here. They are innovative and successful experiments that show the way:

- "Innovation at the BBC: Engaging an Entire Organization," by Mee-Yan Cheung-Judge and Edward H. Powley
- "Whole System Engagement Through Collaborative Technology at World Vision," by Soren Kaplan and Ronald Fry

What to Note in These Cases

In the first case, the British Broadcasting Corporation (BBC) is described as an organization with 27,000 staff worldwide that has experienced many years of organization change initiatives. Nevertheless, the new director general wanted to change the culture at a deep level. He wanted the BBC to become "the most creative organization in the world."

In "Innovation at the BBC: Engaging an Entire Organization," Mee-Yan Cheung-Judge, the external consultant engaged for the project, and Edward Powley describe her high-risk strategy of proposing that they use the Appreciative Inquiry (AI) Summit and accepting a contract that only assured that they could take the first step in the process—the Discovery phase—that occurs in the first day of the summit. Cheung-Judge was working with an internal change leader who was very doubtful that AI as a method would work well at the BBC because of the skeptical, even cynical, mind-set of journalists. This situation reminds us that, years ago, a colleague of ours who was very imaginative decided to propose to the small training group he was facilitating that at the end of each day, they could decide if he should get paid for his work that day. The group was astonished but agreed, and the nature of the work in the group picked up energy and engagement.

The standard contractual arrangement of change agents is to have a contract that will provide time and resources through the implementation of the change. The BBC contract was almost no contract at all. Everyone was "flying by the seat of their pants," or in more contemporary language we could say that this project was "emergent" or even "self-organizing." Each phase had to earn the right to proceed to the next phase. The project goals were also what another British author in this book, Julie Beedon, calls "big hairy audacious goals." They intended to involve all 27,000 employees!

There are several unique features to notice in this case. First, the AI Summit process was spread out over a period of a year, with four to five months between each phase. This gave the opportunity to push each phase of the process down into the divisions of the organization and really engage all the employees. At the same time, readers will wonder how they sustained energy and engagement over this period of time.

The very strong internal change team is another key to the success of this process. Notice also the very strong use of technology to connect the organization, especially in "the big conversation"—the last phase of the AI Summit. Finally, there is a very insightful and useful discussion of what the role and dilemmas are for the lone external consultant in a project this big. The authors discuss how to live with uncertainty, the importance of building relationships and internal capacity, and the external consultant's role to hold the vision for the client, even in times of anxiety. They also describe the importance of using a shadow consultant and mentor in large, complex projects.

The second case in this chapter is "Whole System Engagement Through Collaborative Technology at World Vision." World Vision is a widely dispersed food relief organization with 20,000 employees and volunteers in 100 offices worldwide. World Vision wanted to set big goals for the next ten years, and they wanted to involve as many of their employees and stakeholders as possible. However, their budget only made it possible to bring 150 people to the four-day AI Summit in Bangkok. Soren Kaplan (from the technology firm that used interactive video to engage the online community) and consultant Ronald Fry describe the creation of a collaborative online community that included both face-to-face regional meetings and individual input before, during, and after the conference. So interactive was this event that every morning the delegates in Bangkok received summaries of what the online community had to say overnight. The audio and video proceedings in Bangkok were sent to everyone online at the end of each day so that they could send reactions and suggestions. Groups introduced themselves to each other online using pictures and stories. The feeling of community was palpable. In the end, 4,500 people helped World Vision set its new goals for the next ten years.

Our Ideas

These cases are intriguing because they foreshadow what is possible and what is yet to come in many organizations. We have not begun to exploit the possibilities for being connected technologically, and both of these cases illustrate in a practical way what can be done. In fact, the leaders at World Vision felt that they got better goals and plans, more rapid alignment of the organization, and increased readiness to implement the plans as a result of their Bangkok AI Summit. One leader is even reputed to have said, "There is no going back!" We think this is a correct intuition. It may even suggest new models of organizational governance. Kaplan and Fry suggest, provocatively, that in the future it may be possible to create such a strongly connected online community that the real decision makers will be online and "Bangkok" may be just a coordination center for the decision-making process.

Unfortunately, however, not enough executives realize the impact on the whole organization and its employees of a fully engaging process like the ones described in these cases. Expectations about the future are raised. This means that people expect actions to be taken in line with their planning, and they expect to be involved in it, not just once but whenever there are important decisions that affect the organization and its employees. These are not one-time events. If they are, they can lead to cynicism and greater resistance to change. We need to educate our clients about the dangers of asking people to participate in setting goals or solving problems and then not including them in subsequent activities.

INNOVATION AT THE BBC

Engaging an Entire Organization

Mee-Yan Cheung-Judge and Edward H. Powley

The Challenge

During the decade of the 1990s, the British Broadcasting Corporation (BBC) had undergone a number of nonstop changes. Then in the summer of 1999, Greg Dyke arrived as the newly appointed director general of the BBC. He found the BBC to be sluggish, mired in costly bureaucracy, unresponsive due to multiple layers, risk-averse, and internally too complex. He envisioned a flatter organization, greater collaboration among the top executive committees, increased funding for programming, more visible risk taking, and more agility in an already burgeoning multimedia and entertainment industry.

Four months after his arrival, Dyke launched "OneBBC: Making It Happen"—an organizational change program to cut costs, streamline the business, and encourage teamwork. Organizational layers were removed. More representatives from programming were given a place on the executive committee (called ExCo) that runs the BBC. Dyke demanded more and better teamwork at the very top of the organization. In a move that won huge support among program makers, he vowed to cut overhead. Then between April 1999 and October 2001, overhead decreased from 24 percent to 13 percent, and the savings were channeled into programming output. Nearly eighteen months after the launch, revenue had grown 23 percent, and viewership was at a high: 97 percent of television viewers tuned in to its programs, and BBC Radio broadcasts were reaching 67 percent of the U.K. adult population.

The results from this change effort, however, posed new challenges for the BBC. Internal and external indicators gave cause for concern. Public perceptions suggested that (1) younger viewers were moving away from the BBC, (2) minority and ethnic groups did not feel programming was relevant to them, and (3) in digital homes with greater choice for programming, the BBC had a smaller share of viewers. Moreover, the public felt the BBC was remote, out of touch, and a bit disconnected from reality.

After the reorganization, internal staff felt less valued and thought the BBC was a difficult place to be creative and innovative. Staff surveys revealed a perceived disconnect between the rhetoric of organizational leaders and their behavior. The BBC leadership had, up to this point, made radical changes that led to "losses" of control, destiny, turf, roles, teams, customs, and practices. In response, Greg Dyke recognized the need for profound and radical change to improve creativity, understand market audiences, value staff more, build trust and collaboration, improve leadership, and improve internal communication.

In February 2002, the BBC engaged in a second systemwide, culture-change program when it announced a five-year goal: to become the most creative organization in the world (Burke, 2002; Kanter and Raymond, 2003a, 2003b; Berrisford, 2005). To engage an organization with the scope and scale of the BBC meant more than cosmetic changes to programs and polices; it mandated that strategic decisions align with existing organizational processes, established cultural norms, and business and industry imperatives.

Selecting the Change Method

Managers and directors chosen to lead the change effort understood the challenge. They knew that in order to achieve real culture change, they needed a different method to help capture the hearts and mind of the 27,000 employees. The external consultant (Cheung-Judge), when asked to assist in this change process, proposed a Large Group Method based on Appreciative Inquiry (AI) (Cooperrider and Srivastva, 1987; Srivastva and Cooperrider, 1990; Cooperrider, Whitney, and Starvos, 2003; Whitney and Trosten-Bloom, 2003; Watkins and Mohr, 2001). The AI approach was deemed an attractive alternative because it is inclusive; it is democratic and engages the whole organization in the change process, obtains buy-in from every level of the organization, and enables change by empowering staff to take more risks and demonstrate creativity. Most of all, it would inject energy into the change process, which the organization desperately needed if it were to sustain any change initiatives. Given AI's successful track record in other organizations (Powley, Fry, Barrett, and Bright, 2004; Fry, Whitney, Seiling, and Barrett, 2002; Ludema, Whitney, Mohr, and Griffin, 2003), it offered a fresh approach to large system change.

AI at the BBC

Typical AI Summit Meetings follow a four-day format in which each day represents one phase of AI. At the end of four days, attendees have experienced all phases of the change process. After the Summit Meeting, participants continue to work in teams on follow-up actions. Up to now, those using the summit approach have assumed that organizations must work through AI's four phases sequentially, that is, in four consecutive days. The work at the BBC calls into question this assumption about the summit process (a modified model is described below).

At the BBC, the collaborative partnership between the external consultant and the lead internal change team manager (referred to here as the BBC change leader or internal change leader) played a significant role in determining how this Large Group Method was adapted. The BBC change leader was skeptical of the AI approach. As a senior, experienced program maker, she knew staff would not embrace the AI method. BBC core staff members are journalists, whose instincts are to look skeptically on and cast doubt on the facts presented to them. This means that they favor a deficiency mode for analyzing and engaging in organizational change. In the face of this powerfully skeptical and cynical culture, the introduction of AI and its underlying philosophy would be too challenging an intervention to the system's culture. Her intuition was that this change process would build up resistance early in the change program.

Another reason the BBC change leader worried about using AI was that she knew, as part of the group who had gone through nonstop radical changes with the previous director general, that there was "change fatigue" among BBC staff. The system was still coping with losses from a number of changes such as the radical shift to the internal market way of operating, deep restructuring, and endless efficiency-driven changes. The internal change leader felt that an overly positive approach would cause BBC staff to feel the incongruence between reality and this "new" round of change in the organization. Finally, a four-day off-site event was not only counter to the 24/7 business culture of the BBC but would be viewed as an inappropriate use of financial resources and logistically impossible to create.

The external change consultant and the internal change leader decided to forego a traditional AI Summit approach. They adopted an alternative approach, which, in essence, only involved Discovery (described next). The external consultant felt that engaging employees in the Discovery phase would help establish a path toward more involvement in the rest of the AI Process. Hence, the risk in introducing AI in a piecemeal fashion, even without any guarantee whether the other phases would be continued, was deemed worthwhile. With that, the change leader and consultant designed a pilot phase of just one Discovery session.

Other BBC change leaders agreed to pilot the session, which enabled them to experience and see the potential of AI.

Within a few months of the initiation of the Phase I project, the unimaginable happened: the pilot of Phase I was successful. As a result, the change team was permitted to carry out the rest of the phases, and twelve months later the AI Process had included nearly 17,000 of the 27,000 employees in implementing strategic changes (for a timeline of major phases, see Figure 2.1). Separating out the phases of the AI Process was not planned but emerged as the organization became more familiar and comfortable with the method. The external consultant used the Watkins and Mohr (2001) five-phase model of AI (see Figure 2.2), as well as consultation with Jane Watkins, to help her guide this emerging design.

Definition: Business Case

In the beginning of "OneBBC: Making It Happen," the BBC worked with another external consultancy firm to identify seven areas that the culture-change initiative needed to address. These foundational themes for the process included (1) inspiring creativity everywhere, (2) connecting with all audiences, (3) valuing people, (4) "we are the BBC" (values), (5) great spaces, (6) lead more, manage well, and (7) "just do it" (a reference to changing bureaucratic processes). Articulation of these themes became the basis for discussion in the

FIGURE 2.1. TIMELINE OF THE ROLLOUT FOR ONEBBC: MAKING IT HAPPEN

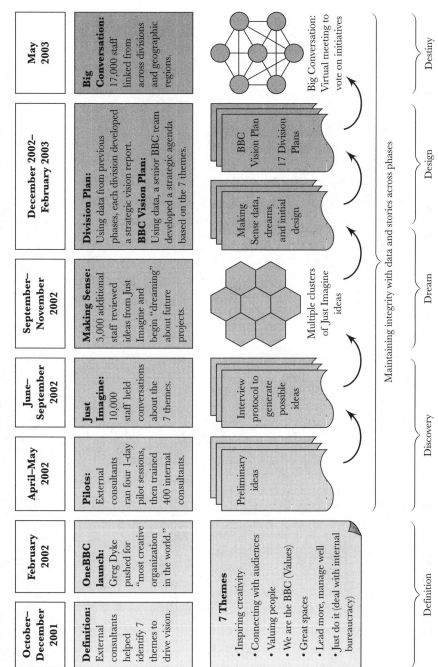

October–December 2001	February 2002	April–May 2002	June–September 2002	September–November 2002	December 2002–February 2003	May 2003
Definition: External consultants helped identify 7 themes to drive vision.	**OneBBC launch:** Greg Dyke pushed for "most creative organization in the world."	**Pilots:** External consultants ran four 1-day pilot sessions, then trained 400 internal consultants.	**Just Imagine:** 10,000 staff held conversations about the 7 themes.	**Making Sense:** 5,000 additional staff reviewed ideas from Just Imagine and begin "dreaming" about future projects.	**Division Plan:** Using data from previous phases, each division developed a strategic vision report. **BBC Vision Plan:** Using data, a senior BBC team developed a strategic agenda based on the 7 themes.	**Big Conversation:** 17,000 staff linked from across divisions and geographic regions.

7 Themes
- Inspiring creativity
- Connecting with audiences
- Valuing people
- We are the BBC (Values)
- Great spaces
- Lead more, manage well
- Just do it (deal with internal bureaucracy)

Preliminary ideas

Interview protocol to generate possible ideas

Multiple clusters of Just Imagine ideas

Making Sense data, dreams, and initial design

BBC Vision Plan 17 Division Plans

Big Conversation: Virtual meeting to vote on initiatives

Maintaining integrity with data and stories across phases

Definition	Discovery	Dream	Design	Destiny

FIGURE 2.2. MODIFIED FIVE PHASES OF AI USED AT THE BBC'S MAKING-IT-HAPPEN PROJECT

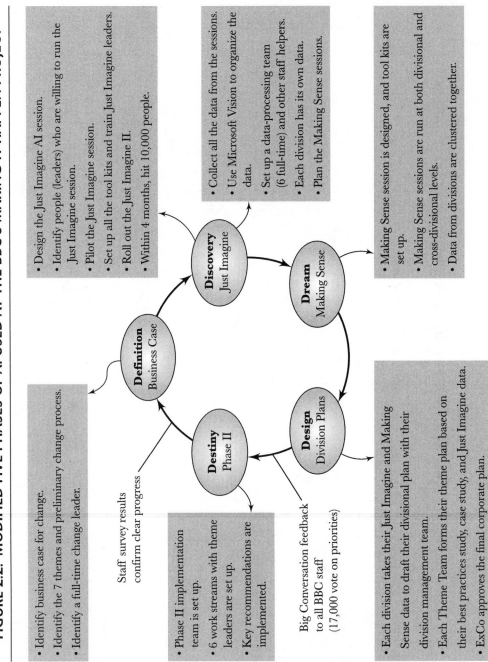

- Design the Just Imagine AI session.
- Identify people (leaders) who are willing to run the Just Imagine session.
- Pilot the Just Imagine session.
- Set up all the tool kits and train Just Imagine leaders.
- Roll out the Just Imagine II.
- Within 4 months, hit 10,000 people.

- Collect all the data from the sessions.
- Use Microsoft Vision to organize the data.
- Set up a data-processing team (6 full-time) and other staff helpers.
- Each division has its own data.
- Plan the Making Sense sessions.

- Making Sense session is designed, and tool kits are set up.
- Making Sense sessions are run at both divisional and cross-divisional levels.
- Data from divisions are clustered together.

- Identify business case for change.
- Identify the 7 themes and preliminary change process.
- Identify a full-time change leader.

Staff survey results confirm clear progress

- Phase II implementation team is set up.
- 6 work streams with theme leaders are set up.
- Key recommendations are implemented.

Big Conversation feedback to all BBC staff (17,000 vote on priorities)

- Each division takes their Just Imagine and Making Sense data to draft their divisional plan with their division management team.
- Each Theme Team forms their theme plan based on their best practices study, case study, and Just Imagine data.
- ExCo approves the final corporate plan.

Discovery
Just Imagine

Dream
Making Sense

Definition
Business Case

Design
Division Plans

Destiny
Phase II

later phases. This is what, in Watkins's and Mohr's model (2001), is referred to as the "Definition phase." These themes became the seeds for proposals on how to achieve strategic goals.

During the Definition phase, understanding the enormity of carrying out a large system change project that would be led mainly by internal staff, the BBC set up support teams at different levels in the organization to carry out specific tasks.

- A central full-time change team of about thirty-five members
- Seven Theme Teams, each headed up by a senior manager with six to ten members and serviced by a project manager who was a member of the central change team
- Seventeen divisional teams, each headed by a senior manager from the division with six to ten members
- A data-processing team, which was responsible for collecting and synthesizing key information from the division teams and the teams associated with the seven themes

Discovery: Just Imagine

In April 2002, the BBC gave permission to proceed with the pilot session of the Just Imagine workshop (Discovery). Four one-day pilot workshops preceded a workshop with four hundred managers. Afterward, when the pilot was deemed successful, plans moved forward to roll out the event in full scale at the divisional level, and more internal change agents

were trained in the methodology—but only the Discovery phase.

Employees from across the organization were invited to participate in similar Just Imagine workshops in their own divisions. In these workshops, participants interviewed each other and identified themes from their group discussions; because the rollout of the Just Imagine event was done in a decentralized fashion, each division adapted the interview guide and discussion topics to fit their divisional culture. Within four months (June to September 2002), workshops with 50 to 200 participants occurred in 120 locations involving over 10,000 staff.

These workshops generated many ideas, themes, and project proposals (what we call "the data"), which were sent to the central data-management team to be collated and processed. Uniform data report-back sheets for each theme, by division, were used. When they were returned to the data-management team, the data collected could be easily categorized by division, according to the seven themes.

To demonstrate that the leadership was behind the initiative and supported the ideas and proposals of the employees, the BBC immediately implemented some of the ideas generated from the Just Imagine sessions, and they publicized the results widely. This also helped maintain momentum and create credibility for the change process. For example, a four-day introductory course for new employees called "Upfront" was implemented, as was job shadowing, job swap, and quick-fire commissions (taking production ideas to actual production quickly).

Dream: Making Sense

In this phase, we were pursuing answers to these two questions:

> What should we do with the impressive data we got from the Just Imagine workshops?
>
> What should we do to continue to increase the number of people who will engage with this change process?

To begin finding answers, the external consultant designed and obtained approval in September 2002 to run the Dream phase of the AI methodology. This event was labeled as the "Making Sense Event." This next step targeted staff that had not participated in any of the Just Imagine workshops. The purpose of this event was to involve them in "making sense" of the data in preparation for the Design phase. A second set of meeting guidelines was designed, and divisional and corporate BBC staff members were trained to conduct these sessions.

The prerequisite for the divisional Making Sense Event was the completion of the divisional data organization (from all the Just Imagine sessions) so that delegates would be able to mine the data for interpreting, dreaming, and identifying action. Data were organized by using Microsoft Visio in which the data-management team organized themed ideas using hexagon diagrams. In preparation

for the Making Sense sessions, each division received a sizeable packet of their summarized ideas in this hexagon format. These were used in the Making Sense sessions by staff members unfamiliar with what had occurred in the Just Imagine sessions.

When BBC staff met for the Making Sense sessions, they were asked to (1) review and interpret the categorized data from the Just Imagine sessions, (2) dream about what the image of the future of BBC would be like if all the ideas generated came true, and (3) determine the priorities and actions needed to make the dreams realities. These Making Sense sessions took place as one-day meetings in October and November, with the majority taking place over a two-week period in a large, rented space. The four-hundred-person sessions ran continuously for ten days, involving approximately four thousand staff members.

Design: Divisional Change Plans and Corporate Change Plan

After the Making Sense sessions, each of the divisions constructed their divisional change plan, based on the actions and priorities identified by the delegates in their individual division sessions. At the same time, seven Theme Team leaders developed specific proposals that formed a corporationwide plan to achieve the BBC vision of the seven themes. They used two primary sources to help them do this work: (1) corporate data that the external consultant produced by pulling all the divisional data together for each theme and (2) both internal and external industry best practices, which BBC benchmarked.

By January 2003, all the divisional change leaders submitted change plans to the ExCo, and the Theme Team leaders submitted to the ExCo an overall, corporationwide plan. Combined, the seven Theme Teams made forty-five actionable recommendations. By then it was obvious to the change team that one more event was needed to increase the ownership and commitment of staff to this change program. A consultation event called the Big Conversation was planned for May 2003.

Destiny: Big Conversation

In May 2003, the BBC held what they called the Big Conversation. Using the Internet and their programming capabilities, they linked up offices and bureaus across the globe. The event was a virtual and face-to-face meeting, where BBC management and staff responded to the ideas generated and shaped by the first three phases of the process: Discovery (Just Imagine), Dream (Making Sense), and Design (Divisional Change Plans). They then gained organizational members' commitment by asking them to vote on priorities; 17,000 of the 27,000 BBC staff voted that day.

After the Big Conversation event, five key streams of work were identified as the top priorities, and new leaders were appointed in June 2003 to oversee the implementation of the five streams (Phase II). Each of the stream leaders

formed new change teams to carry out the implementation, while the central team was reinforced in order to give the stream leaders the necessary support and coordination during the implementation phase. The Big Conversation represented closure for AI. Participants from previous sessions and other BBC staff members from across the BBC had the opportunity to see how the process came full circle, as employees gave input and immediately saw how their ideas were part of the bigger picture.

Holding the Change Process Together

Separating the four phases of the AI method between April 2002 and January 2003 posed a great challenge to the continuity of the change effort. The external consultant and the BBC change team leader were concerned about maintaining continuity of a complex, multifaceted change program and connecting this process to action. They relied on Watkins and Mohr's (2001) five-phase model as a stimulus to develop the following strategies to maintain the integrity of the AI methodology at the BBC.

Role of Internal Change Agents

One of the most important strategies for managing the separation of the AI phases was to create a critical mass of four hundred internal change agents, who held what we call a "continuity baton" over the nine-month period. This group of agents included individuals who were in the theme and divisional teams (most were senior managers), as well as a central project team, which included a production team in charge of audiovisual and film production of the events, a dedicated internal communications team, a team of project managers supporting Theme Teams, and an internal logistics team.

These four hundred key change agents were instrumental in leading the change effort; they acted as the continuity baton by maintaining energy and transferring information throughout the process. They accomplished this by leading on the front lines, demonstrating personal commitment, and fluently telling the "Making It Happen" journey. This latter point was critical to giving participants at every stage a clear story line so that all employees understood how their work related directly to the change initiative. Most important, these change agents served as personal "recorders" of people's voices, thus ensuring that the ideas and innovations of the participants were communicated from one phase to another. They literally became critical "holders" of both the energy and the participants' voices; in this way they played a critical role in sustaining the overall change momentum.

The Linking Role of Data

Reconnecting the AI phases required more than internal change agent teams. Although these teams relayed key information about the progress and process of the change project, the data generated from each phase enabled the change agents to maintain important connections throughout the process. Data generated by the participants of the Just Imagine sessions were mined by the participants in the Making Sense sessions, which, in turn, generated many ideas and proposals for the Design phase and the Big Conversation.

Unlike a traditional AI Summit, managing the data from fragmented stages required the following steps. First, meeting summary posters were designed (for both the Just Imagine and Making Sense sessions) so that attendees could capture the ideas from their conversations. Second, these posters were collected at the end of each session and then sent to a central data-management team (six full-time staff members hired specifically to catalogue and content-code the ideas after each session). Third, the data-collection team used Microsoft Visio to organize the ideas discussed from sessions across the BBC during the nine-month process in connected hexagons (see Figure 2.1) design. At the end of the Just Imagine phase, the external consultant summarized the data for each division and trained the data-management team to conduct a data-facilitation meeting with each divisional team. This process helped prepare the divisions to run the Making Sense event. Then at the end of the Making Sense phase, each division received from the central team their division data in the form of a book from the previous two phases and a guide for drawing up a divisional plan based on the data. Using these resources, each division then created their own division plan that was later submitted to the ExCo.

Managing the data in this way was a significant step in keeping the fragmented AI phases connected. By the end of nine months, the data-management team, under the guidance of the external consultant, had filtered and categorized over 97,800 individual comments into 25,000 ideas and suggestions on how to make BBC the most creative organization in a turbulent and competitive global media market. The huge amounts of data had the potential to be overwhelming, but the data-management process allowed the organization to systematically cull and sort important ideas and proposals that were eventually implemented.

Virtual and Face-to-Face Voting

The third mechanism to hold the process together was a virtual face-to-face digital link-up that spanned the globe (Big Conversation), which the central facilitation team established and managed. In this link-up, the BBC ensured that all employees witnessed how the phases led to specific outcomes. Even though the change process was segmented, in the final phase, the whole organization was involved in co-constructing the future by participating in this one-day consultation. On one day in May of 2003, seventeen thousand employees from across the BBC took part in a live, simultaneous, interactive, BBC-wide conversation in more than four hundred meetings in the

United Kingdom and overseas. Greg Dyke asked his staff to pose their questions and vote electronically on which recommendations should receive immediate attention. Employee reactions were overwhelmingly positive, as people knew they had direct input about the messages that emerged from the AI process.

Assessing the Strategies

Drawing on feedback throughout and at the end of the process, the consultant and internal team leaders assessed the process and the strategies used to reconnect the discrete phases of AI. Those who only attended the Just Imagine sessions did not feel alienated from the process because their ideas and voices carried through to the Big Conversation. Participants read about outcomes of their sessions on the BBC intranet, thus seeing the "whole" picture.

Employees who only attended Making Sense sessions were curious and impressed by the number of ideas that had been proposed in preceding sessions. Even though they did not generate the ideas themselves, they were encouraged by the fact that they could review the Just Imagine data and thus help the organization "make sense" of current and future challenges. Based on the divisional change plans, divisional leaders and their teams decided on the actions the participants identified in the Making Sense sessions. Likewise, each of the seven theme team leaders and their teams decided on the collated actions of all the divisional

Making Sense sessions as the basis of their theme change plan.

The organization began shifting its overall perceptions and experiences of the organizational culture. Within one year (2001–02), opinions started to change. By 2003, responses to twenty-five out of twenty-eight staff survey questions showed marked improvement. As the BBC continued to learn from its employees, the organization responded by implementing many of the ideas proposed during the sessions. For example, they launched a leadership program for all managers and executives. They introduced flexible work schedule programs and flexible leave policies to encourage more work-life integration. The organization developed "creativity training" for those developing programs and appointed "audience insight" teams to gather feedback about programming. One team that studied the redesign of physical working space organized a bus tour to visit all BBC buildings and develop new space plans.

Modifying the AI Summit

From this case, one learns that even when the traditional format is not followed, organizations can remain true to the fundamental principles of the change process and model. Due to the alternative strategies employed in this case, wholeness was achieved through an interview protocol and data that connected organization members. This occurred when the employees saw the data from other people, participated in the Big Conversation, and found points of resonance with others' ideas. Even though they were not in the same room, others were engaging virtually and across time and space.

AI has an expansive effect in organizational change, first because it places emphasis on the emotional-affective experiences and cognitive exercises of those participating together in focused inquiry. In addition, the AI process worked in this setting, using this format, because participants sensed and came to know that they were part of something larger than their organizational unit. As participants listened to experiences of persons from across the organization, they realized that they were part of something bigger than their division. This is particularly revealing for employees occupying the lower echelons of the organization. Participants from across the professional, technical, and staff core, however, understood their role within the larger system and contributed the bigger picture that was encouraged in the change initiative. All this occurred in public forums where everyone saw and heard the thinking, debating, imagining, and enacting of the "whole system in the room."

Although we have focused our attention on an innovation of the AI Summit, we believe that the same principles regarding the modification and separation of the large group process applies to other methods (Axelrod and Axelrod, 2000; Owen, 1997; Axelrod, 1992). We do not always advocate separating the AI process over time, but due to organizational concerns, this approach made the most sense for the BBC. Moreover, the alternative process that emerged at the BBC achieved positive and sustainable outcomes because of a primary concern to stay true to the change model. For example, when we stayed true to the AI change model, fundamental freedoms were sustained: the freedom to belong, to be heard, to dream, to co-construct, and to contribute. By connecting stories and experiences in the data across time, organizations highlight important voices, distribute critical information across the organizational boundaries, and infuse energy as participation grows. The role of internal change agents, as those who carry the "continuity baton," becomes important because they hear and incorporate organization members' feedback.

From this case, we have also learned about the need to develop change agents from within. Those leading the change from the inside had the social capital necessary to nurture virtual and often disconnected networks. They interjected energy as they paid attention to organizational dynamics, processes, and politics that were often hidden from those on the outside of an organization.

We were surprised by what we learned when large group change is not a consecutive two-, three-, or four-day process. A drawn-out change process brings more people into the process, with different kinds of people at different phases across time. The innovation of the method in this case draws the entire system into the process, not just representa-

tives. Because the process is expanded across time, the focus was less about getting done and getting people back to work. People see that they have more than one chance to influence the outcome, and they become involved in the priorities for which they voted.

Personal Reflections (Cheung-Judge)

As I reflect on an intellectually and emotionally challenging project like BBC, I feel that the following issues and characteristics are important to consider in my role as an organizational change consultant.

Our Ability to Hold On to a Vision During the Ups and Downs of the Project

As organizational change agents working for clients in large and complex organization systems, we need to help our clients surface and hold on to their vision. We also need to develop a clear vision for the project ourselves. Often the client system may not be able to do so, for a number of reasons: the power dynamics (especially between their own position and other power figures), their reading of the political reality, the grip of the existing paradigms, or the overfamiliarity of the cultural context, for example. One of the unspoken motives for using external help is that, more often than not, client systems want not just our competencies and experiences but also our aspiration on their behalf. While there is potential danger for us, as practitioners, to be too far ahead of the organization and hence become too disjointed with them, the lack of personal vision is an unacceptable alternative. Our job is to hold a vision clearly in our own mind for the system (especially when their current reality prevents visionary thinking) and then work out the best way to engage them in the process, helping them move step-by-step toward that vision.

Throughout the BBC project, it was clear that AI could offer much to the BBC. I was convinced that the benefit of such methodology would increase the BBC's ability to help the system face future challenges. Holding on to the vision of AI for the BBC meant working hard to persuade key organizational leaders to buy into the vision piece-by-piece, despite the fact that it was never clear whether or not the process would pay off and lay the path for the next step. I am convinced that if those holding the vision of the change process had given up and caved in to the fear of failure, the change program would never have worked.

Increasing Our Tolerance for Ambiguity

Another key lesson for consultants is the ability to live with ongoing ambiguity and uncertainties. Ambiguity is the constant and predictable factor throughout any change project. The need to con-

stantly live in the "in-between space," the incessant "not sure," the ubiquitous "maybe," the "could be a better fit, or not," the duality of being both right and wrong at the same time, or the duality of "I am right and so is she" truly tested limits when dealing with multiple paradigms, personalities, and preferences of those at the BBC. I learned that not giving in to the urge to terminate the consultant-client relationship prematurely because of the chaos and ambiguity led to unimaginably positive results. Throughout the process, resolutions to difficult decisions often turned out to be what was needed at the time. This occurred because of the patient and consistent practice of *not* rushing into a premature decision.

Choosing the Right Mode of Client-Consultant Relationship

One of the most valuable lessons involves managing client-consultant boundaries, specifically, how to balance personal relationship building and professional relationship distance. In the West, we often are reminded of the importance of maintaining clear boundary distinctions with clients in a professional way. In the BBC context, three critical factors require the external consultant to instinctively go against that rule.

First, I used AI, a highly relational methodology that emphasized building personal relationships; the organizational community focused on working together to honor all the voices in the system. Personal relationships are an important part of living out the AI methodology. Next, the BBC is a highly value-based organization in which people need to understand where people come from (in terms of their values) before they are willing to develop personal working relationships. Third, a long-term relationship requires that people be willing to go beyond their professional role or way of relating. Such contextual realities reminded me to re-think boundary maintenance protocols and to develop relationships with those I worked with closely. Part of the trust-building process with the client, particularly in situations where the client seeks a closer relationship based on their values, requires us to give up the need for maintaining boundaries and getting to know them beyond the professional relationship without breaching ethical boundaries. The relationship between some of the BBC personnel and me, particularly the BBC change leader, was one of the cornerstones for the success of the project and its outcomes. The amazing personal benefit at the end of this project is the strong friendship that was developed through an authentic way of relating between the change leader and me.

Building a One-to-One Supportive Relationship with Change Leaders

In addition to building personal relationships is the need to spend a disproportional amount of time and energy building up the capability and confi-

dence of the internal change agents. Dedicated time with a lead internal consultant may seem to be an "expensive" way to deliver the change program, but without one-on-one sessions where perspectives are discussed, experiences are debriefed, and emotions are vented, it is probable that the change leaders would not have endured as long as they did, nor would they have done so as brilliantly. The real learning here is that when this type of individual support (both task and process focus) is carried out effectively, the internal change leaders, in turn, instinctively make this kind of relational support the norm, the culture of the change project. In this sense, the individualized and tailored approach to facilitating and working with change agents at the BBC cascaded down to the theme and division team leaders, which proved to be critical in sustaining their energy and motivation for the project.

Building Sufficient Internal Capacity for the Client System to Be Self-Sustaining

Building organizational capacity for self-sustaining change represents one of the key lessons for consultants. One key principle for organizational development and change is to help clients become self-sustaining—to make change and increase their capacity to adapt to change. When we find talented staff to lead the change internally, we need to increase their ability to deliver systemic change, coach them throughout the delivery, and open their understanding of the "whole" system. We enable the client organization to build long-term change capacity, and the development of leadership throughout the system is enhanced.

Mentoring Support for the External Consultant

Finally, an important aspect of working on this complex, large-scale project was finding support in a trusted and valued mentor. Mine was a fellow organizational consultant. For the project to be a success, I knew that it was critical not to lose heart and to stay clear and courageous until the end. In order to do that, I needed support from a mentor or shadow consultant. The mentor provided encouragement at difficult times during the process and supplied support to keep things in balance. Each time doubts arose or the internal cynical and skeptical voices kept pushing back, the mentor asked the right questions, listened empathetically, and provided guidance. Working alone as an external consultant in such a large system required a support system to help through the difficult times. This mentor played that vital role for me.

References

Axelrod, R. H. (1992). Getting everyone involved: How one organization involved its employees, supervisors, and managers in redesigning the organization. *Journal of Applied Behavioral Science, 28*(4), 499–509.

Axelrod, E. M., & Axelrod, R. H. (2000). *The Conference Model.* San Francisco: Berrett-Koehler.

Berrisford, S. (2005). Using Appreciative Inquiry to drive change at the BBC. *Strategic Communication Management, 9*(3), 22–25.

Burke, W. W. (2002). *Organization change: Theory and practice.* Thousand Oaks, CA: Sage.

Cooperrider, D. L., & Srivastva, S. (1987). Appreciative Inquiry in organizational life. *Research in Organizational Change and Development, 1,* 129–169.

Cooperrider, D. L., Whitney, D., & Starvos, J. M. (2003). *Appreciative Inquiry handbook: The first in a series of AI workbooks for leaders of change.* Bedford Heights, OH: Lakeshore Communications.

Fry, R. E., Whitney, D., Seiling, J., & Barrett, F. J., (Eds.). (2002). *Appreciative Inquiry and organizational transformation: Reports from the field.* Westport, CT: Quorum Books.

Kanter, R. M., & Raymond, D. (2003a). *British Broadcasting Corporation: OneBBC.* Boston: Harvard University.

Kanter, R. M., & Raymond, D. (2003b). *British Broadcasting Corporation: Making it happen.* Boston: Harvard University.

Ludema, J. D., Whitney, D., Mohr, B. J., & Griffin, T. J. (2003). *The Appreciative Inquiry Summit: A practitioner's guide for leading large-group change.* San Francisco: Berrett-Koehler.

Owen, H. (1997). *Open Space Technology: A user's guide* (2nd ed.). San Francisco: Berrett-Koehler.

Powley, E. H., Fry, R. E., Barrett, F. J., & Bright, D. S. (2004). Dialogic democracy meets command and control: Transformation through the Appreciative Inquiry Summit. *Academy of Management Executive, 18*(3), 67–80.

Srivastva, S., & Cooperrider, D. L. (1990). The emergence of the egalitarian organization. In S. Srivastva & D. L. Cooperrider (Eds.), *Appreciative management and leadership: The power of positive thought and action in organizations.* San Francisco: Jossey-Bass.

Watkins, J. M., & Mohr, B. J. (2001). *Appreciative Inquiry: Change at the speed of imagination.* San Francisco: Jossey-Bass.

Whitney, D., & Trosten-Bloom, A. (2003). *The power of Appreciative Inquiry.* San Francisco: Berrett-Koehler.

WHOLE SYSTEM ENGAGEMENT THROUGH COLLABORATIVE TECHNOLOGY AT WORLD VISION

Soren Kaplan and Ronald Fry

The Challenge

When Lars Gustavsson, vice president at World Vision,[1] was asked to lead his organization's Big Goals strategy process, he knew he faced one of the greatest challenges of his professional career. With over twenty thousand employees, World Vision is the world's largest distributor of food, and the agency feeds over seven million people each year through its international relief programs. It is known for its participative approach to leadership and management. World Vision's headquarters, in fact, actively channels decision making to its regional offices, which are distributed across almost one hundred countries throughout the world. Only by driving decision making to the local level can the greatest impact be achieved.

Lars was chartered with engaging the entire organization in a planning process to set World Vision's goals for the next ten years. Having had some prior experience with Appreciative Inquiry (AI), Lars quickly selected AI to guide the approach. The challenges were related to cost, time, scale, and continuity. The budget for the project would only allow 150 stakeholders to come together, face-to-face, for an AI Summit. Different parts of World Vision's organization had already been engaged in various deliberations related to strategic planning: a leadership group had begun the process of environmental scanning; another had begun to question "who we are" in terms of Collins's Hedgehog analysis, the *one unifying idea that allows you to organize everything under that idea* (Collins, 2001); and yet another senior group had begun the long process of considering major work redesign. All these dialogues were revealing implications for strategic goals and objectives. Finally, after spending the past two years in a systemwide participative process to revise and renew their vision statement, the World Vision leadership was adamant about aligning new strategic goals with this vision in an equally engaged process but in a dramatically shorter time span. Lars had only four months to pull it off and was mandated to find a way to invite every employee and stakeholder group to participate, somehow, in the process.

Background

The challenges that faced Lars and World Vision are not uncommon. More and more companies, nonprofits, and communities must do more with less, within shorter time frames. At the same time, the benefits of engaging the whole system in strategy development and organizational change are often recognized, but many "large group" interventions in very large systems are limited to involving representative samples of organizations or communities. As a result, the challenges are often the same:

- How to tap into the knowledge, contributions, and resources from the broader organization
- How to "bring along" those who are not able to be fully involved
- How to engage stakeholders in an experiential process so that new strategies are wholeheartedly embraced and new processes rapidly implemented

The world has changed significantly since the initial introductions of Future Search (Weisbord and Janoff, 1995), AI (Cooperrider and Srivastva, 1987), and other methods applicable to large group work. It is now possible to invite and engage the whole system—literally—to participate in strategic change processes. The benefits of involving an *entire* community of stakeholders extend and enhance the many positive contributions already inherent in many large group interventions (Bunker and Alban, 1997).

The Internet, e-mail, and Web collaboration tools have created new possibilities for engaging people across time and space, both within and across groups, organizations, and communities. Integrating collaborative technology that is focused on expanding the possibilities for participation can allow for broader stakeholder engagement in ways that facilitate learning, input, dialogue, creativity, and action. No longer does the quality of a project or intervention need to be limited by the "size of the room" or by travel constraints.

Questions naturally emerge from the collective awareness of today's interconnected, global environment—questions that underlie the growing inspiration to use technology as a tool to support organizational change:

- How can we most effectively capture, share, and use the knowledge and insights of the entire organization to support our goals?
- How do we most effectively engage the entire organization and set of stakeholders, even when time constraints exist and not everyone is able to meet together face-to-face?
- How do we sustain and grow the momentum created through face-to-face meetings and events so it leads to true innovation and inspires positive change?

- How do we accelerate the adoption of new strategies and organizational changes in ways that are supported by participative values and practices?

Voting and polling technologies frequently support many face-to-face large group meetings, capturing the pulse of a group and accelerating decision making. We are now on the cusp of a new generation of methodologies that apply technology to facilitate new forms of collaborative interaction that extend the reach of these large group events or even stand alone as virtual interventions in themselves.

World Vision's "Big Goals" Initiative

Four months before World Vision's AI Summit, Lars Gustavsson and the World Vision Big Goals steering committee established a bold game plan. The summit would be held in Bangkok, Thailand, and would involve 150 representatives from the organization's 100 field offices and other stakeholders, including partners, donors, and even the voices of children (children receive the bulk of World Vision's services). The objective of the summit was simple: to establish a set of "big goals" for the next ten years to guide the organization as it redesigns its global and regional strategies and work processes. Though the objective was simple, the approach would push the boundaries beyond what had ever been done before.

The Big Goals steering committee included the organization's top leadership, from World Vision's president to vice presidents and directors responsible for international development, human resources, organizational development, knowledge management, and information technology. The committee also incorporated support from two key partners: (1) Ronald Fry, a professor at the Weatherhead School of Management at Case Western Reserve University,[2] along with a group of doctoral students, and (2) a team from iCohere[3]—a software and consulting firm focused on creating collaborative online communities that apply Web-based tools for supporting AI and other organizational development processes.

The steering committee defined a highly inclusive process for engaging the broader organization in setting the big goals. The process would begin six weeks prior to the scheduled summit and would consist of a cascading top-down inquiry and involvement strategy, coupled with a bottom-up invitation to every World Vision employee to participate in the process. Beginning four weeks prior to the summit, regional inquiry groups would join together once a week for four weeks to explore questions and topics and provide summaries of these discussions online, through the iCohere online community.

Each weekly inquiry was designed around the AI 4-D Process: Discovery (when World Vision is at its best), Dream (our preferred future), Design (our goals to help achieve the preferred future), and Destiny (changes we can begin now to make our goals a reality). Employees without groups to join could participate individually by providing input directly online. And though the Bangkok AI Summit would only include 150 participants, opportunities would be provided to any employee who wanted to "participate" through the online community during the four-day event. Because World Vision is a truly global organization, all these activities had to be supported in English, Spanish, and French—the most pervasive international languages.

Preparing for Engagement

Preparation involved creating a detailed "inquiry guide" that established framing and context for the initiative, outlined inquiry group activities for each of the four weeks leading up to the summit, and provided instructions on how to participate online, either as a group or as an individual. Communication channels were identified, including strategies for "cascading" invitations to participate, originating with World Vision's president and being forwarded down and out through the various levels of leadership and regional offices through e-mail and voice mail.

Because stakeholders around the world possessed varying levels of technical capabilities and sophistication, the online environment had to be easy to access and use, while at the same time supporting an experience in which participants would feel that they were truly part of a global community working together on a common, exciting goal. It was equally important to make the online participation consistent with the organization's normal culture of dialogue and work. The inquiries and invited stories were thus framed, first in the context of biblical stories and reflections that begin all major World Vision meetings, anywhere in their complex global system. These were followed by AI questions related to the upcoming work of the Big Goals Summit.

The online community was configured to reflect the spirit of the initiative (see Figure 2.3), with graphics and photos of children from around the world sprinkling the site; the summit topic was focused on *changing the world with children.*

The site was designed to support a range of pre-summit activities, including

- The ability to view a streaming, narrated PowerPoint presentation by the president of World Vision about the importance of the project and of online participation, as well as the anticipated outcomes from the project
- A space for individual and group introductions, including the ability to upload photographs, so that individuals and groups could share their hopes and aspirations
- An area for entering inputs related to questions from the inquiry guide, including stories about "what gives life to World Vision when it is at its best"
- A document library of resources, the AI guide, summit logistics, and other

supporting materials such as the preliminary reports of various task forces

Because the online community needed to support multiple languages, participants were provided with the option of logging on to the site and reading all material in English, Spanish, or French.

Pre-Summit Engagement

Five weeks prior to the Bangkok summit, all twenty thousand employees received an e-mail with an invitation to participate in the Big Goals Summit online. Specific instructions for contributing stories and other inputs through the Big Goals Web site prior to the summit were given.

Individuals were encouraged to go to the Big Goals Web site and respond to a series of questions posted each week for the four weeks preceding the summit. Regional office managers received inquiry-group facilitator guides, which provided detailed instructions on how to orchestrate small group discussions in preparation for the summit. Regional groups that were able to meet in person met once a week, discussed the weekly questions, and then assigned a representative to provide their collective input online on behalf of their group members.

During the first week, for example, individuals and groups were encouraged to enter stories of exceptional service and amazing results from experiences working at World Vision. For each story, core success factors that were seen to

FIGURE 2.3. WELCOME TO WORLD VISION BIG GOALS

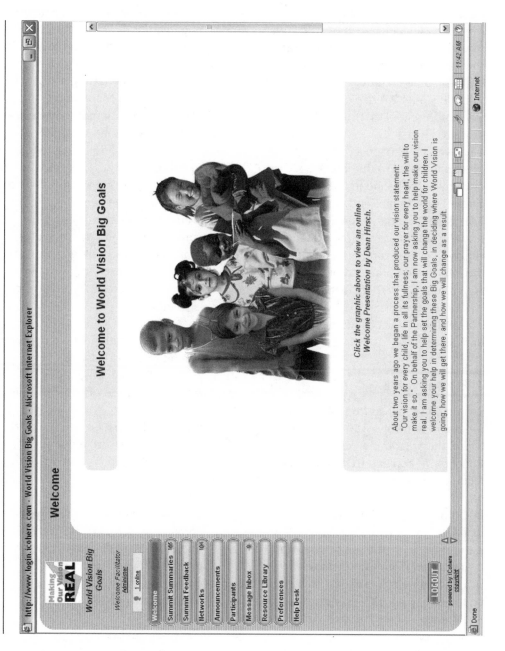

illustrate "what gives life to World Vision when we are doing our best work" were shared, providing further insight into the core strengths of the organization—input that would be used during the Bangkok summit. Figure 2.4 depicts the online AI story-capture tool that supported this process.

Over 3,500 people from forty countries contributed to this important pre-work by participating in the month-long cycle of face-to-face and online dialogue. Prior to the summit, a team of doctoral students from Case Western Reserve University searched, sorted, and exported the information provided online and created a summary report that was used as input during the summit.

And then it was time to fly to Bangkok.

The Bangkok Big Goals Summit

With representatives from all geographies and functions, 150 leaders from across the organization converged on Bangkok. In addition to World Vision's leaders from across its offices around the world, other key stakeholders convened in Bangkok as well, including a number of key donors, external consultants, and partners. Prior to the summit, several World Vision members collected on video comments and stories from the children they serve to interject throughout the summit so that their voice was always present.

The summit, designed around the AI 4-D Process Model, was structured as a four-day event, with each day focused on engaging both face-to-face and online participants in the 4-D process: Discovery, Dream, Design, and Destiny (Cooperrider and Whitney, 1999; Ludema, Whitney, Mohr, and Griffin, 2003). The integration of the face-to-face summit with the virtual online process was thoughtfully designed by a team led by Soren Kaplan from iCohere and Mark Kelly, World Vision's director of knowledge management.

Although the idea of using live streaming video and other real-time communication technologies was considered, several factors necessitated a more creative approach to engaging participants:

- Online participation would occur from around the world, across every time zone, so to expect those participating remotely to do so on "Bangkok time" was unrealistic.
- Remote participation needed to involve more than just a one-way broadcast of presentations and discussions.
- An objective of the Big Goals initiative was to create a participative process that established a feeling of global community across the organization. Virtual participation had to include elements of "community building" like collaborative learning, knowledge sharing, and relationship building.

The Big Goals Summit established a model that expanded participation by weaving together face-to-face and

FIGURE 2.4. Online AI Story-Capture Tool

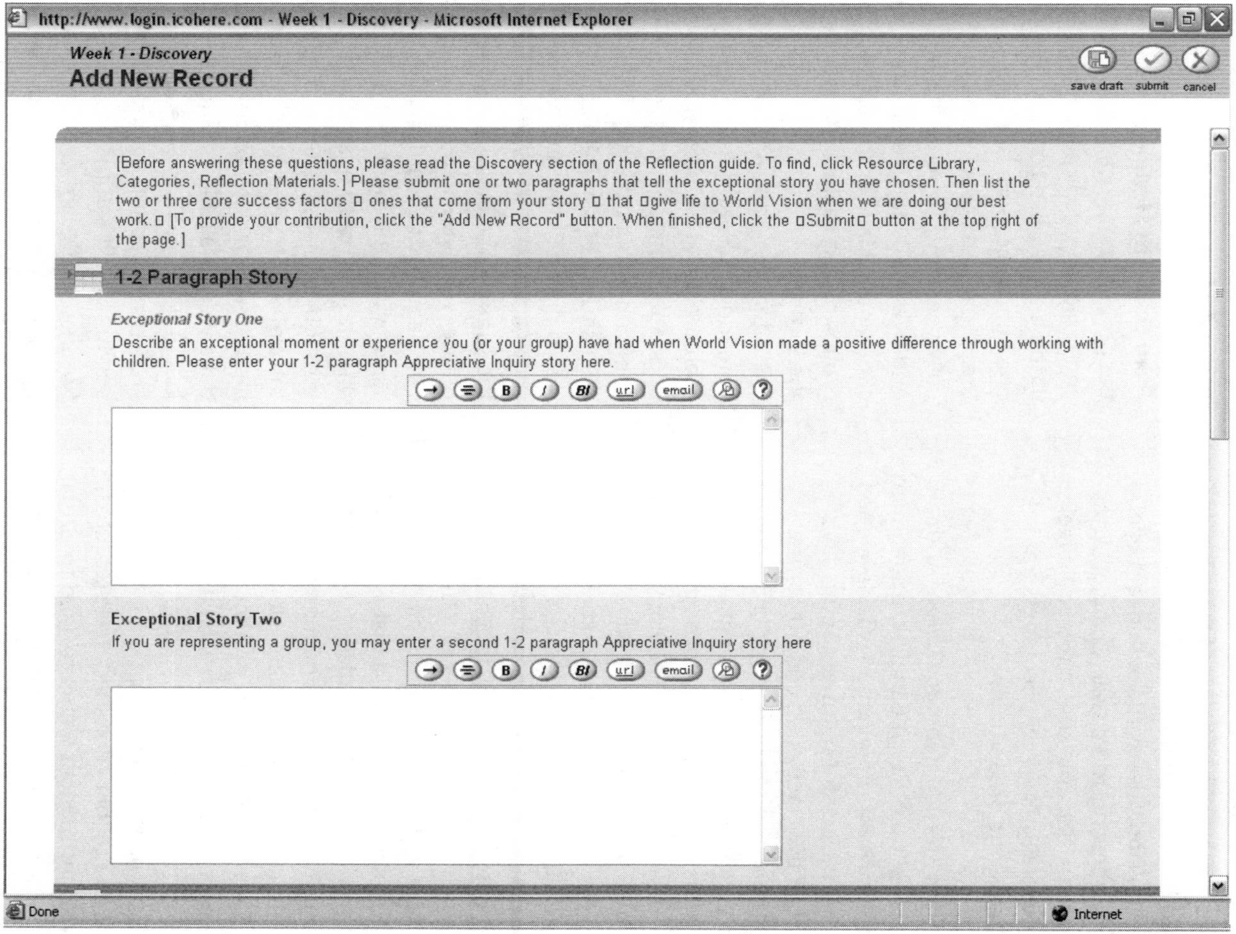
http://www.login.icohere.com - Week 1 - Discovery - Microsoft Internet Explorer
Week 1 - Discovery
Add New Record
save draft
submit
cancel
[Before answering these questions, please read the Discovery section of the Reflection guide. To find, click Resource Library, Categories, Reflection Materials.] Please submit one or two paragraphs that tell the exceptional story you have chosen. Then list the two or three core success factors □ ones that come from your story □ that □give life to World Vision when we are doing our best work.□ [To provide your contribution, click the "Add New Record" button. When finished, click the □Submit□ button at the top right of the page.]
1-2 Paragraph Story
Exceptional Story One
Describe an exceptional moment or experience you (or your group) have had when World Vision made a positive difference through working with children. Please enter your 1-2 paragraph Appreciative Inquiry story here.
B
I
BI
url
email
Exceptional Story Two
If you are representing a group, you may enter a second 1-2 paragraph Appreciative Inquiry story here
B
I
BI
url
email
Done
Internet

virtual participation. This model supported an ebb and flow of information and interaction that established a spirit of collaborative participation far beyond the meeting-room walls in Bangkok. As one participant put it, "You could feel the energy and connectedness from across the organization."

From Meeting Room to Online. At the end of each day in Bangkok, a streaming PowerPoint presentation was developed that included a summary of the day's objectives, activities, and outcomes. Photographs were interspersed within the PowerPoint presentation that gave virtual participants a glimpse into the meeting room and collaborative spirit of the Bangkok summit. Meeting notes were summarized, and additional supporting materials were placed online. For example, during the second day, which focused on "Dream," Bangkok participants created a number of letters that were written to children. These letters outlined the ideal world that will exist in ten years, which essentially embodied participants' vision of the future. These letters were placed online, alongside the streaming PowerPoint presentation in English, Spanish, and French. Figure 2.5 provides a screen shot of the "Summit Summaries" area within the Big Goals Web site that contained these resources.

Instructions were provided to virtual participants on viewing the streaming PowerPoint presentation about how to provide "unstructured" comments and feedback, as well as how to provide input through the structured format that

organized and prioritized inputs related to the day's specific outcomes.

From Online to Meeting Room. Just as in the pre-summit process, both individuals and regional groups participated online in the four-day Bangkok summit. Over one hundred groups from fifty-two countries organized collective viewing of the daily streaming PowerPoint summaries. And over 4,500 people provided input, either individually or though regional groups during each of the four days of the summit.

After viewing a summary presentation, individual participants and group representatives were provided with the option to submit general reflections and comments about the day. Participants then clicked a "Summit Feedback" button to provide more structured input. Early each morning, prior to the start of the summit, the inputs from the night before were tabulated and synthesized. A two-page "virtual participation report" summarized the inputs from the broader organization, both quantitatively through tabulated votes and qualitatively through quotes and themes. Structured inputs, such as votes and demographic data, were available instantly in all three languages. Qualitative feedback in French and Spanish was translated into English, which was then divided up between a small team of doctoral students for thematic analysis. Because individuals had the ability to upload documents, photographs, and other resources, in addition to entering text, many contributions contained rich illustrations of World

FIGURE 2.5. Daily Summit Summary Area

World Vision Big Goals - Microsoft Internet Explorer

http://www.login.icohere.com - World Vision Big Goals - Microsoft Internet Explorer

Making Our Vision REAL

World Vision Big Goals

Welcome Facilitator
Administer

1 online

- Welcome
- Summit Summaries 102
- Summit Feedback
- Networks 104
- Announcements
- Participants
- Message Inbox
- Resource Library
- Preferences
- Help Desk

LOGOUT

powered by iCohere
copyright

Day Two Summary

Show Last 10 items   Include Hidden   go

Top Previous Next Bottom

Introduction

The following is a summary of Day Two of the Bangkok Summit. **Click** the graphic image below to view a narrated overview of the day. If you have a low bandwidth connection, click the "view" button at the top right of this page to download a PDF file of this same summary.

After you are finished viewing the presentation, please click on the "**Summit Feedback**" button on the left side menu and look for *Day 2 Bangkok Summit: DREAM* area to provide your feedback. There are also instructions in the presentation.

back   search   apply   manage   contribute

12:36 PM

Done   Internet

Vision's existing activities that supported the emerging Big Goals. Figure 2.6 illustrates a contribution that originated from Nicaragua that describes a local activity that closely ties to one of the identified big goals.

When the summit participants entered the meeting room each morning, they were given the virtual participation reports. After the daily agenda overview, a presentation was given that summarized the participation report, showed screen shots of the various contributions and interactions within the Big Goals Web site, and outlined implications for the day's activities. Establishing a clear linkage between the work to be done in the room and the inputs from around the world instantly created feelings of deep connection and community and of having the whole system truly involved; also clear was that the ideas and outcomes from the meeting reflected the contributions of the broader organization.

Impact and Results

The Big Goals Summit produced sixteen strategic opportunity areas that World Vision could commit to in order to "Change the World with Children." These were fine-tuned over the following month into three, overarching ten-year goals and eight strategic priorities to reach those goals. World Vision's approach illustrates the power of tapping into the collective learning and wisdom—seeking of an organization through weaving together face-to-face and remote, online participation in the appreciative

spirit of positive change.[4] According to one of World Vision's senior vice presidents, the integration of technology into the Big Goals initiatives resulted in

- Higher-quality goals and strategies
- Faster decision making
- Rapid alignment of stakeholders around the world
- Enhanced organizational readiness for implementation
- A new model of organizational governance and whole-system participation

Input from across offices, time zones, and cultures elevated the quality of the conversations in Bangkok because meeting participants could assimilate the stories, insights, and recommendations of the broader organization into their work. Confidence in the specific outcomes of the summit—the big goals that will drive the organization's future—was significantly elevated, and broad organizational alignment was achieved as a natural part of the summit process. Today, World Vision points to the Big Goals process as a turning point for the organization, as it strives to significantly increase the positive impact it has on children, families, communities, and the world (Tandon, Fry, Gustavsson, and Kaplan, 2005).

Reflections

To our knowledge, World Vision's Big Goals initiative was the first of its kind to marry the AI Summit methodology for

FIGURE 2.6. Online Participant Contribution from Nicaragua

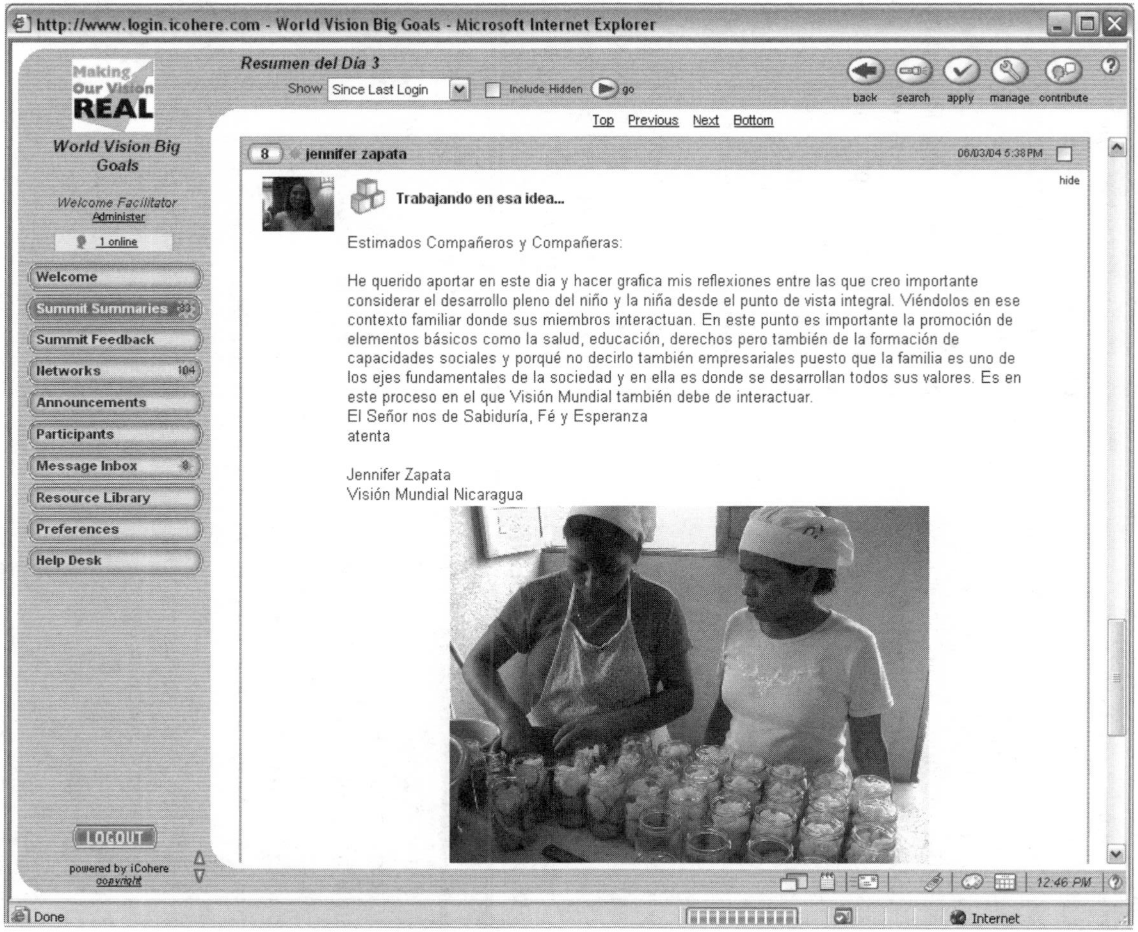

large groups with an online technology to dramatically expand the number of participants and scope of dialogue taking place during a multiday summit. The results of this integration appear to be positive in both the short and long term. World Vision was able to achieve its goal and translate its new vision into strategic priorities and opportunity areas in slightly less than six months, while enabling the same level of involvement as they had in creating their vision statement over a two-year period.

Among the numerous lessons learned and possibilities for future applications, several observations stand out. First is the need for an internal coordinator.

• *Establishing an internal coordinating role drives execution.* It was critical for World Vision to designate a person to guide and coordinate the preparation and customization of the online Web space, pre-summit inquiries, summit design, and daily export and import of online participation (with translation) during the summit. The allocation of this resource—almost full-time for three months preceding the summit—was essential in coordinating the numerous design and technological decisions required.

• *An online with face-to-face dialogue increases engagement.* As the summit progressed, it became evident that the inputs from so many online participants were adding to the momentum and energy surrounding the work of the participants in Bangkok. Each morning, as

those in the room received the summary of the online input overnight, one could sense the connectedness and interest in "doing good for the whole." The magnitude and content of the online input heightened the fatefulness and importance of the work at hand.

• *Encouraging appreciative feedback creates common ground.* During the Bangkok summit, it was helpful to solicit specific feedback from the online participants but in a way that honored existing work in Bangkok while encouraging positive feedback and input. This was done using three basic questions:

1. Please describe what you like most about this (statement, proposition, aspiration) as it is. What stands out to you, or attracts you the most?
2. What would you add or edit to make this statement more powerful and attractive?
3. What, if any, additional comments or input would you add to the list or summary provided?

This format invited the online participants to participate in a similar way to those in Bangkok when they were asked to comment on each other's work with the same appreciative questions. The intent of these questions was to continuously search for common ground and areas of agreement from which to work and build.

• *Encouraging visual input catalyzes a sense of connection.* The online input that stimulated the most interest and enthusiasm in Bangkok came from photos of the groups and children's drawings that were part of the online messages. They brought a sense of personal connection to the proceedings.

• *It is important to know the origin and characteristics of online data.* It was important, in retrospect, to include a way for online participants to indicate how many were responding and from what parts of the globe, particularly if they were including the voice or opinion of children in their responses. When the Bangkok participants could see data that showed that many children (or small groups of male and female staff with children) had met overnight to review and react to their work, it brought a sense of credibility and responsibility to the work going on in Bangkok. The demographic data also allowed World Vision leadership to see if they were getting a representative input from online participants. For example, after Day 1, the input from French-speaking areas was quite low, so the appropriate leadership made phone calls to regional offices to make sure people had access and information about how to connect to the summit.

• *The right Web context encourages the emergence of informal grassroots community.* With the availability of various communication and collaboration tools to support the initiative, the Big Goals Web site became much more than a vehicle for soliciting input and collecting feedback. At any given time, for example, one could see the names of others logged on to the site and invite one or more individuals to a live, online

meeting. Throughout the four-day summit, hundreds of individuals came together for ad hoc, spontaneous discussions focused on further exploring the themes of the summit, as well as fostering new relationships and rekindling old connections. These conversations were outside the formal agenda but were ultimately integral to the strategic effort. The context of the Web site and its simple-to-use tools, along with a clear time frame for participation, allowed for the emergence of grassroots communication and collaboration.

• *Honoring the enduring power of the collective voice sustains alignment.* The message sent to leadership through having such a significant portion of the total system achieving a consensus on a recommended list of key strategic objectives was unprecedented. In a subsequent meeting of global leaders to refine and prepare the summit outcomes for review and endorsement at their upcoming World Council meeting, there was a tendency by some to want to rework the ideas and change their language to fit with the views of a few senior leaders who had not been able to attend the Bangkok summit. At a powerful moment in these proceedings, one leader commented that they must keep true and consistent with the spirit and message from the "whole system's" voice, which had been heard in Bangkok. This was a turning point in the conversation, after which the group was able to reach agreement on the three overarching, ten-year goals and eight strategic priorities to achieve them.

One Final Question

This initiative used a virtual work space to support a face-to-face summit process, which allowed the summit attendees in Bangkok to validate their work and to achieve a sense that they were "representing" the whole system. The question we are left with is the reverse: Can a face-to-face group be in service of the whole system working virtually together? In other words, could the major activities involved in the AI 4-D process have been given to all online participants and then have the smaller group attending in Bangkok be the "staff" to summarize, theme, cluster, and feed these summaries back to the larger virtual group. Although we approached this summit with the Bangkok group being the "figure" and the online community being the "ground," we wonder now if the opposite is possible, if not desirable. Instead of viewing the larger online group as the observers, commentators, or validity checkers, it seems just as possible and feasible now to have them be the focal work group, using the face-to-face group to provide summarization and feedback. In this way, the five thousand that were participating could truly be "in the inner circle of strategy"—arguably a necessity for the fast-changing, knowledge-based global organizations of the future.

As stories like World Vision's become more widely known, more and more organizations will see the benefit of expanding the definition of "large group" in the context of strategic planning and change processes. Organizational development practitioners, strategists, and change consultants who apply collaboration and community technologies to the complex organizational systems in which they work will ultimately establish new expectations for what it means to engage the "whole system." Until that time, we can relish the positive examples set by organizations like World Vision that take bold steps to embody the principles of full participation in the spirit of serving its stakeholders and driving positive change.

Notes

1. World Vision International Web site: www.wvi.org
2. Weatherhead School of Management, Case Western Reserve University: www.weatherhead.case.edu.
3. iCohere Collaboration Software and Appreciative Inquiry Online Tools: www.icohere.com.
4. For a narrated online overview of the World Vision Big Goals process visit http://www.icohere.com/presentations/worldvisioncase/player.html.

References

Bunker, B. B., & Alban, B. T. (1997). *Large group interventions: Engaging the whole system for rapid change.* San Francisco: Jossey-Bass.

Collins, J. (2001). *Good to great: Why some companies make the leap . . . and others don't.* London: Random House.

Cooperrider, D. L., & Srivastva, S. (1987). Appreciative Inquiry in organizational life. *Research in Organizational Change and Development, 1,* 129–169.

Cooperrider, D. L., & Whitney, D. (1999). Appreciative Inquiry: A positive revolution in change. In P. Holman & T. Devane (Eds.), *The change handbook: Group methods for shaping the future.* San Francisco: Berrett-Koehler.

Ludema, J., Whitney, D., Mohr, B., & Griffin, T. (2003). *The Appreciative Inquiry Summit: A practitioner's guide for leading large-group change.* San Francisco: Berrett-Koehler.

Tandon, A., Fry, R., Gustavsson, L., & Kaplan, S. (2005). Making our vision real: From vision to goals. Presentation at the Christian Management Association Annual Conference, Long Beach, CA.

Weisbord, M., & Janoff, S. (1995). *Future Search: An action guide to finding common ground in organizations and communities.* San Francisco: Berrett-Koehler.

CHAPTER THREE

ORGANIZATIONS IN CRISIS

The community organizer, Saul Alinsky, was famous for saying, "Your enemy organizes for you." By this, he meant that people will forget their differences and unite to face a common foe, be it sociopolitical, a natural disaster, war, or any other great danger to their well-being. Defeating the external threat becomes the superordinate goal. But first, the peril must be understood and the climate to fight it created. Remember the frog that cooked to death in a pot of water because he did not recognize the danger of the gradually rising temperature and thus remained to die placidly rather than jump out? The leadership in the cases included in this chapter recognized the crisis and helped their organizations understand it and see why acknowledgment and action were imperative for survival.

Certainly, all of us have witnessed organizations in which leadership denied or ignored the realities of growing danger. In the "Money" section of *USA Today* (September 14, 2005), Marilyn Adams and Dan Reed write, "The slide into bankruptcy of two of the USA's largest airlines is more a result of the carriers' bad assumptions and *slowness to act* than the recent rise in fuel prices or the terrorist attack four years ago" (italics ours). There are many industry examples of market leaders who ignored new technology as it entered their business: the shift to the personal computer (PC), away from mainframes, is a prime example; the move to digital cameras from film-based cameras is another. The threat of new, lower-cost entrants into the marketplace is a constant; if not acknowledged, they can upend the rules and take greater and greater market share. The article in *USA Today* goes on to say, "They counted too heavily on the hope that business conditions would improve, oil prices fall, airfares rise and weakened competitors would fail." It is difficult to predict the future, but it is completely impossible to do so if we do not monitor trends. Clearly, it can be very costly and unsettling for companies to revamp a product, reduce costs, or implement new technology. All the same, there is a time to step up to the plate before reaching the bottom of the ninth.

The first three cases are examples of leadership recognizing the need to take action as the crisis occurs. The fourth case is an example of the leadership at the Boston University Dental School preventing a crisis by using a methodology called Scenario Planning.

- "Back from the Brink at American Airlines," by Beth Ganslen
- "From Fragmentation to Coherence: An Intervention in an Academic Setting," by Rosemarie Barbeau and Nancy Aronson
- "Creating a World-Class Manufacturer in Record Time," by Richard Lent, James Van Patten, and Tom Phair
- "Planning Strategically for an Uncertain Future: The Boston University Dental School," by Gilbert Steil Jr. and Michele Gibbons-Carr

It is legend today that Winston Churchill, during World War II, was able to articulate the external threat while aligning and inspiring the English people to action. To a certain extent, management has to acknowledge the issue while risking being vulnerable to criticism either for failing to battle earlier or for creating a false crisis. Taken together, the articulation of the threat and the invitation to all hands to work together to overcome the challenge provides people with the sense that they are valued members who can make a contribution. It is remarkable how people rise to the situation and how energized they can be by the opportunity to participate.

Two requirements for success in such endeavors are transparency and openness about the situation. These factors are even more critical when there is distrust of the leadership group. Sharing financial data, being open to questions, and educating people on the key issues all increase leadership's credibility. This is what allows leadership to clear the hurdle of complacency that "this too will pass" or "we are OK as we are" (or "the water isn't really that hot").

In the School of Education case, "From Fragmentation to Coherence," there was a wise move to include outside stakeholders in the meetings. This is typical of most of the Large Group Methods. Although an organization's leadership may recognize the need for change, the outside stakeholders may often help drive home the message. The outsider is harder to ignore and, somehow, often has credibility not granted to internal voices.

A small manufacturing plant is very different from a widely dispersed organization like American Airlines, so it is appropriate to use different approaches in each of these instances. Yet these are characteristics at the core of all four cases:

- *Focus:* Whether it was becoming a world-class manufacturer, avoiding bankruptcy, transforming an educational institution, or planning for a very uncertain future, there was clear purpose to bringing people together to engage the challenge.
- *Involvement and engagement:* As Beth Ganslen says about American Airlines, "No one group, including management, could fix the problem: it had to involve everyone." In the School of Education the authors say, "It was important for the whole system to grapple with the pressures for change that they saw in the external world."
- *Openness:* In each case there was commitment to sharing information, to "open the books," thus encouraging employees and participants to question processes, procedures, and products, as well as to explore context. Management also dared to acknowledge shortcomings and to be vulnerable.
- *Diversity of stakeholders:* Each case includes a diversity of internal stakeholders, regardless of level or function. Two of the cases included external stakeholders.

What to Note in the Cases

It is interesting to see how, in "Back from the Brink at American Airlines," the company engaged its employees to help avoid bankruptcy. The company used a face-to-face meeting in Dallas, as well as online surveys and information sharing about the financial situation, to involve the staff in working collaboratively to achieve the cost reduction necessary for financial survival. All departments were involved in the process, providing their knowledge and expertise. The Dallas meeting helped the leadership understand that flexibility was needed in how changes in vacation days, salaries, and work rules were approached. Different levels and functions had different preferences. What is significant is that they allowed work groups to make their own decisions. A new CEO was named during this process—one who embraced a program to discuss and share the turnaround strategy with all levels of the organization. Today, American is the only major airline that has not declared bankruptcy.

"Creating a World-Class Manufacturer in Record Time" describes a specialty chemicals manufacturer that had gone through two plant mergers and then was acquired. It is an intriguing story, and the consultants' approach was to start the turnaround process with a Future Search, following up with a Gemba Kaizen, an action learning method for workplace improvements that creates lean productive manufacturing. A very clear set of guiding principles was used to set the process in motion. As you read it, note that the Future Search was titled "Agree Meetings." In part because it was not jargon, the name sent a message that there would be no move forward without consensus. Over the first year, there were a series of meetings to improve the work environments where production took place. There is a good description of the follow-up meetings with the action teams, using simple questions to start the conversations that provided an action-reflection format.

The third case, "From Fragmentation to Coherence: An Intervention in an Academic Setting," takes place in an educational institution where power is diffuse and academic freedom strongly defended—a clearly challenging setting in which to create a new focus and a curriculum change. The authors outline the steps they took, including their work with the dean, who created a road map of the change process that gave a sense of direction to the meetings. The authors also include their System Coherence Framework, as well as some questions based on this framework that can help a group to focus on where best to direct energy. It is fascinating that in such a highly fragmented system, working with the dean and staff, they were able to infuse the institution with a new sense of identity and purpose and get agreement on the changes that would support this new environment.

The last case in this chapter is "Planning Strategically for an Uncertain Future: The Boston University Dental School." This is not a case about an organization in crisis but an example of an organization taking preemptive action to avoid a crisis. This organization engaged their stakeholders with regard to the dangers of assuming that the future would not be a continuation of the present trends or an extrapolation of the past.

Several Large Group Methods use activities that analyze current external trends affecting an organization or community; they do not reach as far as Scenario Planning, which explores possible futures and asks the group to make explicit the future scenarios that could have the greatest potential impact on the school. Strategies are developed for each scenario; strategies that work well across scenarios are given precedence. The authors take the reader through their own thought processes as they struggled with what would be most helpful to the client challenged with an uncertain future.

The school had used Large Group Methods for many years. These methods encouraged faculty and staff at all levels to become involved in decisions that affected them and to identify and solve work-related problems. The question was how to design an intervention that would allow planners to see future possibilities and prepare for change when the character of the future is in doubt. They purposefully did not determine a method or design until they had immersed themselves in the external environment of the client system. They also worked at a thorough understanding of seeing the world through the client's eyes. They developed a method that combined a Large Group Method with a scenario-planning process. The authors say in the beginning of this case that they have probably designed a new form of large group intervention. A particular aspect to note is how the reports to the various academic committees were handled; this is particularly important in an academic setting, where responsibility for implementation rests with different academic committees.

Our Thoughts and Reflections

One important opportunity that arises when organizations and communities are faced with a crisis is that silos and divisions disappear. People can then work together to surmount incredible difficulties. Years ago I (Billie) witnessed an event like this. There was a fire at New York Telephone Company's 14th Street switching station. Almost all of lower Manhattan was without phone service. Everybody in the phone company pitched in; executives left their enclaves and worked side-by-side with the regular workforce to restore service. The retirees' organization—The Pioneers—was also asked to help. If family, friends, neighbors notified them, they were available to visit shut-ins and do grocery shopping for those who needed help. It was an astounding effort. After the telephone service was restored, one of the executives said to me, "Is there a way we could work like this all the time, or is it only possible in crisis?" In Chapter Seven, "Embedding New Patterns of Working," there are insights that provide a partial response to the executive's question.

BACK FROM THE BRINK
AT AMERICAN AIRLINES

Beth Ganslen

The Challenge

Good companies sometimes fall on hard times. The test of their mettle is how they respond to the challenges they face. This is the story of how American Airlines (AA)—a seventy-five-year-old industry veteran—came back from the brink of bankruptcy when faced with pervasive low-cost competition and the devastating aftereffects of the events of September 11, 2001.

Background

The airline industry experienced dramatic change after deregulation in 1978. Low-cost carriers like Southwest, Jet Blue, and others challenged industry icons such as American, Delta, and United with increasing success. They entered the field as innovative, lower-priced competitors and slowly but surely chipped away at the market share of industry giants. Over time, new entrants gained a foothold in the field, and new and innovative practices married to lower infrastructure costs created a sea change in the industry.

Carriers like Eastern, Pan Am, Braniff, and TWA, once industry icons, were driven out of business. In fact, 140 airlines have sought bankruptcy protection since deregulation, and only one—Continental—has emerged with a sustainable business model.

In early 2001, American Airlines was faced with low-cost competition in 70 percent of its markets. The pressure was on to reduce costs in order to generate profits in a low-fare environment. Simultaneously, instability in the Middle East was driving up fuel costs, and the economy was faltering. As a result, business travel—AA's bread and butter—declined significantly, further reducing revenues. AA posted second-quarter losses of $105 million ($148 million annually), or $.68 per share. The outlook was not favorable, as the economic downturn converged with this fundamental industry change.

Then the unthinkable happened. On the morning of September 11, 2001, American Airlines flight 11 was hijacked and flown into the World Trade Center; flight 77, also commandeered by terrorists, was flown into the Pentagon fifty-three minutes later. One hundred and fifty people lost their lives on the flights, including twenty-three members of the AA "family." Losses on the ground were devastating and unimaginable. The country ultimately went to war, and American Airlines began the fight for its very survival.

Within days, critical portions of AA's liability insurance were cancelled. In the weeks and months to come, 70 aircraft were retired, future orders were deferred,

20,000 of approximately 109,800 employees were laid off, and the company's usually strong credit rating was reduced to junk bond status. Eventually, its stock (listed as AMR on the New York Stock Exchange) was removed from the S&P 500. At year-end, AA posted a $1.8 billion net loss, or $11.43 per share.

The following year (2002) was equally challenging. US Airways and United Airlines filed for Chapter 11. The economy declined further, passenger loads remained depressed, and pricing elasticity was flat. To control losses in excess of $5 million per day, company leadership sought to remove $2.2 billion in infrastructure costs. This was attained through increased schedule efficiency, fleet simplification, streamlined customer interaction, in-flight product changes, operational adjustments, reduction in administrative expenses, vendor concessions, and pricing and distribution enhancements. However, this was not enough. At the close of 2002, AA posted losses of $3.5 billion, or $16.22 per share.

As 2003 began, the negative spiral continued. Oil prices continued to climb, and revenue remained flat. Facing imminent bankruptcy as well, AA needed $1.8 billion in wage, benefits, and work-rule changes to survive. In the spring of 2003, AA management realized they could not stem the tide alone and asked the employees to help. The company's goal was to collaboratively restructure employee pay, benefits, and work rules to survive *without* bankruptcy, thereby maintaining investor, market, and customer confidence.

Method

An active-engagement approach was launched, designed to leverage the participation of all employees to save $1.8 billion; $1.62 billion of the savings needed for the company to survive was attained from 70,000 pilots, flight attendants, and Transportation Workers Union employees through pioneering, collaborative, and accelerated union negotiations. Independent employee groups contributed the remaining $180 million.

The participative process described here focuses on efforts surrounding the 29,000 independent employees who were geographically dispersed: U.S.-based agents, management, and support staff at AA.

The active-engagement process involved a series of bold initiatives, including surveys, educational meetings, interactive feedback sessions, and ongoing debriefs. All efforts were targeted to

- Achieve participative results in an unprecedented five-week time line
- Secure $80 million in savings from nonunionized agent groups and $100 million in savings from management and support staff employees
- Redesign the agent, management, and support staff employment policies, based on employee input, to ensure long-term financial improvements and competitive advantage

- Implement revisions by a targeted date approximately ninety days from project inception

Intervention Phases

The process evolved in four key phases: (1) identification, (2) preparation, (3) participation, and (4) implementation. The success of each phase was dependent on the clarity, coordination, and completion of the previous phase. As such, ongoing education and communication underpinned each phase and acted as threads to weave key content, processes, and people together.

Identification. The intervention began with the *identification phase,* in which the project goals, aggressive time line, and process were defined. Leadership determined that American Airlines needed $1.8 billion in pay, benefits, and work-rule savings in order to survive. Further, leadership publicly committed to using an active engagement or participative approach to involve all employees in the design of needed restructuring efforts.

Next, the project team was assembled. Director-level leaders were assigned to scope the project and alert key stakeholders to the pending challenge and process. Each work group selected key players to form the roughly forty-person project team; HR assumed the overall project design, management, and communication roles. The finance organization quantified the financial targets by specific work group, based on group size, work rules, and market parity. HR then determined potential pay, benefits, and work-rule options, while the legal department anticipated feasibility issues and constraints. Operational leaders promoted the process, helped coordinate work-group participation, and functioned as a steering committee.

A letter from the chairman and president alerted all agent, management, and support-staff employees of the need and the process, as well as their responsibilities. The message was clear that all employees were in this together and that the future of individuals and the corporation was at stake.

Preferences Surveys. As a first step, an external consulting group initiated a preliminary online benefits survey on behalf of the compensation-and-benefits organization. Employees accessed the survey through a link, which was reached via the company Web site. The survey was formatted to help narrow employee pay and benefits preferences in advance of upcoming focus groups and a final survey.

This survey was lengthy and complicated and received mixed reviews at best. Although some found it helpful, many employees found the survey difficult and confusing. This may have reduced participation in the phases that followed, but for some employees, it was the first step in their recognition of the hard challenges that lay ahead.

A solicitation survey was also conducted via the company Web site to solicit volunteers to participate in

upcoming agent InterAction sessions and management focus groups. InterAction sessions are an internally branded, interest-based problem-solving process. The process was trusted and had a five-year history of creating results through collaboration. Agent InterAction and management, as well as support-staff focus-group participants, were selected from the volunteer population using a stratified random sampling methodology. Key agent factors included work group, geographical location, seniority ranges, age, gender, ethnicity, and marital status. In addition, management specialists considered job levels, operational-versus-staff assignments, and manager-versus-individual contributor roles. Support staff were also defined by job levels and job titles.

Qualitative Feedback. Second, employees were given the opportunity to provide free-text qualitative feedback, regardless of their interest in session participation. Survey comments were primarily submitted regarding potential changes in pay, health benefits, vacation, sick days, holidays, work rules, retirement, unpaid time off, travel benefits, and business improvements. Feedback and recommendations were captured daily, categorized by topic, and sorted by work group. Content was used in designing initial pay, work-rule, and benefits-change options that were presented to participants in the InterAction and focus group sessions. A total of 2,397 employees responded to this survey.

Preparation. Substantial preparation was required to coordinate and run the InterAction and focus group sessions, which laid the qualitative foundation for the final input survey. Project leaders and senior management defined targeted participation levels. Invitations were sent to volunteers. Logistical coordinators secured meeting rooms, transportation, necessary media, and supplies.

Sessions were designed to foster employee education and qualitative input. Facilitators, scribes, pay-and-benefits subject matter experts, and work-rule subject matter operational experts were trained and coached on how to support the process. Finance calculated costs associated with various options so employees could make informed recommendations. An affinity diagram tool—MindGenius—was used, to allow for data sharing and capture in the sessions (www.ygnius.com).

Participation. A total of 29,496 agents, management, and support staff had the opportunity to participate in the survey processes; 366 (1.2 percent of the 29,496 eligible employees) were invited to participate in InterAction or focus group sessions—a number approximately three times greater than any previous focus group initiative at AA. The agent groups included airport agents, reservations sales representatives, cargo agents, premium services representatives, travel center representatives, maintenance and engineering coordinators, and weight-and-balance planners. Support staff included administrative assistants, AAdvantage customer service assistants, skycaps, and Admirals Club stewards. Management participants ranged from entry level to director and were differentiated by staff or operational focus.

Sessions were timed and scheduled in Fort Worth, Texas, to allow for attendance from the domestic airline system. International destinations were not included because they are governed by local regulations regarding pay and benefits. The company provided transportation, accommodations, and travel and incidental expenses to remove any potential barriers to participation.

HR professionals who had been trained in facilitation skills led the sessions. Scribes from HR communications captured all data.

A total of 311 volunteers participated in three six-hour sessions designed to educate the employees, gather qualitative input, and enable people to be heard (ice storms prevented others from traveling to Dallas–Fort Worth). Comments and interview feedback indicated that attending the sessions was meaningful and valued.

InterAction and Focus Groups. The sessions, conducted over a three-day period, opened with auditorium-style, "big tent" presentations, followed by question-and-answer periods. Leadership feedback indicated that having everyone in the same room helped people both hear and understand different perspectives and realize that it would be difficult to come up with solutions that would satisfy every individual.

To set the tone, a financial overview, an industry update, and a business plan review were presented by a senior vice president. That was followed by a comprehensive benefits overview, explaining AA's current strategy vis-à-vis the practices of other Fortune 100 companies. The concluding presentation detailed lost time and sick leave practices, which were associated with approximately 20 percent of AA's daily financial losses.

Overall survey results and comments showed that presentations were generally viewed as more helpful to agents and support staff than to management, who typically already had access to much of the data. The majority of participants stated that the information shared was educational and eye-opening, that speakers were direct, and that the discussion clarified key issues and concerns. A few thought there were too many numbers and percentages to digest in a short period of time.

Following the presentations, employees attended facilitated break-out sessions for their specific work group; average session size was twenty-five employees. Agents attended these InterAction sessions. Management attended focus groups, as their issues typically were not addressed via the InterAction process. Both sessions, although titled differently, used the same process.

One participant stated, "I felt that my issues mattered when they broke us down into [work] groups. We [as agents,

management, or support staff] were not overwhelmed by other work groups' issues." Another commented, "Including support staff and management for the first time worked well, as opposed to simply making the decisions for those groups."

The sessions opened with an agenda overview, followed by group introductions highlighting job function and seniority to allow participants to recognize the diversity of the people in the room. Employees then participated in an interactive review of viable pay, benefits, and work-rule options to reach targeted cost savings. Options, with associated savings calculated by the finance group, were pre-populated in the MindGenius affinity diagram tool. This created an organized way for employees to visualize, weigh, and provide feedback on various options. Since employees had different interests, all feedback was captured on the screen in the note section of the MindGenius tool; this allowed all feedback to be validated. Facilitators attempted to determine overall preferences when applicable, without polarizing the group around special interests. An agent leader observed:

> The energy and enthusiasm of the facilitators helped develop an environment of trust and cooperation. The subject matter to be discussed was full of emotion and passion. The facilitators, recognizing this, allowed the emotions to flow, monitoring only when they became too inflamed. Allowing this "flow of

emotion," if you will, allowed for the development of trust.

In addition, facilitators attempted to drive the groups toward accountability for the targeted goals, since minor accommodations were often volunteered, yet major reductions were required. "The way the facilitators stepped in to 'turn the tide,' bring the group to the reality and urgency of the situation, facilitated the urgency of cooperation among the group to come up with solutions that would truly help the cause."

Subject matter experts and subject matter operational experts were available to clarify questions or concerns in each session. Core team members met after each session to combine results, identify trends, and recommend process improvements. Project leaders shared daily feedback with operational managers and senior leaders. A communication team kept the companywide population at large informed of the process and participation outcomes.

Approximately one hundred participants completed feedback forms at the end of each day to evaluate the overall experience. Data were reviewed daily after each session to identify trends and facilitate continuous improvement. Ratings were on a scale of 1 to 10, where 1 was "not very effective" and 10 was "very effective." On average, in all work groups, over 70 percent of respondents rated the sessions as 7 or better as an overall experience; 85 percent or more in each work group rated their willingness to volunteer to attend a future InterAction or focus group sessions as 8 or better.

Final Input Survey. AA's consumer research group observed the sessions and collaborated with the whole core team to design the final input survey. Cumulative data were used to develop a pay, benefits, and work-rules post-session input survey for the entire agent, management, and support-staff population. Survey question design and wording was tested by senior leadership, core team, and nonmanagement advisory board members. This helped avoid potential problems and ensure that the content was true to InterAction and focus group feedback.

Five versions of the survey were created: one for support staff and two each for management and the agent groups. This was necessary because the groups had different work rules and financial targets. Employees automatically received the appropriate survey on the company Web site, based on demographics associated with their employee number. These demographics were also used in data analysis.

The survey incorporated four key design factors: (1) demographics, (2) target accountability, (3) rank ordering, and (4) qualitative feedback. The first series of questions captured demographic data. The next addressed pay, benefits, and work-rules options and allocated points, which equated to dollar savings (1 point equaled approximately $2 million) to each response. The sum of each employee's contributions had to reach the targeted amount, that is, agents equal 40 points ($80 million), and management and support staff equal 50 points ($100 million). Employees who did not reach that amount were directed to review their responses and to find and contribute additional savings. To increase employee comfort, the survey allowed participants to calculate multiple options before finalizing and submitting their response.

The next section enabled employees to prioritize which pay, benefits, and work-rule issues were "most important" to "least important" to them. This category included active-employee medical benefits, retiree medical benefits, dental benefits, pensions and 401(k) plan, work rules, base pay, premium pay, sick pay, and vacation.

The last section of the survey solicited open comments. This gave employees who had not participated in the previous surveys or focus groups an opportunity to be heard. It also provided a final opportunity for all employees to provide qualitative feedback on the process or content. Comments were analyzed by content category, employee status (management or nonmanagement), and support or opposition to change in the existing policies and procedures in each area.

A total of 11,588 employees (39.29 percent of the eligible population) completed surveys. Results were calculated by arithmetic mean and analyzed by topic, demographics, and work group. Results were scrutinized for cumulative financial effects because reductions in one

component could potentially devalue the savings in another. For example, relinquishing a vacation day was valued at a certain amount (based on salary); however, that figure would decrease if a 5 percent pay cut was also selected and applied. Results were cross-referenced to the survey ranking questions to calibrate financial selections with intuitive preferences. Emphasis was placed on identifying changes employees *wanted least,* to avoid implementing solutions that would disengage the workforce.

Agents' survey results were compared with management and support staff data. Overall feedback also was shared with Employee Relations personnel who were involved in accelerated union negotiations. All survey data were viewed as preferences and recommendations rather than votes.

Decision Making. Final results were submitted to senior management, who made the ultimate decisions. Decisions were based on financial impact, employee preference, and long-term strategies. Work groups were permitted to take different paths to reach their financial targets. An employee commented:

> AA did not say everybody had to do the same thing. We said this is your target; you decide how to get there. For management, support staff, and agents, we were able to do that through the survey process and gather people's input and reach the targets, and it did not have to be done the

same way the TWU [Transportation Workers Union] did it, the same way the pilots did it, or the way the flight attendants did it. And every group ended up with, in some respects, dramatically different outcomes, but it was up to each group.

For example, management, support staff, and agents took different approaches to achieving targeted goals. Each work group agreed to different methods and percentages to reduce base pay. Management and support staff took deeper pay cuts and kept vacation, while agents sacrificed a week of vacation to take smaller hourly pay reductions. Management and support staff increased medical benefit contributions and retained paid holidays, while agents relinquished five paid holidays and reduced holiday pay. All groups opted to reduce sick time accrual and tighten up attendance standards, yet leave per-day sick-pay rates unchanged.

Implementation. Policy, work-rule, and cost reductions were implemented immediately when possible. Other changes were implemented with upcoming pay periods or when infrastructure or programming changes could be completed. Benefits changes were completed following an interim enrollment period to allow employees to evaluate various AA plans in conjunction with their spouse's benefits offerings. Headcount reductions were swift, but employees were given approximately sixty days to plan for pay cuts.

Constant communication through management and the company Web site kept employees informed of changes, time lines, and any action that was required on their part. National media coverage also was significant due to the state of the industry, prominence of the company, and magnitude of the active engagement process.

Debriefing and Interviewing. Once implementation was in progress, core team members and key stakeholders met to debrief the overall process. Interviews conducted with participants, project team members, and key leaders also determined positive and constructive feedback about the active engagement process.

Reflections

Comments revealed a combination of success factors and challenges for future practitioners. Five specific factors were key to the success of the project: (1) focus, (2) time, (3) openness, (4) involvement, and (5) preferences. Challenges were inherent in them as well.

Focus

A singular focus enabled the company to mobilize the energy of the organization to reach needed goals. A senior leader stated, "I felt that everyone at a management level, especially senior management, knew that it was not *a* priority, it was *the* priority." As such, resources were allocated to the project, and nonessential efforts were put on hold to allow for needed commitments.

Time

An aggressive five-week time line created a sense of urgency and drove momentum. One leader characterized the implementation of the process itself as an outcome by saying,

> I think one thing that worked really well was the incredibly collaborative environment that was created with multiple departments coming together to work at such a fast pace. People were willing to take on whatever was necessary to accomplish the tasks at hand. I think normally we would look back and say "Wow! In past practices, we have not had that type of cooperation or responsiveness."

On the other hand, the time crunch made it difficult to scope the project in advance or plan and prepare for and execute each phase of the process. To be successful, executive leadership should respect the process by giving it enough time. The project leader role should manage expectations and ensure that communication keeps people connected and informed about the process and outcomes.

Openness

American Airlines opened its books to employees to help them understand the severity of the challenge and the reality of the company's financial situation. This was a bold move, which heightened the organization's vulnerability yet significantly increased trust and collaboration. Giving employees the costs associated with pay, benefits, and work-rule options also increased their ability to understand the business and make informed decisions about their financial futures.

The active-engagement process nearly derailed, however, when it was viewed that sensitive financial information about executive compensation, while discussed, had not been fully disclosed. Many perceived this as a breach of trust. Within a week AA's CEO, Don Carty, resigned, stating, "It is now clear that my continuing on as chairman and chief executive officer of AA is still a barrier that, if removed, could give improved relations—and thus long-term success—the best possible chance." He was succeeded by Gerard Arpey, who instituted the "Turnaround Plan" and pioneered the Involve, Discuss, Share "Working Together" strategy. Ten months later, AA was the subject of a cover story of the January-February 2004 edition of the *US Business Review.* The headline read "Gaining Altitude: Transparent Decision Making and Aggressive Cost Cutting Have AA Flying Toward Profitability" (Krukowski, 2004, p. 18). The move to complete transparency reinforces that "We just need to be more open and honest, and I think that will create more credibility in the process. People would have felt like they could support it more if nothing was being withheld."

As the old adage says, honesty is the best policy. Openness from the start

could have improved results and prevented unnecessary emotional effects.

Involvement

Employee involvement was noted as a
key factor in the success of the active engagement process by over 65 percent of
feedback respondents. Employees commented, "This process reached out and
grabbed a lot of people" in a "we're all
in this together approach." And a manager stated, "In this aspect, no one
group, including management, could
fix the problem. It had to involve everyone. Everyone had to participate in both
identifying the problem and coming
up with alternatives and in the end the
solution to the problem." A project
leader also remarked, "Including support
staff and management for the first time
worked well, as opposed to simply
making those decisions for those work
groups."

Employees reported that being involved helped them better understand
the problems, consider alternatives, and
appreciate each other's perspectives. Further, employees stated that the opportunity to have a say in the outcome
minimized negative feelings and increased their sense that they "might
have made a difference."

Managing passionate dialogue
about people's livelihoods, however, requires skilled facilitation and grace under
fire. Focus group design and data capture must respect all input and promote
employees' feeling heard rather than

feeling challenged or confronted by peer
participants.

Preferences

Half the respondents said that offering
preferences by work group was an important factor in the active engagement
design. An operational manager noted,
"What really worked well, even though
[the circumstances] were less than opti-
mum in many ways, was clearly there
was a sincere effort to solicit preferences." Breaking the overall employee
base into work groups ensured that there
was "flexibility of choice work group to
work group." An employee said that "we
[as agent, management, or support staff]
were not overwhelmed by the pilots' or
other work group's issues." A project
team member expressed that the "menu
approach was a huge factor toward
achieving something that was optimized
as best we could."

Providing options by work group increased buy-in and the probability of
reaching an agreement with all work
groups. The options-menu approach also
added "a certain amount of complexity
around implementation of different
changes for each work group." Complexity increased the need for detailed
communication to both leaders and employees who had to be apprised of and
prepared for changes. Half the respondents mentioned problems or challenges
associated with communicating, receiving, or understanding needed messages.
Feedback indicated that extensive logisti-

cal coordination was required to align systems and processes with final decisions, and because final agreements with each work group were not shared publicly, individuals question whether sacrifices were shared equitably.

Conclusion

According to Beckhard and Pritchard (1992), "Competitive supremacy will be a function not only of increased profits and performance, but of the organization's capacity to innovate, learn, respond quickly, and design the appropriate infrastructure to meet demands and have maximum control over its own destiny" (p. 2). The active engagement process incorporated employee involvement strategies with proven large-scale change methods to respond quickly to the threat of bankruptcy at AA. It used a systemic approach and leveraged a critical mass of employees to redesign the employment contract—a crucial underpinning of the company's financial infrastructure. In doing so, the process ensured that people affected by the process were involved, which increased ownership, decreased resistance, and enabled the company to accelerate implementation. A project leader noted, "People were resolved that changes were going to take place and appreciated that they had a say in their destiny."

In the context of large-scale change, active engagement also reinforced the principles of the engagement paradigm: (1) widening the circle of involvement, (2) connecting people to each other, (3) creating communities for action, and (4) embracing democracy (Axelrod, 2000). Every agent, management, and support staff employee had the potential to be involved through surveys or focus groups. Survey participation was high, and InterAction sessions included larger numbers of employees and a broader range of work groups than ever before. The process brought people together, and shared goals reinforced the democratic objective to balance individual interests with the greater good.

Industry discontinuities, political upheaval, economic shifts, and new laws created conditions that required transformational change. Leaders envisioned the targeted goals for survival and promoted the sense of urgency (Kotter, 1996).

The active engagement design itself fostered significant changes in involvement, transparency, understanding, and collaboration. These process changes were combined with active engagement outcomes and resulted in real changes in how people act and think at work. The company achieved strategic transformation in an effort to regain a competitive advantage. In doing so, AA avoided bankruptcy and retained control of the company's reputation, business practices, and future.

Quotes from business analysts regarding AA's fourth-quarter 2004 performance reinforce that the process and results had significant impact. For example, Gary Chase, an analyst with Lehman Brothers, said AA "posted another solid quarter highlighting the company's progress in turning its operations around. AA shares anticipated some of this surprise, but the numbers are nonetheless impressive." Further, Susan Donofrio of Deutsche Bank Securities upgraded AMR stock from "hold" because of "not only the airline's impressive cost performance, but also . . . its willingness to not rest on its laurels and passively participate in a revenue recovery from an improving economy."

"Organizations that use the engagement paradigm develop the capacity not only to address current issues but to meet further challenges as well" (Axelrod, 2000, p. 197). Through active engagement, American Airlines survived an unprecedented business crisis and laid a foundation for sustained success in the future. In doing so the company and employees proved that *given the chance, ordinary people can achieve extraordinary things.* The challenge for leaders and organization development practitioners is to believe in the power of people and to create opportunities for them to excel. As Gerard Arpey, current CEO of AA, eloquently stated September 11, 2003,

"The power and vibrancy of this great company is not in our airplanes, our buildings, or even in our long-storied history. Rather, the power and vibrancy of AA is in its people" (Corporate Communications, 2003).

References

Axelrod, R. H. (2000). *Terms of engagement: Changing the way we change organizations.* San Francisco: Berrett-Koehler.

Beckhard, R., & Pritchard, W. (1992). *Changing the essence: The art of creating and leading fundamental change in organizations.* San Francisco: Jossey-Bass.

Corporate Communications (Producer). (2003, October). *AATV: September 11, 2003, memorial service* [video]. (Available from American Airlines, Inc., Dallas, TX 75221.)

Kotter, J. P. (1996). *Leading change.* Boston: Harvard Business School Press.

Krukowski, J. (2004, January-February). Gaining altitude: Transparent decision making and aggressive cost cutting have American Airlines flying toward profitability, its leaders say. *US Business Review,* pp. 18–19.

FROM FRAGMENTATION TO COHERENCE

An Intervention in an Academic Setting

Rosemarie Barbeau and Nancy Aronson

The Challenge

The Rossier School of Education (RSOE) at the University of Southern California (USC) in Los Angeles needed to move rapidly to become more coherent, improve its reputation, and be more fiscally viable. When the new dean, Karen Gallagher, arrived in the summer of 2000, she found a highly fragmented organization, characterized by a loose confederation of programs, with little connection or collaboration across departments. The school had twenty-three degree programs and thirty-five full-time faculty members; there were many adjunct faculty members. The culture was extremely entrepreneurial, with little sense of a *collective* identity. The school had once enjoyed a positive reputation, but its position in the field had declined considerably over the past few years. A balanced budget had eluded the organization for the past seven cycles.

A University Committee on Academic Review identified serious problems confronting the school and recommended that the new dean develop a strategic plan to address them. This report, coupled with RSOE's bleak financial picture, helped create a sense of urgency in the system. Dean Gallagher knew she had a brief window of opportunity in which to undertake significant organizational change. She had two assets. One was that the faculty had been part of the hiring process and had chosen her as a leading candidate for the position. Another was that USC's administration expected positive change and was willing to provide support for it.

Background

Academic settings, by their nature, are characterized by diffuse decision making and unique forms of governance, in which faculty-versus-administration decision-making rights are deeply rooted. At RSOE, the curriculum was solely within the domain of faculty. Any change to the curriculum as a whole and courses in particular had to be approved by the faculty body. Henry Mintzberg speaks of these settings as "professional bureaucracies"—organizations characterized by "operator autonomy," with core professional operators (faculty) who work closely with clients and largely independently of colleagues. Those in professional bureaucracies have specialized knowledge and tend to think convergently, organizing new trends into existing frameworks (Mintzberg and Quinn, 1991). These characteristics make innovating in academic institutions extremely challenging.

The dean elected to use a Future Search conference to support strategic planning and begin a process for redesigning the school. She chose this methodology because she wanted to engage the whole system, particularly the faculty. She knew the importance of faculty ownership of the outcomes. In addition, getting external stakeholders in the room would provide important reality checks and create opportunities for support and partnerships that would enhance the school's future. She knew that charting a new course for the school went far beyond listing problems and developing solutions. The challenges facing the school were too complex and interrelated. What was required was a complete transformation of RSOE.

Description of What Was Done

The time line described here (see Table 3.1) outlines the activities undertaken by RSOE as they began their change process. We entered the system in August 2000 as consultants to facilitate the planning and implementation of the Future Search. We stayed actively engaged in the system through the Integration Meeting in March 2001.

TABLE 3.1. TIME LINE OF ACTIVITIES

August 2000	Karen Gallagher becomes dean of the RSOE; consultants contacted about doing a Future Search.
November 2000	First two Future Search Planning Group meetings are held.
December 2000	Third Future Search Planning Group meeting; faculty-staff meeting is held to review details of Future Search and larger picture.
January 2001	Final Future Search Planning Group meeting is held.
January 25–27 2001	Future Search Conference takes place.
February 2001	Action planning teams are chartered.
March 30, 2001	Integration meeting is held.
April 25, 2001	Faculty meets to discuss and provide feedback on the conceptual framework.
May 10, 2001	Faculty unanimously approves the RSOE mission, four academic themes, and conceptual framework.

Table 3.1 lists the major milestones leading up to faculty approval of the new conceptual framework. This conceptual framework became the foundation for subsequent decisions related to curriculum and course development, budget, and infrastructure. A more detailed description of these activities will be provided in the next section.

Methods Used During Our Intervention

Our role in the journey of RSOE had five major components:

1. Working initially with Dean Gallagher to support her in articulating the purpose of the work to be done and the parameters of the effort

2. Working with the planning group to tailor a Future Search to meet the needs of this system, including developing a compelling purpose, selecting the invitees, and creating a customized meeting design

3. Implementing the Future Search: how far we intended to get, how far we actually got, and the critical outcomes that were foundational for the school's future

4. Chartering of implementation planning teams—groups that took the outcomes of the Future Search to deeper levels of meaning and relevance for the school

5. Facilitating an Integration Meeting to ensure that the work of the implementation planning teams became connected, integrated, and coherent

Working with Dean Gallagher (Summer 2000). As part of her entry into the system, the dean shared the report of the University Committee on Academic Review with faculty and staff and discussed the need for change with them. Although there was growing recognition of the need for change, there was less agreement about what the change should be. The complexity of the situation—how to address interrelated issues around academics, budget, morale, and infrastructure—made it challenging to identify a path forward. The dean played an important role in containing the anxiety of people in the system and shaping tasks to get the organization moving. The provost's office was both supportive of the new dean *and* wanted to see results.

At the beginning of the consultation, we helped the dean articulate coherent, integrated messages about the initial direction of the change effort. Because of our distance from USC (we live in Pennsylvania and northern California, respectively), much of our work was done via telephone conference calls. We continually summarized these conversations in writing, highlighting key thoughts, emerging directions, and action items. We e-mailed these notes immediately after each call, and they became both an orienting tool for the dean and the start-

ing point for our next phone or face-to-face meeting with her.

These summaries went considerably beyond meeting minutes. We have come to call the process *dynamic documentation.* By *dynamic,* we mean that this documentation captured and articulated the iterative nature and changing shape of the change effort. It allowed both a retrospective look at how the work was developing and pointed out a clear direction for what needed to happen next. Given the complexity of the situation, this process was helpful to us as consultants and extremely helpful to Dean Gallagher.

We asked the dean a series of questions related to the purposes and boundaries that would be shaping the work of the Future Search and the larger change effort. A sample of the questions we posed to her included the following:

- What key milestones have led up to this? Why this? Why now?
- How does the Future Search fit in the larger planning process? What has come before and what will come after?
- What will be different as a result of having done this?
- Why are you using this approach?
- What are the boundaries of this effort? What's fair game? Is there anything off-limits to the group?
- What are the "givens" (for example, financial, programmatic, operational)?
- Is the mission, "Excellence in Urban Education," a given? How does that fit into the conference?

As we documented her answers, this process helped the dean develop clear, coherent messages that could begin to focus the energy of the system.

Working with the Planning Group (Fall 2000). In the planning group, RSOE took its first step in operating differently by bringing together all the relevant stakeholder groups, internal and external, whose involvement would be needed for this change effort to succeed. Participants included RSOE faculty, representing all the existing divisions of the school, a staff member, an assistant dean, several students, the dean, and an administrator from USC's provost's office; K–12 administrators were represented in this group by both a principal and a superintendent.

This diverse group represented many different perspectives—truly a "blind man and the elephant" situation. The key was to see if they could find enough of a common purpose for the Future Search that they, and hence the system they represented, could move forward together. The work of developing a common purpose took a great deal of discussion and was accomplished over the course of several full-day meetings. In one early conversation, we asked each member of the planning group to speak to their *stake* in the future of the school. Because this type of dialogue happens rarely, it was illuminating for all of us. A particularly poignant comment was made by one of the faculty members: "The whole of this faculty is less than the

sum of its parts. We need an identity as a school, something that will enhance the whole."

As the work of the planning group continued, tensions surfaced around what types of decisions would be made at the Future Search. Faculty began to ask whether decisions would be made in the meeting about their own work. As one person said, "Are a hundred people going to vote 'yes' or 'no' on my program?" Although they would not be going into great detail in the Future Search, it became clear that the intent was, indeed, to narrow the focus of what was currently being done at the school.

Over the course of the planning group's meetings, they also talked about the nonnegotiables of the Future Search. One key issue was around the current mission of the school: Redefining Excellence in Urban Education. The planning group did not have a shared understanding of what this mission meant and raised a question about commitment for it across RSOE. Some wondered whether the mission was open for change at the Future Search. The dean made it very clear that this mission was nonnegotiable. Two other nonnegotiables were the need for academic priorities to help focus the work of the school and the university's expectation that RSOE would be ranked in the top ten schools of education in the country.

There was also confusion about which of the four elements requiring change—the academic program, the budget, morale, and infrastructure—would be dealt with in the Future Search. This discussion led the dean to develop a road map of the overall process, with four different paths, each addressing one of these distinct elements. It became clear that the Future Search would be focused solely on the academic program.

Initially, the dean created a handwritten graphic of the road map. We eventually had the road map re-created and enlarged by a graphic artist. We used this enlarged version of the road map to kick off the Future Search. It was also used in subsequent meetings and large group events to continually reorient people as to "where we have been, where we are, and where we are going."

This road map was a useful orienting tool for both the dean and for those she asked to participate in the process. It included the "givens" about the change process, described the support for the change effort that would be coming from different parts of the organization, and helped people "see the whole" in time and space, through a detailed timetable. The road map brought initial coherence to the change effort because it described the dean's thinking about the change process in such a way that others could quickly and easily understand it, add to it, and know how to participate in it. We discovered that when a change effort is complex and multifaceted, a picture such as this road map is, indeed, worth many words.

The planning group crafted the theme of the Future Search: "Redesign-ing the RSOE Together: Leadership in Urban Education." They also determined the desired outcomes:

- Determine *academic themes* that will serve as a framework for decision making.
- Begin to map the implications of these themes for reviewing current degree programs and identifying new degree programs, identifying potential research priorities, developing nondegree programs, and promoting professional development opportunities.
- Organize for follow-up and action immediately after the conference.
- Do so in a way that engages the faculty and reconnects the RSOE to the larger educational community and practitioners in the field.

In order to meet these outcomes, the planning group determined that 50 percent of the attendees would be external stakeholders.

Implementing the Future Search (January 2001). The Future Search was held from January 25th to 27th, 2001. The one hundred participants included RSOE faculty and staff, USC administrators, current students, K–12 and higher education representatives, as well as community and foundation representatives. Given the importance of these topics, there was high faculty turnout.

The flow of the conference followed the traditional time frame and activities of the Future Search methodology (Weisbord and Janoff, 2000). As it unfolded, the conference created and agreed on four academic themes: (1) diversity, (2) leadership, (3) learning, and (4) account-ability. However, we had an interesting experience in the development of these themes. After the future scenarios on the afternoon of Day 2, groups were asked to use the common themes from the fu-ture scenarios as a backdrop to identify the academic themes. As the groups were doing this task, the energy began to drain out of the room. It was not the usual energy dip that people can experi-ence from being tired at this point in the conference, nor was it the feeling of anx-iety that can begin to creep in as people realize they are moving toward commit-ting to a particular future. The feeling in the room was different. The small groups had come up with themes, they were posted, and we were ending for the day, but it was as if a plug had been pulled and the energy was just seeping out.

After the session, we met with the planning group and consulted with the dean. There were different views about what was going on and how to address action planning the next day. As facilita-tors, we were experiencing a great deal of tension and anxiety. On the one hand, the purpose of the conference was to identify these academic themes and begin mapping their implications. On the other hand, it did not seem that there was a lot of enthusiasm for the themes.

It was difficult to know how to pro-ceed. Should we reopen the dialogue around the common ground and run the risk (as we had heard from the planning group) that the group might start spin-ning and undo any agreement they might have had? Should we just move ahead as planned, using the themes to map implications? We went to sleep undecided. At 6:00 A.M. we met for breakfast. We looked across the table at each other, and this was the opening of our conversation:

"So, what do you think we should do?"

"I have no idea."

"Neither do I!"

Surprisingly, that acknowledgment and the long pause that followed created an *empty space.* The space was actually anxiety-free. Once we started talking again, we reflected on where the group had left off at the end of the day, and we realized that the themes did not reflect the richness of the dialogue that had oc-curred or the possibilities embodied in the future scenarios. This gave us some ideas about how to begin the final morn-ing session.

As we opened the session on Day 3, we started with a large group dialogue. We described our realization about the richness that might have been lost and encouraged the groups to take the themes and add more depth to them. As the work began, the energy level went up. Break-out groups organized around themes, generated ideas, received feed-back and suggestions from others, and then outlined the next steps for going forward out of the conference.

The conference output was not as specific or as comprehensive as initially hoped. In particular, we were unable to fully map out the implications of the academic themes for reviewing current degree programs and identifying new degree programs, identifying potential research priorities, developing nondegree programs, and promoting professional development opportunities. However, there *was* energy for the academic themes that were identified, as well as some beginning agreement about what was at the school's academic core for the future. As Karen Gallagher said,

> The Future Search was invaluable when the USC Rossier School of Education was seeking to chart a new course. As a result, we were able to refocus our mission around four themes of accountability, learning, diversity, and leadership. It also provided the foundation from which we redesigned our academic programs—launching a new Ed.D. program and reconstructing our Ph.D. program.

As facilitators, we learned something about a group being able to move only as fast as it *can* move. In retrospect, we suspect that some of the difficulty in identifying the academic themes probably was related to the high degree of fragmentation that had existed in RSOE. Few dialogues like this had occurred before. With the academic themes as the foundation, this was the beginning of the conceptual journey for the school. Many more conversations would occur over the next few years to gain a deeper

understanding and shared ownership of the themes.

Chartering of Implementation Planning Teams (February–March 2001). Following the Future Search conference, the next task was to charter four implementation-planning teams, each commissioned to clarify and refine one of the four academic themes (diversity, leadership, learning, and accountability). Each group was asked to write a five-page white paper on their theme and develop a presentation. The papers were to include

- A vision for the specific academic theme, including what the theme means for the RSOE
- The link between the specific theme and the mission of RSOE
- The connection between the specific theme and the other academic themes

The teams also were charged to work collaboratively. They were asked to keep all meetings open and to encourage input from all stakeholder voices. Suggested activities for the implementation planning teams included focus groups, input forums, and faculty meetings.

These groups had a four-month time frame, culminating with the last all-faculty-staff meeting in May, where it was expected that they would be presenting their position papers. Early on, it became clear that not only would it be important to develop a deeper understanding of each theme but also to understand the connections *across* the themes. It was suggested that a second large group meeting be held to hear from each team and to begin building an understanding of the meaning of these themes *across the groups.*

Facilitating the Integration Meeting (March 2001). Approximately seventy people participated in the all-day Integration Meeting, which was held on March 30, 2001. This came at the halfway point in the implementation planning teams' work. Once again it involved diverse stakeholders, many of whom had attended the Future Search conference. The purpose of the meeting was to move toward a *signature* for the school—an integrated statement about what makes the Rossier School of Education unique. Specific goals included

- To more deeply understand the four academic themes
- To more clearly see the connections and interrelationships between and among themes
- To weave the four themes together to create a unique signature
- To maintain the dialogue across all stakeholder groups

Throughout the day, white papers were presented for each of the four themes, followed by small group discussions about connections across the themes. The small groups also created graphic representations of the integration of the four themes. The Integration Meet-

ing identified many common linkages that clarified the relationships among these themes. Participants recommended drafting an integration document. Based on these results, the implementation team leaders and executive council determined that the major work of the implementation planning teams had been completed, and it was time to integrate the themes into the conceptual framework. One writer, with the help of others, created a draft for faculty, staff, and administration to critique in April.

RSOE Approves and Implements the Conceptual Framework

At the staff and faculty meeting on May 10, 2001, faculty unanimously approved the conceptual framework. This two-page document contained the following sections: (1) The Primary Educational Challenges of the 21st Century, (2) What Is Urban Education? (3) Mission Statement, (4) Four Themes, and (5) The Future of the RSOE.

From May 2001 forward, the conceptual framework served as a powerful reference point, as implementation proceeded and key decisions were made. A tremendous amount of task-focused collaborative work occurred. Faculty, staff, and administration engaged in a variety of activities to implement the conceptual framework and redesign the school, with external stakeholders serving as reality checks along the way. A sample follows:

- In the fall of 2001, criteria were developed and approved for academic program review. An external evaluation team reviewed the doctoral programs using these criteria. The results influenced changes in course offerings and offered guidance for the future.

- In the early winter of 2001, two teams were created to plan the Ed.D. and Ph.D. curriculum frameworks. Because the Ed.D. was to be the signature program for RSOE, as well as a major source of revenue, tremendous energy and faculty focus was put into its development.
- In December 2002, the faculty unanimously approved the Ed.D. curriculum framework.
- A steering group reconceived the infrastructure of the school to support the academic programs. A staff subcommittee redesigned the support staff structure.
- In April 2003, the university approved RSOE's plan to restructure the academic support staff.
- Faculty partnered with a local school district to field test a critical change in the Ed.D. program.
- The dean initiated a comprehensive communication plan to the larger educational environment. Included in this plan was an urban education newsletter.
- Faculty and administration increased the visibility of RSOE at statewide and national meetings.

All the work of implementing these changes at RSOE was completed after we left the system. It unfolded over the next three years and continues today.

Outcomes

When we checked back with Dean Gallagher two and one-half years after the Future Search, she reported dramatic results. RSOE's random collection of courses had been transformed into streamlined, coherent degree programs, with core courses based on the conceptual framework. The doctorate in education (Ed.D.)—long the traditional trademark of the school—was redesigned and became the school's signature program. A clear distinction was made between the Ph.D. and Ed.D. This differentiation is now receiving national attention.

The core courses, organized around the four academic themes from the Future Search, combined with an integrated, problem-based delivery, replaced the old "It's my course and I'll do what I want" approach. Faculty created these new core courses collaboratively. Standards for what is taught and how it is taught were developed. Twenty months after the Future Search conference, the redesigned Ed.D. program was implemented, and faculty were teaching the newly designed core academic courses.

In addition, for the first time in many years, the budget was balanced. Enrollment targets were established and met. The school's infrastructure was redesigned to support the new academic programs.

As of this writing, the RSOE had jumped twenty places in the *US News and World Report* rankings of schools of education. Another indication of the school's revitalization is the hiring of thirteen new full-time faculty—an increase of almost 30 percent.

A 2004 midterm Academic Program Review acknowledged the great strides that had been made at the RSOE since 2000. One recommendation for improvement that was made in the report was to ensure that there are enough faculty and infrastructure to support the new Ed.D. program. Another was to strengthen the intellectual foundation of the curriculum by engaging the faculty in the next level of work to identify a *distinct* Rossier USC interpretation of the four themes and the mission around urban education and excellence. They challenged RSOE to fully incorporate the four defining themes of accountability, diversity, learning, and leadership into every aspect of the school and to make the school a living laboratory in which these themes can be studied, interpreted, and enacted.

The theme of diversity and how it could be lived out was a particular focus for 2005. A "Future Search Conference II" is being planned for early 2006 to continue the work of deepening the understanding of the school's mission and the meaning of the four themes for the curriculum, research, faculty hiring, and make-up of the student body.

What the Case Authors Learned

Through the process of reconnecting with Karen Gallagher and having the unique opportunity to track the school's

progress in a detailed way over a number of years (Aronson, Barbeau, and Gallagher, 2005), we have come to a deeper understanding of what it takes to support long-term, complex change efforts. We also better understand the role of Future Search and other Large Group Methods in that journey.

As we talked in depth with Karen about her school's change process, we came to see that some of the same principles and ways of working that were instituted before and during the Future Search were also key to Karen's effective leadership of the change process in the years following the Future Search. These core elements are illustrated in Figure 3.1.

Moving from left to right, this visual depicts the high level of fragmentation that often exists before a change process begins. At RSOE in 2000, fragmentation was particularly pronounced. There was no common sense of direction or agreed-upon approach to solve the deep, systemic problems facing the school. Then the new dean arrived.

As Karen took stock at the school, it became clear to her that there would need to be *shared* direction for RSOE to become a strong, viable, and nationally respected organization. One of her first steps in bringing directional coherence was to reaffirm the identity of the school and the mission around leadership in urban education. She connected people and groups through the Future Search to collectively determine the academic themes that would form the foundation for the strategy—or "how we will get there." She used the themes and the

FIGURE 3.1. SYSTEM COHERENCE FRAMEWORK FOR CHANGE LEADERSHIP

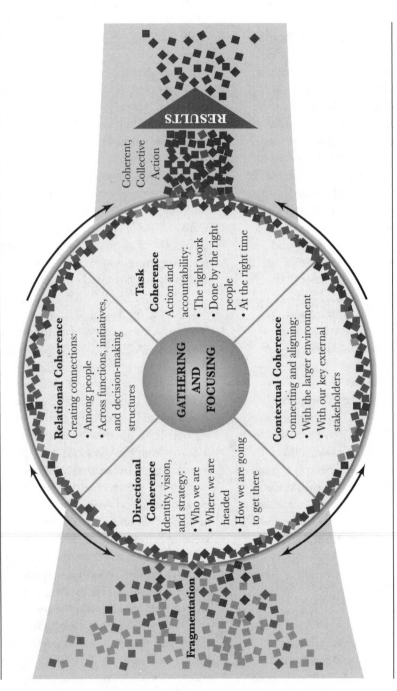

Relational Coherence
Creating connections:
- Among people
- Across functions, initiatives, and decision-making structures

Task Coherence
Action and accountability:
- The right work
- Done by the right people
- At the right time

Directional Coherence
Identity, vision, and strategy:
- Who we are
- Where we are headed
- How we are going to get there

Contextual Coherence
Connecting and aligning:
- With the larger environment
- With our key external stakeholders

GATHERING AND FOCUSING

Fragmentation

Coherent, Collective Action

RESULTS

conceptual framework to orient decision making about the future of the school throughout the following years.

The arrows in the figure depict the interplay among directional, contextual, and relational coherence. *Directional coherence* refers to the *content* of the change effort. *Relational coherence and contextual coherence* inform *how* direction is set by paying attention to the larger environment and engaging internal and external stakeholders. Through the planning group and then in the Future Search itself, RSOE had an opportunity to gather its internal and external stakeholders together to become clear on direction. The involvement of external stakeholders helped to develop contextual coherence—an understanding about what was happening in the broader environment and what key external stakeholder groups needed from the school. Further contextual coherence was developed, as representatives of these external groups participated in the Integration Meeting and in task groups over a several-year period.

Relational coherence refers to connecting and coordinating across diverse internal stakeholder groups. The Future Search provided an opportunity for faculty, staff, administration, and students to interact, understand their different points of view, and jointly contribute to the shaping of the direction of the school. Relational coherence in this case also dealt with the issue of governance, or established structure, roles, and processes for decision making. For example, Dean Gallagher acknowledged the key responsibility and right of faculty to shape curriculum by bringing the conceptual framework to the full faculty for approval.

These three dimensions—directional, contextual, and relational coherence—form the foundation for a change process that is feasible, well designed, and externally relevant. Finally, task coherence builds the bridge to coordinated, collective action and to tangible results by identifying the work to be done, who will do it, and in what time frame.

Dean Gallagher, in collaboration with her staff and key faculty members, identified the tasks that would move the change process forward, beginning with the work of the planning group, moving through the Future Search, the follow-up activities of the implementation planning teams, the Integration Meeting, and the many task groups chartered over the next several years. These are all examples of coherent, collective action leading to concrete results: the redesign of the academic program, the creation of a core curriculum, the restructuring of the infrastructure of the school, and a balanced budget.

Working with Karen Gallagher gave us a much clearer picture of the type of leadership that is needed in highly fragmented systems when transformational change is the goal. This work further reaffirmed for us that methodologies like the Future Search can be pivotal events. It has been useful for us to more deeply understand some key principles that underlie both the Future Search *and* the other activities that followed at RSOE—principles we have organized as the System Coherence Framework. We believe that no matter where a system is in the change process, the framework can guide leaders and others supporting the change by asking diagnostic questions that help the system determine where it needs to focus its energy to build or sustain momentum for change. Some examples of these questions include the following:

- *Directional coherence:* What do people need to know about where we are headed and how we will get there? What is our road map for change?
- *Contextual coherence:* What are the important trends in the environment that affect our customers and us? Which external stakeholders do we need to engage to ensure that we have a reality check? What do external stakeholders need from us now? How can we partner with them to achieve the results of our change effort?
- *Relational coherence:* Who needs to have ownership in this change process in order for it to be successful? Who needs to connect, with whom, around what, in order for effective action to occur?
- *Task coherence:* What are the next concrete action steps in our change process? What is the broader path forward? Do we have the right people in key roles to accomplish this work?

Based on our work with the RSOE, we believe the System Coherence Framework is most useful in organizations where

- The *change is transformational,* that is, when it requires a fundamental shift in the organization's purpose, identity, structure, and operations.
- There is a *high level of fragmentation* at the beginning of the change effort, that is, people are operating in silos, organizational units are isolated, or the culture of the organization is highly individualistic, with little sense of "the whole."
- The *support of a critical mass of the organization* is required for the change to be successful.

The planning and implementation of a Future Search creates what Dean Gallagher calls an *incubator* in which the directional, contextual, relational, and task coherence dimensions can ripen and evolve. Because the Future Search gives a system the experience of working together in a more coherent, integrated way, it provides a picture or model for operating this way after the conference. However, for this way of working to be *sustained,* ongoing leadership intention *and* attention are required. Dean Gallagher put it well when she said, "We would not be where we are today without the Future Search, and the conference alone would not have been enough." As a leader, she helped continually gather and focus the attention and energy of this system over time to keep the change process coherent and moving toward results.

References

Aronson, N., Barbeau, R., & Gallagher, K. (2005). Transforming a school of education: Building system coherence. In R. Schweitz & K. Martens (Eds.), *Future Search in school district change: Connection, community, and results.* Lanham, MD: Scarecrow Press.

Mintzberg, H., & Quinn, J. (1991). *The strategy process: Concepts, contexts and cases.* Upper Saddle River, NJ: Prentice Hall.

Weisbord, M., & Janoff, S. (2000). *Future Search: An action guide to finding common ground in organizations and communities.* San Francisco: Berrett-Koehler.

CREATING A WORLD-CLASS MANUFACTURER IN RECORD TIME

Richard Lent, James Van Patten, and Tom Phair

The Challenge

At the start of this change effort in 1999, Emerson & Cuming (E&C)—a specialty chemical manufacturer—had just been acquired, and its two plants had merged into one facility. Though the merger resulted in immediate operational cost savings, it also caused significant confusion and disorganization. Raw materials were difficult to locate and inventories difficult to gauge with any certainty. Production areas were disorganized and cramped, creating safety and environmental concerns; employee productivity and morale were poor. Many customer orders had to be rushed to make up for poor production scheduling, and customers complained more frequently. The plant's financial performance was disappointing.

The situation needed to be turned around quickly. However, the plant's state was the result of many interacting technical, cultural, and organizational issues. There was no single "root cause," no missing skill or piece of information, no organizational dysfunction or defective management routine. The key question was, How can we address all the interacting issues simultaneously to quickly improve business results?

Background

E&C manufactures epoxies and other formulations used in demanding electronics, automotive, and aerospace applications. The company has plants in several countries. Its Canton, Massachusetts, facility produces about four million pounds annually of almost 1,800 different products.

In 1999, the plant was organized as a typical "batch and queue" manufacturer, with an emphasis on producing large batches of product, following production schedules based on manufacturing resources planning (MRP) software. As a result of combining the two plants into this one site, there now were two product lines, with different histories, and two distinct work cultures under the same roof, with little cooperation or trust across the workforce.

Approach

As the consultants planned the approach to the plant's improvement effort, they thought it important that the change effort begin with the cultural (or social side) of change, rather than with a program of technical interventions. They used four guiding principles to develop the eventual transformation process:

1. *Engage the whole system.* The two existing cultures had to evolve into one new culture. A new culture could not be taught, but it could be learned in action if enough members of the organization were involved.

2. *Let the workplace inform action.* Operators, supervisors, and managers need quick feedback on the impact of their actions and efforts to improve. Ongoing, direct experience in the workplace would be essential.

3. *Focus on what all agree on for the desired future of the plant and the workplace.* A focus on a common future would be more energizing than a focus on current problems to be overcome. Beginning with areas of common agreement would be more productive than trying to resolve the multiple areas of disagreement.

4. *Aim for incremental improvement (getting better) rather than a programmatic push (implementing "perfect").* Many in the plant had already been through quality and safety programs that taught them many tools and concepts. What they needed was enough persistence over time to produce visible differences in the safety, quality, and productivity of the plant.

The consultants decided that Future Search (Weisbord and Janoff, 2000) would be the initial intervention. Action teams, some using Gemba Kaizen action learning techniques, would begin work on the improvement efforts identified during the Future Search. The consultants would provide limited but focused support to the teams. Follow-Up Meetings would be held periodically to reinforce the progress of the change throughout the whole plant.

Taken together, this set of Future Search, improvement activities, and Follow-Up Meetings were to provide "whole-system action learning." That is, E&C's organizational change would be supported through a cycle of plantwide actions, discussion to understand the results of those actions, and subsequent planning to create still more change (see Figure 3.2).

FIGURE 3.2. A CYCLE OF LEARNING AND CHANGE

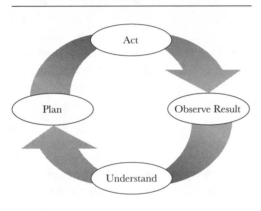

Over the course of the first year, the whole organization was involved in a series of actions to improve the workplace and conversations to understand the impact of those actions. In all, the plant un-

derwent at least five cycles of learning and change (see Figure 3.3).

Within six months of the Future Search (called the Agree Meeting), managers and operators began to see concrete results of their improvement efforts across all measures of safety, productivity, and efficiency. Within a year, they had achieved a major turnaround in all key performance areas. Five years later, the E&C Canton plant is considered by its parent company (National Starch) to be an outstanding production facility and has won worldwide recognition for its record in safety, quality, and improvement. The plant's current rate of safety incidents (OSHA recordables) is 0; its order-to-delivery lead time is three days; its quality issues (all-inclusive) are below 110 per million shipped, and its inventory turns over sixteen times per year. With the space saved in the plant through reduced inventories, two new businesses have been added, which now represent one-fifth of the plant's total revenue. Throughout this period, the operation manager's leadership was critical in supporting continuing cycles of plantwide learning and change.

FIGURE 3.3. CYCLES OF WHOLE-SYSTEM ACTION LEARNING ACROSS THE FIRST YEAR

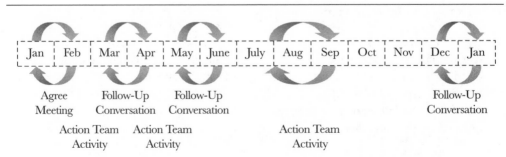

What Happened

Just after they met, the operations manager and the consultants walked through the plant. What they saw was a crowded, disorganized, and messy facility. People worked with little enjoyment and less eye contact. The recent merger had moved all the material and equipment from the previous site into this building. Raw materials and finished goods were stored in several locations. Tools and excess materials were everywhere. Production, raw materials, finished goods, and various support functions were scattered throughout the facility.

Data Gathering, Design, and Management Commitment (Fall 1998)

As they continued their tour, the operations manager explained his vision of a lean, efficient operation. He explained that, to him, "lean" meant free from unnecessary activity, supplies, and materials that did not contribute to meeting customer needs. More important, "lean" meant helping employees work safely and effectively in producing what customers wanted. He felt that such a plant would not only be safer but would improve financial performance and customer satisfaction. The plant he envisioned was also a *long* way from the dirty, disorganized facility and unhappy employees that they saw around them that day.

Shortly thereafter, the consultants met with a cross-section of employees in a series of focus groups. They found that operators and supervisors felt frustrated in their ability to work effectively in the plant. Necessary materials were hard to find, and orders had to be expedited frequently. There were few standard procedures, and there was a "them and us" feeling between the two product lines.

The consultants then met with supervisors, staff managers, and the operations manager to develop and agree on the overall approach. Together they reviewed recent business results, along with comments from the focus groups and outcomes of an employee questionnaire. They discussed the importance of building the energy and commitment of employees from within; improvement activities could begin with whatever was causing the most frustration. The tools and concepts of lean manufacturing would be the *means* used to achieve the *ends* identified by the employees in the Future Search.

Agree Meeting (Winter 1999)

The first major effort to help the organization change its culture and results was a Future Search. This was held with about one-third of the plant employees, as well as people from sales, R&D, and corporate functions. The Future Search followed the standard design, with one exception. To avoid consultant jargon or any suggestion of another program "launch," the session was called an Agree Meeting. The stated focus was to agree on the ". . . safest, highest-quality, most productive workplace . . ." Forty managers, supervisors, and operators were grouped into five stakeholder teams to represent all aspects of the plant, as well as sales, corporate, and R&D functions. Operators represented the largest group of participants. This was partly because they represented the biggest group of employees but also because their views had typically been overlooked in planning for previous changes.

The final vision for the plant's future, as generated in this meeting, included a number of specific agreements about what all wanted for the future of their plant. Among these agreements on the future workplace were the following:

- Satisfying customer needs, particularly critical customer needs
- Clean, neat, orderly workplace
- Reproducible, reliable, consistent processes and instructions
- Cross-training between departments

As the meeting came to a close, participants identified twelve specific projects to help them achieve their vision. Action teams were formed around each project, with each team including a cross-section of employees. Some of these teams and their initial goals were as follows:

- Product line management team: eliminate low-revenue products.
- Inventory reduction team: reduce inventory by half within six months.
- Improve the workplace team: sort, straighten, scrub, and standardize the entire workplace.

- Reorganize work flow team: complete a model line within twelve months that demonstrates the new way of working.
- Improve quality and safety programs team: develop and implement new quality and safety standards.

In addition to the action teams, a cross-functional and cross-level (from operator to manager) steering committee was created to help coordinate the various projects. The operations manager would act as chairman of the nine-member steering committee.

Action Team Activity and Gemba Kaizen (Winter 1999)

The plan was for participants to take quick initial actions and then reflect on the results of those actions. Teams were told that they should spend a few weeks trying to implement their project plans and then meet again to share their successes and frustrations. Some of these efforts were planned to provide immediate, visible signs of progress to demonstrate that change was under way. In addition, the intent was to engage as many employees as possible as soon as possible. Over the first month, well over half of the plant employees were involved in the Agree Meeting and the subsequent improvement activities.

Gemba Kaizen Activities

Gemba Kaizen is an action learning method that quickly identifies and implements workplace improvement by working directly on and in the work-place (Imai and Heymans, 1999). Specifically, a team is set up to study the workplace, develop improvement ideas, implement trials of these ideas, and gather data about their effectiveness. Some of the action teams set up in the Agree Meeting provided an opportunity for conducting improvement projects using this approach.

Two action teams used Gemba Kaizen activities to reorganize a warehouse and simplify a production area. Each team included a cross-section of managers, supervisors, and operators, some of whom did not normally work in these areas. Both projects were conducted over four days using the "5S" approach (a lean manufacturing technique where a workplace is Sorted, Straightened, Scrubbed, and Standardized, and the new practices are Spread). This provided immediate, visual progress in making the workplace safer, easier, and more efficient. It also provided a framework that the teams could use when they were presented with similar problems in the future.

Follow-Up Meeting and Subsequent Actions (Early Spring 1999)

The first Follow-Up Meeting was held a little over a month after the Agree Meeting and two weeks after the completion of the initial Gemba Kaizen projects. Members of all action teams were present, along with other individuals from the plant who had not attended the

original Future Search. Each action team reported on the initial progress they had made. Everyone toured the two areas that had undergone the Kaizen efforts to see the very visible results.

Several of the action teams had made considerable progress toward aspects of the vision developed at the Agree Meeting. However, two teams had difficulty getting started. The three key questions for this Follow-Up Meeting were:

- What have you accomplished so far?
- What haven't you accomplished that you thought you would?
- What are you learning about leading improvement from both the successes and the difficulties so far?

The consultants used this meeting to reinforce the fact that the change process was the responsibility of everyone in the plant. After sharing their reflections, the group planned their next actions and asked for a second Follow-Up Meeting in five weeks.

After this first Follow-Up Meeting, the steering committee decided to launch more projects in every department. They also chose to further explore lean thinking, especially "pull scheduling" (making to order, not to inventory). The consultants were asked to return to assist with three projects: (1) develop a "focused factory," with pull scheduling, (2) develop a "self-managed work team," and (3) improve the order-entry process. Projects were completed over the next two months, with periodic cycles of meetings across the teams to review and reflect on what they were learning about creating change.

With the steering committee taking over the governance role, the consultants looked for others in E&C to take over their role as "lean experts" and facilitators. Several employees were prepared to be internal experts by "apprenticing" with the consultants during the three improvement activities identified earlier.

Steering Committee Sponsorship of Improvement Projects (Spring to Late Fall 1999)

A number of improvement projects were conducted according to the vision developed in the initial Agree Meeting. The following projects were sponsored by the operations manager and the steering committee, with only occasional involvement of the consultants (including support for one of the Gemba Kaizen efforts from consultant Derek Kotze).

Using the 5S Approach. The whole facility was reorganized and standardized following the 5S approach. By organizing the workplace to support the work, the entire facility improved safety and quality while reducing nonproductive office, lab, and warehouse space to make way for additional production equipment. This way of thinking became characteristic of the new culture. For example, a project was launched to use the 5S process to rationalize the product offerings from 3,000 SKUs to fewer than

1,800. Products were sorted (needed, not needed), then organized into families, then scrubbed (checked for presence of good manufacturing practices) and standardized. This use of 5S surprised the consultants for its creative use of the concept.

Streamlining Order Entry. The order-entry process was mapped and analyzed to help reduce order-to-delivery time. As a result, the organization developed a new appreciation for this important role, which led to a change in focus, goal, and even name—from "order entry" to "customer service."

Improving the ECO Process. Using the same techniques as the order-entry improvement project, an improvement team analyzed the engineering change order (ECO) process. The ECO process controls changes made to the manufacturing standards, called *batch cards,* used to produce products. As the batch cards were reviewed and improved, the ECO process became the bottleneck to improvement, so it was improved as well.

Rationalizing Products and Service. Customers and products were differentiated in an effort to provide the priority and focus the group desired. Although all customers would receive good quality and timely service, the group decided that they would "jump through hoops" only for the high-volume or growth-oriented customers. Similarly, the almost 1,800 products were classified by production volume. High-volume products would be produced on a steady, often daily basis, based on demand, while low-volume products would be produced only as required.

Developing Lean Supplier Relationships. "Lean" requirements for suppliers were negotiated into agreements so that small, frequent shipments and consignment inventories became the norm. If suppliers were unable or unwilling to comply with E&C's requirements, the purchasing team worked to develop new suppliers in the greater Boston area who could.

Over this period, the consultants led one more Follow-Up Meeting to help the organization learn from the activities and results of the various team efforts. The design of this meeting was similar to the first and occurred about the third month after the Agree Meeting.

One-Year Follow-Up (January 2000)

At the one-year anniversary of the initial Agree Meeting, the consultants facilitated a one-day meeting where participants from all areas of the plant reflected on their vision, goals, activities, and progress.

Although the organization had made great progress, participants agreed that they still had room for improvement. Some of their observations were as follows:

- Although the 5S activities had made a lot of progress, there was no "shining" example.
- Team skills were not as well developed as they needed to be.
- Clarity of overall vision was not as good as it could be.
- The steering committee was not operating consistently.

The group recognized the weak areas that needed more attention and were also very positive and excited about their success so far. E&C had learned to "welcome problems" as opportunities and learn from the results of its actions.

During this Follow-Up Meeting the group revisited some of the items that had not been included in the original vision or action plans because they had not been agreed to by everyone. Some of these items had once been points of real contention. But after a year of progress, it was clear that many of these issues were not as important as once thought, and several were no longer relevant at all.

At about the same time as this meeting, the National Starch newsletter (E&C's Canton Facility Gets "Lean," 2000) published an article about the changes at the plant. The operations manager and his boss, Charles Call, reported:

> As the end of the first year [of improvement activities] approaches, the results achieved by the E&C teams are impressive. . . . And more significant than these individual

results is the development of a culture of continuous improvement in such a short time. Where most companies plan on a three to five year plan to implement this type of culture change, E&C has managed to dramatically change its culture in less than a year.

Among the first-year results they reported were the following indicators of progress:

- Productivity improved from 12 to 50 percent across different production areas.
- Warehouse space utilization improved by 23 percent; productive floor space showed gains of 35 percent across all areas.
- Lead time to delivery was reduced by 30 to 60 percent for major customers; on-time delivery improved from 86 to 95 percent.
- Cross-training of all applicable staff across all product families was complete.

Four Years Later

Over the last few years, E&C has become a recognized flagship manufacturing facility for all of National Starch and its parent company, ICI. E&C has received international recognition for its safety record and manufacturing effectiveness and has accomplished this with very little change in technology or personnel.

In January of 1999, the employees of E&C envisioned their future and agreed to work together to attain that future. In time, their achievements far surpassed the expectations of their corporate managers or the consultants. Here are a few indicators of their achievement:

Indicator	January 1999	December 2004
Recorded safety incidents	9	0
Safety suggestions	0	500
Number of employees	101	93
Hazardous waste generated	7,675 lbs.	748 lbs.
On-time deliveries	86%	98.4%
Customer issues (in parts-per-million)	400 PPM	110 PPM
Batches produced	5,236	9,063
Inventory turns	6.5	16 (21 in 2004)
Working capital as % of sales	21.3%	8.3%
Sales	$X million	$1.5X million
Order-to-delivery lead time	15 days	1 to 3 days

What Was Learned

Learning occurred for everyone during this process. E&C employees learned about each other and about their capability to make improvements. Along the way, they learned about lean manufacturing, about productive workplaces, and about talking together, even around areas where they held different views. Some learned about trust in the workplace. By following a completely transparent process, the operations manager and the consultants were able to provide a model for everyday interactions. Meanwhile, the organization learned to adopt a new culture—one of lean thinking. Even if employees could not exactly define the new culture, they recognized that it had changed. One of the senior supervisors quipped, "I'm still not sure why this lean stuff works. But as long as I keep [shipping] on time, I'll keep doing it."

Finally, the consultants learned more about the effectiveness of the four principles they used to guide their overall approach. In hindsight, they can reflect on how those principles operated in this situation: (1) engage the whole system, (2) let the workplace inform action, (3) focus on what all agree on for the future, and (4) incremental improvement can be more successful than programmatic push. The operations manager also adds his own views on his learning as the manager responsible for leading change while managing ongoing business performance.

• *Engage the whole system.* From the beginning the consultants and the operations manager recognized they had to involve everyone from across the two original plants if the effort was to succeed. In 1999, the plant had approximately one hundred operators and employees. Although everyone could not attend the Agree Meeting (Future Search), over one-third of the plant's managers, supervisors, and operators, as well as representatives from key corporate functions, were involved from the beginning. Those operators and supervisors that had to remain at the plant to keep things running all had an opportunity to get involved, see initial change begin, and share their own ideas within the first thirty days.

Not everyone supported the change effort. In particular, one supervisor and one functional manager seemed to provide only minimal compliance with new ideas and initiatives. The operations manager had to work with these individuals to keep them from slowing down the overall change effort.

Another important way in which this effort "engaged the whole system" was in the work of the action teams, particularly the Gemba Kaizen events. In the first month people saw real change, as areas of the plant were cleaned and reorganized to better serve the work being done at these locations. Members of these teams included a cross-section of managers, supervisors, and operators, in addition to the operators from that immediate work area. It made quite an impression on people to see the operations manager and other influential individuals spending three days on the shop floor cleaning and organizing an area. People later shared stories of how they saw the operations manager on his hands and knees cleaning a fitting with a toothbrush. His actions provided very visible top management commitment and made it "safe" for others to support and participate in the improvement activities.

• *Let the workplace inform action.* From the beginning, managers, supervisors, and operators were encouraged to ask questions about the workplace and the results produced there. Why was that machine located at that distance from the work station? Where were the raw materials stored? Why were things dirty? When did production orders arrive? Why were so many orders expedited? These questions were asked openly to build understanding and encourage lean thinking about how the workplace was—or was not—supporting the work in a safe and efficient manner.

The answers to these simple, direct questions came as equally direct and powerful improvement ideas. For example, when conducting a Gemba Kaizen activity in the warehouse, one consultant asked, "How did all of these out-of-date products get here?" The team discussed the question and realized that most items were due to cancelled shipments. With some research, they found that most of the cancelled shipments were for distributors. A high priority was placed on better managing their distribution network. Once the warehouse was reorganized and out-of-date products re-

moved, a severe shortage of warehouse space was resolved.

• *Focus on what all agree on for the future.* The warehouse improvement story was one chapter in a fairly contentious issue when work began. At the Agree Meeting, a number of people held that their vision for the future of the plant included a larger warehouse so that product could be more easily stored where all could find it. Considerable attention was given to a plan for acquiring more space so that enough material could be removed from the plant to make it easier and safer for people to do their jobs. While agreeing with the vision of a less cluttered workplace in which materials and products were easier to store and to find, other people disagreed with the need for additional warehouse space. These people felt that lean thinking could help them achieve the same goal in their existing space. Because there was no common agreement on whether additional warehouse space was needed, no action was taken on this idea. However, because all agreed that the workplace had to be neater and easier to work in, several Gemba Kaizen efforts were devoted to creating some initial improvements in key areas, including the warehouse. Six months later the warehouse had so much extra room that some space had been turned over to production. Looking back, the group recognized they had achieved this aspect of their vision without getting stuck on one of the more contentious ideas.

Disagreements on means of achieving the vision arose a number of times.

Plant management and staff learned to respect the areas of disagreement but not to focus all their efforts on resolving them. They learned that by moving ahead on areas of agreement, areas of disagreement might be resolved in time.

• *Incremental improvement can be more successful than programmatic push.* By the end of the Agree Meeting, eleven action teams had been identified and formed. Two of the teams implemented their projects with consultant support, while the other nine teams worked on their own, using the improvement tools and concepts they already knew. This meant that the change effort was widely distributed across the plant. The message always was that this was their change to create. The consultants' role was that of support in a few focused areas.

The Follow-Up Meetings were explicitly designed to emphasize the improvement and learning occurring from both successes and disappointments across all the teams. Achievements were celebrated. A few of the achievements were surprising to all. At the first Follow-Up Meeting, some of the most exciting progress came from one of the most unexpected areas: updated instructions for making core products and plans for training people across product lines. These issues had been considered almost insurmountable problems. At the same meeting, some teams reported that they were stuck or had otherwise failed to achieve some plan for the period. Such "disappointing" results were framed as useful and important, and helped the whole group to learn about the difficulty

of making improvement and leading change at this plant at this time.

Reflections from the Operations Manager

Looking back over the five-year period, the operations manager reached the following conclusions from his experience:

• *His boss (the vice president, Charles Call) played a critical role in creating space for change.* Charlie made it clear to the surrounding company that the plant needed to focus on its own improvements. This was to be done from inside, by the people in Canton. Charlie demonstrated visible support through his personal involvement in the Agree and Follow-Up Meetings.

• *Ground rules for respecting disagreements were helpful.* By establishing a ground rule (in the Agree Meeting) that areas of disagreement should be acknowledged but not worked, the plant established a way to work through decisions more productively. Such focusing on areas of agreement is now firmly entrenched in the culture of E&C.

• *The plant was able to achieve small but observable and meaningful improvements within the first month.* These helped to make the outcomes of the Agree Meeting real for the whole plant. More important, these early successes said "we can do it" to a workforce that was bruised and jaded from all the changes to which they had been subjected.

• *Persistence was important to deal with resistance.* Many in the plant were used to seeing any change as only temporary—the "change of the month." It was through a persistent focus on the vision for the plant's future that the natural resistance to change could be kept from stopping forward motion.

• *It was important to change everyone's perspective from that of a narrow functional view to a wider view of the system.* Until this effort, managers and operators saw their work from the perspective of their own departments and responsibilities. A number of the activities in this change effort helped people see the broader processes and recognize how important it was to serve their internal customers as well as their external ones.

Conclusion

E&C's Canton plant is thriving today. It is so efficient that it can compete effectively in the global marketplace. Their parent company has recognized them as an outstanding example of lean manufacturing, and they have been sought out by others looking for ideas and lessons. The consultants have not been

involved with the plant since 2001, and the continued improvement has all been led from within.

Canton's difficult situation in 1999 seems like a long-ago dream. Change, once seen as a "flavor of the month" is now seen as "the way we work here." It is expected and welcomed. The plant is growing in new ways, while still working with the same physical plant and many of the same people it had in the past. They continue to complete cycles of learning and change. Today they are truly world class.

References

E&C's Canton facility gets "lean." (2000). *EEM News, 2*(2), 3–4.

Imai, M., & Heymans, B. (1999). Gemba Kaizen: Organizational change in real time. In P. Holman & T. Devane, *The change handbook: Group methods for shaping the future* (pp. 109–122). San Francisco: Berrett-Koehler.

Weisbord, M., & Janoff, S. *Future Search: An action guide to finding common ground in organizations and communities* (2nd ed.). San Francisco: Berrett-Koehler, 2000.

PLANNING STRATEGICALLY FOR AN UNCERTAIN FUTURE

The Boston University Dental School

Gilbert Steil Jr. and Michele Gibbons-Carr

The Challenge

In 2002 we were asked to assist the Boston University School of Dental Medicine in preparing its strategic plan for the next decade. We were faced with a post-9/11 world in which there was a palpable sense of uncertainty in everything that was done and said. Although we had a seven-year history of consulting at the dental school, we faced a very different school. The role of research at the dental school had grown and exploded in importance, the school had grown in size, and the emphasis of the school had shifted from a predominantly postdoctoral educational institution to include a significant focus on predoctoral education as well.

The authors extend special thanks to Dean Spencer N. Frankl of The Boston University School of Dental Medicine, whose support and cooperation made this chapter and the work it describes possible.

Background

The fortieth anniversary of the school was coming up, and to celebrate, the school hosted the Goldman Symposium on the Future of Dental Medicine. This event provided the opportunity to immerse everyone in what was going on in the world of dentistry—outside the walls of the institution. Dental colleagues from many other institutions presented dental research and the latest scientific advances in an examination of the future of dental medicine. We picked up some of the buzz: the technology exists today to grow replacement teeth in the lab, potentially eliminating the need for false teeth; saliva may soon be used as a diagnostic tool, replacing the use of blood tests; links can be drawn between whether or not people floss their teeth and systemic health problems; revolutionary new tools are about to come to market; in the United Kingdom, some of the work traditionally being done by dentists was being done by practitioners with only a year of training.

In summary, the symposium provided glimpses into what might become a transformative future for the profession, driven by science and technology and changes in the economy and complex geopolitical events. It raised important questions for faculty and administrators who would have to meet the challenges of a world very different from the one for which their academic and prior experience had prepared them. It raised questions about what the dental school can and should be in the future, what it should prepare students for, how it should keep abreast of what is happening in science, technology, and dental medicine, and whether it should focus on adapting to transformative change on the horizon or participate in shaping it. The school had important choices to make and questions to explore about how it would engage its future. The goal was to continue to thrive and be successful, regardless of the external conditions that might unfold. But which of the embryos of change were about to unfold, and which would prevail?

The Method as Challenge

The more we talked about what was happening in dentistry, the more confirmed we became in our conviction that for this client at this time, we needed a new large group intervention for strategic planning. We had previously led seven successful large group interventions for the school (Frankl and Gibbons-Carr, 2001), addressing everything from creating the culture of a learning organization to organization design, but this situation felt qualitatively different: the future of dentistry in the world could take several different paths, and these paths were poles apart. How could we help the school plan for the future when the future path for dentistry itself is yet to be chosen? The typical large group "futuring" and "common ground" exercises, where the future of dentistry and the future of the school were addressed simultaneously, did not feel robust enough. What if the whole system reached common ground on the future of the school, but their collective assumptions about the future of the profession were wrong? We needed to be able to help the school see what was happening from different perspectives, push the limits of conventional thinking, face uncertainty, and arrive at a shared view of its meaning.

We had both read *The Art of the Long View* (Schwartz, 1991, 1996) years before, and we began to talk about the possibility of building on traditional scenario planning as the basis of our intervention. It appealed to us because it shared with our whole-system consulting philosophy the aim of producing both mutual understanding and organizational learning. Most important, it provided a tool for handling very difficult questions about the future through dialogue about differences. By developing multiple views of the future, it offered us the opportunity to help the school embrace uncertainty.

In the two-year traditional scenario planning process described by Ringland (1998), multiple future worlds are made explicit, strategies are created for each, and then the strategies that work well in more than one future world are given precedence. Convinced that we had found an answer, we now faced a technical challenge: How do we blend the structure of a scenario-creation strategy with the high-engagement strategy of Large Group Methods? How do we do, in two *days,* much of what traditional scenario planning does over two *years?*

We awaited the appointment of a steering committee.

The Steering Committee's Work

The dean convened a fourteen-member steering committee that brought together leading faculty, staff, and administrators who represented every component of the school's mission to think about what lay ahead. This diverse group brought strong and divergent viewpoints about the challenges ahead and the direction to be taken. The steering committee included the dean, the associate deans of Clinical Services, Academic Affairs, and Postdoctoral Programs, co-chairs of the curriculum committee, the director of the Office of Educational Research and Evaluation, the executive director of the Office of Admissions and Student Services, research faculty from the Oral Biology and Health Policy departments, predoctoral clinical and didactic faculty, administrative staff, and two chairs of departments. There were men and women; some members had been at the school fewer than five years and some longer than ten.

The key tasks for the planning process were to grapple with where the profession was headed, decide the important questions facing the school, consider the decisions that must be made today in order to prepare the school for tomorrow, and make solid recommendations to the dean and the key groups within the school that would be responsible for implementation.

As we worked on adapting traditional scenario planning to a large group format, we saw that we needed three full days if we were to start at the beginning and proceed all the way to a set of agreed-on strategies. We had a firm budget of two days, so we decided to have some of the tasks done by the steering committee, and those tasks crucial to large group interaction at the event itself.

The committee first explored their own vision of what it would take to be successful in 2013, and then formulated three decision questions to be the focus of the large group and scenario planning process:

1. How do we evolve the curriculum in a way that translates science into better oral health?
2. How do we build, maintain, and enrich a committed faculty and staff?
3. How do we attract, maintain, and support quality students?

The steering committee then identified ten factors as having the broadest influence on the outcomes of the decision questions:

1. Changes in the provider-delivery paradigm (granting independent status to auxiliary practitioners and expanding their function)
2. The access-to-care crisis in the United States
3. Changes in regulatory-licensure issues
4. Third-party influences on delivery of care and reimbursement
5. The dynamics of the national economy of the United States

6. Impact of scientific advances and research
7. Expectations of the public for oral health providers
8. Student indebtedness and available aid for future students
9. Dentistry as a favorable career choice
10. Changes in demographics; immigration regulations affecting student recruitment

Each factor was then rated for its importance and its predictability. Factors that were considered predictable (inevitable or nearly certain to unfold) were set aside for later consideration, even though they were felt to be important. Schwartz (1991, 1996) calls these "predetermined elements."

The two unpredictable factors that were felt to have the broadest and most overriding impact on the decision questions were then selected, and their polar possibilities articulated. Schwartz (1991, 1996) calls these "critical uncertainties." The two factors chosen by the school were (1) the dynamics of the national economy of the United States and (2) the nature of the provider-delivery paradigm (traditional provider or expansion of oral health providers). Traditional providers would include the spectrum of dentists we see today: general dentists, orthodontists, endodontists, and so forth. The expansion of oral health providers would include auxiliaries such as denturists, dental nurses, or independent dental hygienists.

Four future worlds were then defined by the polar possibilities of the chosen unpredictable factors. The four worlds became

1. Strong economy, traditional provider model
2. Strong economy, expansion of oral health providers
3. Weak economy, traditional provider model
4. Weak economy, expansion of oral health providers

At this point the process of creating future scenarios had just begun.

The remaining trends and driving forces were organized into themes. The two critical uncertainties and three sample themes are shown in Tables 3.2 and 3.3. Table 3.2 shows polar possibilities and a range of possible outcomes. Table 3.3 contains descriptions of the different ways each theme might influence the future and provides the working definitions of each of the themes developed by the dental school steering committee. The tables together constitute what Schoemaker (2002) calls a "scenario blueprint."

Each one of the four blueprints was next transformed into a scenario. The roles of the critical uncertainties for each scenario were already defined within each of the four worlds. The other themes of the scenario blueprint were then considered, and for each theme a decision was made as to what role that theme might plausibly play in the future world being envisioned. Each scenario was based on how these factors might interact. A narrative that took all the themes into account was then created. Each scenario was an integrated structure that could be apprehended as a whole. A narrative description of how two of the four future worlds might evolve is shown on pages 131–132.

TABLE 3.2. DENTAL SCHOOL SCENARIO BLUEPRINT: FORCES AND RANGE OF POSSIBLE OUTCOMES (A SAMPLING)

Factors	Range of Possible Outcomes
Economy	Strong... Weak
Provider-delivery paradigm	Traditional model... Expanded oral health workforce
Provider-delivery level of access to care	Universal.................Majority.................Limited.................None
Role of new oral health technologies	Breakthrough..........................Incremental..........................None
Role of dentists	Continued control and dominance... Entry of new providers, independent status

TABLE 3.3. WORKING DEFINITIONS OF DRIVING FORCES (A SAMPLING)

Driving Force	Working Definitions
Dynamics of the national economy	**Strong:** characterized by high employment, thriving middle class, increased demand for health care, better government funding for those in need, money for investment in research
	Weak: characterized by unemployment, increase in applications to dental school, stronger quality of students, increased need for a safety net, budget cutbacks on funding to dental care
Impact of provider-delivery paradigm on cost, quality, and access to care	**Traditional:** dentist as supervisor of nondentists, fee for service, direct reimbursement model, dominated by disease-treatment model
	Expansion of providers: expanding function of existing roles among auxiliaries independent hygiene practice, creation of new and/or different roles, such as dental nurse, denturists, focus on prevention, and broader view of health
Level of access to oral health care	Access is defined as obtaining care to maintain oral health within a one-year period.
	• **Universal:** Neither cost nor geographic distribution of providers is a barrier.
	• **Majority:** System is differentiated by ability to pay, but most of the population has access.
	• **Limited:** Access is beyond the reach of the average citizen because of cost.
Role of new oral health technologies	**Breakthrough:** Innovative technologies transform dentistry. **Incremental:** Some new technologies provide improvement. **None:** New technology fails to live up to promise.

Scenario 1: Strong Economy, Expanded Oral Health Workforce

Orthodontic care knows no age limits. The inevitable graying of the population prompts the development of geriatric-aesthetic clinics and increased marketing to the elderly. With a strong economy and increased government intervention, access to oral health care is dramatically improved. Some disparities do continue to exist among seniors. To address this disparity, Medicare creates an optional Part Den (Dental) and Part Rx (Rx). Dental schools develop a clinical focus on the frail elderly. Government involvement in legislation to expand the oral health workforce has paved the way for geriatric hygienists to work as independent practitioners and to do triage in community clinics and nursing homes. New dental professionals such as dental nurses and dental therapists emerge, and many of them practice independent of dentists. There is reciprocity in licensure nationwide. Dental schools participate in providing training for the expanded duties of the allied health practitioners.

CODA is eliminated and replaced by the Department of Prevention and Oral Health Promotion of the National Institutes of Health. The heavy focus on prevention and health promotion is fueled by reimbursement for prevention being higher than that for restorative work. Government legislation leads to increased community-based prevention programs and care clinics in needy communities (dentists are forced to go to the needy rather than vice versa). Employers run dental centers to provide therapeutic preventive care for employees.

Multiple diagnostic and therapeutic preventive breakthroughs occur due to increased funding in research. Major studies show that oral health improves general health and well-being. Fifty percent of dental procedures are done without rotary instruments. Saliva replaces blood as a primary diagnostic tool. Industry forces the use of evidence-based care. Dental school curricula evolve around evidence-based dentistry, expanded-duty practitioners, and multilingual capabilities.

The role of the dentist shifts to becoming more integrated with other health care providers, including physicians and expanded-duty practitioners. Dentists diagnose, evaluate outcomes of care, coordinate care, apply evidence to decision making, and function as team leaders for expanded practitioners who are able to take care of various needs.

Immigration increases, and there is a strong need for bilingual and multilingual providers.

Scenario 2: Weak Economy, Traditional Dentist-Driven Provider Model

Dow Jones closes at 7900, NASDQ at 290. The Federal Reserve Bank chairman announces that interest rates remain at 0.75 percent. With high unemployment, increasing numbers of the middle class are losing their insurance coverage and are unable to pay for dental care on their own. The cost of oral health care is becoming beyond the reach of the average citizen. With record numbers of retirements of practicing dentists, access to care is becoming a crisis because of both cost and geographic distribution.

Organized dentistry has been effective in restricting the move to expand the duties of auxiliaries or to allow nondentists to practice independently. This has slowed the movement to focus on prevention and health promotion. The disease-and-treatment-oriented model of care prevails. Concern is growing, however, that failure of the profession to address the access-to-care crisis may invite government intervention to change regulations and expand the number of providers.

Dental schools increase their marketing to engineering and computer science majors. The American Dental Association announces that the number of students taking the Dental Aptitude Test increases by 15 percent over the previous year.

Distance learning, teleconferences, and computer-based learning increases, and education improves. Dental students outperform medical students in critical thinking. Partnerships between higher education and industry increase and influence the development and use of educational technology to lower the costs of higher education.

The BCL-2 gene is found to be a reliable predictor of oral squamous-cell carcinoma. Other breakthrough technologies that have been in the pipeline also become available but are adopted into practice only if they affect efficiency or profitability.

Dental schools experience sweeping changes in the makeup of the class of 2013: 90 percent of the students are female; 75 percent of the dental faculty is female.

Terrorism has resulted in increased government regulations on immigration. As a consequence, immigration has decreased overall. An increase is noted from Africa, South America, and Asia.

Baby Boomers—the largest cohort in history—are now seventy, and access to oral health care for this senior population is growing and is related to cost and geographic distribution factors.

The governor of Massachusetts embraces local dental schools as Third-Party Administrators as a platform for re-election. The dental licensing board is found to be barbaric and subsequently is abolished.

The Two-Day Conference

About one hundred individuals were invited to participate. They represented nine stakeholder groups, including students, faculty, administrators, department chairs, staff, the Board of Visitors, Boston Medical Center administration, and several "strategic partner" organizations. Every school department was represented; all steering committee members were included, as were the full membership of all standing committees with responsibility for areas related to the decision questions. Standing committees play a key role in decision making and governance at the dental school, in some cases having the last word. The standing committee structure became the focus for follow-up action.

On the morning of the first day of the two-day large group meeting, the first task was to build a shared understanding of the history of the school for the purpose of understanding its momentum. We chose to focus on how answers to the three decision questions had evolved over time. Participants created time lines for how the curriculum evolved, how faculty and staff were developed, and how students were attracted and supported over a forty-year period. Small groups analyzed the time lines for insight.

Next, it was important for the whole system to grapple with the pressures for change that *they* saw in the world external to the school. The pressures for change were brainstormed and sum-marized by a straightforward small group exercise, with a sampling of the outcomes reported to the large group. No new significant forces emerged from this exercise, but it enabled the whole system to relate easily to the future scenarios, as constructed by the steering committee.

The dental school distributed the four scenarios to participants prior to the start of the conference, but each scenario was presented at the meeting in the form of a humorous skit.

It was now time for total immersion into the four future worlds. The dental school conference of about one hundred participants was divided into four separate worlds of about twenty-five. The four worlds were physically separated within the same room and differentiated by the color of their table coverings (participants were seated at tables of eight). As a way of helping this immersion, small groups were asked to envision what dentistry would be like in their world in 2013 and to describe the role and life of the dentist in that world.

At this point, a sense of shared context had been established among the participant planners: they were immersed in a world of the future, and they had an understanding of the historical momentum of the school (Pepper, 1942). The time had come to answer the decision questions, in which we invested the largest amount of large group meeting time.

The task of designing a new curriculum was the most challenging. Each of the four separate worlds was asked to design an imaginative four-year curriculum, based on their vision of the role of the general dentist in the future and taking into account three criteria: (1) a curriculum that makes the best use of research and science in improving oral health, (2) a curriculum that maximizes the use of technology for both education and practice, and (3) a curriculum that maximizes the satisfaction and commitment of faculty and staff, as well as student commitment to learning. For this, the Axelrod Conference Model Design Conference (Axelrod, 1992, 2000) provided an excellent basis for the process that participants used to create their designs. Each of the four world groups focused first on brainstorming designs that addressed a single criterion, then on integrated designs that addressed all criteria, then on the selection of the best integrated design for a base, and then, finally, on a "treasure hunt" to discover the best ideas.

A sample single-criterion curriculum design, devoted to making the best use of research and science in improving oral health, is shown on page 135. This is an intermediate result that became input to the creation of an integrated design.

When each of the four worlds had completed its curriculum designs, the conference focused on the questions of faculty and staff enrichment, and student recruitment and support. This work was done in small stakeholder groups.

At this point, participants had been working in their separate worlds for eight full hours, and they were quite conver-

sant with life in their world and the trends and driving forces that shaped it. But now it was time to bring participants back from their four worlds to share their designs and answers to the decision questions. Each world prepared its "tour"—a presentation that engaged the other participants in the essence of their designs and answers. Participants took notes during the tours. These presentations spelled the end of the separate worlds, as we needed to get on with the task of finding what designs and strategies had a good chance of working, regardless of which future world emerged.

When dental school participants returned from a well-earned break, they found that their four worlds had disappeared and that they had new table assignments in a now-unified world of 2013. At each table there were two participants from each of the four worlds. Each table then focused its attention on what had been learned and on which of the many ideas presented were the most robust, that is, the ideas that worked in more than one world. Each table prepared its recommendations for presentation to the curriculum committee, admissions committee, and the committee on faculty and staff development. In this way, we built a bridge from the temporary planning community that had been assembled to those structures in the school that would have the responsibility for carrying the work forward. Over the years we have developed a bias toward empowering and challenging the existing structures instead of inventing

---

Example of a Single-Criterion Curriculum Design: A Science- and Research-Based Curriculum

Clinical and basic sciences are integrated across all courses for all four years of the DMD program, in order to prepare students to provide science-based care. Basic sciences, such as biochemistry, physiology, and microbiology, are prerequisites to acceptance to dental school and a national ADA requirement. The program begins in the first year with a case-based teaching model. This educational model requires that students access basic medical and clinical sciences to make decisions about care. Biomedical sciences are taught with a streamlined approach, concentrating on biological systems and information relevant to clinical practice. The impact of genomics, proteomics, and meta-bolomics on dental biology is a part of the first-year study, along with population research. Actual patient contact in a group-practice setting begins second semester of the first year to bring science chairside. Second-year dental students do cavity preparations in the clinic. First-year students place restorations using the EFDA model.

A scientific externship experience (including medicine and research) occurs, where students leave school for four to six weeks all four years, to allow students the opportunity to learn the science behind diagnostics, to do research, study science, and be part of a project with scientists in a lab and to learn how to use new technologies: nanotechnology-proteomics-bioengineering, gene transfer, and bioinformatics. There is increased emphasis on clinical research, the oral-systemic connection, and how to access, sort, and evaluate scientific information. Students move from observing and gathering information to evaluating information and being more active in the lab.

Second-year work is more patient-focused. Research impact is emphasized. The impact of technology research on preclinical training (simulation) and the impact of pharmacology research is studied. In the fourth year, the focus includes expanded knowledge on medically compromised patients and evidence-based clinic decisions.

---

new ones, although there are occasions when a new structure that crosses previously uncrossed boundaries has been appropriate.

Reports were given first to the curriculum committee (a standing committee of the school), which took special seats at the front of the room, then to department chairs and the committee on faculty and staff enrichment (a task force),

then finally to the admissions committee (standing committee) and the Office of Admissions and Student Services.

Although the discovery of common ground was not made an explicit step in this large group meeting, such common ground became abundantly clear when group after group supported identical or similar ideas in their recommendations.

What the Client Gained

With a relatively small investment (several steering committee off-sites and a two-day large group meeting) the dental school took a large step toward crafting a strategic plan responsive to the dynamic changes in the world and in dentistry. As a critical mass of the school participated, the whole system was unfrozen, and there was solid agreement about strategies that could work in several different future worlds. A plethora of ideas and information emerged to inform those choices yet to be made. New life was breathed into existing committees and staff groups, and significant challenges were made to them. Everyone participating (faculty, staff, students, others) learned much about the working of the school as a whole—a consequence of working together on planning that will provide many benefits down the road.

What We Learned

Drawn to the scenario planning process as a methodology for understanding the future, we began exploring this work from the perspective of Schwartz (1991), Ogilvy (2002), Ringland (1998), Schoemaker (2002), and van der Heijden (1996), all of whom had their roots in a Royal Dutch Shell Group planning department. While there were fundamental similarities, each emphasized a particular aspect of the process from its philosophical underpinnings to its applications in

practice. Each shared the tools they had developed and provided a perspective on how the discipline evolved. Taking them together, we were able to develop a road map for achieving the result of creating scenarios in a way that lent itself to large groups.

We learned for ourselves the value of exploring the external environment of our client system. It was our immersion in the world outside the dental school that led us to the conclusion that a new method was needed for our intervention—one that put much more energy into dealing with critical uncertainties outside the school. We were fortunate to have a relationship with the school that permitted this. One of us attended the Goldman Symposium on the Future of Dental Medicine.

We also relearned the value of not settling on a method or a design until we had thoroughly listened to the clients and understood, through their eyes, the dilemma they faced.

We were able to use a bold new design for the first time with this client, as a result of the confidence obtained over seven years of using large group interventions for applications ranging from organization design to accreditation.

Our objective in using scenario planning was more limited than the objectives of Schwarz, Ogilvy, Ringland, Schoemaker, and van der Heijden. We wanted to divorce our clients from the tendency to think of the future as an extrapolation of the past and to introduce a degree of safety into the strategies they chose to implement (by considering how they would work out in different future worlds). The traditional scenario planning authors are more earnest in their researching of the drivers of change that create the alternate future worlds—to the point that each future world is eminently plausible. While we encourage clients to plan for the future in the context of all future possibilities, there is nothing in the methodology to prevent a client from placing a bet on a single future.

We did not start out to invent a new large group intervention, but that is how it turned out. After a colleague pointed out the value of what we had done with the dental school for other client systems, we redesigned what the steering committee did on behalf of the school, so that the whole process can be done in a large group setting over a three-day period. The result is a generic Large Group Scenario Planning intervention for any client system facing significant uncertainty in the world in which it plans to prevail.

An early draft of this case included a list of design principles we use for custom large group interventions, which received a tepid response from our editors. "Everyone has his design principles," they said. They were right. We, like others in the OD consulting community, are adept at putting together a quasi-theoretical model in an attempt to convince our clients and ourselves that what we are doing is based on more than caprice.

So instead of listing design principles, we would like to pay tribute to two scientists and a philosopher whose years of dedicated research inform every design for large groups that we create: Steve Pepper (1942), whose illumination of "Contextualism" made plain the importance of context in human interaction; Solomon Asch (1952), whose experiments at the University of Pennsylvania demonstrated the effect of context on human interaction in groups; and Fred Emery (1977, and also in Emery, M., 1993), who adapted the work of Pepper and Asch to create Open Systems Theory, still one of the best science-based tools for organization development. We believe that being grounded in these principles enabled us to move outside of individual large group models and take risks in order to customize the design (Steil, 1998).

Conclusion

How should an organization plan long-term strategy in the face of significant uncertainty about the future of the world in which that organization must live? Scenario planning is a core tool for developing multiple views of the future and setting out a successful course in the face of several different but plausible future worlds. Large group scenario planning is a tool for engaging a critical mass of an organization in scenario planning over a two- or three-day period.

Scenario planning in a large group format is a fast and effective way for a client system to include a shared understanding of possible futures in their planning process. Large group scenario planning is an antidote to the toxin of thinking of the future as an extrapolation of the past and present.

References

Asch, S. (1952). *Social psychology.* New York: Prentice Hall. (Republished by Oxford University Press in 1987.)

Axelrod, R. H. (1992, December). Getting everyone involved: How one organization involved its employees, supervisors, and managers in redesigning the organization. [Special issue]. *Journal of Applied Behavioral Science, 28*(4), 499–509.

Axelrod, R. H. (2000). *Terms of engagement.* San Francisco: Berrett-Koehler.

Emery, F. (1977). *Futures we are in.* Leiden, the Netherlands: Martinus Nijhoff.

Emery, M. (Ed.). (1993). *Participative design for participative democracy.* Canberra, ACT, Australia: Centre for Continuing Education, Australian National University.

Frankl, S., & Gibbons-Carr, M. (2001, November). Creating a school without walls and building a learning organization: A case study. *Journal of Dental Education, 65*(11), 1253–1263.

Ogilvy, J. (2002). *Creating better futures.* New York: Oxford University Press.

Pepper, S. C. (1942). *World hypotheses.* Berkeley: University of California.

Ringland, G. (1998). *Scenario planning: Managing for the future.* New York: Wiley.

Schoemaker, P. (2002). *Profiting from uncertainty.* New York: The Free Press.

Schwartz, P. (1991, 1996). *The art of the long view.* New York: Doubleday.

Steil, G. (1998). The magic is in the principles. *Consulting Today,* Ardsley-on-Hudson, New York.

van der Heijden, K. (1996). *Scenarios: The art of strategic conversation.* New York: Wiley.

CHAPTER FOUR

WORKING IN POLARIZED AND POLITICIZED ENVIRONMENTS

We live in a world constantly confronted by the ease with which differences escalate into polarized conflict. We are not just talking about the kinds of national and international conflicts that are always in the newspapers. Organizations are full of balkanized groups that do not like each other and may not talk to each other. Interest groups in communities fight to get what they want, often at the expense of the common good. Even interpersonal relationships are not immune from withdrawal, misunderstanding, anger, and distrust. The challenge that we are facing at every level is to find a better way of dealing with differences so that they do not escalate into polarized conflict.

One of the most important and intriguing topics in this book is the potential of Large Group Methods for bringing together people and groups with different interests into a common understanding of the issues they are facing. It is easy to imagine that if you bring people together representing divergent interests and perspectives, you are bound to have conflict. What keeps these methods from blowing up? So many aspects of organizational and community life disintegrate into shouting matches or worse. Why don't these events?

The proposition underlying this chapter is that Large Group Methods have a *different way of dealing with differences*. They use a different process. In order to make this proposition clearer, we present four case examples of this way of managing differences. After we point out the interesting or unique aspects of the cases, we describe the theory underlying this way of working.

- "Trust and Transformation: Integrating Two Florida Education Unions," by Sylvia L. James, Jack Carbone, Albert B. Blixt, and James McNeil
- "Bringing Multiple Competing National Health Service Organizations Together," by Julie Beedon and Sophia Christie
- "Clearing the Air: The FAA's Historic Growth Without Gridlock Conference," by Marvin Weisbord and Sandra Janoff
- "Working with Corporate Community Tensions on Environmental Issues," by John D. Adams and Ann L. Clancy

What to Note in These Cases

The first case, "Trust and Transformation: Integrating Two Florida Education Unions," is about a one-year process to address issues and change the culture of the Florida Teachers Association. The merger of two previously rival unions created this union. Despite four years of being in one organization, no real integration of operating styles had occurred, and the old cultures and norms created mistrust and a union that was not functioning at its best. A combined internal and external consulting team worked with a "Futures Committee" that was a microcosm of the groups within the union to diagnose the situation and plan for changes. Over the year, large group events were held that built a dynamic leadership team for the union, addressed old sources of conflict within the union, and created recommendations for new forms of governance for the organization. The case describes how the process unfolded, critical moments when the culture shifted, and evidence of success.

We were impressed with how the consultants dealt with the conflict and mistrust that re-emerged and threatened the process. "Whatever happens is the only thing that could have" may be a rule of Open Space, but consultants who continually get feedback from the system and deal with whatever emerges, even when it temporarily stops progress toward the goal, are more likely to create real change. These consultants stayed focused on the goal, but not so rigidly that they ignored issues that required them to stop and replan. In so doing, they believe that they modeled for the system how to deal with difficulties that emerge and thereby strengthened the capacity of the system to deal with its own difficulties. They also include a useful description of the role of consultants in helping leadership manage its own anxiety during such a long-term process.

The second case, "Bringing Multiple Competing National Health Service Organizations Together," is a three-year effort to create a new and more collaborative and positive culture in a new health care organization that was created from four Primary Care Trusts (PCTs) that are part of the National Health Service in Birmingham, Great Britain. The authors, the external consultant, and the CEO of this health care organization decided that the process of creating goals and strategies for the new organization needed to model the kind of organization they wanted it to become. So, in this historically very politicized and competitive environment, they engaged all the stakeholders in a series of participative events to break down barriers, create relationships, find out what people believed were the goals that the organization should strive for, and determine how plans could be developed to get there. This series of large and small group activities over a three-year period changed the culture and what the organization was able to deliver in important ways.

The third case, "Clearing the Air: The FAA's Historic Growth Without Gridlock Conference," is a description of a conference using a modified Future Search of the key players who manage and use U.S. airspace. Potentially, all the stakeholders want to have this system organized for their own benefit. Currently, the airspace is so crowded that the old rules no longer lead to anything but gridlock in the skies. In this critical time period, people representing very different interests were able to get the whole problem on the table, learn more about it than they knew before, and take some major steps toward changing the rules for the benefit of the larger system. This is a remarkable achievement, given the previous history of unproductive infighting at meetings. Of great interest in this case are the reflections of the consultants about how they thought about what was happening as they moved through the two-day event.

Finally, the fourth case in this section, "Working with Corporate Community Tensions on Environmental Issues," describes an off-site meeting of the refinery managers of a recently merged petroleum company and representatives from local action committees that are concerned with the impact of the refinery on their lives and community, as well as larger environmental issues. In this case, The World Café process was used after a presentation by the consultant to get issues on the table that were of concern and to begin to anticipate dealing with them.

In these four cases, we have two very big projects with a series of large group events that take months and affect the way the whole system engages differences and interests, and we have two cases about two events that, as large group events, brought stakeholders together to begin to address important issues. In all cases, open conflict was in the history and potential in the events. No event was difference-free, but all created a different way of dealing with conflict.

Our Ideas About How Large Group Methods Manage Conflict

In all large group events where diverse stakeholders are present, there are differences—real differences and many of them. But all these events have a different process for dealing with differences, which is to *focus on finding common ground*. They operate under a different assumption from, say, a traditional town meeting or a hearing in front of the city council. The key here is the *search for common ground*. People are asked to focus their minds and energy on what is shared. Early activities in all these events create a shared database of information, as well as knowledge about the views of those present; sometimes invited experts and relevant outsiders provide information that contributes to the shared database. People are encouraged to notice and take differences seriously but not to focus on them or to give a lot of energy to conflict resolution. Rather, they try to discover what they agree on, and this becomes the base for moving forward. Usually, people are surprised by how much agreement there actually is when they look for it. This is because the usual process of noticing and focusing on differences is disrupted.

Merrelyn Emery's thinking about the relationship between conflict and common ground in her writing about the Search Conference makes these issues very clear (Emery and Purser, 1996). She sees the conference setting as a "protected site" where people can come together and search for commonalties, despite their fear and natural anxiety about conflict. She believes that "groups tend to overestimate the area of conflict and underestimate the amount of common ground that exists" (p. 142).

"Rationalizing conflict" is the important process that takes conflict seriously when it arises so that the substantive differences are clarified and everyone understands and respects what they are. If the conflict is rationalized, and everyone is clear about exactly what the agreements and disagreements are, it is possible to allow a short time to see if it can be resolved. Then people who come with a position are encouraged to explain more about why they believe what they believe. The idea is to get behind the position to understand the thinking and ideas that underlie it. If an issue cannot be resolved, it is posted on a "disagree list," meaning that the issue will not receive further attention, but the differences are acknowledged.

Structuring Encounters with Diverse Ideas

The preassigned heterogeneous table discussion groups of about eight people create a microcosm of the differences in the room at any large group event. Making sure that each group is truly representative and mixed is a key part of the planning process. This means that people do not spend all their time in clusters with like-minded people. Rather, they meet and engage in a series of discussions and activities with people of different views under strong norms of respect for differences and allowing differences to emerge. In many discussion activities, the structure is to do a round robin so that everyone has expressed their views before the group moves on to a dialogue about the issue. This process of getting all the views on the table first helps the group know from the beginning where people are and what issues the group needs to deal with. Because the roles of facilitator, recorder, and reporter are rotated for every activity, it is difficult for any one person or subgroup to dominate. Even in Open Space, where people are not assigned to groups but select ones of their own interest, the diversity of views is unavoidable, as one surveys the agenda of diverse topics posted on the Community Bulletin Board.

In short, the structure of these events makes it very difficult to maintain the idea that there is only one view. Participants are continually confronted with alternative views, but in an atmosphere of open discussion and developing personal relationships in small groups. When participants are free to discuss their views openly, polarization and escalation around differences are much less likely. Two reasons for that are that (1) hierarchies are disregarded and (2) differences are managed in a constructive way.

Reducing Hierarchy

In these events, people interact as people more than from role or status. Everyone is on the same footing with everyone else in the structure of the small group discussions. People have influence based on knowledge or by making a cogent argument, rather than by having authority in the hierarchy. This is sometimes described as "a level playing field." When hierarchy is absent, the well-worn patterns of manipulation and control are disrupted. There is no decision structure or way of getting power. The normal way of doing business is suspended, and people are asked simply to follow their own energy and commitments so that they both get and give.

Large Group Principles for Dealing with Differences

The following seven principles underlie the way Large Group Methods are structured and account for their effectiveness in dealing with differences and managing conflict (Bunker, 2000).

- *Focus on common ground*—areas of agreement rather than differences or competitive interests.
- *Rationalize conflict,* which means acknowledge and then clarify conflict rather than ignore or deny it. Agree to disagree and move on to areas of agreement.
- *Manage conflict* by avoiding incendiary issues or issues that cannot be dealt with in the time available.
- *Expand individuals' egocentric view of the situation* by exposing them to many points of view in heterogeneous groups that do real tasks together collaboratively and develop group spirit. This broadens views and educates.
- Allow time to acknowledge the group's *history of conflict and feelings* before expecting people to work together cooperatively.
- *Manage the public airing of differences and conflict.* Treat all views with respect. Allow minority views to be heard but not to dominate discussion. Preserve time for the expression of views of people "in the middle" as well as those who are more extreme.
- *Reduce hierarchy as much as possible.* Push responsibility for working together and for managing conflict down in the organization so that people are responsible for their own activity.

Interventions using Large Group Methods tackle conflict in different ways at different points in its development—sometimes dealing with past history, sometimes putting differences aside and simply managing them, sometimes directly addressing and resolving issues that divide people and groups. The principles described here are primarily at the systems level. These processes, however, simultaneously affect the group and the individual level, as reflected in the fourth principle.

References

Bunker, B. B. (2000). Managing conflict through large group methods. In M. Deutsch & P. T. Coleman (Eds.), *The handbook of conflict resolution: Theory and practice.* San Francisco: Jossey-Bass, 546–547.

Emery, M., & Purser, R. (1996). *The Search Conference: A powerful method for planned organizational change and community action.* San Francisco: Jossey-Bass.

TRUST AND TRANSFORMATION

Integrating Two Florida Education Unions

Sylvia L. James, Jack Carbone, Albert B. Blixt,
and James McNeil

The Challenge

How do you bridge a thirty-year chasm of conflict between two
competing organizations that must merge in order to survive?
For the Florida Education Association (FEA), the challenge was
enormous. The success of the FEA merger required bringing
together two distinctly different cultures and healing old
conflicts, wounds, history, and polarized philosophies of doing
business. Conflict that continued was based on three
fundamental cultural differences:

1. *Structures:* centralized versus decentralized
2. *Operating styles:* flexible and adaptable versus traditional,
   hierarchical, and procedural
3. *Modes of decision making:* direct versus indirect participation by
   local union presidents

   Four years after the official merger, FEA president Andy Ford
recognized that the integration process was not working. There

was continuing conflict over future direction, how decisions were made, and the role and participation of key stakeholders. "We said we put it [the merger] together," Ford says. "In reality we did what we needed to do to get the deal done in the beginning. We did not deal with the practicalities of integrating it." The promise and opportunities of the new organization were not being realized. The real challenge facing FEA was building relationships and trust while designing structures and processes for the newly integrated organization.

Background

The FEA split in the early 1970s after nearly one hundred years as a single organization. The two resulting unions engaged in bitter competition for members and influence until 2000, when Florida's state affiliates of the American Federation of Teachers (AFT) and the National Education Association (NEA) merged. The new organization represents more than 250,000 teachers and education staff professionals in Florida's sixty-seven school districts. A six-year transition agreement was established.

In March of 2004, Ford commissioned a "Futures Committee" to recommend changes that would accelerate real integration and create a unified organization with a shared vision of the future. He appointed a cross-section of union presidents from both former organizations representing small, medium, and large locals, as well as members of the staff. FEA chose Whole-Scale[1] as the transformation process to use.

The Whole-Scale process involved a series of small and large group meetings

that addressed both underlying conflicts and fundamental organizational and strategic issues that had proved intractable in the past (see Figure 4.1).

Among the major challenges were:

- How to overcome, integrate, and transform twenty-six years of pre-merger and four years of post-merger culture into a new, single, cohesive culture.
- How to build the trust that was needed for healing, cohesion, and forward movement.
- How to accomplish this in the course of one year with only four Friday evening–Saturday sessions, and one 2.5 day session with a cross-section of 65 people who had other full-time jobs and assignments and were geographically dispersed.

The Story

The purpose of the first meeting was to launch the Futures Committee in a way that would ensure that it achieved its purpose.

FIGURE 4.1. FUTURES COMMITTEE PROCESS ROAD MAP

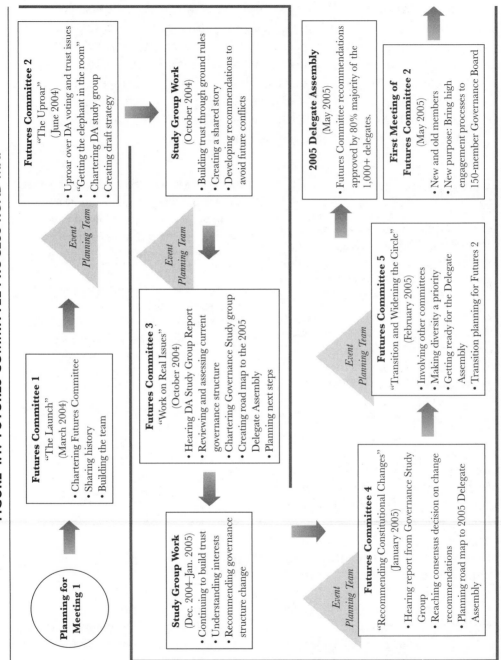

Planning for Meeting 1

Futures Committee 1
"The Launch"
(March 2004)
• Chartering Futures Committee
• Sharing history
• Building the team

Event Planning Team

Futures Committee 2
"The Uproar"
(June 2004)
• Uproar over DA voting and trust issues
• "Getting the elephant in the room"
• Chartering DA study group
• Creating draft strategy

Event Planning Team

Study Group Work
(October 2004)
• Building trust through ground rules
• Creating a shared story
• Developing recommendations to avoid future conflicts

Futures Committee 3
"Work on Real Issues"
(October 2004)
• Hearing DA Study Group Report
• Reviewing and assessing current governance structure
• Chartering Governance Study group
• Creating road map to the 2005 Delegate Assembly
• Planning next steps

Study Group Work
(Dec. 2004–Jan. 2005)
• Continuing to build trust
• Understanding interests
• Recommending governance structure change

Event Planning Team

Futures Committee 4
"Recommending Constitutional Changes"
(January 2005)
• Hearing report from Governance Study Group
• Reaching consensus decision on change recommendations
• Planning road map to 2005 Delegate Assembly

Event Planning Team

Futures Committee 5
"Transition and Widening the Circle"
(February 2005)
• Involving other committees
• Making diversity a priority
• Getting ready for the Delegate Assembly
• Transition planning for Futures 2

2005 Delegate Assembly
(May 2005)
• Futures Committee recommendations approved by 80% majority of the 1,000+ delegates.

First Meeting of Futures Committee 2
(May 2005)
• New and old members
• New purpose: Bring high engagement processes to 150-member Governance Board

Source: Copyright © Dannemiller Tyson Associates, 2005.

First Futures Committee Meeting (March 2004)

The challenge in the first meeting was to establish cohesion, a sense of purpose, and a charter for the committee. A set of processes, tools, and methods were established in this first meeting that would continue throughout all the meetings:

1. *A meeting planning process:* A microcosm of a Futures Committee created a purpose statement, desired outcomes, and design for each meeting.
2. *A converge-diverge group process:* We created a design for the journey and for each meeting that takes into account the need for small group work (for example, study groups, meeting planning) and large group work that lets the system tap the wisdom of the whole, to make decisions, and to plan actions.
3. *A time for design to emerge:* We provided the time to confront the issues, to change conversations and activities, based on new data that surfaced and that affected the way we would achieve the meeting purpose and desired outcomes.
4. *A way to build trust in every meeting:* This required demonstrating that there were no hidden agendas in the process. Total transparency was required about how meetings were designed, and willingness to hear all voices was demonstrated. We surfaced and worked on those things that occurred and were breaking trust or reinforcing the lack of trust.

5. *An internal-external consulting team:* To simultaneously see and process the complexity of this transformation requires a team. We built an internal-external consulting team to plan and facilitate this process. The team decided the timing and sequencing of activities and constantly assessed the state of the group.
6. *Daily feedback and written evaluations:* At every meeting, each participant completes a written evaluation at the end of the day. The planning team, leadership, and consulting team read these and make changes to the next day's agenda. The next morning, a summary is shared with everyone to make the meeting totally transparent, build trust, share information on how to work differently, and make visible how the participants' shaped the new agenda.

As the sixty-five members of the Futures Committee gathered for the first time at four o'clock on a Friday afternoon, the atmosphere ranged from caution to outright skepticism about what was about to happen. Most of the members were local union presidents, and some were FEA staff. All presidents, elected to serve their local membership, would have to be convinced about the value of this group process.

The sixty-five were seated at round tables of eight. Seating was predetermined so that each table was a microcosm of the entire room: elected leaders from each of the former unions, different-size locals and staff, and different occupations in education represented by FEA. President Ford and the Futures Committee co-chairs convened the meeting, describing why this committee was formed, what it was intended to accomplish, and the way the group would work together to maximize participation.

The design of the meeting moved from creating common data to a vision of the future to first steps for action. Participants began creating a common database by introducing themselves, sharing their individual perspectives about their hopes and fears for this process, and agreeing on the outcomes they needed for this first meeting. Then a merger history time line was placed on the wall, and everyone wrote their memories about the history of the merger. A whole group discussion followed about the events leading up to and following the merger and the feelings, experiences, and learning that came as a result.

Friday evening and most of Saturday morning was spent agreeing on a vision of themselves and their role as a committee. The framework for this discussion was the proposed group charter. The purpose of a group charter is to clearly identify the group's purpose, role, authority, and tasks, and how it will do its work. After considerable discussion, a consensus was reached and the charter was adopted:

> The purpose of the Futures Committee is to design a process to gain maximum input and

participation from FEA elected leaders, constituency groups, members, potential members, FEA staff, and local staff, in order to make recommendations to the appropriate governing bodies for change as we define our desired future.

Finally, as part of next-steps planning, there was discussion on whether to have an all-stakeholder meeting in June in order to gather input on building a shared vision for the future direction of FEA. The group decided that it was not ready to sponsor the all-stakeholder meeting until the committee had more time to become familiar with the key issues to be addressed, the target audience for such a meeting, and the intended outcomes for it. They decided instead to reconvene as a committee for three days in June to continue the dialogue. Before adjourning, they agreed on outcomes and a series of questions to address at their June meeting, and selected members to work with the internal-external consulting team to plan the agenda.

Each person completed a written evaluation, which was summarized and communicated to everyone. Participants described the most significant outcomes of the two days: "We worked out several areas that could have derailed the process. Discussion of merger timeline (telling the story)."

Their response to the question, "What surprised you?": "We came up with a timeline that had such impact . . . Personal agendas . . . How much everyone cares about FEA!"

To maintain momentum, they recommended: "Communication in the room, not the hallway. Don't let up."

Second Futures Committee Meeting (June 2004)

The two-and-one-half-day session that became known as "The June Meeting" was planned by a microcosm of the Futures Committee and facilitated by the internal-external consulting team. In April, this planning team spent two days together creating a purpose statement, desired outcomes, and a design for the flow of the meeting. The purpose statement was, "To build a dynamic, committed and knowledgeable leadership team that creates a comprehensive work plan that will help shape the desired future of FEA." The agenda that they created together was expanded into a "minute-by-minute" detailed design by the consultation team. That design was then shared with the microcosm planning team and finalized, based on their reactions and input.

Day 1. As the June Futures Committee meeting was about to begin on Tuesday afternoon, the planning team alerted us that the "elephant in the room" was how voting had been handled at the May Delegate Assembly. The annual Delegate Assembly elects FEA leadership and votes on other business of the association. Approximately one thousand delegates attended the 2004 Delegate Assembly (including all members of the Futures Committee), and several important issues

were to be decided. A dispute arose over voting procedures. Confusion about the rules for voting had created dissention, and many leaders felt they had been treated unfairly. During the first afternoon, there was obvious tension.

At the end of the day, the planning team reviewed the day's evaluations, which confirmed how significant the issue of trust was within the Futures Committee and within FEA. Many people felt that if the trust issue was not directly confronted, the work of the committee would not be productive. The planning team revised the event agenda to conduct dialogue on the main trust issues within the room and within FEA.

Day 2. The morning of the second day, the whole group discussed the sequence of events around voting at the Delegate Assembly. The original agenda included a morning activity to hear from the top official from each of the two national unions. The consultants described the situation and the urgent need to have a whole-room discussion before everyone would be ready to listen. The national leaders quickly understood and endorsed the decision to engage in this conversation. The resulting conversation was spirited and free-flowing. People began to realize that the conflict surrounding the Delegate Assembly voting procedures was the result of both different perspectives and different amounts of information. As people began to feel heard, they agreed to move on with the agenda.

By mid-morning, the agenda resumed with "Expanding Our View," which included a look at the external forces and trends affecting the future of education and an internal view from small, medium, and large-size locals. Using this information, the entire group created a draft high-level strategy for FEA, including mission, values, and goals.

That evening, the microcosm planning team and the consultants sat down with the co-chairs to read the day's evaluations. Despite the morning's attempt to clear the air about the Delegate Assembly conflicts, we learned that one faction was holding a "meeting outside the meeting" that evening, and others were holding frequent huddles in the halls. The planning team members shared their own conflicts and emotions; they mirrored the larger organizational conflict. People were really bent out of shape and polarized about how they saw the sequence of events. There was incredible tension within each individual about their personal choice to demonstrate loyalty to their colleagues by attending the evening "meeting outside the meeting" or whether to show support for the process by not attending and keeping all conversations within the Futures Committee meeting. It was clear that the conflict was still festering. Trust was still an issue. The events were analogous to the entire merger struggle: mistrust between the two former cultures, about inclusion (who was in, who was out), as seen in the issue of who had the information about how voting was going to take place at the Delegate Assembly. Each side of the conflict felt that the

other side had information it did not have. It appeared that the committee was suddenly unraveling. They were asking themselves, "What are we doing here? Why did some people have the information about the voting procedures and others did not? I'm not sure I want to be part of this group."

The consulting team shifted the conversation to the question: "How do we want to deal with this tomorrow morning?" The planning team realized that the conflict needed to be directly confronted. "We have to have this same conversation in the whole room tomorrow morning. Look what we have learned from each other tonight. Tomorrow let's describe our conversation to the whole group. We'll read the concerns expressed in the evaluations by some people about a 'meeting outside the meeting' being held off-site tonight." Then the planning team and consultants redesigned Thursday's agenda so that everyone could spend the next morning in a conversation about trust that paralleled the conversation that the planning team had on Wednesday evening. The planning team decided, "We cannot talk at tables of eight. We must have a sixty-five-person conversation so everyone hears everyone to begin to build the trust."

Day 3. When the entire Futures Committee reconvened the next morning, the co-chairs talked candidly about the conversation the night before, how they felt personally, and how critical it was that we openly talk about the trust issue. In that moment, the room went silent. The consultants let silence continue. Then someone spoke. The group spent the next two hours in roomwide conversation. Sixty-five people "told their story." Finally, the entire elephant was on the table and visible to all.

In the end, the group agreed to charter a subcommittee of the Futures Committee to review the events leading up to and during the Delegate Assembly on the issue of the voting procedures. The purpose was to draw lessons and recommend changes to next year's voting and communication process. The charter discussion defined "conflict" as occurring when "my expectations don't meet yours." Everyone wanted a voice in writing the subgroup's charter. Having built enough trust to resume work in small groups, each table of eight discussed what had to be in that charter. These drafts were then consolidated in the whole room, resulting in a clear set of expectations for the subcommittee. In "Advice to the Subcommittee," everyone stressed that this was not a witch hunt, not about placing blame, but about learning from it. For that reason, the subcommittee was called the Delegate Assembly Study Group.

This was the critical turning point in the process and the catalyst that allowed the full process to play out successfully over the next year. After the group fully addressed the Delegate Assembly issue, everyone was able to set it aside and return to work on FEA's strategy. They reviewed the goals they had drafted the day before. Energy was high!

The evaluations for the June meeting reflected the hope that was restored. People described the most significant outcomes: "Start on honesty issues . . . bringing out issues that are still lurking. . . building the trust . . . discussing the undiscussables . . . more comfort with people in the room."

To maintain momentum, they recommended: "Continue to work on the trust issue, keep talking, keep big picture in mind, and keep confronting the issues . . ."

Preparation for the third meeting was thorough. The Delegate Assembly Study Group met for two days prior to it. Through a six-hour "Telling Our Stories" process, they created a common picture of what actually happened in the Delegate Assembly. On Friday evening, they planned to give their progress report to the entire committee.

While the Delegate Assembly Study Group was meeting, a separate group created a visual of the year-long time line of what needed to happen in order for recommendations from the Futures Committee to be voted on at the May 2005 Delegate Assembly. Although the Futures Committee was a microcosm of the system, their work had to go through the normal approval channels in order to adhere to FEA's constitution and bylaws, as well as state and federal labor regulations. Since the approval process was not commonly understood by all Futures Committee members, this time line would have to be shared at the third meeting.

Third Futures Committee Meeting (October 2004)

By the time of the third meeting, trust levels had reached a point where the group could begin tackling the real work of planning for the future of the association. The October meeting began Friday evening with the Delegate Assembly Study Group telling their story. The report was very positive in terms of the process and telling the story. The Study Group shared how they had spent most of the first day talking about and agreeing to ground rules for how the conversation was going to take place by continuously asking themselves, "How are we going to have the conversation with each other so others can hear?" The conversation to agree on ground rules helped create a safe place for people to begin telling their stories about the events surrounding the Delegate Assembly voting conflict.

The Study Group members described how they spent two days reconstructing the sequence of events leading up to and during the Delegate Assembly. They told it as a story. They talked about how they had worked together, what they had learned, and how they had finally converged on a picture that explained but did not blame. Flip charts captured all the information from their conversations and filled two walls in the meeting room. When the rest of the Futures Committee saw how this diverse group was connected, energized, and honest with each other, there was a palpable shift in attitude and affect from lurking distrust to excitement.

Saturday, working as a whole group, the Futures Committee finalized the strategy and turned its attention to the ongoing debate surrounding "organization governance." Many considered the current structure ineffective and onerous. The multilevel structure, made up of executive officers, the governance board, the executive cabinet, and the Delegate Assembly, had been created in order to facilitate the merger, not necessarily to best manage the organization. Because of general dissatisfaction, this issue had been flagged by the FEA president as one area that needed to be reviewed. Most others agreed.

Opening up discussion of governance also opened up the possibility that some forces would gain power and influence while others would lose it. Passions ran high and ulterior motives were suspected. The challenge was to discuss the issues in an open and honest way and arrive at solutions that would be supported by the rest of the organization.

Creating a Governance Study Group. By now, the Futures Committee had become more willing to trust smaller groups to tackle specific issues and bring back recommendations for the whole group's consideration and approval. They identified a subgroup of fourteen Futures Committee members and called it the Governance Study Group. Members were nominated and chosen by the full Futures Committee, based on the following criteria that properly reflected the various interests within the organization: small, medium, and large locals; elected and staff; governance levels; gender-ethnic diversity; opinion diversity; historical perspective; people without historical perspective; constituency group representatives; and nonpresidents. Once the group was chosen, a charter was developed by the entire Futures Committee, through table work and then whole-group agreement (Figure 4.2).

Soliciting Input from the Futures Committee. The next step was to solicit input from the entire Futures Committee. We asked the members at their tables to identify the issues that the Governance Study Group needed to address for each of the four governing levels (executive officers, governance board, executive cabinet, and Delegate Assembly) in order to serve the organization's needs three to five years into the future and those that must be brought to the Delegate Assembly for approval in May. This process generated nearly a hundred responses, which formed the basis for the committee's work. They voted on which issues were most critical and which recommendations were most powerful.

We suggested using Interest Based Problem Solving[2] as the process for exploring governance issues because it was familiar and favorably viewed by most FEA members. Interest Based Problem Solving (sometimes known as Win-Win) had been used in several contract bargaining sessions. The underlying principles of Interest Based Problem Solving had provided ground rules for the

FIGURE 4.2. GOVERNANCE STUDY GROUP CHARTER

Purpose: To accelerate Futures Committee work on governance structure by developing draft changes to the constitution and bylaws

Deliverables:
- Draft change language
- Rationale changes
- Constitution
- Transition thinking

Deadlines—Work Plan:
- Feedback process to Futures Committee Nov.-Dec.?
- Futures Committee—January 7–8
- Gov Board Meeting—January 28–29

Givens—Boundaries:
- Align with FEA mission, vision, goals, and values

Advice:
- Use Web-based collaborative tools
- Start with areas of agreement

all-room discussion in the highly charged June meeting. The committee trusted that these principles would again provide a healthy, shared framework for the governance discussions. To support the study group, they agreed that it would be facilitated by one external consultant and one trusted staff member, both experienced in Interest Based Problem Solving. Choosing a familiar and trusted process, led by experienced and neutral facilitators, laid a foundation for the Governance Study Group that was open, transparent, and trusted by all Futures Committee members. Equipped with both a structured way to safely explore options and a means to listen and learn from each other, the group was ready to engage in meaningful dialogue.

Fourth Futures Committee Meeting (December 2004, January 2005)

Constitutional changes were recommended at this meeting. Two Governance Study Group sessions were held, each three days long, using the Interest Based Problem Solving process to fully deliberate the issues and arrive at recommendations. Once completed, the subcommittee's recommendations were brought back to the full Futures Committee for discussion in their January meeting. The final recommendations contained significant constitutional changes in the election of union leadership, policymaking responsibilities, and alignment of organizational structure and decision making.

Remarkably, all recommendations were adopted, with only one Futures Committee member voicing disagreement. The meeting ended with a group commitment to support all the Governance Study Group's recommendations through the required approval process. They planned how they would present these recommendations to the governance board for review and action, starting at the governance board's January meeting. Given the level of mistrust and the number of differing opinions in the beginning of this process, the Futures Committee talked about how they had succeeded in staying true to their values and principles while forging a plan for the future.

A cross-section of the Futures Committee presented all the recommended constitutional changes at the January governance board meeting. Modeling the interactive processes they had learned, after they presented, Futures Committee members asked the 150-person governance board, in their small groups, to discuss what they had heard and their reactions, and to identify their questions of understanding. Then they facilitated a whole-group open forum. A Futures Committee member, who was also a governance board member, was seated at each table for the small group conversations to provide background and answer questions. The governance board was the final decision maker on which recommendations of constitutional changes would be voted on at the May Delegate Assembly. Even though they did not have to agree on this until their March meeting, that January 150-member governance board recommended the Futures Committees' proposal to the Delegate Assembly as a complete package! In addition, they agreed to integrate the work of the Futures Committee into the governance board, adopting Whole-Scale processes as their new way of leading as a strategic body. They saw the possibility of their own meetings becoming meaningful and participative.

Fifth Futures Committee Meeting (February 2005)

This meeting began the transition of integrating the Futures Committee into the governance board. They broke into small groups to create a charter for the new role of the Futures Committee, to create plans to engage the rest of FEA in understanding the recommended constitutional changes that would be voted on at the Delegate Assembly, and to plan their own presentation at the Delegate Assembly.

The evaluations from the February meeting are the Futures Committee's powerful testimony of their learning journey to alignment and commitment. Their responses to the question, "What were the most significant outcomes of the 11-month Future's Committee experience?" included the following:

> To see FEA moving forward with a positive attitude . . . it's made me a better leader . . . gaining new and wider perspective . . . building

of meaningful and trusting relationship . . . the growth in trust and listening . . . really listening to each other . . . validation . . . an ability to hear both sides . . . being given a process to have a difficult/important discussion and a way to come to resolution . . . the recommendation of changes were well thought out and good for the organization . . . the idea of ALL voices being seen and heard . . . alignment of purpose and structure . . .

When asked, "On a scale of 1–10, how comfortable are you that your opinions were considered in shaping the committee's recommendation?" the average response was 9.3! This was a tremendous leap from an average response of 6.9, eleven months earlier, to the question, "How confident are you that we will carry out our commitments to each other?"

The Result

In May 2005, the FEA Delegate Assembly was presented with the recommendations. Nearly 80 percent of the one thousand delegates voted to accept the changes to strategic goals, budget, governance structure, and dues. In the words of one leader, "This process has transformed our union for the better."

In June 2005, the 150-member governance board, in a two-day meeting planned by a microcosm, "relaunched" itself, using the participative processes to agree on strategic objectives for the next fifteen months, to identify the subgroups to get started, and to tackle "hot topics" that required real-time conversation and action. They described the meeting this way:

> The best we've ever had . . . first time I ever held a microphone . . . being able to speak my voice to the concerns of the organization . . . met more of the Governance Board members and heard their perspectives by thinking in large group process . . . information for everyone, regardless of size . . . I believe in this process.

They wrote recommendations to the microcosm planning team that would design the agenda for their next meeting. FEA has a shared process to sustain its organizational learning.

Reflections

This section describes what we—the internal and external consulting team—learned about the trust that had to be built within the transformation infrastructure in order to sustain success. We decided to write from the "view of the internal consultant" in order to stimulate thinking about additional ways external consultants might support the internal consultant.

• *Help leadership manage the anxiety about the process and the uncertain-*

ties. Having committed leadership and supporting the leaders in their commitment was critical to the ongoing success of the project. The greater challenge was helping the president and co-chairs manage their anxiety as they headed off into the unknown. FEA President Ford was determined to make it work! Like any leader, he took a leap of faith in the beginning. He wanted to engage others in redesigning the merged FEA, but he did not know what the process would hold, how it would unfold, or what the outcome would be. He knew the risks. His appointments to the Futures Committee put the key personalities, opinion leaders, and resisters into one room—a potentially volatile mixture. He realized the potential for him to become the target for all the pent-up anger and frustration. Ford understood the risks but was willing to accept them in order to integrate the merger and build a strong, united organization. His commitment would be seriously tested if the process spun out of control and the polarization intensified so that FEA split apart yet again. He knew that, if he wavered or walked away from the process, it would send the signal that the merger was not salvageable.

At several points, Ford was feeling ready to give it up. There were a number of reasons for his feelings: the uncertainty about where it was all heading; the feeling of loss of control and predictability; the apparent lack of clear, definable outcomes; challenges to his leadership, and an organizational culture that did not confront differences and conflict openly and directly. The organization's culture was used to working in linear and predictable ways. Conflict, when it was confronted, usually resulted in a win-lose result. The fact that conflict and chaos were necessary and that they preceded any sense of order was unsettling.

From the beginning, I continuously nurtured Ford's commitment by building trust and maintaining credibility with him so that he believed we could manage any uncertainly and that we had the skills and experience to help the group through anything that emerged. I was candid about the realities. I focused on helping Ford feel knowledgeable and having the information to answer the inevitable push-back and questioning he would get from committee members. In addition, I ensured that the president and the co-chairs stayed connected as a team, by bringing them together to share information, anxieties, and expectations.

The June meeting uproar tested both Ford's and the futures committee's resolve to continue. Everyone emerged hopeful about the process. At the same time, the Delegate Assembly Study Group, which was an outcome of the June meeting, put Ford dead center of the lingering controversy. In conversations I had with him before the Delegate Assembly Study Group meeting, I learned how anxious he was because he would have to relive all the events, and he could become the target for all the dissatisfaction and anger, even though the Study Group's charter described that the purpose would be to learn and to make recommendations, not to place blame. Through our conversation, he re-gained trust that we would design the Study Group meeting in a way that all the information could be shared in non-threatening ways—constructively, with ground rules. I continually made sure he was informed about what the design was, what his role would be, and what he needed to do at any given moment to support the process.

The next test for Ford was in October, when the entire Futures Committee would decide who would participate in the Governance Study Group. It was the moment when it became clear what "control" and "being participative" really look like. Again Ford confided that he felt he had lost control of the process and his constitutional authority as president because he had no control over the task and the composition of the group. I continued helping leadership understand how uncertainty and temporary chaos are part of the process and how staying focused on purpose is critical to keeping it all going.

Another insight was that Ford needed to be in the room for all these subcommittee conversations, even though he was not part of the decision making. In the early stages, he chose to stay out of conversations, to turn this process over to the large group so he would not be seen as manipulating this process or having a hidden agenda. With our nudging, by December he was comfortable being with the Study Group, contributing to conversations without controlling the outcomes.

If Ford had felt, at some point, that he did not trust me in this process or that I was working some other agenda, or that this was just too volatile, too unpredictable, and that these consultants did not really know what they were doing, then this would have all been different. As I look back, I'm glad I was candid and kept confronting and challenging the president and co-chairs. I'm glad I kept constant reality checks with the co-chairs and president to keep them grounded in what was going on, grounded in the process; at the same time building the trust level and credibility in the process so that in time he would say, "well these folks know what they're doing . . . and in the end it's going to be okay."

• *Work at staying calm.* In order to build trust and maintain hope and perseverance within the leadership, as an internal consultant, I had to have confidence that the process was going to work. I could have just as easily gotten derailed when those bumps in the road surfaced. I told myself "Stay calm. Do not react to everything." Then I had to take my own leap of faith. Sometimes it did feel scary and dangerous working on the edge of chaos. In addition to confidence in the process, I had to have perseverance, mechanisms that ensured that no one would get hurt, and processes that kept the leadership committed through the process: educated, confident, and comfortable with the push-back that would come from whatever direction.

In the earlier days, I would have panicked and said, "This isn't going to work! How do we get out of this gracefully?" Instead I said, "This *is* going to work. It will all come out in the end." And it did! It helped to partner with external consultants who have experience in doing this, who have flexible design processes, who value enabling the system to reach its own solutions, and who are committed to transferring their methodology. We built a relationship in which I trusted them to support me internally and to keep me on track. At times, I had to say, "No, I do not have the skill level to do XYZ. That's why we have you here."

• *Build critical mass, with capacity to facilitate and lead change.* If the Futures Process was to be more than an event, then we had to approach our role as one of helping to build the system's capacity to sustain the changes for doing work differently. Learning was ongoing, experiential, and grounded in the "real" work of the organization. It included everything from learning how to design high-engagement meetings, to developing skills for dialogue and reaching consensus, to gaining clarity about roles and responsibilities. We learned how important it is to transfer processes and underlying principles to a critical mass of leaders by making transparent everything we were doing to design and facilitate meetings.

When the Futures Committee took their recommendations to the governance board, they designed the meeting using the processes they had learned from their own highly participative meetings. By sharing the process, they demonstrated transparency and openness. In turn, the governance board experienced how a large group can work together to create results and adopted Futures Process as a way of designing and leading their own 150-person meetings. Several presidents are using these processes in their locals, and many others now attend FEA workshops on "Futures Process."

Notes

1. Whole-Scale® is a registered international trademark of Dannemiller Tyson Associates.
2. Interest Based Problem Solving (IBPS), also called Win-Win or principled bargaining, is based on deciding "issues on their merits rather than through a haggling process focused on what each side says it will or won't do" (Fisher and Ury, 1991, p. xviii). The methods are devised to obtain wise, durable agreements, efficiently and with goodwill.

References

Fisher, R., & Ury, W. (and for the 2nd ed., Patton, B.). (1991). *Getting to yes: Negotiating agreement without giving in.* New York: Penguin Books USA.

BRINGING MULTIPLE COMPETING NATIONAL HEALTH SERVICE ORGANIZATIONS TOGETHER

Julie Beedon and Sophia Christie

The Challenge

The challenge here was to create a high-performing, coherent health organization from a merger of five predecessor organizations—one that could operate effectively in a highly politicized and complex environment and deliver health improvement and effective services to a disadvantaged and diverse community.

Background

The United Kingdom's National Health Service (NHS) operates in a complex, political, polarized environment. Founded in 1948, the NHS is one of the largest organizations in the world (it employs over one million people) with a clear, single

identity in the public mind; the NHS is accountable to the secretary of state for health, who reports directly to the prime minister. This direct connection to politics at the highest level and the important place, in the public's mind, of the institution makes the NHS a highly politicized environment. The principle of health care funded out of general taxation and largely free at the point of delivery provides daily fodder for media scrutiny and political spin.

At a local level, NHS organizations have a high profile. They are often the major local employer, after local government. Many local politicians sit as lay members (nonexecutives) on the boards of NHS organizations. The public health improvement role requires a close formal relationship with local government, and delivering services to vulnerable adults requires collaboration with Social Care, itself an agency commissioned by local government. The typical NHS organization operates against a backdrop of political intervention, public scrutiny, and competitive dynamics, facing a series of challenging polarities such as the following:

- Provide universal access yet operate within a limited budget
- Strive to serve the greatest good while offering individual and personal choice
- Provide professional clinical expertise while offering patient-driven services
- Offer the latest specialist interventions, as well as a full range of services for local health care

When the Labour government came into power in 1997, they saw a NHS at the point of collapse, with long waiting lists for basic treatments, degraded physical facilities, and a demoralized workforce. A comprehensive review resulted in the creation of 303 new local delivery organizations: the Primary Care Trusts (PCTs).

PCTs are statutory bodies managed by a Board comprising seven lay people and six NHS executive directors, including the chief executive. The core functions of a PCT are to:

- Improve the health of the population they serve
- Commission a range of primary care and hospital services to meet the needs of that population
- Deliver a range of community-based services, usually including community nursing, therapies, and rehabilitation

Birmingham is the largest metropolitan council in Europe (1.1 million people), and in that city the changes mentioned resulted in the disaggregation of a single Health Authority, with a public health and commissioning role, into four PCTs and a single (having merged eighteen months previously) specialist-provider of community services. The focus of this story is Eastern Birmingham PCT (EBPCT), which had five predecessor organizations.

Eastern Birmingham PCT

All PCTs have to manage a complex balance of activity between health improvement, commissioning, and service delivery, but EBPCT has developed as a particularly complex organization that:

- Serves a diverse and deprived population of 250,000 people in an

inner-city area with a history of underinvestment and challenges in recruitment
- Has the largest turnover for a PCT in England and Wales and a complex series of commissioning relationships to manage (the budget is £260m for core services and an additional £340m for specialized services, and commissioning is done on behalf of twenty-nine other PCTs)
- Has delivery responsibility for community services (over 1,100 staff), including intermediate care (in partnership with Social Services) and a hospice
- Hosts the Shared Services Agency for the city, providing provision and maintenance of facilities, as well as information technology (IT) and financial services to the four Birmingham PCTs
- Supports three hundred independent contractors delivering family medicine, dentistry, pharmacy, and optical services, who in turn employ some five hundred other staff in their businesses

Beyond Structural Change

The NHS Improvement Plan laid out a radical agenda but sought to deliver the change largely through a structural solution. This focus on structure at the expense of culture and other aspects of organizational design has been typical when political imperatives drive policy. During the first term of the Labour government, a number of government bodies had begun to experiment with Large Group Methods and whole systems ap-

proaches, notably the Employment Service, the Cabinet Office, the Health Service, and some local authorities. These collaborative and inclusive approaches were by no means widespread. It was not surprising that on her first day as chief executive, the second author (the CEO) was presented with a paper proposing the more traditional approach of a "Board Away-Day," when the top team would describe a mission and prioritize activity. The CEO was immediately struck by the limitation of such an approach. Having inherited five "legacy" organizations with complex and competing priorities and knowing that the multiple stakeholders in these organizations were facing the tenth reorganization in almost as many years, she realized something else was needed.

So the CEO decided that the *process* of mission development and prioritization was as important as the content. She contacted the first author, a consultant specializing in large-scale interactive approaches to change, with whom she had previously worked. The process of change should reflect the type of organization she wanted to create. Broader participation would allow people to move beyond past conflicts, develop an understanding and appreciation for the broader picture, and build a common agenda for a stronger partnership. An immediate decision they made was to use whole system approaches to:

- Define the mission of the new organization
- Establish core strategies

- Clarify organizational values
- Build a collaborative culture internally and with partners (including contractors and hospital and local government staff)
- Surface and respond to hopes and fears among the workforce

In effect, the decision was to move from a structural intervention to one that would build a strongly collaborative organizational culture beyond the boundaries of the new structures. Key events are as follows in Figure 4.3:

The First Hundred Days

In convening the first series of three events in 2002, EBPCT embarked on what has become a continuous process of planned and emergent events spanning some three years to date. They knew that they wanted to develop an approach in which the interventions would be designed and delivered to model participation, empowerment, and partnership—key themes that the CEO believed to be essential to a high-performing organization operating in a complex environment. The program has been characterized as balancing the political need for concrete plans and actions tied to targets with the organizational need to respond to emergent issues.

The work started by convening a planning team, which included the CEO and the chairman of the board, a range of people from the legacy organizations who would care about the future and would have a personal investment in the impact of the changes, and a sprinkling of cynics. Including cynics, rather than introducing conflict, allowed the CEO to model new ways of listening and enabling people to develop common agendas.

FIGURE 4.3. KEY EVENTS

	2002	2003	2004	2005
Drop-In Fair	★		★	
Structured annual stakeholder events	✸	✸		✸
Leadership alignment	→			
Dialogue development		→		
Polarity management		→		

This team mapped out a three-month plan that would take the organization from its inception on April 1, 2002, to the ratification of a business plan by the Board early in July. The agreed-on aim was "to have a set of interventions that would give people voice, develop cohesion and move to action." This plan included:

- A Drop-In Fair (exhibition style) for all staff
- A leadership team alignment session
- A stakeholder visioning event
- A communications strategy

An additional event was added after the stakeholder event to synthesise the outputs.

Drop-In Fair

The fair was held on April 11, 2002—seven working days after the inception of the new organization. The idea of this intervention was to send two clear signals: (1) that everyone was already doing valuable work that could be carried forward and (2) that this would be an organization in which everybody had an important part to play. The planning team knew they needed to create a whole new set of networks and to learn about each other, as well as to let people help create the solutions so that things would be different. Expectations were high, and people welcomed having more influence.

All staff were invited to come, and any group that wanted to could have an exhibition space to display what they were doing. Over twenty-two groups brought exhibits, and over three hundred people attended. The CEO and chairman were available throughout the day to talk and discuss their ideas, with the CEO presenting twice during the day.

Because the day provided unique access to a much larger group of people than constitutes a typical "event," two typical Real Time Strategic Change (Jacobs, 1994) design team activities that gather ideas and input were turned into interactive graphics that people could engage with. One very large graphic was a change model showing the journey forward as a path, the ultimate vision as shining over the distant hills, the steps that would need to be taken as footprints, a bin for what should be left behind, and a well for the capacity they would need to draw on. The graphic facilitator, Don Braisby, discussed the images and people's thoughts about change and enabled them to leave their ideas as post-its or drawings on the graphic. The other graphic was designed to engage early interest in the upcoming stakeholder event and seek input to inform the planning. People wrote and stuck post-it notes describing the incoming issues, the desired outcomes, and ideas for activities on the graphic.

This event gave a strong, early signal that the new organization would work in a different way, emphasizing learning, listening, and participating.

Leadership Team Alignment

PCTs are required to adopt a three-pronged system of governance, which includes the following:

1. Nonexecutive directors (NEDs), led by a chairperson, to provide external perspectives and oversight
2. A professional executive committee (PEC), led by a PEC chair, to provide clinical leadership
3. An executive team, led by the CEO, to provide management

Each of these groups has potentially conflicting views and perspectives. The leadership alignment challenge for the system is to develop strategies that honor and integrate all of these in a way that can provide leadership to the whole system of internal and external stakeholders. One of the mechanisms that provides for integration across the three bodies is a regular "three at the top" meeting of the CEO, PEC chair, and chair.

By the first week of May, all the people for these roles had been identified, if not appointed. The consultant used a semi-structured questionnaire, which had been developed by the planning team, to interview all these new leaders over the phone about their views on leadership vision, behaviors, the roles of the three groups, and communication and consultation.

The data were used to plan an alignment event focused on their individual and collective roles. The design allowed the team to get to know each other and use the aggregated answers from the interviews to explore how aligned they were. An interesting assumption was that there would be many differences because of historic conflicts. The data showed that there was a lot more align-

ment than might have been anticipated. The conversations were deliberately designed to allow participants to see clearly the similarities in their viewpoints and to highlight and discuss the differences.

It was recognized that it was too early for this team to be providing direction to the rest of the organization. They needed time to become an aligned team, and they needed input from the wider system. Each conversation allowed the group to test and develop a collective understanding of who was in the team and how they might operate. No decisions were planned other than agreeing on how they needed to act at the stakeholder event and what they wanted to get from it. They explicitly agreed that it "was critical that they be ready to listen to the stakeholders" and "be ready to allow them to shape the future of the organization."

Stakeholder Event

The planning for this event started at the Drop-In Fair in April and continued with a small team representative of all stakeholders. The day was designed to take the first steps toward a shared vision for improving the health and well-being of people in Eastern Birmingham. This was a one-day event but clearly billed as the start of a longer participative process. Using a Real Time Strategic Change format, approximately 240 people worked together at mixed tables of eight stakeholders. About two-thirds came from all levels and functions within the PCT (a diagonal slice), and one-third were drawn from a wide group of potential partner organizations, including local hospitals, Social Care, the city council, and community and voluntary sector organizations and patients.

This was a very large, broad collection of people who were known to be cynical about structural change and who had some past conflict among them. The start of the day was designed to allow everyone to speak as individuals and then begin to connect with each other and take on the identity of the new PCT. People shared how they were involved in the PCT and what they brought to it. They created four large group mind maps (described in Chapter One) to explore the issues, trends, and developments facing them as a PCT and used dot voting to identify important themes.

At this stage the size of the challenge began to emerge, and a sense of collective responsibility was starting to develop. In working on the vision, there was a desire to build a common agenda and to understand that different stakeholder groups might, for valid reasons, want different things. The process was intended to ameliorate potential political conflicts by allowing people to see how the mixed groups understood each others' hopes and desires. At max-mix tables, people were challenged to think themselves ten years into the future, responding to the issues to develop their ideas about vision. Each table expressed this vision from the perspective of a different stakeholder group (for example, local people, the hospital) and presented their ideas to the room in the form of a

news report for TV or radio. The media in the United Kingdom have been perceived as a common enemy for the NHS. Having the reports in the form of media-based presentations evoked the sense in the group of a common enemy being overcome by their collaborative action. The final action of reflecting on the common themes from all the presentations proved a further reinforcement of the common agenda. Participants reflected on the common themes emerging, which were then sorted and arranged into action themes, and people signed up to lead or participate in taking them forward. Calling out the "news reports" gave very powerful expression to collective aspirations, and participants at the synthesizing workshop a few weeks later drew very heavily on this content in formulating the next steps—the "audacious goals."

In identifying the action themes, a strong commitment emerged to the idea that this same approach of a cross-section of stakeholders should develop the detail of the purpose, goal, and values statements.

Strategy Synthesis Event

Some twenty people chose to sign up at the Stakeholder Event to work on the theme of "Vision and Mission." All those who had volunteered were invited to this session and were supplemented with invited people to ensure that the complexity of the PCT and its key partners would be included. Thirty people participated over the two days, although at times there were as few as seventeen in the room. The "three at the top" opened the meeting and then empowered the team to use the data available to create the core purpose statements for the PCT. The key to this was a trust that the team would use the data that had been generated and captured in all the work to date, including the ideas generated on the interactive graphics at the fair, the outputs of the leadership interviews and leadership alignment event, and the outputs of the stakeholder event. Having introduced the event, the "three at the top" left.

The focus of this workshop was to synthesize the information already generated to create the mission, vision, and strategy rather than to generate new ideas. An ongoing source of conflict in the NHS is the polarity of stability and change. The notion of "modernization" is widely used and gives rise to fears that much of what is traditional and valued will be lost. The format for the vision was the one used in *Built to Last* (Collins and Porras, 2000), which shows the value of the tension between a stable core and a stimulus to progress. This led to the team developing a core purpose for the new organization and to describing core values and three "big hairy audacious goals."

The audacious goals have been particularly powerful in establishing an organizational identity characterized by aspiration and challenge. Their existence has served to differentiate the approach and style of the organization from its neighbors and provided an accessible

framework for prioritization and decision making. The outcome can be summarized as follows:

- Core Purpose: Working together to enable health and well-being in Eastern Birmingham
- Core Values: Caring, committed, and competent
- Big hairy audacious goals

  To be so responsive to customer needs that there is no waiting for health care in Eastern Birmingham

  That the health and well-being of the population of Eastern Birmingham has improved so much that people will live ten years longer than they do now

  That, by working in partnership, Eastern Birmingham Primary Care Trust is regarded as the employer and partner of choice and will have the most involved, informed, and empowered community in the country

The audacious goals provided a basis for the identification of five key themes, which became the core strategies of the PCT and were adopted as the focus of five subgroups of the PEC: service redesign, primary care development, clinical governance, partnerships first–saving lives, and organization development.

On the afternoon of the second day the "three at the top" returned, and the synthesizing team presented their work as the basis for a dialogue to test willingness to move forward. The event closed with a promise that the CEO would write up the work into the first organizational business plan to be presented to the board in July 2002 and that it would form the basis of an organizational development strategy.

Fully Engaging the System

Whole system working has continued to be a cornerstone of the way the organization operates; a range of planned events over the last three years have taken place that include internal and external stakeholders in planning and implementation, support business planning, and sustain learning and dialogue.

A Communications Strategy

The very first planning group identified the need for an active, thoughtful approach to communications. In practice, the approach has been both planned and emergent. The planning group determined that the key events and communications should create an early feel for a new culture that is

- Participative, with communications going up down and across the organization
- Different—being creative, taking risks, challenging, and ready to be challenged
- Getting early wins—using information generated to tackle issues
- Connected and networked—putting partnerships first and creating a strong sense of belonging

In the first few months they developed news briefs and help lines, which would keep the people at all levels and in all divisions of the organization in touch. The briefs developed into an organizational newsletter, called *In Touch,* which is now published about every six weeks, and a newspaper for local people served by the PCT called *Health News,* which goes to some 50,000 households twice a year. The statutory requirement to hold an Annual General Meeting developed into an opportunity to create a regular participative event that would recognize and celebrate the achievements of individuals and teams within the new organization and in partner organizations.

Stakeholder Events

May 2002 was the first of a series of stakeholder events. Each year a new representative design team is convened to review the current issues and identify stakeholders, to create a compelling purpose and desired outcomes for the event, and to plan the process for the event and support delivery.

One year after the inception of the organization, the second event in May 2003 was an Open Space. The design team invited people to "help us work out future tactics for improving our performance in Eastern Birmingham." They felt that the free format of an Open Space would help achieve their desired outcomes:

- Building a strong team
- Sharing good practice

- Breaking down barriers
- Advancing the goals of "employer and partner of choice" and "health improvement," developed the previous year

Over three hundred people gathered in a premiership football ground, which was great for metaphors of goals, success, and scoring! A theater group set the day off with a lively performance dramatizing achievements of the first year. When the Open Space was called, the chairman and CEO held their breath, but within moments a nursing team leader stepped forward, closely followed by a surgeon from one of the local hospitals; the agenda was created within minutes. With some twenty-six subjects in the morning and twenty-two in the afternoon, extra spaces were needed to accommodate all the sessions people wanted to hold. The sessions were very practical and action-oriented, with people working on subjects such as "developing community-based diabetes clinics" and "improving the process of discharge from hospital." The day ended with people seated in their "locality groups," sharing what they had learned from the day and taking responsibility to deliver local follow-up. Each session produced a flip chart highlighting three key actions, and the output from the sessions was used to flesh out the detailed business plan being developed.

The third event in April 2004 was a more traditional exhibition, with shorter workshops. About 250 people joined over the course of an afternoon and evening. Taking the title of "Inform and Empower," it focused on the third audacious goal of "having the most informed, empowered and involved community in the country." The exhibits were supported by a choice of workshops running throughout the day. The day was designed to enable staff and members of the community to attend workshops related to key current decisions, and it enabled people from the community to input ideas and opinions.

The fourth event took place in May 2005 and was designed to emphasize the personal role of everyone in the PCT and key partners for high performance. The theme was "Choosing Health: Our Goals and a Role for Everyone." It was designed: "To bring together a wide range of stakeholders in the work of the PCT to understand the opportunities for everyone to make a difference through choosing health." By 2005 the whole system was one in which people were keen to understand each other's roles and how they could work together better. In a typical three-day RTSC event, there is a session near the end that uses the newly created sense of vision and common purpose to facilitate inter-organizational feedback. This day was, in effect, a larger-scale "valentines" process. It took a key current NHS theme of Health Improvement and used it to enable participants to explore the important roles that different people play at all levels in the system for making progress on the core organizational purpose and goals. The emphasis on personal contributions was emphasized by the culmination of the event in a "parade" in which stakeholder groups proudly organized themselves behind banners proclaiming their team commitments, including:

> Acute Trust Staff—"Wanting to Work with You"
>
> Community Nurses—"For health not just for illness . . ."
>
> General Practice—"Proactive not Prozac"

An interesting twist to the introduction of the NHS Choosing Health agenda was the use of interactive theater rather than the more traditional PowerPoint presentation. The theater group introduced the characters by showing them shopping and using the shopping basket to highlight health issues. After lunch when the characters returned for a deeper discussion of health, the tables were invited to "stop action" and advise what the characters should ask and explain further. This allowed people to reflect on how they might explain some of the more controversial issues.

Business Planning Events

Engaging with the system needs whole system tools to look at traditional tasks. The first business planning event in 2002 used the Star Model (Galbraith, 2002) to take a broad look at all aspects of the system, including strategy, structure, processes, metrics and rewards, and people. It was another form of Leadership

Alignment Event allowing key managers, clinicians, and leaders to understand what it would take to build the organization and to check progress to date. The model has remained an important tool in designing action and chasing progress within the organization.

In the summer of 2003, an extended leadership team met to look at six key priorities in the business plan and imagine that a government inspection was going to take place within a six-week time frame. This enabled them to explore the interdependence between the business plan and current team commitments, with a focus on performance improvement. The purpose was "To work together in new ways to deliver the Business Plan and improve health and well-being in Eastern Birmingham." It enabled the wider management team to focus in on the delivery of key government targets. It was at this event that "polarities" were first introduced as a concept, as potential conflict arose between those preferring to keep strategy high level and open to change (emergence) and those who wished for specific and robust objectives (planned).

Following this, polarity mapping has become another important system tool in discussing and managing conflict in the organization. First, the conflict is clearly highlighted and drawn out in ways that allow people to fully express their values and fears. In this instance, we asked people to stand on either side of a line and share why they took that position and what they fear about the people on the other side of the line. This was also designed to find out how both aspects of a polarity can be used and valued. The business planning conversation committed the organization to developing more formal planning and performance management processes, in addition to the emergent methods that currently existed. It also highlighted the need for work on individual skills in system thinking and dialogue, particularly within the leadership team.

Developing Dialogue Across the System

An underlying theme of all the large whole systems events is enabling dialogue that moves beyond conflict and enables people to find common ground. Following the tense conversations at the business planning event, the CEO approached Rob and Bridget Farrands (organizational consultants with a Gestalt background) to work with the executive leadership team on their conflict and conversation skills. This would enable individuals to be more skillful in both interpersonal and system conflict situations in expressing their views and inviting inquiry and in enquiring about the deeper assumptions of others.

This focus on dialogue has been particularly important in managing local politics, especially when designing new systems of care with the acute sector. Any change to historic forms of delivery is typically associated with high levels of staff and public anxiety and significant

suspicion of motives. The combination of large group events that have engaged patients and politicians directly in imagining a new and better future in which they are collaborating rather than competing or fighting, and building individual relationships across organizational boundaries, has enabled significant positive change in service delivery without the usual political noise and challenge.

What Happened

An organization with a deprived population, low profile, low investment, and poor performance has become a high-performing system, affecting many local stakeholders and building a national and international profile. The UK NHS has a complex system of targets with a balanced scorecard and a star rating system. The first year saw this organization earning one star, the second year two; in July 2005 it achieved the highest accolade of three stars, placing it in the top 19 percent of PCTs in the country.

The big hairy audacious goals, which looked so shocking in July 2002, are already coming within reach; the PCT has some of the lowest waits for acute services in the country, hits all key targets, and has significantly reduced waiting even in areas not measured by the government. Deaths from coronary heart disease are falling faster than the national average (despite having high levels of long-term illness in the population), and the PCT has attracted significant numbers of able and enthusiastic clinicians to work in areas where it has traditionally been difficult to recruit. A strong culture of partnership working across multiple boundaries has been established and embedded, with the EBPCT regularly seen as the "partner of choice" by local government. The medical director in one local hospital consistently uses the metaphor of marriage to describe the depth and commitment of the relationship. Nobody talks about the "way it used to be" or about the five legacy organizations. Perhaps most significantly, the CEO has been asked to take on the additional role of CEO in a neighboring PCT, leading to a merger of the two organizations—a process being managed through the use of whole systems approaches.

Reflections

Large-scale interactive processes, combined with whole system ways of thinking, can bring people together within a large and complex politicized system to move beyond conflict and political and polarized viewpoints into a new spirit of partnership, which uses differences constructively.

Being in one room is, in and of itself, a powerful intervention. An effectively designed event can enable hundreds of people to clearly express their unique perspective, listen to others, and work to find common ground. In this context people shift in their appreciation of what the issues really are. Participants feel their

voice is heard, and they remember the individual voices of others, as well as the common ground they had to work hard to create. People learn to share their information and use it to create desired outcomes for themselves and others. Conflict moves to the background when they see goals worth achieving together.

It is important to plan time for people to connect and get to know each other. This matters as much in the overall process as it does in individual events. Creating space for the leadership team to understand each other and listen to the system before being required to lead helps to forge early partnership commitment. Large systems reflect the dynamics of intimate relationships. It is important to develop skills in conversation and relationship building through dialogue alongside creating opportunities for dialogue and inquiry.

This work needs to focus on both getting real work done and on relationship building, as well as managing the tension between the two. Some people will be frustrated with time committed to relationship building for its own sake. However, the power of a common task that people want to get done can help people work through their conflicts.

Watch out for polarities and expect them to arise. When planning interventions, explore fully what polarities are likely to be at play, and plan to talk about them explicitly. Plan the flow of activities to see the polarity as something to work creatively with rather than to solve or have one "side" win. Have fun with the opposing viewpoints without ridiculing them. Build ways of looking at the polarity from the extremes and see the value in each, the movement needed, and the ways both sides can be enhanced and developed. In one event, which brought together two potentially compelling perspectives, we used the metaphor "breathing in and breathing out" to demonstrate the value and necessity of two extremes. Pay close attention to compromises. They may not make anyone happy. Support people in being creative in thinking up ways in which they can have both poles and use their differences to move the whole system forward.

Finally, the personal qualities and skills of the CEO are critical. Sometimes they are natural and sometimes coaching is essential. In this situation, the CEO had characteristics that forwarded the process. She was always open to the possibility that what emerged from the large collaborative process might not be what she wanted but was likely to be what the system needed. She was aware of her own biases and ready to listen to the opposing viewpoint and find some value in it. She made it clear with every group that she trusted them. Most important, she engaged wholeheartedly—implementing what was developed with drive and energy, following through on commitments, and holding people accountable.

References

Collins, J. C., and Porras, J. I. (2000). *Built to last: Successful habits of visionary companies.* London: Random House.

Galbraith, J. R. (2002). *Designing organizations: An executive guide to strategy, structure, and process.* San Francisco: Jossey-Bass.

Jacobs, R. W. (1994). *Real Time Strategic Change.* San Francisco: Berrett-Koehler.

CLEARING THE AIR

The FAA's Historic Growth Without Gridlock Conference

Marvin Weisbord and Sandra Janoff

The Challenge

This is a tale of political, technological, organizational, geographical, economic, and human complexity that defies the most sophisticated planning methods. In the spring of 2004, officials of the Federal Aviation Administration (FAA)—a U.S. government agency whose mission "is to provide the safest, most efficient aerospace system in the world"—were worried about a summer crunch in the skies. To head off this near-certainty, they invited a cross-section of the aviation community to a two-and-one-half-day meeting. The participants—cynical and jaded by years of frustrating encounters—considered changes that would upset decades of accepted practice. Could a diverse slice of system users, regulators, and technical experts, despite their profound skepticism, collaborate to make unprecedented course corrections in the way air traffic is managed in the United States?

While planning and managing this meeting, we were supported at every stage by Steve Bell and Paul Branch, FAA traffic controllers and trainers. Future Search Network members Sandy Silva and Michael Randel served as recorders, capturing all small group reports and much verbatim dialogue. This chapter draws heavily on their report (Randel and Silva, 2004).

Background

Consider this. Airspace—FAA's highway system in the sky—is finite. So are the numbers of airports and runways. At a given moment there are 5,000 to 6,000 aircraft competing for altitudes, routings, and airport landing slots in the U.S. airspace, which includes large parts of the oceans off both coasts. The United States has 600,000 certified pilots. A small, personal "Very Light Jet" (price tag $1.4 million) has generated 2,400 orders. That is more planes than are flown by the three largest passenger carriers—American, United, and Delta Airlines—combined. Four businessmen wanting to meet with a client 1,500 miles away and be back the same day can fly as high and almost as fast as a jumbo jet carrying 400 people. So, for that matter, can four golfers off to Florida for the weekend. All compete for airspace with an even-larger general aviation fleet, discount passenger carriers, and a military fleet that is the largest of all.

But for the unfortunate events of 9/11, this situation might have reached a crisis in 2002. The FAA had been working for some time on updating its operations to take advantage of fast-changing technologies. Today, for example, modern business and commercial jets can take off, fly to distant airports, and land without pilots touching the controls. Pilots can maintain safe altitudes, speeds, and headings independent of ground control. Global positioning technologies make possible "point to point" flight

without reference to radio signals from the ground. The FAA, in theory, could manage the whole system from a single control room rather than its twenty regional centers. Yet few technological advances are useable in the near term on a scale likely to resolve the air traffic system's paradoxes.

The reasons are at once economic, political, and logistical. In a time of shrinking federal budgets, the ideal air traffic system carries an astronomical price tag. The politics include the U.S. Congress and the National Air Traffic Controllers' Association (NATCA), both seeking to preserve employment. The logistics are tied to mind-boggling systems complexity. In the short run, keeping the system going and growing is, despite a welter of rules and regulations, dependent to an extraordinary degree on voluntary cooperation. Jack Kies, in 2003 the FAA's program manager for Air Traffic Tactical Operations (essentially chief controller), was considering a National Airspace Services Summit, bringing together perhaps twenty key leaders of the aviation community to seek agreement on systems improvement.

Past experience suggested such a meeting with "the usual suspects" was likely to lead to the usual outcome: controversy without resolution. Steve Bell, an air traffic controller and former controllers' union president, now a training consultant on Kies's staff, had been investigating cooperative solutions. He urged Kies in the fall of 2003 to consider a Future Search as a way to break with past precedent. The motivation for people to attend would be the near-certainty of coming aerial gridlock. In a meeting with Kies and other FAA staff not long after that, we listened at length to a tale of task forces, committee reports, meetings at many levels, and increasing frustration. Another summit might well be seen as just "the feds" calling another meeting,

This, the FAA executives iterated, was exactly what they did not want. The clock had ticked well past the hour for talking. Air traffic patterns over the United States, said Kies, had become an interlocking web. Delays anywhere in the system could ground planes thousands of miles away. For decades, air service providers had expected the FAA to live by the slogan "first come, first served." Traffic controllers honored flight plans in the order submitted. No aircraft, in theory, should be favored over any other. (In practice there were many ways to "game" the system for individual advantage.) There were a few exceptions. If a storm over Chicago, for example, backed up airplanes in Los Angeles, New York, and Miami, controllers held some planes, expedited others, and rerouted traffic to minimize delays for as many people as possible.

Planning the Future Search

It was in this context that Kies, in November 2003, convened several aviation experts to help plan an unusual multistakeholder conference. The initial group included two executives from the Na-

tional Business Aviation Association (NBAA): senior vice president for operations, Bob Blouin, and director of air traffic services and infrastructure, Bob Lamond. Also included were a senior vice president at MITRE Corporation, Amr ElSawy, who was working with the FAA on new technologies; the FAA's deputy director of air traffic plans and procedures, Sabra Kaulia; a Northwest Airlines executive in charge of air traffic control matters, Lorne Cass, and David Watrous, president of RTCA, a private corporation seeking consensus solutions to aviation issues. In support roles were Steve Bell and his colleague Paul Branch, a traffic controller and trainer.

Kies got right to the core issue. "The United States is the global leader in aviation," he said, "but to stay that way we need to rethink airspace design and traffic control. We need to increase the capacity of the airspace. We're at a point in time when we need to change the course of this mighty river. That means giving up our parochial positions. Like it or not we are interdependent."

This meeting, he continued, would not be simply another session to surface issues. It would involve both FAA staff and air traffic system users with the authority and resources to make substantive decisions. The meeting would succeed, he went on, only if they could collaborate for the greater good. The emphasis would be on discovery, not argument. Could airspace users agree on a set of "minimum critical specifications" to avoid gridlock? In short, would they be willing to seek common ground?

This was a startling proposition for executives accustomed to the politics of airspace management. All agreed there was a problem that required substantial participation by diverse airways users. How many and who they should be were not so obvious. There was considerable skepticism that any meeting design was equal to the treacherous crosswinds of aviation controversies.

For us, the question was not about finding common ground, which we were confident could be done. Rather, we wondered about our ability to adapt Future Search, which we had aggressively maintained was not a problem-solving process, to short-term problems. In conversations with Bell and Branch, we got a blinding flash of the obvious. Though Future Search asks people to imagine planning five to twenty years into the future, the outcomes are usually immediate action on critical issues. We decided not to alter our generic meeting design. We would look at the system's past, present, and future as a necessary precondition for acting on common ground.

It took two all-day meetings to work through the implications. The planners decided that the title had to instantly capture the attention of the aviation community to the urgency of the problem. After more than an hour of brainstorming, they settled on "Growth Without Gridlock: Systems Operations in the 21st Century." Next, the planners spent some hours listing possible participants, settling at last on ninety-two stakeholders: national and regional airlines and freight carriers; private, business, and military flyers; technical organizations, consultants, unions, FAA staff, and other government officials.

In their second meeting the planning group was joined by Russell Chew, former operations head at American Airlines, now the first chief operating officer of the newly created Air Traffic Organization (ATO) that combined FAA's air traffic operations under a single head. Chew had determined to create a professionally managed, economically sound, data-based system, emphasizing safety and customer service.

Chew, like all the others, had no Future Search experience. He acknowledged that no ideal way existed to head off what Kies anticipated would be a long, hot, delay-ridden summer. He accepted on faith that with the "whole system in the room," new actions might be possible. He would put his credibility on the line to get key airline executives in the room for three days. Still, he had no illusions. The event was a gamble. Chew's boss, Marion Blakey, FAA Administrator and chief executive of the 30,000-person agency, agreed to kick off the conference and to be present for the action plans. Chew and Kies had full authority to act on operating proposals that emerged.

The Meeting

Some sixty stakeholders showed up—a good cross-section of invitees. All had been to endless meetings. Few had experience with large group, interactive dialogue. Chew was concerned. "I promised people that this would be a meaningful use of their time," he told us. "If we see that we're not going in that direction, I want to let them go home." As great believers in ending meetings that go nowhere, we found Chew's orientation reassuring.

Administrator Marion Blakey opened by noting this was the first time ever for the FAA to bring in diverse customers to challenge the status quo, identify priorities, and develop new collaborative strategies. Russell Chew challenged participants to address gridlock and capacity growth over the next twenty-five years as economic concerns, not simply operational issues. FAA costs were expected to exceed revenue, and the Aviation and Airport Trust Fund was dramatically declining. Merely "throwing money" at the current air traffic system would not solve the problem, for the money was not available. He urged conference participants to accept responsibility for collaborative decisions and take action now.

Jack Kies presented a startling two-minute computer simulation of traffic density on the busiest day of 2003, compared to forecasts for 2020. He showed how limited gridlock already present in the system would increase in the future. He was looking, he said, for system strategies that maximized existing resources. "We need to look at ourselves to see the solutions to the problems."

We briefly described how we would proceed. The agenda consisted of five segments requiring a half day, a full day, and a half day. People would pool their experiences of the past and present, dramatize their desired futures, assess their common ground, and decide what, if anything, they wished to do. The main method was dialogue in small groups and among the whole group. We made three points crucial to Future Search. First, we would do no problem solving until all issues—global and systemic— had been explored by everyone. Second, we considered conflicts and past problems information, not action items. Third, participants would manage their own small groups, reach their own conclusions, and do their own analysis and summaries.

No one needed to change their mind for this process to succeed. We were looking for common ground that already existed. We also pointed out that people learn in different ways, so we would be patient if everybody was not always at the same place. Indeed, having worked in many cultures, we knew that if people did not fight or run away, their anxiety about differences and confusion over what was going on would lead to greater clarity.

The Past

To review the past, we asked that people write key points on three long "time lines" on the wall covering the last thirty years: Personal, Global, Air Traffic System. The purpose was to get diverse people into a shared context that included everyone's experiences. Each of eight groups, all consisting of diverse stakeholders, was assigned a time line to study. Each was to present a brief story and their understanding of what the story meant for the work to be done here. Observing the Personal time line, one group noted that most people in the room had at least thirty years in aviation and brought a diversity of operational experience. "We're skeptical of change— but we're also in leadership roles and can't pass the buck any longer." A second group reaffirmed their commitment, ownership, and accountability for the future of aviation. "If we don't have it," they asked, "who does?"

From the Global time line, groups noted thirty-year trends toward globalization and advanced technology, as well as higher security concerns, cyclical conflicts, and fluctuating fuel costs—a more complex world, harder to predict. From the Air Traffic System time line, groups observed that competition had increased along with consumer demand. They highlighted industry deregulation, "hub and spoke" operations, low-cost carriers, route congestion, bankruptcies, mergers, and alliances for "code sharing." They acknowledged the centrality of collaboration, as well as its paradoxes.

The Present

Next, participants were invited to identify present trends that affect Air Traffic Operations. Recorders wrote these on a six-foot by twelve-foot mind map. The whole group faced the map, one person speaking at a time so that all could see and hear the relevant trends. Nobody could say that an issue was "left out" un-

less every person chose to overlook it. The map made possible a feat hard to accomplish in large groups: getting everybody talking about the *same* world, one that included all perceptions. Thus sixty people quickly developed a rich portrait of a world in flux, one that no single person could detail alone.

To help focus their conversations, people were asked before breaking to place colored dots on those trends they believed ought to be addressed the next day. This was *not* a priority-setting exercise. The dots (each stakeholder group had its own color) provided visual information about concerns. Participants put most of their dots on eleven trends. A major one was shrinking budgets. Against this was the increase in demand for services, fueled in part by the rise of regional jets. Another was increasing use of RNAV—a navigational system that allows each aircraft to fly its own course independent of ground navigation aids. Many groups noted congested skies and airport delays. Moreover, people noted a decades-old institutional resistance to change that many doubted could be altered.

We have found that such issues can be related to one another. So we asked stakeholder groups to make their own maps showing the connections among the key trends of greatest concern to them. In addition, they were to note what *they* were doing now about these trends and what they were *not* doing and wanted to do. This provided clues—unavailable until now—about all other stakeholders' hopes, fears, and commitments. It's hard to summarize the detailed observations of nine stakeholder groups. One striking pattern was linking technical changes to systemic social issues.

Many groups cited "demand exceeding capacity," not easily addressed because of system inertia. Another group added that "the challenge we must learn to meet is how to integrate conflicting viewpoints. How do we move from the status quo of 'muddling along' to assuming an objective long-term viewpoint?" All observed that the march of technology and consumer demand made the future increasingly unpredictable. The group including private, business, and military flyers, with the largest fleets of high-technology aircraft, made the point that the airlines were not the only ones competing for airspace.

Several groups acknowledged the importance of good labor relations (the many unions involved in aviation) as critical to a well-functioning system. The conversations ranged across every level of concern. Some stakeholders, conversant with the politics and economics of air travel, had little understanding of the system's technical complexity. Others patiently sought to explain. Still others fidgeted in their chairs at talk that seemed to go everywhere and nowhere at once.

Soon a coherent story emerged. Air travel declined after September 11, 2001, but by early 2004 had almost returned to previous levels. Consumer demand would soon exceed the system's capacity, and the summer of 2004 could be the worst yet. The previous four years

had produced some responsive changes. CDM (Collaborative Decision-Making)—a joint industry-government traffic management initiative—had been helpful, but it had not increased en-route capacity. Even with funding, many busy airports could not add runways. What most people saw as essential to the future was something few had yet been able to do: problem solve in a spirit of collaboration and interdependent support from all stakeholders. This was a political as well as pragmatic imperative.

Said one executive, "It is time to demonstrate together to Congress and the public that the FAA and the industry as a whole will produce as promised, will be prudent and productive with funding, and will be responsible to consumers."

Prouds and Sorries

We now asked people to take responsibility for their concerns. What were they proudest of in their own behavior, and what were they sorriest about? The purpose was to help people own up without blaming or breast beating, thus reducing defensiveness and enabling greater objectivity and mutual acceptance. In response, stakeholders validated justifiable pride in their emphasis on safety, training, and crisis management. On the sorry line, many acknowledged without acrimony several sensitive themes. Groups admitted their own tendency toward finger pointing, difficulty in collaborating, efforts to maximize personal advantage at the expense of the common good, and difficulties in allocating shrinking resources. The FAA directors summed up an emerging theme when they owned up to "parochialism and turf protection—internally and externally."

The dialogue that followed these reports proved to be a pivotal point for the conference. People had given frequent lip service to cooperation. Now its many paradoxes, when practiced by competitors, became manifest. You could feel the electricity crackle as people began voluntarily to soften adversarial positions. One participant, viewing ruefully his "marginally omnipotent" perspective, said he had learned so much from those who were willing to share and that he came to realize how little he knew about the whole.

Several others talked of what they had learned:

> "A review of the last thirty years reveals so many events and circumstances that no one would have been able to predict—weather, labor strikes, and bankruptcies all the way to the tragic events of September 11, 2001. As we look ahead, we must work toward the collaborative design of a system that is supremely flexible and responsive to ambiguity, uncertainty, and unpredictability."

> "In years past we each had the luxury of taking a parochial perspective that was self-serving. As an industry those days are behind us. We must recognize our interdependence and then design, embrace, and implement the actions to support our joint mission."

> "Simply, 'throwing money' at our current concerns or assuming that our solutions will come solely through technology would be erroneous."

One airline executive summed it up: "We have got to be willing to share the pain!"

Dramatizing the Future

Participants returned to the diverse groups in which they had worked on Day 1. They were asked to put themselves six years in the future and imagine an Air Traffic Operations system that would (1) be technically feasible, (2) benefit society, and (3) be personally motivating. "Today is March 3, 2010. Imagine that you have created a system as gridlock-free as you can make it. You have a set of responsive operating norms and agreed-upon procedures for making changes when necessary. Describe this, and identify what actions you took in the summer of 2004 that got you on the right path."

There were eight scenarios, with many common features. One group, for example, offered a graphic showing the net benefits of saving time by seeing the air traffic system as a whole—one plane takes a delay to save another plane a longer delay—based on trust in the system for reliability and predictability. "Express lanes" in the sky have been implemented when demand exceeds capacity to help free up airways and speed traffic.

People imagined that the big obstacle back in 2004 was lack of collaboration. After the Future Search, went this scenario, they agreed to common objectives and measurements and were able to control costs, increase revenue, and put in place needed technology and training. Barriers were overcome by providing incentives to users, educating one another on the positive effects of sharing burdens, using technology to improve collaboration. Organizational stability grew, not from counter-lobbying against one another's interests but, instead, using more transparent financial reporting, improved labor relations, and collaboration to address capacity-demand imbalances. One group proposed a new acronym, CCCA: "Constructive Collaborative Communication Among Stakeholders for 'Systems Thinking.'"

Finding Common Ground

Now people were asked to sit again in mixed groups and write down what they believed was common ground for every person present. Each group posted its items on one wall, and people moved paper strips around until all related issues were grouped together. The following key clusters emerged:

- Further developing System-Wide Information Management (SWIM) and ongoing information exchange among system users
- A daily reporting system, using a 10 A.M. conference call among airspace users and FAA staff (that many had disregarded)
- Broadening and deepening the existing CDM
- Making systemwide efforts to get all aircraft to declare "early intent," giving traffic managers advance warning of demands on the system
- Making a cooperative effort to eliminate "gaming"—the common practice of finding loopholes in the system to benefit your own flight
- Increasing capacity, where needed, on a daily basis through policies and technologies that the FAA would implement with cooperation from other users, including a fair process for allocating capacity when actual demand exceeded projected capacity
- Modifying "on-demand, first-come, first-served" practices to improve traffic flow and avoid extreme delays
- Creating "express lanes" where demand and capacity required them

The list differed in detail, though not in spirit, from the common ground we had seen many times before. It iterated deeply held values: stakeholder collaboration, a wish to create more user equity, a valuing of diverse views, participative problem solving, "transparent" governance, and economic responsibility.

This discussion would not be complete without a nod toward "financing" on the "not agreed" list. All could accept Chew's data showing that the system was in dire financial shape. What they could not agree on was an equitable funding policy. The business and private flyers believed that they were already paying their fair share through fuel taxes. The airlines argued that airline ticket taxes paid most of the price tag for air traffic control. This issue, all agreed, would take a lot more work.

Perhaps the central insight of Growth Without Gridlock was that the U.S. air traffic system, with twenty control centers, thousands of airborne craft, hundreds of airports, and tens of thousands of individual daily decisions, was an indivisible entity. Optimizing the whole would require a great deal of understanding from those asked to accept small delays for the sake of the greater good. In a few hours of dialogue, Jack Kies's personal aspiration had spiraled into a pledge by diverse system users.

Indeed, ATO's COO, Russell Chew, hardly trusting this turn of events, felt obliged to test people's commitment at the end of the second day. He asked the group whether they would act on their insights. "I don't want to waste anybody's time," he said. "You don't have to come back tomorrow if you don't intend to do something." Nobody said a word. Growth Without Gridlock had landed at a destination never before reached by the nation's flyers: the pain would be shared.

Action Planning

It was with this stark realization that people undertook action planning on the third morning. Participants were asked to select common ground themes to translate into policies, programs, procedures, and structures. Five voluntary groups formed. One wrote an overall vision statement affirming the centrality of stakeholder involvement in ameliorating problems of system capacity and financing. Another wrote a "long-term vision" supporting the FAA's shift toward a business-like entity "based on sound economic principles." They affirmed the intent to grow the system by using technology where possible and by new procedures where constraints existed. They called for performance-based standards and measurements, priority to high-tech aircraft, improvements in the forecasting of demand, and the upgrading of airports. Members agreed to join in educating Congress and the public on air traffic challenges.

A historic breakthrough occurred when one of the airline executives said he was ready to work with Jack Kies in tackling the "first-come, first-served" norm if certain others, whom he named, would participate. He was joined by twenty-one others—private and business flyers, airlines large and small, senior FAA executives—the largest action planning group we had ever seen. No one sat. For an hour and a half they stood around a flip chart exploring, with single-minded focus, what changes they would be willing to make *immediately* to this complex, immovable system.

At length the group proposed an unprecedented "System Access Plan," enabling the FAA to relieve congestion daily, based on data from the whole system. All flyers would accept short delays and longer routes when this made the overall system work better. The system would be implemented on a trial basis within three weeks. Review would take place daily in the 10 A.M. phone call between the FAA Command Center and the users.

The group also recommended that an "Express Lane" strategy be invoked when any airport experienced a ninety-minute delay. In such a plan fifteen or twenty aircraft at many smaller airports might be delayed five or ten minutes to open up "holes" in the air traffic flow for hubs with long delays. That way, FAA controllers could "flush" congested airports rather than indefinitely hold planes on the ground. Moreover (and a vindication for business and private flyers), the policies would apply equally to airports large and small and to planes regardless of capacity.

Another group worked out—for the long-term future—limited conditions under which pilots with the right technology might maintain their own separation rather than have ground controllers do it. Such a plan would hinge on industry and public acceptance and might take years to implement.

Each group read its statements and plans aloud. They were confirmed by all stakeholders. Now a microphone was passed around the room for people to say a few words about what they personally planned to do. Many spoke of closing the door on parochial attitudes of the

past, now realizing they were part of one system. Numerous others committed to follow up, communicate, prepare, educate, and support the agreements with their own organizations.

At this point, a senior FAA executive, with years of experience in conflicted meetings, took the microphone again.

> I was having breakfast this morning with some of you, and I thought to myself that we had been at this for a day-and-a-half. I had my fingers crossed that somehow in the next couple of hours we would come up with something on which we agreed. I thought we would need a miracle. . . . Not a MIRACLE miracle, just a small enough miracle to have this broad customer base really find some common ground and align ourselves to start doing things differently.

He paused for breath. "I think perhaps a miracle did pop out. With these commitments, we *are* doing something different. This is a huge step for the aviation community!"

The conference had, by then, been in session a total of eighteen hours.

At the end, Russell Chew thanked participants for their contributions. He noted that a report would be distributed to all within a few days. Marion Blakey, who had rejoined the group, said how much she appreciated the commitments to immediate action in 2004 and to critical long-term principles. She would address issues that needed to be tackled in other parts of the FAA. She also committed to engaging with Congress and the administration to ensure resources to support the work. At a press conference afterwards, Administrator Blakey said, "Air travelers may experience more short delays but fewer long ones. The plan, if it works, should reduce the total amount of time that all flights are delayed because of bad weather or crowded airspace." She added, "It's not just a question of redistributing the pain; it's a question of lessening the pain for everyone."

Reflections

For years we have thought of Future Search as a way of creating a values-based "strategic umbrella," making possible short-term planning against a backdrop of desired future scenarios. The FAA meeting presented a more complex situation than usual. Experts, committees, task forces, and technical teams had worked for years on ideal systems for the national airspace. Future scenarios abounded. What troubled most of the actors was what to do in the short run.

This meeting, like every other we have done, had to be viewed as an experiment. None of us had been to this place before. Still, we were not flying blind. We had reason to be optimistic that a new kind of summit, based on Future Search principles, would lead to new outcomes. Having the "whole system in the room"—people with au-

thority, expertise, information, resources, and need—had been proven repeatedly to lead to action when people realized they could no longer point fingers, except at themselves (Weisbord and Janoff, 2000).

We also had faith in using differentiation-integration (D-I) theory as a way of managing both the meeting's structure and process. Having people differentiate their views in *stakeholder* groups and then integrate their values and aspirations in *diverse* groups guarantees they will take a spectrum of views into account. As stakeholder groups highlight their concerns, they sharpen rather than blur their differences. Paradoxically, they also reveal uncharted common ground. Many groups discover differences amid apparent sameness and similarities among ostensible differences. People develop a more balanced view of "reality." Integrated solutions become more feasible.

Making conflict a matter of information, not action, enables people to find and act on common ground *that already exists.* This may not always be obvious. Common ground is not the same as pressuring people to go along with the majority in a gesture toward harmony. We seek *real,* not reluctant, alignment. People cannot discover how much they already agree on when they spend up to 80 percent of their time trying to reconcile views on a few problematic issues. We are quite willing to put even a majority position on the "not agreed" list if anyone dissents. That list will not be "worked" unless some people choose to do it at the end while most others are working the common ground.

In a common ground dialogue, people also discover improbable allies. Sometimes conflicts dissolve when they are found to be based on false assumptions and predictions. Pilots and passengers experience only a fraction of the air traffic system—only what happens to the airplane they happen to be in. Observers in the FAA's Virginia Command Center can see on one wall every plane in U.S. airspace under traffic control—thousands of points of light. While even a very large group cannot see it all, people can educate one another to system aspects heretofore unknown, giving each an understanding of the whole that none had at the start.

Beyond understanding, there is the centrality of *interdependence* if joint action is desired. Most "failures" of collaborative methods can be traced to imposing them on people who see no need for working in harness. In the aviation community, the web of relationships and the requisite cooperation became quickly manifest when the "whole system" was in one room rather than in far-flung offices, cockpits, and control centers. Under these conditions, sharing the pain began to look like a better strategy than sharing the gridlock.

We also know that if people won't make the shift toward greater cooperation, we can't make it happen for them. All we can do is offer opportunities they never had before. No group methods so far discovered are equal to the task of reorganizing systems as complex as this

one. Yet the repeated use of such methods surely can ease the traumas of relentless growth and technological change.

A year after the conference we talked to several participants who said Growth Without Gridlock had been a breakthrough meeting. The core agreements—dropping the first-come, first-served policy, and the ninety-minute "flush," combined with "express lanes"—were meaningful steps. The summer of 2004 saw fewer delays than anticipated. The aviation community learned that with simultaneous access to one another, members could cooperate for mutual benefit.

Moreover, they recognized that in a world of ever more crowded skies, no alternatives to cooperation exist. Many hoped they would have follow-up meetings to build on the progress so far made. "There were no guarantees," wrote Bob Lamond, of the National Business Aviation Association, in a report to his members. "But the participants agreed to take a risk . . . to put parochial positions behind for the good of the entire community. Growth Without Gridlock was a one-of-a-kind event."

Postscript on Techniques Versus Principles

Please note that the principles underlying this meeting are more critical to its success than its techniques. You can use time lines, mind maps, and future scenarios until Mars becomes an Earth colony. Without the whole system in the room, exploring everyone's views, putting conflicts and problems on hold, acting on common ground, and inviting people to take responsibility, you are unlikely to get systemic action of the kind reported here.

References

Randel, M., & Silva, S. (2004). *Growth without gridlock: System operations in the 21st century.* A Report of the Future Search Conference at the National Conference Center, Lansdowne, VA, March 2–4.

Weisbord, M., & Janoff, S. *Future Search: An action guide to finding common ground in organizations and communities* (2nd ed.). San Francisco: Berrett-Koehler, 2000.

For more information on the air traffic system, see http://*www.faa.gov*, *www.rtca.org*, and *www.nbaa.org*. For more on Future Search applications see http://www.futuresearch.org.

WORKING WITH CORPORATE COMMUNITY TENSIONS ON ENVIRONMENTAL ISSUES

John D. Adams and Ann L. Clancy

The Challenge

A two-day retreat of an energy company's corporate managers, refinery managers, and Citizen's Advisory Council (CAC) members from eight refinery sites (a total of nearly sixty people) was planned. The purpose of the retreat was to productively engage these groups, following the recent merger of two formerly independent oil companies, to explore progress and raise questions concerning the company's commitment to implementing a variety of sustainable development initiatives. A further purpose was to energize the CACs and to promote their action taking on behalf of the company's sustainability initiatives.

The planning team for the retreat consisted primarily of the refinery manager, sustainability manager, and a team of CAC members of the "host" refinery, headed by the host CAC's external facilitator. In planning for this gathering, the team was cognizant of several challenges that needed to be creatively managed to ensure that the retreat would make a successful contribution to the recently merged company's relatively new commitment to a set of "Sustainable Development Goals." The potential challenges for the meeting included

- The refinery managers' range of interests in and commitments to the company's corporate-level sustainable development commitments and principles
- The wide range of priorities, goals, and activity levels practiced by the different refineries in their engagement with their CACs and their communities
- The unknown degree of completeness of the adjustment to the recent merger of two energy companies with significantly different corporate cultures into the present global energy company
- The potentially disruptive individual agendas of some CAC members who were attending as representatives of community advocacy organizations (for example, people whose families had suffered illnesses they felt were due to toxic releases from the local refinery)
- Varying levels of confidence and trust of the CAC members that the corporate and refinery managers would actually follow up on any concerns, questions, or ideas raised
- The fact that the retreat included nearly sixty people from corporate, refinery management, and CAC stakeholders and was only two days in length
- The presence in the group of three potentially divisive sets of priorities as to how to focus next steps: optimize the business, protect the environment, and develop the community

Background

Following the disastrous chemical gas leak from a Union Carbide plant in Bhopal, India, in 1984, the presence of CACs working at the interface between any organization engaged in potentially hazardous production processes and the surrounding community increased rapidly. These CACs most often represent the community stakeholders living in the vicinity of chemical plants, petroleum refineries, arms manufacturers, and other organizations that may potentially experience significant toxic releases.

As representatives of various constituencies within the communities in which these usually large operations are located, the CAC members often arrive with a variety of potentially competing agendas. To further complicate matters, it is well known in the behavioral sciences that when stakeholders in a situation hold steadfastly to their roles as "representatives of [_____]" their community advocacy groups, NGOs, local government agencies, and so on, as opposed to joining together to represent the greater good of the whole, competition and conflict ordinarily drive out collaboration and discovery of common ground.

In this case, we are focusing on the refinery organization of a global energy company—the third-largest oil-refining organization in the world. The two-day retreat included participants from seven of its twelve North American refineries, one English refinery, and the CACs located in the communities where these refineries operate. The eight locations and their CACs had operated relatively independently prior to this retreat, which included refinery management, CACs, and corporate management; the retreat was held in September of 2004. This was to be the first meeting of the CACs and their respective management teams since the merger between the two large energy companies was completed in 2002. National and regional CAC meetings had been held within one of the merged companies over a fifteen-year period prior to the merger, with increasing focus on that company's sustainabil-

ity efforts. This meeting would be the first to bring both of the merged entities' CACs together with a clear intent of bringing everyone up to speed and furthering the company's commitment to operating sustainably with respect to both the environment and the communities in which the refineries operate.

After reviewing many options for generating data (Future Search, Open Space, and Whole-Scale Change approaches), the host planning team decided that The World Café (for information, see http://www.theworld cafe.com) would be the most effective process for generating useful questions, suggestions, and concerns, in light of the various challenges outlined earlier. The external consultant interviewed several corporate and refinery sustainability managers to develop a larger understanding of the history and context for the sustainable development aspirations of the company. Data were also solicited by the external consultant in survey form from all refinery managers and CAC members to assess their expectations and hopes for the retreat, as well as to fine-tune some of the retreat features.

The Two-Day Conference

On the arrival evening, the host CAC welcomed guests and helped everyone get acquainted. The first full day included presentations by company executives on strategic issues facing the company and the company's sustainable development program; small group activities to discuss the value of CACs, and a "CAC Fair" to share best practices. These activities provided an excellent overview of the background and context for initiating work toward achieving companywide sustainable development, which has been a strong and overt commitment of the CEO. That evening was filled with social and cultural activities designed by a local Native American representative of the hosting CAC.

The second (final) day was devoted to developing a pool of information—concerns, suggestions, and questions—for following up and enhancing the overall community involvement effort at both corporate and refinery levels. The external consultant delivered his keynote on how the company's program in sustainability compares to similar programs across the industry worldwide, what it takes to successfully implement "triple bottom line" (economically viable, environmentally safe, and with attention to development in the community) sustainability initiatives (ninety minutes); then, the consultant introduced and led The World Café process for the remainder of the morning (two hours).

The World Café (Brown and Isaacs, 2005) is a simple, yet powerful series of progressive conversations that help even very large groups (the largest to date is twelve hundred) engage in constructive dialogue, build personal relationships, engage in collaborative learning, and surface key opportunities for action. The World Café uses a set of seven core design principles that, *when used in combination,* create a type of "conversational greenhouse," nurturing the conditions

for the rapid propagation of collaborative knowledge and insight, often across traditional boundaries such as those described in this case study.

Prior to the first round, everyone received a briefing on how the process would work, including instructions about how to participate productively.

In this Café, three conversational rounds of twenty minutes each were conducted. At the end of each round, a "table host" was asked to stay behind, welcome new guests, and briefly summarize what had happened at the table in the previous round, while everyone else moved to a new table, carrying the key ideas generated in their earlier conversation. The only criterion in place for where to move was to maintain a new heterogeneous mix of corporate, refinery management, and CAC members at each table, in order to ensure the cross-pollination of diverse perspectives. In the first two rounds, participants were asked to generate key questions, concerns, and suggestions that people had in relation to the sustainable development direction of the company. In the third round, each group was asked to share and prioritize the concerns, questions, and suggestions that had been brought up in the first two rounds. Using 5 × 7 post-it notes, each individual wrote down the ideas that he or she thought were most important and then posted these in a designated area under one of four signs: CONCERNS, QUESTIONS, SUGGESTIONS, OTHER. Everyone then participated in a "Gallery Walk" to see an overview of what The World Café activity had generated. Posting these items in the designated space brought the entire community together in a "beehive" of high energy and enthusiastic activity.

After all notes were posted, and the CAC participants had gone to lunch, the corporate director of sustainability led the other key corporate representatives and the eight refinery managers in organizing all the post-it notes into eight major themes.

The eight themes that emerged and a small sampling of the key questions, concerns, and suggestions that were generated by The World Café process follow:

1. Influencing Public Policy

- Is the company willing to stand alone or buck the petroleum PACs to support sustainable development?
- Should the company have a role in leading national energy policy change?

Some suggestions were:

- The company should better publicize the fact it is committed to sustainability.
- [The company should] be a strong advocate for energy efficiency in all fields—transport, buildings, and so on.

2. Emissions By-Products

- What is going to happen to all the sulfur being extracted from the fuel?
- Assuming a 60 percent increase in energy demands in the next ten years, will the company stay committed to meeting ecological and social con-

cerns as it ramps up to meet that need?

Some suggestions and concerns were:

- If we're going to continue our dependence on hydrocarbons, we need to focus on investing capital to reduce emissions and minimize impact on the community.
- Low-level heat and used water could be reused for heated water for greenhouses and food production.
- Coking gas will be released in the atmosphere.

3. Economic and Stockholder Issues

- What stockholder support does the company really have for sustainable development?
- Is the company willing to forego short-term profitability for long-term sustainability?

4. Alternative Energy

- What is the company doing to explore the development and use of alternative fuels?
- Where is the company compared to other companies in terms of sustainable development, renewable fuel, alternative fuels?

5. The Energy Challenge

- With the increase in forecasted energy demand, will the company compromise its sustainable development position to meet demand?

- What is the company's dependence on Middle East oil?

6. Corporate Strategy

- Do we meet the strictest environmental regulations of any given country on all aspects within all the countries we operate in?
- Is the company an oil company or an energy company?
- Is the company's planning horizon long term enough?

7. Community and CAC Role

- Is the company just using the CACs to push their position into the community?
- Is there a conflict between the company's long-term sustainability plans and its present practices in my local community?
- What is the impact of increased consumption on the community?

8. Benchmarking

- Will the company measure its success using something like the Dow Jones sustainability index?

Outcomes of the Process

Following lunch, corporate representatives and refinery managers created a panel to engage with the themes that had been generated by The World Café and to answer any additional verbal questions and ideas raised from the remainder of the participants (two hours). A very fruitful and frank whole group dialogue involving all sixty participants ensued. The World Café process had enabled everyone—CAC members and facilitators, corporate people, and refinery managers—to become equally involved and able to discuss the company's sustainable development policies and direction. All participants appeared to feel high ownership for the results of this review process.

Because of the depth and breadth of the items contained within the eight themes generated by The World Café process, it is too soon to chart the ultimate impact of the issues raised at this retreat concerning the corporate implementation of its sustainability initiative. It is clear from reading the earlier list, however, that a variety of very real and important items were generated. The World Café is a powerful process for producing actionable knowledge. It is also essential to have an equally compelling process for follow-up and action taking in order to translate the energy and excitement of The World Café's strategic dialogue process into ongoing plans for implementation, feedback, and continuous improvement.

Reactions of CAC Participants Eight Months Later

The following comments, taken from a much longer list, were generated by members of the attending CACs, eight months following the conclusion of the retreat at which The World Café was held. These responses were selected as being representative of the overall experience, and include general comments and learning, as identified by community CAC and corporate members.

> "The World Café brought a bunch of people together who didn't know each other and got people working together. It was a way of moving things along rather than people talking *at* each other."

> "This meeting generated issues and concerns that corporate and refinery managers responded to publicly; this had never happened at previous meetings."

> "For the company, this was the community talking, involving *all* the people there; whether CAC members, refinery managers, or corporate, we were all the "community."

> "Our CAC was newly formed and, as members, we weren't sure what the function of CAC was supposed to be, much less what our role in that process was. We were allowed the opportunity to ask questions, get wonderful ideas, and even learn from others' already-tried mistakes."

> "The benefit of The World Café, from my perspective, is in bringing experiences into major theme areas that, in turn, can be developed into action areas which, in the case of our CAC, is what we've begun to do."

This small sampling of comments about the process, collected eight months following the actual retreat, indicates that the participants enjoyed the process and found it to be highly worthwhile in terms of getting better acquainted as an extended "community," bringing the newer CACs up to speed, clarifying and focusing the key questions and concerns, building a shared understanding of the CAC role in the overall sustainability policies and strategy of the company, and helping the CACs formulate their own next steps. It is clear in the comments that The World Café experience still remains very much in people's awareness and that the information generated by the process is still very current in their minds. Some of the CACs were making use of the information generated by The World Café, and others were not. In every case, The World Café was apparently a positive and memorable experience.

Reflections

This case presentation is a description of an application of The World Café process in a situation that was potentially quite explosive. We believe that this process helps to manage and contain potential conflict by reducing the likelihood of polarization and by increasing real interpersonal listening and communication. How might this occur?

First, the "Café Etiquette," which all participants are taught in their orientation to the method, establishes norms about contributing one's own real views while also listening with respect. Second, the use of max-mix tables discourages any one interest group from gathering together and talking only to people who share their own views. Third, the presence of a table host, who has remained in place from the previous round and who provides a quick summary of what has previously transpired and also keeps the conversation focused and balanced, helps to keep the conversations focused on exploring the announced questions for the round. Fourth, writing all the points of view on the paper tablecloth with markers makes a big graphic that anyone at the table can add to because everyone has a pen. This "tablecloth art" creates a cumulative legacy of the conversations that have taken place. Fifth, the short time frame for discussion (in this case twenty minutes) makes it hard for protracted conflict to break out. And at the end of each twenty-minute period, the composition of each table changes so that everyone is talking with different people in the next round. Finally, having only four or five people at a small round table engenders a more personal, even intimate, conversation. This keeps the developing conversation from becoming a bully pulpit for anyone's point of view. All these factors in The World Café process help the discussions genuinely engage and explore difficult issues.

A carefully thought-out process and context is one of the primary reasons for the success of The World Café. The host team worked diligently to create a retreat that would be productive and would be experienced as a unified whole by everyone who attended. The pre-work interviews and survey work done by the external consultant provided both background and context for the consultant to use in planning his keynote, which, in turn, framed the conversation in The World Café process and also helped with expectation setting for the participants. Day 1 provided everyone with the corporate background, a sense of best practices across the eight communities in attendance, and community-building aspects. All these features were essential to the success of Day 2.

The keynote presentation, which took up the first ninety minutes of Day 2, was designed by the external consultant, in consultation with the host team, with The World Café in mind. The presentation was crafted to set a solid and easily understood context and rationale for using The World Café. It began broadly with a background on the reasons why sustainability is so important and included several definitions of sustainability. The presentation then narrowed to a review of how well the company's approach (and in particular the implications for refineries) to sustainable development fit in with an industry overview of sustainability best practices by oil companies worldwide. Finally, it converged on the challenges and success factors for implementation of large-scale sustainability initiatives (Adams, 2003). This presentation served both to contextualize and legitimize The World Café process and to develop trust in the speaker as The World Café facilitator. As a result, we moved smoothly and effortlessly into the interactive process, with each table group immediately digging into the first round assignment.

One area that was not addressed in this retreat planning and delivery process was mechanisms to ensure follow-up at the corporate level of the potential substantive action steps "back home." While specific companywide follow-up of actions emanating from The World Café process was not originally included in the purpose and objectives of the retreat, in retrospect some potential effects may have been lost. Since this was the first-ever gathering of the merged company's refinery management and all the CACs, attention was focused on bringing people together, clarifying roles, and sharing ideas in a cooperative and supportive environment. It was decided by the planners that these emphases would be enough to keep track of, and so follow-up action was not mandated. The individual refineries and CACs were left to follow up in ways appropriate to their diverse situations.

Included in the "success factors for successful change implementation" portion of the keynote (Adams, 2003) were a few factors supportive of follow-up action that we chose not to build into the design of the retreat. In order for complex change implementation to be successful over the long term, one important element is that there are champions and stakeholders who are "visible, vocal, consistent, and persis-

tent" in their advocacy for the change. We did not put this feature in place at the companywide level. A second important element for successful implementation is that everyone understands the vision or goal and knows the next step or two that he or she will take. Although we felt confident that everyone left with a good grasp of the longer-term vision, we did not ensure that everyone had a specific next step to act upon.

And finally, we did not clarify specific accountabilities at the corporate level for monitoring and reporting on progress in implementing the ideas that arose from The World Café process and the afternoon review of the information generated. These are a few of the points shared in the closing of the keynote presentation that were not built into the process, that could be included in subsequent World Café experiences in this organization.

References

Adams, J. D. (2003). Successful change: Paying attention to the intangibles. *OD Practitioner, 35*(4), 22–26.

Brown, J., & Isaacs, D. (2005). *The World Café: Shaping our futures through conversations that matter.* San Francisco: Berrett-Koehler.

CHAPTER FIVE

WORKING IN COMMUNITIES WITH DIVERSE INTEREST GROUPS

For those of us who have worked in community settings the analogy, "It is like herding cats," captures some of the difficulties. It is daunting to stand in front of a very diverse group of stakeholders, each with their own perspectives and agendas, who, like cats, want to do their own thing! "How," we ask ourselves, "are we ever going to bring these people to work together?" It is clearly a challenge—a very important one for democratic societies.

Have people in the past been more accepting of letting a few leaders make decisions for the whole community? Did we simply leave community planning to the elected officials? Even if we were not always satisfied with their decisions, we chose to live with them. However we view the past, we are in a different climate today. People want to influence the issues that affect them. More crucial perhaps, is that the federal government has shifted more and more responsibility for services and new initiatives to the local level. School bond issues and other local initiatives have funding requirements that need broad-based public support or they do not pass. Public hearings or old-style town hall meetings often turn into screaming matches. This is why we think many community leaders have turned to Large Group Methods as a way to build understanding and consensus around critical issues.

Since we first started writing about these methods, we have been amazed how often and how effectively these ideas are successfully used in working with community issues worldwide. In this chapter, three cases demonstrate how Large Group Methods work with community groups:

- "SpeakUp!: Bringing Youth, Educators, and Parents Together for Critical Conversations," by Marie T. McCormick
- "Building Coalitions to Create a Community Planning Tool in Israel," by Tova Averbuch
- "Taking Democracy to a Regional Scale in Hamilton County," by Steven Brigham

Differences Between Working with Organizations and Working with Communities

We believe that there are differences in using Large Group Methods with community groups, as compared to working within organizations. Though this seems obvious, it may be worthwhile to call attention to a few of the differences.

First, organizations are bounded. Although they are part of a larger system of suppliers, customers, and community, they have their own rules, norms, and culture. The parts are clearly interdependent; policies and structures make this explicit and bind the parts to the whole. Communities are more amorphous and complex; the ties are much weaker, the boundaries more flexible and penetrable.

Here is an example of using a Large Group Method within an organization. Recently, we worked with a business organization where the information technology (IT) department was working to improve their support of the different business functions. They brought together the stakeholders from different areas of the organization. Naturally, each of these areas had their own agenda—items that they wanted the IT department to implement. The overarching goal, however, was to improve employee productivity through the use of technology for all areas by improving ease of use, ease of input, and access to certain types of data. Though there were multiple agendas, clearly an improvement in productivity would benefit everyone in the organization. Departments might be siloed, but there are bonds and interdependencies that tie them together, not the least of which is the reward and bonus system. The difference we want to emphasize is the level of *interdependence around the superordinate goal.* In communities there is much less interdependence, even when a superordinate goal is present.

The second difference is that in organizations there is a hierarchy of command and authority. Once agreements are reached, there is a process for funding initiatives and making changes. Organizations may have problems getting things done, but communities face different constraints. For example, at a recent community conference on land development, many conflicting agendas were brought to the meeting. There was a group representing the interests of the builders, another group clamoring for low-income housing, an advocacy group concerned about the environment, a group worried about the impact on the school system, a group representing the handicapped, as well as individuals with their own specific agendas. Not only is it difficult to reach agreements and compromises in this type of situation, but a critical issue remains: What structure will we use to move forward? Who or what groups will take responsibility? What are the financial requirements to sustain the initiative?

The Need for Sponsorship and Sustainability

The cases in this chapter are all community-based but have differing degrees of leverage on the participants. In both the Israeli case and the Hamilton County case there is a sponsoring organization or partnership that invites people to participate. In the SpeakUp! case the sponsor is an individual who, because of her experience with her son, feels passionately about encouraging meaningful conversations across generations; she recruits people to help her with her vision. Unfortunately, after a few years there was no organizational sponsor to sustain the initiative. Nonprofit, government, and quasi-government organizations often invite community participation because they need public support and consensus to move ahead. They may have more power and influence with community agencies and groups if they are seen as providers of funding.

In the case of the United Kingdom's National Health Service (see Chapter Four), health delivery agencies and health and social service professionals have a degree of interdependence. They need each other to provide health care to the larger community. The NHS may have the funding, but they need the other groups and organizations to be providers in the health care delivery system. This does not mean that there are not political rivalries, conflicts about goals and methods, and issues around the use of money. There are, however, ties that bind. It is important to recognize the degree of interdependence when working with government, nonprofits, community groups, and agencies.

Even without the leverage of funding, a strong meta-goal, or vision, can help a group recognize their interdependence. "We cannot accomplish this preferred future if we don't work together!" The advantage of a strong sponsor is that the sponsor provides a means for sustaining the effort. When working on community issues, it is important to ask the tough questions about sponsorship. Many groups go after grant money to help finance the initial meeting costs. Grants end, and if the endeavor is worth sustaining, the initiative often requires ongoing time, commitment, and money.

Over time, people who do this important community work recognize these issues and find ways to manage the dilemmas. The first important step occurs in the planning meeting. Time must be spent on identifying the stakeholders who need to be invited and what means will be used to recruit and motivate people to attend. There is often no power to command attendance when community involvement is desired.

The second issue is managing the diverse agendas. In the three cases in this chapter, there is a superordinate goal: What is the quality of life we want for our community. How can we create a planning tool that will take into account important social and environmental concerns in Israel? How can we encourage meaningful conversations across generations? The vision, or goal, provides a context for exploring the diverse perspectives and weaving them into the means to support the vision. If the vision, or meta-goal, is agreed upon, it provides leverage to manage different perspectives and reduce conflict.

The third and most difficult issue is follow-up. The importance of a sponsoring organization for needed continuity cannot be underestimated. What is the process for moving ahead and taking action after the large group event? People make commitments of various kinds at these events, but who keeps track of what is—and is not—happening? Even with a sponsoring organization and sources of funding, implementation and follow-through can still be difficult.

Recently, one of us was doing a Future Search meeting in a town in Connecticut. The title was "Conference on Aging: Focus on the Future." The town's Commission on Aging sponsored the meeting, but the meeting was co-sponsored by the Junior League. The Junior League's commitment was to devote their time, money, and facilitation skills to support the follow-up on agreed activities for at least a year.

Gaining commitment for follow-up is more precarious in some of these cases. In the SpeakUp! case, the author comments that pulling people together for follow-up activity would be impossible. Many of the attendees had come as individuals from all over the city of Philadelphia. They addressed this issue by creating a structured activity where people made a personal commitment to what their follow-up activity would be. At the close of the Parliament of World Religions (see Chapter Six, "World Religions Engage Critical Global Issues"), they were faced with a similar dilemma. They had religious leaders from all over the world; they wanted these leaders to go back and make a difference by exerting influence on a particular global issue. At the close of the Parliament, everyone drew an Opportunity Map by creating a spider diagram, with their name at the center, and adding spokes that represented the different groups they were part of, such as family, friends, work, school, professional associations, community groups, and other memberships—in other words, their network. In trios, people talked to each other about how they could influence, educate, and motivate members of their network on the critical global issues. They had an opportunity, in the trio, to rehearse their approach and receive feedback and suggestions from the other trio members. This type of activity, at the end of a large group meeting, can help start the commitment and follow-up process in a setting where there is no organized follow-up.

What to Note in These Cases

The case examples in this chapter are very different from each other, but each case represents a community effort to promote change. SpeakUp! was a one-day, yearly meeting whose purpose was to bring together parents, teachers, and youth across socioeconomic levels to have meaningful conversations on issues critical to all three groups: drugs, teen suicide, and alcohol. For each of three years, they used a different method. The comparisons of the methods and their conclusion on the elements that had the biggest payoff are worthy of note.

The second case—"Building Coalitions to Create a Community Planning Tool in Israel"—is about a partnership in Israel that purposefully involved a diverse group of stakeholders to develop a community-planning tool that would incorporate the social, environmental, and other community concerns as part of the planning process for community development in Israel. It is interesting to note how the author introduced Open Space to the steering committee by providing them with an experience of the method. Their commitment to the principles was clear in how they managed their meetings. This pattern of working seems to have contributed to their ability to work together and to the success of the event. Convergence in Open Space can often be a challenge. Tova Averbuch describes how, after a long day, she engaged participants to join her and take responsibility for organizing and clustering the data they had produced so that next steps could be taken.

The third case—"Taking Democracy to a Regional Scale in Hamilton County"—involved over a thousand people. Hamilton County cuts across three states and has as its center the City of Cincinnati. As regional planning becomes more and more necessary in many areas, this case study is a demonstration of what can be done with leadership, careful planning, and citizen involvement. Similar to the Israeli case, the factors that need to be taken into account when doing regional planning are enormous. The other fascinating aspect is the political issue, since not much can happen unless groups, institutions, towns, and cities are willing to give up some power and control to serve the larger good. This becomes possible with the achievement of a strong and broad community mandate and commitment, which was developed here through widespread participation.

In all three cases, a great deal of attention is paid to the pre-work and planning process. Recruitment of the right people to attend is a high priority. Who are the stakeholders, regardless of their positions? Who needs to be present? It is critical in community work to have all the voices. We know of an interesting example in one school district where increases in school taxes were a hot issue. A vigilante group who were opposed to all tax increases for education was invited. Someone in the planning group said, "You mean we are inviting the enemy?" The school bond issue might never have passed had this group not been part of the process. This group was able to raise their concern, hear the needs of others, and move to support a proposal that integrated major issues, including some of their concerns. The right people in the room may include the enemy!

What are the core facilitation skills required to do this kind of work? The facilitator needs to help groups listen to different viewpoints, to stay open and explore thoroughly the context and issues before anyone takes positions. The facilitator guides the stakeholders in the search for some common under-standings and agreements—the search for common ground.

Our Thoughts and Reflections

In the beginning of this section, we discussed the challenge of working with community groups and highlighted the differences between working with or-ganizations and working with communities. The following is a summary of elements to keep in mind:

- A sponsoring organization is needed to take responsibility for continuity and follow-up that will support and sustain the initiatives. Funding may be provided by the sponsoring organization, or it may come from grants or foundations. It is important to remember that follow-up requires financial support.
- Representative planning groups are needed—groups tasked with making strategic choices about stakeholder selection and providing ongoing help with recruitment.
- Skilled facilitators and meeting designers who have worked with commu-nity groups with diverse and polarized agendas are needed, allowing for dif-ferentiation of views and providing methods for developing common ground and goal congruence.
- A very important activity at the close of the meeting is to use a method for generating and tracking commitments from attending organizations, as well as individual participants.

We call your attention to Chapter Seven, "Embedding New Patterns of Working." This chapter takes a look at new patterns of interactions that can support implementation in organizations and communities.

SPEAKUP!

Bringing Youth, Educators, and Parents Together for Critical Conversations

Marie T. McCormick

The Challenge

In June of 2000, a potential client came to me with a challenge: design a one-day meeting to bring together youth, educators, and parents from different socioeconomic backgrounds to foster meaningful conversation on issues that are critical to all three groups—issues such as drugs and alcohol, teen suicide, and eating disorders. I was intrigued by the prospect, both because I believed that success would have a tremendous impact on the community and because the idea of a large meeting that focused on conversation between youth and adults was something that I had never heard of being done before. In addition,

- The client wanted this to be a meeting with over one thousand participants. She wanted it to be a prototype and so successful

---

The design team members were Donna Skubis-Pearce, Chris Kingsbery, and Rick Lent. No piece on SpeakUp! would be complete without acknowledging their countless hours and dedication, as well as their tremendous contributions.

that it would become an annual event in Philadelphia and a model for other locations.

- The request for help came after a planning team had already worked for six months. As a result, there were many decisions already made, as well as great expectations.
- The time line for the planning was now three months.

Background

At the time, Martie Gillin was a sixty-three-year-old suburban upper-class grandmother and division manager for a successful limousine and chauffeur business. Ten years earlier, her oldest son, Bob, who had just turned thirty, died of AIDS. Bob had never told Martie or his father that he was gay, had AIDS, or was a drug user. A success on the outside, on the inside he was hurting. Bob spent his last healthy days educating others on AIDS awareness and prevention. His dying request was that his family continue this mission after he died.

Through personal experience, Martie had learned how critical honest conversation between youth and adults can be. She was certain that her family was not the only one grappling with the issues of open and honest conversation. She decided to act to bring youth and adults together to have tough, meaningful conversations. The vision was to speak *with*, not *to* all participants. She called the vision SpeakUp!

SpeakUp! was to facilitate effective communication and interaction among urban and suburban youth, as well as ed-ucators and parents or guardians, and encourage them to assume shared responsibility for improving the quality of life in their homes, schools, and neighborhoods through an enhanced ability to speak more honestly and forthrightly. A series of focus groups identified the issues that youth and the adults most wanted to talk about (but struggled with)—topics such as drugs and alcohol, eating disorders, spirituality, and teen suicide.

Martie had formed a planning team of donors and interested people six months prior to our involvement. Their role was to recruit within their communities and spread the word about SpeakUp! They were also to participate in the design. Some were to serve as presenters in the small group sessions.

From the planning team work, a number of design elements emerged that were considered givens:

- The meeting date was set for September 17 in a college gymnasium.
- Target audience was a large group of at least five hundred.
- Recruitment focused on recruiting - diversity in socioeconomic status, age (youth ranged from twelve to eighteen), race, gender, and

experience—urban and suburban living, public, private, and parochial schools, and a variety of neighborhood settings.

- Small discussion groups during the day would be based on people like Martie sharing their stories on a specific topic.
- The meeting was to be exciting (marching band, fireworks, and a local TV personality as emcee).

Design Challenges

Although I had reservations about the potential success of the approach, I believed in the outcomes. So I resolved to work with the givens as best I could. Some of my specific concerns were these:

- Could a one-day event really make a difference?
- Could we really pull this off in a basketball gym?
- Could the sales-meeting model, based on external excitement and the OD (Organization Development) model, based on systemic exploration and the possibility of change, coexist in harmony?
- Would it be possible to attract so many people?

Meeting Design

I formed a design team with three other OD practitioners. None of us had ever designed or facilitated a meeting of this size or style. We began by agreeing on a set of principles that would guide our design. These principles were:

- Conversation, rather than expertise and advice, would be central.
- Equal voice would be given to youth and adults—this was not about adults teaching kids what they need to know.
- Participants were to be nonjudgmental of others.

We agreed that our design had to accommodate the givens that the client required. In addition, it must be repeatable year after year without redundancy (since we were hoping this would become an annual event, and some of the same participants would return year after year).

Also we needed to create the intimacy that would be required to foster open and honest communication.

The Meeting Framework

The framework we ultimately developed consisted of three major elements: (1) an opening plenary session (about three hours), (2) small group break-out sessions (about two hours), and (3) a closing plenary session (about one hour). We agreed that in order for this to be successful year after year, each element of the framework would need an element of consistency, as well as an element of variation. The consistency would be provided by the framework of the meeting. The variation would be provided by the OD method used to structure the content of the meeting.

We chose Future Search as the underlying methodology for the first year, Appreciative Inquiry (AI) for the second year, and "Decision Making for Teens" for the third year. We did not use the strict formats from each of these methods; rather, we borrowed structures and experiences from each method to serve as a guide for each meeting.

Consistent Elements

The three sessions described next were similar in content.

Morning Plenary Session. The intent of the session was to

- Build trust among the three groups represented: youth, educators, and parents
- Acknowledge that despite the diversity, each group essentially had the same set of concerns
- Promote a feeling that "my voice matters"
- Encourage a rapport that would render participants ready for deeper listening and honest conversation

The room layout was basically the same all three years, with circle groups (eight to ten) spread throughout the gym. These circle groups engaged in a series of activities and then shared their work with the whole group.

Afternoon Break-Out Sessions. Participants pre-selected two one-hour break-out sessions. These sessions began with a presenter telling their personal story and then a facilitator supporting the rest of the group in sharing their stories, feelings, and learnings on the topic. It was agreed that the presenter would not be an expert on the subject and share just facts, but rather would tell his or her heartfelt personal story. The facilitator's role was to monitor the conversation, keep it on track, make sure everyone had a chance to speak, help participants summarize the conversation, and support a brief read-out in the closing session.

Closing Plenary Session. Participants gathered in the gym and shared their experiences and learning from the breakout groups and the day. In addition, participants made personal commitments to make change in their own lives, their school, and their community. Armed with an agreed-on design, we worked with the overall planning committee to take on the practical tasks of detailed planning, recruiting, and training, as well as logistics and meeting operations.

Year 1: Future Search–Based Design

In the first year, the design framework for the conference was based on Future Search. Attendance for this conference was over seven hundred people, including facilitators and presenters. The format of the day revolved around the concept of past, present, future, common ground, and action. In the plenary session, we explored the past with the use of time lines, the present by developing mind maps, and the future through a guided imagery experience and development of pictures of an ideal future. To some extent, we came to common ground through the development of a common list of wishes for the future, and, finally, we moved to action through individual commitments.

A Future Search typically has sixty-four participants, made up of eight groups of eight. For the morning plenary session, SpeakUp! had ten simultaneous Future Search groups of sixty-four people, each sitting in areas designated by different-colored balloons. Each group of sixty-four was made up of eight circle groups of eight participants. The circle group generally included equal numbers of youth, parents, and educators. Each of these circles was given a number from 1 to 8, designated by a numbered balloon. Each group of sixty-four had two facilitators assigned to them. In addition, each group of sixty-four had two sets of large foam-core boards posted on the walls or bleachers near them; one of the boards was for a time line and the other for a mind map. Finally, each circle group had poster boards and markers to create a vision of the future community they wanted. Some of the work was done in circle groups of eight (future vision pictures); some was done in the color groups of sixty-four (time lines and mind maps); other work was done in the whole group of seven hundred.

We began the day with introductions, and then each of the color groups developed their own time lines. Instead of the traditional three time lines (Personal, Organization, and Global), we used only two, with the Organization time line being eliminated. In their circle groups, participants made sense of either the Global or Personal time line of their color group and then shared themes in the color group of sixty-four.

The next experience was the development of mind maps by each color group, with the color group facilitators leading the process and scribing. At the center of each mind map was the topic "Trends Facing Youth-Educators-Parents Today." Still in color groups, participants were each given a strip of dots (youth were one color, parents another, and educators a third) and asked to vote for those issues that they felt were most important. Dots were counted, and a list of key issues was made by each color group. The cofacilitator of the color group copied this list onto a form. These forms were gathered by a runner and given to the audiovisual-PC person. The groups went to lunch while the PC person input the results of the color groups. After lunch, results of the major trends for the whole group of seven hundred were tallied and categorized by Youth, Educator, and Parent groupings.

Future visioning was next. Participants were asked to listen to a guided imagery led from the platform. They made notes of their experience in their workbooks. Finally, working in their circle groups of eight, each group was asked to draw a picture of the relationship they would like to create in their community between youth, educators, and parents. Next, the group created a list of three wishes that they agreed would help create this desired future. A group member was asked to write these on a form, and a runner collected and gave them to the PC input person so they could be tallied. This time the tallying was done during the afternoon and shared at the closing plenary.

The Break-Out Sessions

The break-out topics included Violence, Sex/AIDS, Eating Disorders, Drugs and Alcohol, Teen Suicide, Family Dynamics, and the Impact of the Internet. Because of the large number of participants, there were twenty-one (three each for seven topics) separate break-out groups. In each group, we attempted to balance the number of youth and adults. The break-out sessions also followed the format of past, present, and future.

The presenter shared a personal story on the topic, starting with the past, then dealing with it in the present, and finally sharing wishes for the future. Following the whole group sharing, participants were asked to answer the following questions in their workbooks:

- What are we proud of as youth/educators/parents in terms of how we deal with _____ ?
- What do we regret as youth/educators/parents in terms of how we deal with _____ ?

- What is it that you as youth/educators/parents want to do to move us closer to the wishes being reality?

Next, we had small group participants divided into peer groups, that is, students met with students, parents with parents, and educators with educators to discuss their answers to these questions. Finally, each group shared their discussion with the whole room.

The Closing Plenary

The plenary involved sharing what was discussed in the break-out groups, as well as making commitments about change. We decided that commitments would be made at the individual level, because the logistics of bringing people together from all over the Philadelphia area for post-event action was not feasible.

Reflections on Year 1

We chose Future Search as the methodological framework for the first year, because each of us had used Future Search extensively with large groups with great success. At the core of Future Search is the work toward a shared vision and common ground among people concerned about the future of a common organization or issue. We came to realize that although SpeakUp! had over seven hundred participants in the first year, this intervention was really about individual change and commitment, not about building a shared vision for Philadelphia youth, educators, and parents. Nonetheless, the time lines, mind maps, and guided imagery of an ideal future proved very useful in building toward the individual revelation and growth that we were hoping to support.

Year 2: AI-Based Design

In the second year, the design framework for the conference was AI. The attendance for this conference was the highest of the three years, with over one thousand people participating. Several groups of youth, educators, and parents or guardians met over the summer to begin the discovery process to identify themes for the conference. Hundreds of interviews were conducted and then analyzed for common and important themes. These themes included the difficult and joyous times in life, the importance of making good choices in your life, and the value of community in religion, family, neighborhood, and school.

After discussing these themes, the planning team decided all of this led to a theme for SpeakUp! Thus "The Power of One," that is, the difference one person can make for another person or a group, became the theme.

Plenary Set-Up, Requirements, and Activities

The work in the plenary session began with three groups from the summer presenting skits that were to share the essence of what they had learned through the interview process.

Then pairs interviewed each other on the following question that derived from the summer work: "Tell me a story about a time in your life when you made a difference to someone else, or someone else made a difference to you. What about this made it a joyful experience? Where were you? Who else was there? What was the result? How did you feel at the time?"

As is customary with AI, after partners shared, stories were shared in circle groups, and circle groups were asked to make notes of themes they heard. Topics were then posted on walls around the room. We then moved to the Dream phase of AI. Participants were asked to dream of how their lives would be in the future. They were told: "Put yourself in the future. If you are a student, imagine your graduation. If you are a parent or educator, imagine a community dinner in your honor. Reflect for a moment on the kinds of changes you see in your life, your family, your community, those you care about at this future date. This future has come to be through choices and efforts you have made."

The circle groups shared their individual dreams and then drew a picture that captured the essence of the dreams that were shared in the small group. These were then placed around the room on white boards. As a group, they were asked to identify "dream themes" and write these themes on a white board labeled Dream Themes.

The Break-Out Sessions

These were very similar to the first year except that they used an appreciative frame.

The Closing Plenary

The closing plenary was built around the Destiny stage of AI. We focused on participants making commitments on how they could become the most powerful person they could be. In all three years, we handed out "Connection Cards" so that youth and others could keep in touch with each other after the one-day event.

Reflections on Year 2

The greatest challenge of using AI for SpeakUp! was bringing information into the room from the summer work. The skits were not as successful as we had hoped, for two reasons: (1) it proved difficult to bring people together to write and practice the skits, and (2) the skits did not hold the attention of the people in the large room.

Another difficulty in applying AI to SpeakUp! involved time constraints. Although we had developed many questions as the result of the summer work, we only used one interview question due to the limited time available. Nonetheless, we found the interviews to be rich in content and depth. The interviews provided clear themes of what makes one person powerful. These themes included being a role model of living values, offering friendship and support during a difficult time, and standing up for a friend.

Year 3: Decision Model–Based Design

In the third year, the planning team decided to try something different. Although dialogue would still be central to the design, many members of the team wanted to teach participants something tangible that they could take away and use after the session. One of the small group facilitators from the previous year suggested that we partner with a nonprofit organization that had been offering a Decisions for Teens program for over a decade. In its full form, Decisions for Teens is a twelve-hour interactive training. Vita Education Service's five-step decision-making model formed the framework for the third year. The five steps of the model are

Step 1: See the situation clearly.

Step 2: Know what you want.

Step 3: Expand the possibilities.

Step 4: Evaluate and decide.

Step 5: Plan and act.

Attendance at this conference was around five hundred participants.

Plenary Set-Up, Requirements, and Activities

We began the day by asking the circle groups in the plenary session to discuss the following question: "What are some of the decisions that you and your friends are facing?" After the small group sharing, we did "popcorn sharing" in the large group. *Popcorn sharing* is a term we coined to refer to very quick polling of participants from around the room on a question that had been asked of the whole group. A sample of the issues identified is (1) whether to drink alcohol or not, (2) whether to be honest and share with parents certain activities, and (3) whether or not to attend parties where prohibited behavior would be going on.

We then moved into sharing scripted scenarios developed by the planning group in advance about issues that youth/educators/parents might face. We asked the small groups to work through the five-step process using the scenarios. Finally, we moved to "Making It Real" by asking partners in the small groups to answer this question: "What is a decision that you are currently facing or will be facing in the near future?" and then to use the model to help them with this decision.

The Addition of the Resource Fair

In the third year, we partnered with the United Way of Southeastern Pennsylvania to hold a Resource Fair during the lunch hour. The Resource Fair made information available on the break-out topics, and it also made volunteer opportunities available for those who were ready to make commitments. Tables representing various social service organizations were set up around the cafeteria.

The Break-Out Sessions

The break-out sessions shared the same design as the previous year. A decision was made not to ask small groups to work through the five-step process but rather to have discussions on important decisions related to the break-out topic. We left it to the discretion of the participants to apply the five steps if they chose to.

The Closing Plenary

During the closing plenary, participants were asked to make a personal commitment as a result of the day. In addition, we offered the possibility of continuing the conversation through mini-SpeakUps! in their own school or community.

Reflections on Year 3

The greatest challenge of the third year was integrating a teaching model with a facilitative model. In the end, I don't think this framework had as much life and energy as the other two. To some extent, the teaching detracted from good conversation. However, the flow from hypothetical scenarios to discussions led by participants was useful.

Outcomes and Learnings

SpeakUp! was born in 2000 and continued in 2001 and 2002; attendance varied from about five hundred to well over eight hundred people. Each year, the event was a great success and basically went off without a hitch. We got marvelous feedback from participants in all three years and wanted to continue the event for many years. After the second year, we conducted focus groups to evaluate the impact that SpeakUp! had on attendees. Major findings were that SpeakUp!

- Allowed people to see the validity in other points of view
- Was successful, as all three stakeholder groups felt heard
- Changed the perspective of parents and children of their relationship

SpeakUp! provided a rich and wonderful learning experience for all of us who were involved. Although we couldn't possibly list all our learnings, some of our major "aha's" revolved around recruitment.

Martie and the executive director of SpeakUp!, Kathy Campbell, made hundreds of calls, sent hundreds of letters, gave scores and scores of talks at schools, community centers, churches, synagogues, and other venues. In the end, their efforts paid off, but it was not without a great deal of sweat equity. Recruitment turned out to be the most time-consuming and difficult task of the project. Although the members of the planning team were successful in recruiting groups of students from their schools or other members of the community, the great majority of the participants came to SpeakUp! through the efforts of Martie and Kathy. A major hurdle was that many youth had conflicts with Saturday dates because of sports, religious holi-

days, and long holiday weekends. We considered a weekday event but were unable to negotiate school absence with the various school systems.

Recruiting educators was even more difficult than recruitment of the other two groups. As the years passed, we did offer CEU credits to teachers, and this helped.

Another lesson concerning recruitment was the participation of youth below the eighth grade. As noted, in the first year participants came from sixth grade through twelfth grade. While some sixth-graders seemed ready for the work, others were obviously bored. In the second and third years, we recruited eighth-graders and older.

In addition to the recruitment of youth, educator, and parent participants, there was also a need to recruit twenty-five small group facilitators and another fifty people who would share their stories in the break-outs. For the break-out groups, we recruited story teams consisting of at least one adult and one youth for each of the groups. Again, Martie and Kathy did the lion's share of recruitment for presenters.

The OD design team recruited volunteer facilitators from the Future Search and AI listservs. All these people were generous with their time and talent.

Facilitator and Presenter Training

In the first year, to ensure understanding of intent and consistency in style, we held half-day training for facilitators and presenters a few weeks before SpeakUp!

In the later years, since we had many repeat facilitators, we conducted the training the Friday night before the event. We developed two separate training manuals, one for facilitators and one for presenters. In addition, the training itself consisted of two parts: (1) Part One, in which both facilitators and presenters were provided with an overview of SpeakUp!—a focus on the goals, objects, principles, and logistics, and (2) Part Two, which was customized for each group, depending on their role. (Facilitator and presenter handbooks are available at www.InsytePartners.com.)

Focus on the Individual

One of the greatest learnings was that although there were as many as eight hundred participants at the meeting, the intervention was really about individual learning, change, and growth—not system change. Large numbers do not a system make. When we began, we thought that we could create a SpeakUp! community that would ultimately take action together. We thought hard about how we could form action teams that would cross geographic and age boundaries, but in the end realized that the real action would take place with individuals making commitments to themselves and their communities.

Logistics

The logistics were overwhelming and a very practical element of success. We learned that you cannot do too much advance planning when a large group like this is involved. We made floor maps, detailed time lines, assigned different roles to various members of the design team as well as the planning team, hired a meeting planner, and had a client who was very organized. All this led to success!

All three years we worked closely with a meeting-planning firm—Lead Dog—to make sure things ran smoothly. The planning firm took care of registration, name tags, sound, audiovisuals, and room setup, including color-coded numbered balloons; they assigned participants to color-circle groups, as well as to break-out rooms.

Sound in the gym proved to be a great challenge. For example, we found in the first year that when everyone moved their chairs simultaneously in the gym, the noise was deafening. So in the second and third years, we rented carpets to cover most of the gym floor. Other things we did to help with the noise included hanging flags, which baffled the noise. In addition, we altered the design to lessen the noise level. In the first year we worked at three levels: (1) circle groups of eight, (2) color groups of sixty-four (eight circle groups), and (3) the whole room. In Years 2 and 3, we eliminated the color groups of sixty-four because this eliminated the need for small group facilitators and the tremendous noise level their simultaneous facilitation created.

The layout of the room (circle groups of chairs around the room) remained basically the same all three years. However, the position of the lead facilitators changed. In the first year, facilitators worked from a stage at the front of the gym. In the second year, the stage was moved to the side of the gym to increase visibility to participants. Finally, in the third year, the room became "in the round," with a small platform in the center of the gym and all the circle groups around it. At the four corners of the platform were standing microphones, and a quadrant facilitator was stationed at each of the four microphones.

Another learning concerning logistics was the length of day. The first year, the day went from 8:00 A.M. (registration) to 5:00 P.M., with a dance party following. This was too long, and no one stayed for the party. In the next two years, we shortened the day by ending at 3:00 P.M. This was basically because most students are accustomed to a nine-to-three day.

We also had to grapple with how much technology we really needed. We experimented with using PCs, runners, and large screens to share with the whole group the data that were gathered in small groups. This included the key trends of the mind maps and the wishes generated as part of the future vision. To do this required a great deal of behind-the-scenes work. The effort did not justify the results. People seemed to gain what they needed with the small group sharing in the plenary. We discontinued displaying data in the later years.

A final learning concerned the physical distance between the plenary area and the break-out session rooms. Be-

cause the gym building did not have small break-out rooms, we chose to work in two buildings. Even though they were just a two-minute walk apart, we lost people coming back from the break-outs. A facility that can hold both kinds of meetings in the same building is highly important.

Working with Youth

First and foremost, we were continuously impressed by the insight, energy, and honesty that youth brought to the process. Although we did involve youth as small group presenters, we believe that we could and should have trained youth to serve as small group facilitators as well. This would be yet another way to empower youth and develop capacity.

One of the greatest difficulties for us in working with youth on the design team was finding a balance between honoring the youth voice and honoring our own expertise and professional background. How can we best incorporate the work of the professional OD design team with the inclusion of ideas from youth? We were so careful to respect and incorporate the ideas of the youth we worked with that sometimes we may have stretched outside our comfort area to accommodate their requests.

A final element, in terms of working with youth, was more a confirmation of what we already knew than an actual learning. Excitement for youth and others came from within the conversations, not from external factors such as the fireworks and bands. By the third year, we had eliminated all entertainment except for performances by local youth groups, for example an African American jazz combo.

How SpeakUp! Lives On

While SpeakUp! as a large group meeting did not continue because of a lack of funding, all of us viewed the project as a wonderful success. Martie continues to offer mini-SpeakUps! at schools around the area. People often approach us and ask when and if we are going to resurrect SpeakUp! The SpeakUp! team is currently working to attain funding to create a package available via the Web that would provide detailed designs, instructions, and scripts to hold a similar event in other cities.

BUILDING COALITIONS TO CREATE A COMMUNITY PLANNING TOOL IN ISRAEL

Tova Averbuch

The Challenge

The client was seeking to build partnerships and coalitions with the purpose of creating a structured planning tool that would enable planners and communities to integrate social and community aspects into the process of physical planning in Israel.

Background

Israel is a very densely populated country, with little undeveloped land, and is characterized by a rapidly growing and diverse population. This combination of factors generates tremendous pressure to build and develop in immediate response to emerging needs, on an ad hoc basis, with no master plan and no time or attention for systematic or integrated broad-scope views of social and community considerations.

I am grateful to all steering committee members and OST event participants. Special thanks to the following people for their participation in the development of this case (in alphabetical order): Shai Ben-Yossef, Arza Churchman, Avner Haramati, Peggy Holman, Dalia Lev-Sadeh, Harrison Owen, Mali Reif, Ora Setter, and the Zippori center in Jerusalem.

In 1999, the Knesset (Israel's Parliament) approved a "master plan for building and development." Around the same time there was a stirring of public awareness and increasing civic involvement in regard to these issues coupled with a growing demand for community participation in decision-making processes in areas that directly affect people's lives. The initiative described in this case was one of the first and most revolutionary in terms of public participation and deep democracy—a swallow foretelling the spring.

From Initiative to Steering Committee

The initiative for integrating social and community aspects into physical planning processes came from four sources: (1) government, (2) NGO, (3) a public agency, and (4) academia. Initiative from the government came in the person of Dalia Lev-Sadeh, then director of the Community Work Department in the Ministry of Labor and Welfare. She was joined by members of an NGO who had expertise in creating coalitions between government and civic groups in Israel. These two invited and were joined by a public agency who specializes in community work and participatory democracy; from academia the initiative was supported by Prop Arza Churchman, then the head of a research center for urban and regional studies based at the Technion in Haifa.

This partnership served as a sustainable base for the initiative. The initiating individuals (and a few others) created a spirit of engagement in the project and developed strong personal bonds. The four organizations together created a long-term commitment, generated power and resources, and created the legitimacy and stature that were needed to invite others to join a nationwide, multidisciplinary initiative and project. As a formal step, the partners created a steering committee, making sure that it was made up of diverse stakeholders and, in keeping with that spirit, continually inviting more and different partners to join in.

The Steering Committee Chooses Its Path

Initiating members of the steering committee had a compelling desire to make a difference in the field of physical planning but at the start had no clear vision of how to go about doing it. As all the members were committed to the idea of a partnership, they decided that two key features would characterize their way of being and working together: (1) the steering committee would be composed of all the main stakeholders, and (2) the resulting document would be written collectively.

Another important choice made by the steering committee was to focus on one project: to create a "social and community impact assessment" document that would be a practical tool for physical planners. The choice to focus on creating a tool rather than focus on a specific content was a key factor. Preparing a tool, as well as using a planning tool together, enables people holding opposing positions to join together in the process of exploring and crafting new domains and often keeps them from fighting over details.

As the committee looked for a suitable methodology for the launching stage of the project, Shai Ben-Yossef, one of the initiators, called and asked me to introduce Open Space Technology (OST) as a possible approach. By that time I was already a seasoned organizational development (OD) consultant and an Open Space specialist, but I had never before used OST to work with a multiparty, cross-organizational project that would be open for public participation.

At the first meeting of the steering committee, as I listened carefully to the dreams of the people there and to the challenges they were facing, I realized that OST would definitely be their best choice for the preparatory and launching stage. As most of them were not familiar with OST, I gave a short presentation, but knowing that this method is about making and enabling choices, I suggested that we have a mini-OST so that they could experience this process.

From the beginning, the preconditions for using OST were clearly in evidence: real concern, complexity, conflicting and opposing forces, rich diversity, and urgency (the implementation time was yesterday). Yet the need to make a choice was there as well. The mini-OST meeting, which was dedicated to clarifying the various roles and tasks of the committee as a preparatory team for a large group gathering, served to give the committee members a clear understanding of what opening space for real and vital issues entails. This shared experience enabled the committee to make an informed and conscious choice as to whether and when to use OST in the process.

The steering committee's goals at that time were to:

- Generate legitimacy, as well as practical ideas for the formulation of a comprehensive guiding tool for planners
- Build momentum and energy around this issue, and, more implicitly, to experiment with the large group gathering in OST as an example of a participatory method for potential use in large diverse groups in Israel

The nature of OST, as reflected in the four principles and the law of two feet, which communicate some of the norms for participating in Open Space, is a perfect match for these goals. They create a space conducive to the inclusion of differing and diverse opinions. The equality manifested by people sitting side-by-side in a large circle and the transparency of a real-time agenda and real-time proceedings that are open to everyone invite trust and personal responsibility; thus they tend to promote

the creation of alliances and partnerships. The four principles, by putting
aside shame and blame, unleash blocked
energies, promote playful participation,
and give way to new and practical ideas.
All these elements together generate
more than enough energy to fuel a
launching event—a lift-off.

Pre-Work with and by the Steering Committee

For the preparatory work the committee
met every four to six weeks, for about
five hours at a time, over a period of six
months. I attended about half of these
meetings in my role as an OST expert.
The meetings were full of life and good
humor, yet the work was done very seriously. The preparatory steps dealt with
three key areas:

1. A careful and intentional process of
   invitation and marketing efforts to
   major players in the field, to people
   who care about physical planning in
   Israel, and to the community at large
2. Site requirements and logistical ongoing preparations suitable for OST event
3. Trying to "be the change we want to
   bring," we let OST principles govern
   our decision-making process. Decisions about invitations, fees, registration procedures, and so forth, were
   made in the spirit of Open Space.

As a manifestation of OST principles,
the client group grew from four to eleven
sponsoring organizations, embracing
more and more diversity and consciously
appreciating and finding joy in conversing
with people with different perspectives.

The Launch

Interest continued to grow. A week before the planned convention, we had an
enrollment of 180 people. It was a bitter-
sweet feeling, making us think: "Wait, we
don't have room for that many people."
The steering committee made a decision
reflecting their trust and commitment to
opening more and more space: "We bar
no one. Whoever really wants to be at
the gathering will be invited in. We'll
manage somehow."

On February 20, 2002, while the al-
mond trees were still in full bloom over
the mountains of Jerusalem, the stage
was set for an OST launching event.
Eleven sponsoring entities (government
ministries, NGOs, community agencies,
activist groups, and a variety of local and
national public and professional organizations) took part. A two-day OST gathering convened in a beautiful and
peaceful setting at the Zippori Center in
the Jerusalem Forest. The theme was "Integrating Social and Community Aspects
into Physical Planning: What Should We
Do to Make a Difference?"

On the day before the convention,
inquiries were still coming in. By the end
of the day, 210 people were registered.
In Israel that could mean that any number from 180 to 250 people would show
up. What should we do and how shall
we manage bounty? We took a deep

breath and decided that: This was very good news; there would be a future; the future would be good! After we squeezed three concentric circles into an oval room with a low ceiling, the space was shaped like a long hot dog, but we got everyone in.

Most of the last evening before the actual gathering was spent by steering committee members in connecting and creating a pleasant, welcoming ambience in every way we could think of, from installing a ramp for the one wheelchair-bound person who registered to introducing and briefing the people from cleaning, maintenance, the hotel, and the photographers, who all became peers in the same production. The feeling was similar to what one might experience at the opening of a carnival or while anticipating a large family gathering.

On the first day people began flocking to the Jerusalem Forest at around 8:30 A.M. Within an hour the parking lot was full, and the joy and excitement were overflowing. Around 10:00 A.M., nearly all the seats were taken by what proved to be a rich diversity of people, including "major league players" in the planning field. More than two hundred individuals who cared about the physical planning process in Israel had turned up: urban planners, architects, social and community workers, strategic unit managers of municipalities and communities, neighborhood activists, representatives of three government ministries (Labor and Welfare, Interior, and Environment), four government departments, and

many kinds of NGOs. It was a very experienced and diversified crowd: men and women varying in age, place of residence, profession, education, life experience, and perspective; Jews and Arabs, religious and secular. In all likelihood, most of the people attending had never shared a conversation before and had never conversed as equals.

Dalia Lev-Shadeh, the chairwoman of the steering committee, opened the event with a warm welcome, presented some background and history, and talked about the committee's intentions regarding future development and expansion of the initiative. She finished with, "Be prepared to be surprised," and passed the microphone to me. I also welcomed people to the OST, acknowledging the richness of the group, and drew attention to the two thousand years of planning experience that was present in that room for a two-day interaction—a truly revolutionary potential.

At the opening of the OST proper, the response was lively. About ten people actually jumped into the center of the circle and hurriedly grabbed paper and a marker to create their themes. Within three minutes, there was a line of twenty people waiting for the microphone to announce their issue of interest, and fifteen minutes later the community bulletin board listed some fifty issues, spread over four sessions and seventeen different break-out spaces. There was a bustling, vital atmosphere in the huge "marketplace," and groups convened.

Different issues were discussed in depth:

- Public participation in planning processes
- Trains and changes in commuting habits
- The Israeli seashore as a public asset
- What to include in a social and community impact assessment guiding document for physical planning
- Special planning needs for senior citizens, women, and youth and their involvement in decision making
- Issues unique to Arab society or the rural sector
- Planning flaws in burying pollutants in populated areas as causes of mass poisoning

We added a five-minute "noon news" gathering of the whole to allow new issues to be announced and posted on the community bulletin board. Since we only had one day of conversations before integration into action, the "noon news" helped us to go deeper into the issues.

At around 5 P.M., I noticed that people were beginning to leave at an increasing rate. Some of the participants approached me, suggesting, "When it's over, it's over." I thought perhaps it *was* time to close, but just as I was about to do so, I decided to get my own personal impression first. Taking a short trip around the premises, I was astounded to find four large groups (of about twenty people each) and two small ones (of about seven people) deeply involved in serious discussions; some fifteen people were walking around and talking or writing up the proceedings of concluded

meetings. We continued as planned. About a hundred people attended the concluding "evening news" plenary—totally committed, satisfied, hungry, and tired. We collected the main experiences of the day from all those who wished to speak, informed the group about administrative and logistical issues, and invited everyone to come to the steering committee planning meeting later that evening. The first-day plenary was over.

After dinner, members of the steering committee, joined by seven other participants, set out to fine-tune the planning for the next day. We read all the material created by the various groups, developed subject-matter clusters, and made our choices as to how the day would flow. After midnight our work was done for the day, but the sounds of Zippori Center staff producing copies of the proceedings continued until dawn.

The second day was dedicated to translating the energy and the rich dialogue of the preceding day into an operative plan. In the center of the room, covered with a flowered cloth, lay 120 books that had been produced during the night. Following an unveiling ceremony, everybody started reading. Once the reading was done, we moved on to a presentation of the subject clustering that had been done by the volunteers of the previous night's meeting as an offering to the collective. At the plenary, during the next two hours, all the participants reviewed the work, validating and improving it in one big circle. We were 150 people, keeping track together: "Does subject X belong to subject cluster A or to cluster B?" This phase is not an easy one because implementation work requires a greater degree of precision than conversation. Sensing that *this* is the point at which people may give up on the tedious work of co-creating and of keeping the space open, I turned to the group and asked each and every participant in that plenary to please join me in trying to create a minimal emerging order to help us wade through. By the time we were done, each subject cluster had become an implementation team composed of people who had *selected themselves,* either for championing the team and/or for participating in it.

The "closing circle" allowed every team leader to briefly describe the steps they would follow, and then I invited everyone who cared to share to do so. People shared their insights, conclusions, and gratitude for the opportunity to be part of this process.

What Happened

Following is a chronological review of three years after the launching event (2002–2005):

February–March 2002. A comprehensive literature review of the world's best practices for integrating social and community aspects into physical planning processes was conducted, parallel and right after the OST process. This survey was used as input in the tool-creation process and provided access to a systematic, worldwide body of knowledge as a complement to the local knowledge generated by people who shared (at the launching OST event) personal experience, passion, and responsibility in the field, both paving the way for integration.

February 2002. An initial book of proceedings was produced, which included all conversations that took place during the OST gathering and contact information for all the participants. This book was handed out on the second morning of the launch to all who were present at that moment.

March 2002. A second book of proceedings was issued, which included the entire first book of proceedings after incorporation of the addenda and errata and all the implementation team summaries. It was sent to every participant, made available on the Web, and served as the base for the next product: "The Organizing Document" (an interim document in the making of "The Social and Community Impact Assessment Document").

April 2002. Six weeks after the launch, the steering committee held a meeting to summarize and reflect on the OST process and chart its future course. At this get-together, people indicated that their goals and expectations had been met very successfully and there was joy and satisfaction with the event. Mali Reif, one of the four initiators, expressed her satisfaction:

> We were very pleased with the number and rich variety of people

that showed up. This process drew the attention of people in the field, marked their consciousness . . . and, gave us a lot of issues and ideas for the creation of "a social and community impact assessment" tool.

The committee decided to focus its effort on document creation. Committee members were supported in this process by a few experts and by participants from the OST launch event who volunteered to be "readers" throughout the process of writing.

Looking Back Three Years Later

As my contract was only for the preparatory work and the OST launching event, I had no formal relationship with the project after April 2002. When I was asked to share my experience using Large Group Methods for this chapter, I went back to the people involved to find out what has happened during these last three years and what is happening now. To gain perspective I interviewed thirteen people (in April and May of 2005): five of the steering committee members (all of the initiating organizations included) and eight participants. Six out of these eight participants had formed conversation groups during the two-day OST event in Zippori, and half of them were leading implementation groups on the second day. Half of the interviews were conducted over the phone, and half were face-to-

face. I report what I drew from these interviews in the following section.

February 2002–Onward: The Ripple Effect

The Open Space Technology gathering event at the Zippori Center in 2002 marked the beginning of the pervasive use of OST in the municipal sector in Israel. The year 2002 saw seven OST gatherings dedicated to creating partnerships and involving the public over various municipal and regional strategic issues. The number of events is still growing, and each event seems to be larger in scope, diversity, or number of participants than the one before. The OST gathering in Zippori also made a difference in the field of planning in Israel that same year by effecting the actual integration of social and community aspects into municipal strategic planning through direct and extensive public participation.

At least twelve of the OST events that took place in different regions and communities in Israel in 2002 and in subsequent years were joint projects of the Zippori OST launching-event participants! These individuals joined together, two to four at a time, supporting and empowering one another in co-production, advice, or facilitation of OST gatherings on behalf of one another. The occurrence of so many OST gatherings in the municipal planning field in such a short period of time is quite a remarkable phenomenon, as the participatory methods used in Israel until early 2002 were highly structured, and none employed *large* gatherings that invited the participating public to actually *partner in leading* with the organizers and in taking the co-created desired change together into the future.

How was that possible? Apparently, the new awareness and the perceived need to find avenues for genuine public involvement were growing trends in the country when the 2002 gathering created a new model for participation. It was clear, for the first time in Israel, that vast public participation is a real option and can genuinely be implemented and used. Hanna Heiman-Pessach, a participant who became a sponsor and facilitator of future OST gatherings, expressed it very poignantly: "The OST in Zippori made it clear that it is possible. This was the final thing that I needed, a feasibility study, a full proof of quality that had gained my trust and confidence. All that was left was to run and do it." This diffusion of Open Space is still going on.

2005–The Tool Making Is Complete

The final draft of a detailed, consensual, and comprehensive guiding tool for physical planners—"The Social and Community Impact Assessment Document"—was ready and open to public scrutiny in early 2005. Committee members are creating opportunities for professional feedback, public hearings, and mail comments regarding the final draft, and are revising and improving it as prepara-

tion for implementation by planners. The desired next step is that physical planners will use this document as part of their planning routine.

Along with achieving the primary challenge, the committee had two additional achievements. First, the coalitions and partnerships among organizations and individuals are strong and active. Committee members of all organizations meet and work together, even though quite a few of the initiators have moved to different organizations and different positions. Second—and on the personal level—there is a vivid memory of an empowering experience. The people I interviewed responded willingly and had spontaneous and lively memories.

Why did it take almost three years to produce the document? The steering committee people I asked indicated that writing the document was like a weaving process, that is, weaving local knowledge (as revealed in the OST event) and the world's state-of-the-art knowledge (as reviewed in the literature on planning), and weaving all different points of view and crafting it carefully, like a wordsmith who is creating a nationwide, comprehensive legal process. They took responsibility for precision and comprehensiveness while operating in a culture of inclusion of many diverse partners, respecting differences, and using consensual decision-making processes. All this took time, yet laid the foundation for a structured and possibly legislated countrywide process of integrating social and community needs into physical planning.

What Did I Learn?

First, I reflect on Open Space Technology as a method.

• *Assessing a large group event three years later is an unfolding mystery.* While looking back on this work from a three-year perspective, I have a simple yet strong realization that a large group event is always an unfolding mystery. Yes, the event is over. We are satisfied (or not), and we finish the work and part, yet we can never know or foretell the actual contribution and effect of this single event. The large group event serves as a potent amplifier and the "self-organizing" aspect keeps the ripples going long after the event itself is over. It is both disturbing and rewarding to realize that if not for my work on this chapter, I am not sure when or if I would have noticed the ripple effect that the February 2002 OST experience had on opening the Israeli municipal sphere to the use of Open Space Technology as a methodology that enables and promotes shared leadership and co-creation among people and sectors in our society.

• *There is a simple magic in very different people conversing as equals and self-organizing.* While still in Zippori in February 2002, I was touched by how precious it is to have diverse, opposing, very different people meet to converse as equals—so simple and so powerfully revolutionary, as Shai Ben-Yossef illustrated beautifully three years later:

The most revolutionary moment for me in Zippori was watching a

woman, whom I had never seen before, stand up in the plenary and speak in her clear voice, everybody listening carefully to her wisdom. When she was finished I asked someone next to me: "Tell me, who is this lady?" The answer was: "She is the secretary of the Carmel market [a fresh-food open-air market] in Tel Aviv."

By inviting everyone who cared to come to the launch, two simple but very uncommon things took place: the first was to have this diversity in the room; the second was trusting that they would know how to work together (self-organization). Usually, it is groups of the same profession who meet, and most of the time they are told what to do. It was a breakthrough in Israel in 2002 to have diverse professions and roles in the same room talking eye-to-eye and heart-to-heart. Participants took time to self-organize, rather than being overly structured, and managed with an agenda and a time table imposed by the organizers. In a rich, diversified, and transparent milieu, it is easy for anyone to initiate, to listen, to find allies, to form partnerships, and to join others in making headway together.

• *Pre-work is the real work of space opening.* This was a profound realization while working with the steering committee. We were using every minute of our working time together as an opportunity to experiment and explore living and doing in open space. Letting the four principles and the law of two feet govern and be reflected in everything we were trying to do generated a space for playful inquiry and experimentation. Inviting and including partners with diverse and opposing opinions created a real open space for the steering committee and served to open space for all the rest to join in the launch event.

While reflecting on the challenges of doing the pre-work, the most challenging aspect I recall was the fact that different people showed up at every committee meeting! Under the typical paradigm of what is considered a "productive way of functioning," that was preposterous, but under the OST paradigm and its set of governing principles, whoever came and whenever they showed up was perfectly all right. This was tough at times, both for me and for some of the committee members, but we were all joking and wading through it together. Eventually, I came to think of the steering committee as akin to a riverbed: same river, different waters (members) every month, streaming along in a self-organizing process supported minimally by the ground-project management. This *modus operandi* seems to be the best preparatory training for "trusting the process" of OST before falling into the real "big waters" of a multi-organizational OST gathering open to public participation. In an odd and interesting way, this "riverbed" concept also became a marketing effort: more people bought into it, talked about it, felt part of it, and were witnesses to our ongoing and genuine attempt to practice what we preach.

One last note about OST: in Zippori I recognized the strength of OST as a way of moving people and organizations from care to dare, from concern to action, from "community of care" (that shares passionate concern and interest over the same issue) to "community of practice" (that self-organizes to materialize a joint initiative).

Now, I will conclude by sharing some practical wisdom about creating partnerships and coalitions that I acquired while consulting, reflecting, and writing. Here are eight bits of advice about steps to take while attempting to build partnerships and coalitions:

1. *Make at least one real partner.* This creates an energy field—a potential space—for the emergence of new creation.
2. *Make a coalition composed of organizations and individuals, not a coalition of individuals or of organizations only.* Organizations are essential because they bring qualities such as continuity, steady energy (time and money allocation), clarity of interest, balance, and power in representation. These are very important in long-term processes, where people change positions and too much energy is required from individuals. *Individuals* are essential because they bring passion, free spirit, and their unique abilities and attributes.
3. *A good start for a wide coalition is a diverse partnership of government, NGO, public agency, and academia.*

This base creates a balanced whole that is "top down" (government) and "bottom up" (public agency), anchored by professional orientation (NGO) and a spirit of inquiry (academics) and thus compatible with and able to accommodate the inclusion of many more.

4. *Define a wide enough issue so that everyone can step in and belong if they so choose.* The issue should be wide enough to really invite and embrace a rich variety of opposing and conflicting partners who share passion and interest in the same subject.

5. *Find and engage in a real, specific, and concrete initiative to pursue together.* This keeps the focus and directs the energy in a productive direction.

6. *Support the initiative by adequate resource allocation.* There needs to be enough time and money dedicated to the building and maintaining of the infrastructure to support the self-organizing process. This is even truer in high-conflict situations.

7. *Create a steering committee or preparatory team (as a microcosm) and work with them in open space.* Practice makes perfect. Allow at least six weeks for this preparatory work, preferably several months.

8. *Prepare for an energy blast.* People who share passions seem to generate an abundance of energy when put together in the same time and space, voluntarily self-organizing. If you want to make use of these energies, prepare for "the day after" the OST event by having threads, webs, and infrastructures to assist in keeping it up and emerging.

References

Bunker, B. B., & Alban B. T. (1997). *Large group interventions*. San Francisco: Jossey-Bass.

Holman P., & Devane T. (Eds.). (1999). *The change handbook*. San Francisco: Berrett-Koehler.

Owen, H. (1997). *Open Space Technology guide book*. San Francisco: Berrett-Koehler.

Owen, H. (2000). *The power of spirit*. San Francisco: Berrett-Koehler.

Owen, H. (2004). *The practice of peace*. Circle Pines, MN: Human System Dynamics Institute.

Zippori Center, Jerusalem. Web site: www.zippori.org.il/SIA/index.html.

TAKING DEMOCRACY TO A REGIONAL SCALE IN HAMILTON COUNTY

Steven Brigham

The Challenge

The importance of regional planning has grown in recent years, as more and more communities realize that the issues they confront cut across jurisdictional boundaries. Its importance has increased further, as the federal government shifts more responsibility for services locally, and states and cities have encountered difficult challenges in tackling these new responsibilities without the necessary resources.

In counties and regions with older urban centers, much of regional planning centers on how to address the shortcomings of aging cities and how to engender responsibility in the surrounding suburbs to pay more for regional services, for example, transit and housing assistance and amenities such as stadiums, the symphony, and zoo, that are concentrated in urban centers. Regional planning also focuses on the potential efficiencies of having integrated strategies for economic development, land use planning (particularly "smart growth"), and public transportation—without displacing other functions and powers of local government. Even where the need for collaboration seems painfully obvious, it can be very difficult for jurisdictions to either give up control over functions they have traditionally performed or to expand their thinking beyond their own well-defined and politically critical borders.

Finally, regional planners must figure out how to deal with the citizenry effectively so that the plans garner genuine public support. Some regional efforts do well in engaging citizens in substantive ways but fail to engage large numbers in this way. Other regional efforts do well in interacting with large numbers of citizens but with most of them only in relatively superficial ways. Few surmount the challenge of engaging a significant number of citizens in the development of a vision and plan across a county or region in meaningful and substantive ways.

Hamilton County, Ohio: The Community COMPASS Process and the Planning Partnership

Hamilton County is a medium-sized county situated in the southwestern corner of Ohio, with Cincinnati serving as its urban hub on the Ohio River. Within the county are forty-nine municipalities, including twenty-one cities and sixteen villages and twelve townships. The larger Cincinnati metropolitan area includes counties in three states—Ohio and Indiana and across the river in Kentucky. The factors driving toward more effective regional planning nationally mirror what is happening in the county locally. Michael Gallis, noted planning consultant, has explained that the county's "weakness is in its fragmentation."[1]

To underscore this fragmentation, the county has over six hundred planning and zoning commissioners, twenty-two school districts, and sixteen special countywide districts, all of which contribute to a substantial lack of coordination, making any notion of a collective vision impossible. The county has experienced a population loss of more than eighty thousand people over the last three decades. Cincinnati, like many northern industrial cities, has experienced decline that extends to its inner ring of suburbs. This decline can be attributed to many factors, including the exodus of a younger workforce, an aging population, deteriorating housing stock, loss of jobs, a waning tax base, and intra-metropolitan competition among the forty-nine separate economies. Given these changes, it had become critical that a ground-breaking approach to planning in the county be found.

The Hamilton County Regional Planning Commission introduced the planning process—Community COMPASS—in 2000 as its first comprehensive plan effort in more than thirty-five years. For the uninitiated, comprehensive plans traditionally attempt to guide the long-term physical development of a particular area. More recently, in professional planning circles these plans are striving for a more integrated look at the long-term physical, economic, and social needs of a community. The planning commission wanted to avoid developing ideal concepts and instead create a plan that would directly, positively affect the way people live and work.

According to planning authors Mourad and Ways,

> Most regional solutions rely primarily on voluntary efforts, cooperative arrangements, and mediated agreements. Regional decision making complements, and does not replace, municipal and state governments by providing a mechanism for addressing cross-cutting issues that cannot be sponsored by one government body alone.[2]

A planning commission, then, can be a catalyst for cooperative planning and intergovernmental coordination, but implementation is still largely dependent on endorsement and voluntary cooperation of local governments.

Ron Miller, executive director of the planning commission, inaugurated a collaborative initiative dubbed the "Planning Partnership," which shepherded the county through a strategic and painstaking process that ultimately resulted in unanimous consent for a unified vision by the many collaborating governments and planning commissions within the county. Establishing the Planning Partnership prior to the visioning and planning process enabled ownership of the plan by local jurisdictions, as well as civic and private sector partners. This framework for community engagement and ownership ensured sustainability for long-term implementation of the county's collective vision.

The Planning Partnership, with nearly eighty members in all, served as the advisory board for the long-range, comprehensive approach to planning that the county had chosen. It brought together public (including most of the jurisdictions), private (for example, Procter & Gamble, University of Cincinnati, AFL-CIO, the Homebuilders Association, and the African-American Chamber of Commerce), and civic sector (for example, United Way, League of Women Voters, Urban League, Sierra Club, Leadership Cincinnati) organizations, all of which were engaged in community planning.

The Community COMPASS planning effort officially started in November 2000, when the commission sent a mail survey on community values to 4,500 county residents. The survey (1,158 respondents), designed to gauge the public's opinion on development and a range of other county issues, provided key insights about why many people were considering moving out of the county to find new housing, the degree of concern about poorly performing public schools, and the desire for far more cooperation among jurisdictions on development issues.

Citizen Engagement

The launching of the Planning Partnership and the survey and research activities all set the stage for the citizen engagement work that began in the fall of 2001 and continued intensively for nearly a year. This is where America-*Speaks* first entered the picture.

The planning commission built in an expectation of extensive public participation from the outset, viewing it as a key component of the ultimate viability of the plan. They developed three participation goals:

1. Reach out to all residents of Hamilton County for their participation in the plan.
2. Create a level playing field so all participants have an equal opportunity to express their desires regarding the development of the plan.
3. Involve all participants in a problem-solving instead of position-taking approach to reach "win-win" situations.

The commission hired two organizations to develop and implement the vi-

sioning segment of the citizen engagement: (1) ACP Visioning and Planning, Ltd. (a Columbus, Ohio–based firm that provides comprehensive planning, strategic planning, urban design, and public involvement services) and (2) America*Speaks* (a national nonprofit specializing in large-scale citizen engagement processes). This was a unique partnership among the planning commission and the two firms, and significant time was spent in the late spring and early summer forging effective working relationships. The commission asked ACP and America*Speaks* to work together with their core staff to create a six-month, integrated visioning process that would effectively combine the methods of both firms. Together the two organizations developed a series of distributed, decentralized forums (to be run by ACP) to be held throughout the county to gather ideas, culminating in a large-scale, high-tech, centralized forum— what America*Speaks* calls the 21st Century Town Meeting to synthesize and develop agreement around the most central ideas.

The First Step: Idea Gathering Forums

ACP worked with a core group of Planning Partnership members (and with America*Speaks* in an advisory capacity) to organize and host eleven community forums, which were dispersed geographically around the county, during three weeks in October; these forums involved more than 400 participants, and a countywide youth forum held in Cincinnati attracted 175 young people.

In these meetings, christened "Idea Gathering Forums," citizens were placed into smaller groups of ten to twelve around a series of flip charts to gather ideas and issues concerning their desired future for Hamilton County.

More than 2,800 ideas were collected at these twelve forums and in a multiweek online idea-gathering forum involving nearly two hundred people. Ideas included improving schools, providing more accessibility for seniors and the disabled, creating more bike paths, improving downtown, creating alternative transport options, and changing the current governance structure. America-*Speaks* attended many of these meetings to hear how citizens were discussing their ideas and articulating key issues.

During the time these forums were occurring, America*Speaks* worked with the regional planning commission staff to develop plans and staffing assignments for participant recruitment, preregistration, public relations, facilitator and volunteer recruitment, logistics, and vendor contracting for the larger, countywide town meeting. All these tasks require intensive staff (and consultant) time and extensive staff coordination to effectively prepare for a town meeting. For example, planning for logistics includes finding and contracting for the right-sized site, selecting and coordinating with a top-notch audiovisual firm, arranging catering for breakfast and lunch meals, lining up professionals for language translation, arranging for security,

coat check, signs, and banners, renting equipment, and recruiting day-of volunteers.

The task of recruiting participants and volunteer facilitators was eased somewhat in Hamilton County, as they could recruit directly from the idea-gathering forums (about 25 percent of both facilitators and participants were recruited this way).

Compiling the Regional Goals: The "Goal-Writing Workshop"

In mid-November 2001, the Planning Partnership used the nearly three thousand ideas from these forums and organized them into twelve goal categories for the county during a day-long Goal-Writing Workshop. These categories are traditionally found in most comprehensive plans and include topics like housing, natural resources, economic development, and education. Teams identified common themes, linkages, tradeoffs, and obstacles within the twelve goals. ACP led this workshop, and America*Speaks* participated.

Preparing the Vision for the Countywide Town Meeting

At the end of this workshop, America-*Speaks* had concern about the utility of grappling with such a large number of goals (twelve) in the context of a one-day, thousand-person meeting. From previous experience, we knew it would be too unwieldy to tackle all twelve individually in a seven-hour meeting. What would be critical, then, would be to find a way to articulate these goals into a more integrated framework around a smaller set of what the commission came to call "core goals."

Members of the Planning Partnership, key commission staff, ACP, and America*Speaks* worked for a full day to develop the four core goals—ensuring economic prosperity, balancing development and environment, embracing diversity and equity, and building collaborative decision making—that fully honored the twelve planning goals. Over the next several weeks, as we developed the Participant Guide (background materials that inform the town meeting discussions), the context and language of the four core goals continued to be refined. What emerged as descriptions for the four goals is as follows:

• *Ensuring economic prosperity:* a twenty-four-hour downtown Cincinnati where people can live, work, and play; a strong cluster of diverse attractions in arts, culture, sports, and entertainment; a globally competitive and diversified economy that supports entrepreneurial activities and emerging industries; and attraction and retention of business and industries that provide good-paying jobs.

• *Balancing development and the environment:* preserving and managing natural resources to enhance the unique character of the county; balancing investment and reinvestment around the county, using existing infrastructure to reduce costs; an economical and efficient transportation system; and well-planned, controlled growth that limits sprawl, preserves open space, and fosters neighborhood-focused development and revitalization.

• *Embracing diversity and equity:* clean, safe, integrated communities; high-quality equitable educational opportunities in safe learning environments; affordable housing with a mix of residential choices that provides home ownership and rental opportunities across all economic levels; a high quality of life for all residents, with improved facilities and health and community services; and a multimodal transportation system that enables access by a diverse population.

• *Building collaborative decision making:* effective and efficient government that works cooperatively across political boundaries; effective collaboration between citizens and across all sectors for developing strategies for guiding the future of the county; public input processes that lead to improved public decision making; and a strong sense of community that encourages volunteerism and full utilization of the county's social capital.

These goals served as the backbone of the vision statement proposed at the Countywide Town Meeting, run by America*Speaks,* on January 12, 2002, where the statement was debated and revised, as well as the backbone for the final vision endorsed by the full Planning Partnership more than a year later. In

2005, the four goals provided the essential structure for four implementation campaigns.

Origins and Elements of the 21st Century Town Meeting

America*Speaks* was founded in 1995 to serve as a counterweight to the influence of special interest groups on public policy. It came to believe, fundamentally— and it has found this to be true in its work—that people want to take responsibility for the common good and want to contribute to something larger than themselves in public life.

Through its 21st Century Town Meeting, which was developed in 1997, America*Speaks* began to give citizens voice by taking the traditional New England town meeting to a far larger scale through the innovative use of technology, engaging thousands of people in the decisions that have an impact on their lives. These town meetings provided citizens a chance for direct dialogue with both decision makers and fellow citizens to share ideas and shape decisions. They stand as significant new forays into shaping democratic governance.

In preparing for a 21st Century Town Meeting, several elements are essential for ensuring success at the meeting itself: diverse participants, informed dialogue, and a link to decision makers.

Diverse Participants. 21st Century Town Meeting participants always reflect the rich diversity of the community in

which the meeting is held. Although participants are self-selecting, America*Speaks* helps sponsors design extensive outreach efforts to draw citizens from all walks of life, particularly those who feel disenfranchised and do not normally participate in civic activities. Diverse participation gives decision makers the confidence that the meeting outcome reflects the whole community's needs and views. In Hamilton County, given ongoing racial tensions in the aftermath of a race riot, we worked closely with African American community groups and grassroots organizers to recruit large enough numbers from the community to ensure that we would meet the demographic percentages of the county at the meeting.

We go to great lengths to recruit the right numbers for a town meeting. We begin our planning by using census data to determine the demographic make-up of the community represented and set target participation goals. We take into account demographic measures like age, ethnicity, gender, income, and geographical location, as well as measures related to the specific issue we are addressing in the meeting.

We then go well beyond the passive approaches for outreach, like posters, advertisements, and e-mail invitations, to more personalized and targeted approaches, like community leaders inviting personal friends or colleagues, linking to community-based job-training or assistance programs, and engaging parents and children through school-based efforts. We develop partnerships with community organizations that will be effective recruiters in their particular arenas, and we unfailingly track registration trends so we can make adjustments in the implementation of the recruitment plan if we are light in numbers, such as senior citizens, or away from where we are heavy, such as middle-class whites. It is a delicate dance. Although it is nearly impossible to exactly match all the key demographics for a particular meeting, we are rarely off by more than 5 to 10 percent on any measure.

Informed Dialogue. All participants receive detailed background materials that provided a balance of perspectives on the issues under consideration. These background materials educate participants on the issues and create the foundation for a rich, informed table discussion. In addition to the written materials, issue experts are invited to attend the town meeting to respond to specific questions generated at the tables during the discussion periods. Although much attention is given to ensuring that information is not biased toward particular points of view, we also make sure there is ample room for participants to develop and recommend their own ideas during the day.

Link to Decision Makers. The core intent of a 21st Century Town Meeting program is to provide useful, timely information to decision makers and to allow citizens a genuine method for influencing the decisions or policies

being made. Prior to the town meeting, we involve decision makers directly in the planning of the program so that they know what to expect and are clear and comfortable about how issues and discussions are getting framed. In the meeting, discussion questions and keypad votes are designed to generate the type of information (in terms of content and specificity) that will best inform the decision-making process. Decision makers, in turn, publicly pledge to review and seriously consider the input generated by participants. In Hamilton County, we had all active members of the Planning Partnership involved in the planning of the meeting and its follow-up, and county commissioners were in attendance, as well as involved afterwards.

In the town meeting itself, we carefully structure the room, the program, and the process to ensure high impact. Here, in outline, is the basic set-up:

- Participants, seated at tables of ten (randomly assigned to ensure a good cross-section of the community at each table) openly discuss four to six challenging discussion questions with their peers over the course of the day.
- A trained volunteer facilitates these discussions at each table, ensuring a fair and balanced dialogue.
- A lead facilitator directs the program from the stage, introducing discussion questions, leading keypad votes, reporting outcomes, and responding "real time" to participant input.
- Networked laptop computers at each table serve as "electronic flip charts"

to record the ideas generated during each round of discussions.

- Volunteer recorders at each table record and transmit the views of participants about each of the issues instantly through a wireless network to a group, called the Theme Team, which reads through each report and identifies the strongest themes across them. (All participants receive voting keypads, which allows them to cast individual votes.)

- The results from each table discussion and keypad voting are displayed to participants in rapid cycles. Keypad votes are tallied instantly, and the results are displayed on large video screens.

- The Theme Team reviews table reports as they are sent throughout the discussion period and reports back the strongest themes within ten minutes after each discussion has ended.

- At the end of the day, a Preliminary Report (a three-to-four-page written record of the meeting) is distributed to all participants as they walk out the door.

Countywide Town Meeting: Citizens Working Toward a Shared Vision

Planning commission staff and members of the Planning Partnership were astounded and pleased when more than a thousand citizens showed up to the Countywide Town Meeting on January 12th. It was the largest gathering of its type in county history. Participants were highly representative of the demographic profile of Hamilton County, based on the year 2000 census.

In the first half of the meeting, participants reviewed, refined, and accepted a draft vision developed from themes, goals, and challenges identified at the Goal-Writing Workshop.

The first discussion centered on values, particularly the places they value in their own community and in the county as a whole. After the conversation, participants were polled, and 75 percent agreed that they shared common values about what was important for the county.

Conversation turned next to a set of vision statements that had been written for the four core goals. Participants were asked to review and discuss each vision statement and then vote on their level of support. After indicating their level of support, they were then asked what changes would be required to increase their level of support for the core goal.

For all four goals, about 80 percent of the participants supported the vision. At the end of each discussion, they were asked to provide ideas that would create greater support. Here are examples of what they recommended for each goal:

- *Ensuring economic prosperity:* (1) show stronger linkages between all levels of education and workforce needs, including education, training, and retraining and life skills programs; (2) use economic incentives to retain and attract business; (3) develop economic and education programs that are inclusive of all walks of life to maximize the economic return to the region; and (4) build stronger connections between people to jobs via transportation and the location of businesses.

• *Building collaborative decision making:* (1) have more robust connections and involvement between local officials (including schools) and citizens; (2) eliminate perceived and real conflicts of interest by public officials and be more responsive to citizen concerns; and (3) to expand collaboration beyond the jurisdictions within the county to other counties, both in-state and in Indiana and Kentucky.

• *Embracing diversity and equity:* (1) far stronger promotion of diversity in the county (rather than *assuming* it will happen); (2) greater emphasis on accessibility for people with disabilities; and (3) address economic and social justice issues like income disparities, a fair shake in the justice system, elimination of racial and ethnic profiling, and statutory protections for issues of equity.

• *Balancing development and the environment:* (1) balance in reinvestment and new investment; (2) citizen input into planning and development decisions; (3) emphasize multimodal transport systems, not just roads; and (4) make development and environment decisions with a regional perspective, beyond Hamilton County.

Following lunch, participants discussed the challenges to two of the core goals (balancing development and envi-

ronment; embracing diversity and equity) that hinder Hamilton County's current and future success and progress. In planning the program, we chose these two because the issues they addressed were the most pertinent and the most currently painful of the four goals.

In probing further into the diversity and equity issues, participants wrestled with two questions—one around increasing education and employment opportunities for all county residents, especially for minority and lower-income residents, and the other around increasing the availability of affordable housing in the county, especially for minority and lower-income populations. In response to each question, the gathering developed about a half-dozen strategies to address these issues; when asked, "How much impact will these strategies have in the next five years?" 71 percent of the participants indicated that they believed their strategies would have a significant or noticeable impact on education and employment opportunities, and 65 percent believed the strategies would have a significant or noticeable impact on increasing affordable housing.

In exploring challenges to the goal of balancing development and the environment, discussion centered around the top obstacles to achieving the vision for this goal area for the county over the next decade. The top five were as follows:

• Resistance to change by vested interests
• Lack of leadership from public officials
• Lack of regional land-use planning

- Problem of balancing private property rights with public good
- Policies that encourage sprawl

Participants acknowledged that for the vision to have any staying power, it must address these issues head-on after the town meeting.

At the end of the meeting, 92 percent of participants rated the quality of the town meeting as "excellent" or "good," and 98 percent believed that technology made a real contribution to the value of the meeting. Most important, 55 percent identified themselves as "very confident" or "confident" that they could influence the future of the county, and 75 percent were either "very committed" or "committed" to staying involved in the process. This was demonstrated in dramatic fashion when nearly six hundred people volunteered to serve on action teams to develop implementation strategies to realize Hamilton County's vision for the future before walking out of the room.

COMPASS Action Teams (CATs): Citizens Flesh Out the Vision

Shortly after the Countywide Town Meeting, the regional planning commission took advantage of the extraordinary outpouring of interest from citizens and began organizing COMPASS Action Teams (CATs), to be arranged around the four goals. From the community forums, the Goal-Writing Workshop, and the town meeting, there were twenty-three objectives to be sorted through under

the goals and more than two hundred strategies. America*Speaks* participated in several early strategy sessions about the framework for the CATs and then bowed out of the process, as the commission had a highly capable staff, as well as Planning Partnership members, ready to coordinate the effort.

CAT meetings were held from March to May, 2002. Each goal had three CATs assigned to it, staffed both by volunteers and subject matter experts. Over this three-month period, these groups each met on at least four separate occasions to develop long-term strategies and actions to be reviewed by the Planning Partnership; 320 people participated in all. Each subgroup determined seven primary strategies that were most important to their goal, highlighted the policy implications of those strategies, and, finally, conducted an analysis of what was required to implement the strategies.

Final Results: A Unanimous Vision and an Award-Winning Process

A year after the CAT teams published their recommendations, "The Vision for Hamilton County's Future" was endorsed unanimously by the Planning Partnership and the regional planning commission. It was then certified to the Hamilton County Board of County Commissioners and the forty-nine municipal and township planning commissions within the county, as well as all organizations representing the public, private, and civic sectors, for voluntary implementation.

The vision, as well as initiatives and strategies, was endorsed by the county commissioners in November 2003.

It is important to note that these approvals did *not* constitute any specific agreement or mandate for implementation, funding, or policy change. Therefore, accountability for communitywide results is not assigned to any one individual organization or government but instead must rely on the voluntary actions of the coordinated framework of partners created at the beginning of the COMPASS process.

Beginning in 2003, Community COMPASS became widely recognized for its efforts. The American Planning Association (Ohio Planning Conference) named Community COMPASS and "The Vision for Hamilton County's Future" for its Award for Outstanding Community Planning. The National Association of Counties gave COMPASS its 2004 Achievement Award for innovative programs, while the Ohio general assembly gave COMPASS its 2004 Senatorial Commendation for Outstanding Achievement. The Ohio City/County Management Association also named COMPASS for its 2004 Award for Citizen Participation. And, finally, the International City/County Management Association gave its 2004 Program Excellence Award for Citizen Involvement to Community COMPASS, recognizing its "ground-breaking comprehensive planning process . . . and its innovation in citizen involvement, consensus building, and community decision-making."

The COMPASS process culminated in November 2004 with the roll-out of the county's first comprehensive master plan in almost forty years. An important feature of its implementation will be to increase the responsibility (personal and communal) of citizens, planning commissioners, and organizational leaders (in civic, private, and public sectors) for the whole county. This emphasis was a conscious shift away from total dependence on *traditional* players like professional or expert agencies and government leaders. As of the beginning of 2005, partners in COMPASS had made commitments on over a hundred of the action strategies outlined in the plan, including more than forty specific implementation actions already initiated by Planning Partnership members. The evolving actions are part of four campaigns for implementing the four core goals, as refined and confirmed at the town meeting.

What We Have Learned

Conducting large-scale citizen engagement presents a unique and difficult challenge in community systems, whether that be around planning, policy, or budget issues in a single jurisdiction or in a region. Whereas in organizations, leadership, authority, and outcomes are clearer and under greater control, community systems are far more complex social systems, with a wide range of influences coming from multiple actors and decision makers. Rarely does a single decision maker, agency, or organization control the outcome of a specific issue or set of issues (as was the case with the planning commission). As a result, change on an issue or problem is caused by an accumulation of decisions and actions across diverse groups, organizations, and individuals. This certainly was the case in Hamilton County.

There is a very significant political dimension to the larger public and civic social system. Decision makers in broader social systems must consider that their activities are communicated through a wide set of media lenses not under their direct control. This creates an imperative that the process be conducted in a way that can withstand careful scrutiny. Only in this way will the process and the outcomes be viewed by the public as legitimate.

In addition, the issues in the public sphere represent the full range of questions facing our modern communities, for example, health, housing, transportation, jobs—issues discussed within the twelve community systems in Community COMPASS. Thus in broader social systems, there is a need for deliberation among a much larger spectrum of individuals and groups. With larger numbers, the approach must be carefully designed to ensure the participation of many more groups and individuals than are involved usually in organizational contexts. Issues of language, handicap, and other differences also must be effectively accommodated.

Hamilton County presented a unique opportunity for conducting citizen engagement. They had already made an extraordinary commitment to collaboration and partnership a year before actively embarking on a citizen engagement plan. As a result, they had rallied a significant proportion of the municipal and township governments in the county, as well as organizations and assets from the public, civic, and private spheres to join in the effort.

The regional planning commission was very fortunate to have a thoughtful and dedicated leader in their executive director, Ron Miller. What he and collaborating partners were able to accomplish during this three-year period was impressive. By the time the process had concluded, they had built enormous political and social capital for implementation. Part of their vision was to productively bring more than a thousand diverse citizens into a room for a day to develop and endorse a shared vision for the region. By doing this successfully, they paved the way for another year's worth of dedicated work to put the basics of the vision, goals, strategies, and action plans together with all the partners and hundreds of citizens along the way.

In working with leaders like Ron Miller, we have re-learned several important lessons that are fundamental tenets of our large-scale, citizen engagement work.

First, we do not embark on 21st Century Town Meeting projects until we have carefully and mutually analyzed numerous contexts. It is essential to answer the following questions:

- Who are the key decision makers, stakeholders, and communities, and what is the nature of their stake in the issue?
- What are the decision-making processes already under way?

- How would a town meeting build on previous activity?
- What information is required for the decision-making process?
- What is the history and current political climate concerning these issues?

Second, we do not hold these meetings unless they establish credibility with the public. Citizen deliberation has the capacity for significant impact *if* there is a meaningful, transparent link to decision makers and decision-making processes. Partisanship and bias must be absent from the planning and execution of events, participant mix, and discussion materials. Because citizen deliberation can affect the terms and outcome of a debate, the shape and content of a policy that is enacted, or how dollars are allocated in a budget, it is critical that decision makers be present, listening, and publicly committed to taking outcomes into consideration.

In Hamilton County, Miller and the planning commission had already involved key leaders and decision makers (the Planning Partnership) from across the county in the process. The town meeting wasn't an interesting intellectual exercise dreaming up grandiose dreams for the region. It was an exercise grounded in lots of research, discussion, and reality testing within the community before being vetted at the town meeting.

Third, the event must be designed to seek and ensure fair and productive dialogue and create a level playing field in which individual citizen voices are equal to those representing established interests. There must be ample time for extensive small group discussion, balanced by time for large group synthesis and recommendations. The space should also be made inviting and intimate, whether through the design of the room, the décor used, or the showcasing of art and music.

Finally, the overall strategy must plan for horizons far beyond the town meeting itself. It must be linked to a larger planning, policymaking, or decision-making process, and the strategy must incorporate ways to prompt and track actions among decision makers and to foster a renewed sense of agency among participants. There must be an avenue by which a citizen can continue to pursue and stay active with the issues.

These lessons are true for our work with 21st Century Town Meetings, but they are lessons that apply to a wide range of public sector work and, in particular, for the practice of planning regionally.

Conclusion

We believe a healthy democracy depends on the ability of citizens to directly affect the public policies central to their lives as they were able to do in Hamilton County. We have learned that, despite the myths arguing the contrary, citizens will participate in policymaking, deal competently with complex public policy issues, and rise above self-interest on behalf of the common good. The citizens of Hamilton County—in the process of es-

tablishing a regional vision and plan—
have elegantly proved this point.

Notes

1. As quoted in "Planning: Will It Make a
   Difference?" by Ron Miller, March 16,
   2000—an unpublished article pre-
   sented to Planning Partnership,
   Hamilton County Regional Planning
   Commission.

2. "Regional Planning: An Overview," by
   Moustafa Mourad and Howard Ways;
   online article accessible on The Enterprise Foundation Web site (www.
   enterprisefoundation.org/pubsnews/
   bb/cc3973.asp).

CHAPTER SIX

WORKING CROSS-CULTURALLY

Sometime in the 1990s, we were invited to do a Large Group Methods training workshop in Singapore. We accepted with eagerness and had a wonderful time working with a group of about forty human resources and training and development managers from various business organizations. At the beginning of the three-day event, we talked with the group about the fact that these are methods developed in the West, particularly in North America. We acknowledged the real cultural differences between the situation they faced and ours, and they agreed to talk in more depth about the issue before the end of the workshop.

Ours was an educational mission. They wanted to know about these methods, and we did our best to introduce them, to make clear how and when they are used, how they work, and why they work. We had a thoroughly enjoyable time with much participation, many questions, and great interest. On the last day, we set aside some time to talk about the cross-cultural issues. At one point, we said, "Now tell us frankly, do you really think that you can use these methods in your own organizations?" A quick survey around the room made it quite clear that the probability was very low indeed. We also understood why. Singapore is a hierarchical culture (Hofstede, 1980), where those in charge are expected to make decisions for those reporting to them. If they do not decide, they appear weak in the eyes of their subordinates. Flattening this hierarchy in the way most of these methods do in order to encourage participation on equal footing runs counter to the way business is usually done in Singapore.

However, Singapore is also a relationship-oriented culture. In the special issue of the *Journal of Applied Behavioral Science* (JABS) that we edited (March 2005), Samantha Tan and Juanita Brown write about the extensive use of The World Café method in many different Singapore organizations, from the police to the housing authority. She renamed the method using the name of a favorite type of Singapore coffee house and gathering place, and used it to engage people in important learning conversations that made it possible for people at different levels of the bureaucracy to have real dialogue. Clearly, the answer to whether these methods can be used in non-Western cultures is, "It depends on how and for what you use them."

On another educational trip, this time presenting our work in New Zealand, we were delighted when, from among the participants, a Maori woman arose and told everyone how congruent with Maori culture the principles that underlie these methods are. She felt right at home with these participative processes, and we know that later a Maori group did create some events using these methods.

The challenge that we focus on in this chapter is more subtle than a simple yes or no, these methods work or they do not work. The challenge is to introduce them for compelling work and adjust them appropriately for the culture.

Because of our keen interest in the cultural congruence of these methods, as we began to consult and do educational workshops outside the United States, we have made a special effort in this book to solicit cases from people working in non-Western cultures or across cultures. In this chapter, we present four cases from all over the world:

- "Whole Systems Change in Mexican Organizations," by Michael R. Manning and José DelaCerda
- "From Strategic Planning to Open Space in East Africa," by Theo Groot
- "Training Indonesian Facilitators to Lead Community Planning for Women and Children," by Kim Martens, Rita Schweitz, and Kenoli Oleari
- "World Religions Engage Critical Global Issues," by Ray Gordezky, Susan Dupre, and Helen Spector

After we describe what we think is especially interesting about each case, we will return to some ideas about what we have learned and are still learning about the cross-cultural adaptations of these methods.

What to Note in These Cases

We are extremely fortunate to be able to present a picture of how these methods were used and tested in Mexico and in Central and South America, in the extensive work reported in "Whole Systems Change in Mexican Organizations," by Michael Manning and José DelaCerda—the first case in this chapter. They point out that according to cross-cultural research, these methods should have some problems in Mexican and other Latino cultures because of the practice in these cultures of high "power distance" (Hofstede, 1980). However, their experience in over fifty conferences with some 4,500 participants using Future Search, Participative Design, and combined methods was that the relationship and communitarian values in these cultures made it both possible and effective to involve people in having discussions, planning, and making decisions. They believe that the right focus, the right stakeholders, and a motivated delegate group are more important than cultural differences.

In the case of Instituto Tecnológico de Estudios Superiores Occidente (ITESO), a Jesuit-Mexican university faced with aggressive competition to its previous pre-eminence, the stakeholder community is invited to participate in two large planning and implementing conferences to reverse the downward trend. The unique collaboration between the Mexican consultant and his English-speaking "external" consultant who helped with event design and shadow consultation is intriguing. Readers will also find interesting a number of minor cultural adaptations that made these interventions more congruent with the host culture. The authors also point out that their research does not answer questions about whether or not the widespread participation that occurs in large group events is transferable back to the workplace. (For more on this topic, see Chapter Seven.)

Another crucible for testing these methods cross-culturally is in the work of NGOs in developing countries. They are always looking for ways to involve people at the grassroots level in improving life, health, and agriculture. In his chapter "From Strategic Planning to Open Space Technology in East Africa,"

Theo Groot describes his frustration with the traditional planning methods he learned to use as a strategic planner. Then he discovered the much less structured and more informal Open Space and decided to risk using it in an African village to see if it would move the work forward. His delightful description of his first attempt at Open Space should spark memories in many practitioners. Note that although he had some difficulties with those in power who expected more deference than this method allows, most villagers took to it easily. Notice also the adjustments he made for those who could not write and for limited supplies and facilities. His experiences with Open Space caused him to rethink his approach to community development and also to draw fascinating parallels between Open Space and traditional African healing rites.

In another part of the world—Indonesia—a team of Future Search practitioners (Kim Martens, Rita Schweitz, and Kenoli Oleari) agreed to help the United Nations train Indonesians to run Future Searches in provincial villages. Their mission is "Training Indonesian Facilitators to Lead Community Planning for Women and Children," in order to promote the health, safety, and development of these women and children. These trainers did not speak the language and arrived to do the training just as a coup d'état was threatening. Their candor in discussing the issues they confronted working across culture, language, and political barriers is both refreshing and immensely helpful to practitioners going into a really different cultural situation.

At still another level of cross-cultural immersion: What do you do when you not only have to cross cultures, but you have four hundred delegates representing most of the major religious traditions—cultures of the world—together for several days discussing highly contentious issues? Both the Assembly and the Parliament of World Religions held in Barcelona in July 2004 used Large Group Methods to help delegates discuss four very difficult issues confronting the world and what faith communities can contribute to resolving them. In "World Religions Engage Critical Global Issues," Ray Gordezky, Susan Dupre, and Helen Spector talk about the pre-work that went into creating a method that would help people bridge their cultural differences and be able to talk deeply with each other about what their own values and tradition could contribute to the discussion and to the solution. They stood on the ground of their own consulting traditions to work with others, using the principles of Large Group Methods to create a new process for the Parliament. The ideas and processes they developed are a rich resource for people working in very diverse gatherings.

Our Ideas About Working Cross-Culturally

Most of us confront diversity at home as well as abroad. We work in organizations that are increasingly diverse or in communities with diverse stakeholders. Even if we never leave our home country, the principles underlying Large Group Methods allow us to be more appropriately inclusive. This is not about learning the customs of all the cultures of the world, though certainly people working across cultures need to do their homework and know something about the cultures they are working in. We believe that planning large cross-cultural meetings involves both a relevant framework and an inquiring attitude. In the concluding section, we provide some concepts, rules of thumb, and two possible frameworks for planning cross-cultural large group meetings.

The first rule of thumb is to be constantly aware of what you do not know about other cultures. When you live in a culture that is not your own for a couple of years, as we both have done at various stages in our lives, rather than becoming an expert, you become acutely aware of how much more there is to know that is out of your awareness. This is particularly true in the "high-context" cultures—cultures where people read nonverbal cues to understand what is going on and what is expected, rather than being told explicitly in words. If you take this attitude with you into new situations, it will serve you well. You will listen better, ask better questions, and probably learn faster.

More specifically, when proposing to work with a group, always think about the match between their culture and the format of the Large Group Method you are proposing. When going to talk with an Israeli foundation in New York City in the early days of our consulting work in this area, Billie waxed eloquent about the Future Search process and began to describe it in some detail. As she did, she could read in the face of the executive that something was amiss. She stopped and asked him what his reactions were. He said to her, "Well, if you start with our history, we will never get any further!" She understood immediately that he was right and began to talk about the Search Conference as a similar method that begins with the desired future state rather than with history. That got his attention as a real possibility.

We believe that many managers find themselves needing to plan large meetings that may include several cultures. Planners of global meetings need to step back and ask, "How can we be sure that we create an experience that takes into consideration and responds to the cultural norms and assumptions of all the participants?" The first answer is that we can't. Some of the cultural assumptions that people bring run counter to each other. This means that planners will need to thoughtfully consider how to deal with these differences.

The first step here is a heightened consciousness that many of our ideas about what a good meeting is derive from very Western values. This means that others from different cultures may not share these ideas. In fact, research results about how group processes work may not be true in other parts of the world! For example, the demonstrated Western tendency in groups toward "social loafing," that is, not putting in as much effort when others are present as when you are alone, is absent in collectivist cultures. In fact, in collectivist cultures people work harder in groups rather than less hard.

Another example is the idea that open communication works better and that more communication in organizations is valuable. But in some Asian cultures, there is a strong value on what is *not* said, on reading nonverbal cues. In these cultures, less is more.

A Framework for Approaching Global Meetings

How will we know whether the values that are implicit in much of our consultation practice lead us to propose structures inhospitable to persons of different cultures? We have found it useful to do a slight rephrasing of the well-known work of Geert Hofstede on dimensions that underlie different customs and behavior to provide a general map for understanding cultural differences. Because customs and behaviors are only the surface evidence of deeper cultural differences, anyone who is working with culturally diverse groups needs a deeper framework than just learning the easily observable customs of the countries at issue.

Our framework has four key dimensions. The first dimension is the priority placed on work, as contrasted with social relationships. In the United States, the expression "business before pleasure" picks up this value. Americans want to get right down to business and have the satisfaction of concluding their work and then going on to some pleasant social event. Unfortunately, many Americans do not realize that 85 percent of the world holds another value. Most of the world is relationship-oriented. "How can I do business with you if I do not know you?" they ask. This means that social events—getting acquainted, knowing about your life, your family, your views—are all part of developing a working relationship. Only after that groundwork is laid are they interested in talking about the business at hand.

In global meetings, Americans must understand and participate in social events that they may experience as extraneous to the business at hand. It also means that a great deal of attention must be given to the settings in which people interact. The "meeting" is the whole day, not just the time spent on work.

The second dimension has to do with reactions to authority and hierarchy. Anglo cultures emphasize independence. People try to reduce the distance between levels and treat others as co-equals or peers. We prefer the flat playing field. In other cultures, particularly but not exclusively some in Asia, the natural distance between superiors and subordinates is experienced as normal and desirable. The person in authority has a special role to fulfill. To pretend that one is equal would be confusing. What is interesting about this clarity of roles is that in some ways it facilitates social interaction. Professors in Japan have considerable social interaction with their student majors. They go out for social occasions, weekend trips, and drinking after class, yet no one is confused about who the professor is and who is a student. The roles prescribe a social distance that is always clear and makes it possible for different levels to have fun together without becoming confused about roles. How different this is from the United States, where young assistant professors are often admonished not to spend too much time with the graduate students lest it be said of them that they are not taking on their new role very well!

The third dimension has to do with how comfortable one is taking risks, with uncertainty, as compared with preferring a structured and unambiguous world. Americans admire decisive decision makers, especially when their snap decisions turn out well! In Japan, however, decision making is slow and involves many people. When it is accomplished, everyone knows what has been agreed to and how to move ahead.

In the global meeting, this dimension may cause difficulty with regard to what a meeting "means." In some cultures, meetings are ceremonial public announcements of decisions that have already been made and everyone knows about. In others, they are places where decisions are hammered out and actions decided. Clearly, these different perceptions of the purpose of meetings need to be negotiated.

The fourth dimension is probably the best known and the best researched. Individualism and collectivism describe the way we think about ourselves. Individualists conceive themselves as unique persons with particular characteristics. Children of these cultures are reinforced for standing out, for achieving, for being different and better than others, as well as for being able to stand alone. People raised in more collectivist societies see themselves as members of groups and as defined by their roles in those groups. Standing out is antagonistic to group harmony; therefore, one strives to fit in, to support, to participate, and to bring honor to your family, your school, your company.

In meetings, this means that people from individualistic cultures make themselves heard, have little difficulty expressing their views or uncertainties. But those from more collectivist cultures may be acutely uncomfortable being asked for individual views. They are much more comfortable participating in groups and having the group express a collective view. All this is important background for the design of any meeting.

The Four-Worlds Framework

How do we think about these cultural differences as we plan the meeting? We have found Ronnie Lessem and Sudhanshu Palsule's *Managing in Four Worlds* (1997) a useful framework, or mental model, as we plan. Theirs is a much more complex analysis than we present here, but simply stated, they use North, South, East, and West to represent four essential quadrants that encompass the whole, be it person or organization—a four-worlds framework. Within our world are people whose dominant world is North, or South, or East, or West. We need to understand each of these worlds and take them into consideration as we design global meetings.

The world of the North is the world of the intellect. It is conceptual, rational, heady, systematic, linear, left-brain. A "Northern" meeting is full of presentations, PowerPoint slides with models, figures, and supporting financial data making "the case." It is full of discussions where being smart and winning the point is important, where people say things like, "Now, let's be rational about this" or "I still haven't heard a good argument for why we should do this." The assumption is that ideas meet on the playing field of the meeting and may the best ideas win. The currency of discourse is ideas.

In sharp contrast, the world of the South is the world of feeling and of energy. In that world the organization is experienced as personal, so each member must sustain personal relationships. The organization is a community with an important history. People expect to know others they work with personally. They expect to take time to know about their life outside the organization.

Who you know—your network of relationships—is important to getting work done. People expect to take time for relationships in meetings. In fact, "the meeting after the meeting" or "the party after the party" may be more important than the so-called main event. People value situations in which they can know who their colleagues are, not just by role but in person. Westerners seldom realize how important relationship building is or how much time Southerners feel needs to be given to it.

The world of the East is the world of intuition, of right-brain thinking, of spirit. It is holistic; it contains opposites and holds them in balance. It is reflective, inward moving. Rather than getting and doing, the Eastern world is about being able to let go so that the future can emerge. In some Eastern cultures, meetings do not occur in the form we know them in the West. Rather, they are literally ceremonial occasions, the work having occurred previously. The idea of active participation, discussion, and decision making in public may not be at all comfortable. Advocacy for one's own point of view is frowned on in many Asian cultures. However, if people meet in groups and then the group asks a question or suggests a remedy, the stigma is reduced because the individual does not stand out. Pace is another important concern. Eastern approaches are not as fast-paced and driven as in the West. There is much more time for consideration, reflection. It is more like the motto over the fireplace in a Vermont woods cabin: "Here time is slow and gracious, a companion rather than a master." This becomes an interesting dilemma to be managed by the design team.

Finally, the fourth world—the world of the West—is pragmatic. Organizations are focused on survival and growth, or structure and boundaries. Movement is outward and active. Western meetings are action-oriented, and people feel frustrated if discussions go on too long without closure and decisions. Jokes like "Ready, fire, aim!" capture this tendency when it becomes exaggerated and dysfunctional.

How do we balance all these forces in a single meeting (and in ourselves)? The four-worlds framework allows us to ask of meeting designs: Is there enough East in this design? If not, what can we do to create more time for reflection, a more leisurely pace? Is there enough South? Do we have plenty of time for people just to talk with each other and get to know each other, or are we moving too fast into the agenda? Are we using the "free time" (a Western idea) to make it easy for people to do things together and get better acquainted? What kinds of group activities would do that best? Is there enough North? Are we introducing what is known about this topic? Do we need an expert to increase our expertise? Are we using our best thinkers to lead these discussions and make presentations? Is there enough of the West? Are we reserving enough time to decide on clear actions and how they will get implemented?

Using the points of the compass as a way of reviewing the design of meetings can help us plan events that consider different cultural values at a deeper level. Members of the design team who come from these cultures can act as a check on how the team is doing.

As you turn now to the cases that follow, we think you will both enjoy reading about the experiences of these consultants and increasing your awareness of what issues need attention when working across cultures. If you find these cases interesting, check The Matrix at the end of Chapter One for other cases that contain cross-cultural material.

References

Bunker, B. B., & Alban, B. T. (Eds.) (March 2005). Large group interventions. Special issue of *The Journal of Applied Behavioral Science, 41*(1).

Hofstede, G. (1980). *Culture's consequences: International differences in work-related values.* Thousand Oaks, CA: Sage.

Lessem, R., & Palsule, S. (1997). *Managing in four worlds: From competition to co-creation.* Oxford, UK: Blackwell.

WHOLE SYSTEMS CHANGE IN MEXICAN ORGANIZATIONS

Michael R. Manning and José DelaCerda

The Challenge

Our challenge has been two-fold. First, we are challenged to apply Large Group Methods, such as variations of Future Search, Open Space, and Whole-Scale Organization redesign, within various business and social sectors of Mexico. Being aware that cross-cultural research suggests that these participative and egalitarian methods were inconsistent with the culture of Mexico added to the challenge.

Second, we report a particular case where we applied Large Group Methods in an effort to help a Jesuit university facing severe competition create a strategy for the future.

Large-Scale Change in Mexican Business and Society

In an effort to help Mexican organizations deal with pressing business and societal issues, we have been applying whole systems change methods in Mexico for more than six years, conducting over fifty Large Group Methods events since 1999 (see Manning and DelaCerda, 2003, for a detailed summary of our work). The primary purpose of our work is to help communities and organizations bridge the present-future gap by focusing on change processes that utilize participatory whole systems approaches. These methods produce active and intensive participation with techniques that use simultaneous dialogue of all stakeholder groups and elements of a system (Manning and Binzagr, 1996).

Mexico's economy has been revolutionized over the last fifteen years. Moving from a closed, technologically dependent economy that was externally financed by public debt and had huge import-export deficits, the Mexican economy is now one of the freest markets in the world. No other country has been more active in opening channels of international commerce.

Although this trade liberalism has its benefits, it also creates a situation where Mexican businesses must now compete with many international competitors, even within their home market.

This must be done without the necessary infrastructure and economic reforms to help industries and business leverage their costs with foreign competition. Transformation is absolutely necessary within the business and social sectors in order to compete in a free-trade economy.

In addition, Mexicans have enormous social problems that have yet to find innovative and effective solutions. The main challenges of the twenty-first century in Mexico are as follows:

- To solve the rampant poverty and improve the lack of education that inflicts disadvantageous economic conditions on at least half the current 95 million population
- To stop the increasing devastation and restore natural resources in most of the Mexican territory
- To effectively and rapidly build missing infrastructure to be competitive with those countries party to Mexico's free-trade agreements
- To find more effective ways of fighting and decreasing corruption and unequal competitive practices
- To reform bureaucratic government and business organizations to become flexible and innovative

Our interventions have been applied in very different organizations: public and private institutions, profits and nonprofits, and small, medium-sized, and very large organizations. Most of our interventions have taken place in two types of organizations: (1) small business communities (forestry, fishery, food industry, livestock breeding) looking for forms of inter-firm cooperation and value-added integration and (2) government institutions (city and state governments, public health institutions, infrastructure construction, and education) looking for improved performance on behalf of their communities. A few interventions have been conducted as well with private business firms or specific community organizations. See Table 6.1 for a summary of these interventions.

Interventions have taken place in differing geographical areas of Mexico: small towns and very large cities located in northern, southern, and central Mexican states. Sizes of conferences have also varied, from sessions of forty to forty-five people to sessions larger than five hundred persons. According to our attendance records, more than five thousand people have participated in one of these large group interventions.

Most interventions have been conducted by a group of three facilitators, who are part of a team of trained consultants, assisted by logistics teams. Techniques applied in conferences have been mainly of two types (Bunker and Alban, 1997): (1) methods for creating the future together and (2) methods for participative work design. More specifically, two particular whole systems change techniques have been most influential in our practice: Future Search (Weisbord and Janoff, 1995) and Participative Design (Emery, 1995). We do not claim, however, pure application of any

model; as a matter of fact, most interventions need a sort of "methodological-cultural adaptation" in order to fit the intervened system limitations, usually related to time, money, or information restrictions. The work by Dannemiller and Tolchinsky (Dannemiller Tyson Associates, 2000) has been particularly helpful to us on issues of strategic planning and work design.

We present our general findings and learnings on Large Group Methods through a case of whole system strategic planning in a Mexican university. We also address the issue of culture.

Hofstede's research, in 1980, was a watershed in cross-cultural organizational studies. His findings suggest that the Mexican culture is characterized by high power distance, high risk avoidance, high collectivism, and moderately high masculinity. These traits are usually the basis for explaining cultural influences on corporate behavior, leadership, and performance.

Generally speaking, most cultural researchers support Hofstede´s statement that participative leadership behaviors are neither frequent nor effective in cultures like that of Mexico. This conclusion suggests that basic assumptions and methods of whole systems change could find cultural resistance. We will suggest that cultural influences can be dealt with in simpler ways that do not consider culture as a major restriction for participation in large group processes. Our experience using Large Group Methods contradicts the caution implicit in the cross-cultural research.

TABLE 6.1. WHOLE SYSTEMS CHANGE IN MEXICAN ORGANIZATIONS

Sector	Type of Organizations	Type of Intervention	Number of Conferences and Attendance	Typical Stakeholders	Conference Length in Days	Geographical Scope	Profit or Nonprofit
Small business, inter-firm cooperation	Small firms within forestry, fishery, agriculture, livestock breeding, and food industries	Future Search	18 conferences and 2,000 participants	Firms' owners and independent producers and growers Industry experts and analysts Government officials Educators and trainers Engineers and technicians Researchers Suppliers and customers	3 days (3) 2 days (12) 1.5 days (5)	State (4) Regional within a given state (5) Local (9)	Profit
Government	City, state, and federal government institutions	Future Search and Participative Process Redesign	10 conferences and 550 participants	Elected political representatives Top government officials Top and middle public management officials Employees at all levels Community representatives	3 days (1) 2 days (6) 1 day (3)	National (1) State and regional (2) County or city (7)	Nonprofit

TABLE 6.1. WHOLE SYSTEMS CHANGE IN MEXICAN ORGANIZATIONS, *continued*

Sector	Type of Organizations	Type of Intervention	Number of Conferences and Attendance	Typical Stakeholders	Conference Length in Days	Geographical Scope	Profit or Nonprofit
Community and socio-political organizations	NGOs Political parties Urban communities	Future Search	10 conferences and 750 participants	Community and organizational leaders and members	2 days (1) 1 day (9)	Local (10)	Nonprofit
Education	Universities and technological institutes	Future Search, Participative Strategic Planning and Process Redesign	9 conferences and 800 participants	Governing board members and university officials Deans and department heads Researchers and professors Employees at all levels	2 days (8) 1 day (1)	Organizational	Nonprofit
Business	Software design Land developers and housing Construction industry	Participative Strategic Planning and Process Redesign	5 conferences and 350 participants	Members of the board Top management Engineers and technicians Employees at all levels Suppliers and clients	3 days (2) 2 days (1) 1 day (2)	Organizational	Profit

Large-Scale Change at ITESO University

Many Latin American countries have become very attractive for global investment in higher education. Mexico is perhaps the best case example. Fifty years ago higher education was almost exclusively limited to public universities, with a few private institutions fighting for social legitimacy and a small market share. Now university education in Mexico is undergoing an irreversible process of privatization. There were only five private universities in Mexico in 1950; today, there are over one thousand institutions of higher education registered with the Public Education Ministry. The market share for these private institutions is more than 32 percent of the 1.9 million active university students.

The most prestigious private universities, like the *Tec de Monterrey,* the *Universidad Iberoamericana—Instituto Tecnologico Estudios Superiores de Occidente System* (ITESO), the *Universidad Panamericana,* the *Universidad de las Américas,* and the *Universidad de Monterrey,* have earmarked investment in infrastructure and improving academic quality in order to shore up their market position. But the race for market share is extremely aggressive. Over the last ten years, new groups and strategic alliances have appeared, bent on securing a significant market position.

ITESO—the Jesuit University in Guadalajara, Mexico—had to plan for its organizational strategy for a period of three years (2004 to 2006). An institution historically committed to community development and social justice and equality, ITESO intends to be as socially and culturally diverse as possible. At the same time, it has to ensure the income needed to sustain educational operations, research programs, and community development projects. Founded in 1957, more than 93 percent of its income comes from the tuition of 7,846 undergraduates and about 5 percent from the tuition of 701 graduate students; the rest comes from other university programs such as continuing education (1,500 students), research funding, and community development funding. Today ITESO has 285 full-time and 853 part-time faculty that serve twenty-five undergraduate degree programs, thirteen master's-degree programs, and three doctoral programs, distributed in the fields of engineering, social sciences, and business administration.

In early 2003, ITESO found itself in the midst of increasingly aggressive competition in the western region's higher education market. Besides some traditionally prestigious private universities like *Tec de Monterrey* and *Universidad Panamericana,* the three most aggressive new for-profit institutions—*Universidad del Valle de Mexico* (UVM), *Universidad Tecnologica de Mexico* (UNITEC), *TecMilenio*—had settled within a ten-mile radius of ITESO. It is likely that, given ITESO's dominant position in this region, most of the newly arrived institutions are deciding to locate their facilities as close as possible to their main competitor. The upshot is that old players and new entrants have made Guadalajara a prominent center for higher education in Mexico and Latin America.

Although ITESO is regarded by some analysts as being among the top ten most prestigious educational institutions in Mexico and a definite leader in the western region, student enrollment had been declining steadily for five years. The university faced problems of market differentiation due to the arrival of dozens of new entrants, with aggressive advertising and marketing strategies offering novelties such as dual degrees and similar products at a lower price. Nevertheless, it was evident that the real issue for differentiation went well beyond marketing: both ITESO's academic and organizational systems needed strategic changes to ensure adaptability to the new market conditions.

ITESO's Whole Systems Strategic Planning Process

Although the topic of stiffer competition had been discussed in the past, it was not until the strategic planning for 2004–2006 that the governing board, the rector's council, and the planning commission decided to focus on the crucial issues of competition and the weakening market position. It was also decided that the new strategic process should be as participative and inclusive as possible.

ITESO went beyond simply increasing participation by opting for whole systems planning methods. For ITESO, the whole system includes professors (835

part-time and 285 full-time), students (10,047 undergraduate, graduate, and continuing education students), alumni (approximately 33,000), the Jesuit community, collegiate bodies and academic and administrative authorities, university service personnel, business groups and employers, state-city and educational authorities, high school principals, *Sistema Universitario Jesuita* (UIA-ITESO) system representatives (the five sister educational institutions throughout Mexico), the Mexican Province of the Society of Jesus, some outside researchers and intellectuals, and parents. Stakeholders from all these categories were solicited to participate in the process of collective thinking and planning.

According to the mandate given by the university governing board, the new strategic plan should specify a three-year formulation of goals, programs, and actions for all ITESO divisions, departments, centers, and offices. However, the mission and the fundamental principles of the institution were not under revision. The whole systems strategic planning process would need to be designed to involve all stakeholders in order to jointly define the core strategies for ITESO's near future. Figure 6.1 provides an overview of the ITESO's strategic planning process.

Work with the Governing Board, Planning Commission, and Consultants

The governing board of ITESO University is the highest decision-making body in the university. It is composed of twelve

FIGURE 6.1. WHOLE SYSTEMS STRATEGIC PLANNING AT ITESO UNIVERSITY

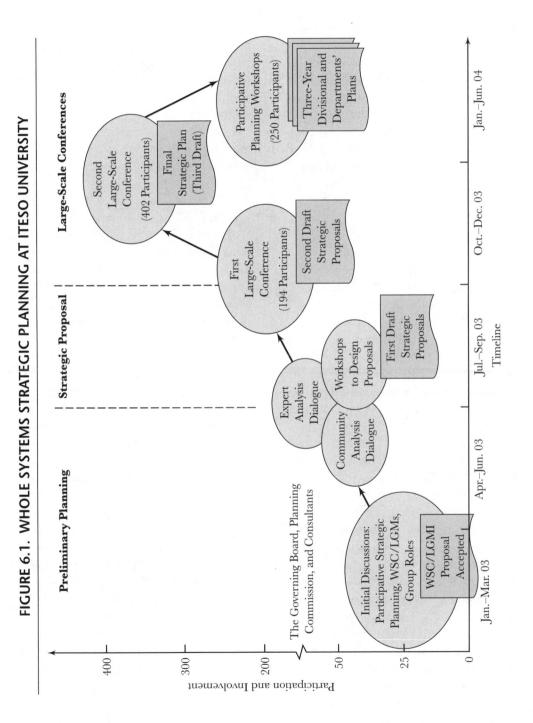

members representing the faculty, the administration, and ITESO's ownership association members. The rector of the university personally heads this board. The governing board makes decisions about strategic issues such as growth, investments and finance, tuition levels, establishment of scholarships, construction projects, and yearly budgets. Every three years the board is charged with creating a strategic direction for the university. In 2000, a task force was appointed by the board to create the strategic plan for 2001–2003. A strategy document of future-desirable scenarios was created and approved, setting the next three-year strategy for ITESO (2001–2003).

The document, although rigorously written, did not influence decision making as much as was intended, so the board decided to create a permanent planning commission to facilitate implementation. Soon the commission had to start a new three-year strategic planning process. The chair of the planning commission decided to invite a former part-time professor of ITESO's MBA program (the second author, who is Mexican) to be part of this body as a local internal consultant. He had experience applying large-scale methods for strategic planning and organizational design in Mexico. After a few meetings, the internal consultant recommended opening participation to as many managers of the organization as possible, in order to enable organizational learning for both strategic formulation and implementation. He presented videotapes of Mexican organizations using Large Group Methods and educated them about these methods. Many members of the commission felt attracted to these ideas of "engaging the whole system in the strategic thinking process." Although some members of the commission were reluctant to try such a large gathering in one room at the same time, the general idea of having a highly involving strategic formulation process was approved by consensus.

The next step was to discuss the specific stages of large-scale strategic design. In this stage of the process, the Mexican consultant initiated frequent e-mail communication with an experienced international consultant (the first author, who is from the United States). He wanted his colleague from the United States to be aware of this situation, in the event that he was invited to be part of the intervention team. (The international consultant also had worked with Mexican organizations using Large Group Methods, but he was not fluent in Spanish, making it difficult for him to work at an implementation level without simultaneous translation.)

The commission presented a process-oriented proposal using Large Group Methods that involved representatives from all of the university's stakeholders. These representatives were to engage in a conference that would analyze the context of higher education in Mexico. Emphasis would be placed on the competitive environment and how ITESO would successfully face these new challenges.

At the first meetings with the governing board, board members asked many questions, and most looked very skeptical. At the same time, they were very much aware of the difficulties emerging with competition all over Mexico, especially in the city of Guadalajara. Finally, after three meetings, the board approved the methodology and decided to proceed immediately.

Responding to the internal consultant's proposal, the planning commission approved hiring an experienced third party to help scrutinize and shape the final design of the large-scale conferences. The board accepted the commission's proposal of having a third party, but not as direct facilitator. They were clear that they wanted this consultant to help design the process, be a detached observer (not facilitator), and be in charge of evaluating the large-scale conferences. It was decided that it would be more "proper and practical to the process" if insiders would conduct the conferences. Simultaneous translation was considered risky for conducting large groups; in addition, it was argued that "particular manners of ITESO's culture could be better dealt with by local consultants." Both consultants worked with the planning commission for over three months (April through June, 2003), helping to design the whole systems intervention.

Formulation of the Governing Board's Strategic Proposals

It was decided that the board would develop a proposed strategic plan that would be used as the springboard for the

two large group interventions. To facilitate this, all board members participated in a series of strategic workshops to formulate the content of a strategic proposal. This process began with a series of dialogues (three to five hours) among selected university stakeholders and national experts on education, science and technology, economy and marketing, and government policy, which created a list of crucial topics in the field of higher education in Mexico and Latin America. A report with the most important conclusions of the talks with outside experts was made available to the university community for consultation and feedback over the Internet. To provide additional preparation for workshops and conferences, an expert market-and-economic analysis relating data on enrollment and tuition to several economic variables was performed. This document was widely distributed to faculty and other stakeholder groups at the beginning of the strategic planning process.

The next step was to open the process to the whole ITESO community. The university governing board invited everyone to propose key issues for the immediate future by logging in to an online forum that was created to incorporate proposals. The main topics contributed related to teaching methods, research projects, competition and market position, quality of education, cost structure and financial situation, operational efficiency, technological innovation, management, personnel policies, and facilities and physical plant. A total of forty-two documents were received, which were then compiled on a CD for distribution among all members before the strategic workshops and the large group conferences.

Strategic workshops (one and two days in length) were required for the board to develop the strategy proposal. The chair of the planning commission and the local consultant acted as facilitators. The international external consultant was invited to observe and provide feedback during one of these workshops, supported by simultaneous translation. The workshops were attended by both members of the board and the planning commission.

The first task of these workshops was to select the strategic issues for ITESO's immediate future. Groups were assigned to work on each of these issues. Selected groups were asked to formulate a first draft of a strategic proposal for their issue. Each draft was thoroughly discussed by all participants by pre-assigning relevant groups to each strategic issue. In a second round of discussion, participants had the opportunity to join groups about the specific issue they felt most passionate about. The final consolidation of proposals consisted of several rounds of small group discussions. Participants in each group were asked to look for common themes as much as possible rather than vote to solve differences. At this stage, one of the original key issues was dropped, and two more strategic issues were added.

During the workshop, the international consultant commented mainly on process issues rather than content issues. Some board members said that they were expecting ideas about how good, precise, or adequate the strategic orientations looked to him. He clearly indicated that he was not in a position to add value to the content of the strategies being developed but that his role was to help create the right environment, processes, and designs to ensure that a good strategic plan was developed and would have wide acceptance.

After these workshops, the international consultant was in a better position to help design the two large-scale conferences. His interactions were through e-mail and phone calls. The original design was proposed by the local consultant and reviewed by the planning commission. The local consultant made sure that everybody got involved in the design.

Here is one example of the communication between the international consultant, the local consultant, and some members of the planning commission:

> José, I thought in our discussions that we focused on this management conference as prioritizing and identifying the units that need to address each of the institutional priorities, clarifying what these priorities might mean, as well as some preliminary thoughts about what a future for ITESO might look like. If the objective of this conference is what you have written, what will the next conference (with faculty, students, alumni, employers,

and so on) do—the same? If so, why two conferences? The second large conference, as I see it now, could focus on operationalizing the priorities and identify how these can be implemented into each unit.

Here is another good example of dealing with more specific details of the conference:

> I might suggest that the Rector presents these institutional directions and then participants sitting in groups around small tables could do an exercise: what we heard, questions of clarification, concerns that we have. The Rector (and others) should be available to respond to these three rounds.

Once the large-scale conferences were carefully designed, a logistics team was trained by the local consultant and some colleagues. Everything was prepared the day before the first conference. The international consultant and the local consultant supervised the room arrangements, the materials, the sound system, and other matters the night before the conference.

First Large Group Conference

The first conference (October 20–21, 2003) opened with 194 members of the ITESO community participating within twenty-three heterogeneous work groups. The purposes of this conference were (1) to identify the opportunities

and risks implied in the implementation of the proposed strategic guidelines, (2) to imagine the future of ITESO and the various university divisions in light of the proposal, and (3) to propose changes to improve the strategic guidelines.

The local facilitators assumed the main role, and the international consultant sat at a table close to the front of the large room to have a clear perspective of what was going on during the two days of the conference (he was assisted by a translator). During the conference, the facilitators had chances to meet with the international consultant and share perceptions of the process. Some minor adjustments were made in the process as a result of this interaction. At the end of the first day, a meeting took place to discuss the conference and decide if the process was on the right track. No major adjustments were made, but comments on the roles of the facilitators were very useful. The second day of the conference followed more or less the same path.

The Monday after the conference, the international consultant attended the planning commission meeting to comment on the process and results. Five topics were addressed and discussed in that session: (1) stakeholder representation and how representative this first conference was; (2) the degree of participation, involvement, and energy aroused during the conference; (3) the depth of the suggestions made to the strategic proposals of the board; (4) what might be done to ensure high levels of participation in the second conference, and (5) comments on diverse topics such as logistics (which were highly rated), the role of facilitators, and the length of the conference.

The results of the conference were entered in their entirety into Word and Excel files. Then a summary was drawn up of the most relevant aspects for possible inclusion in the strategic proposals, especially all the suggestions for modifications or additions.

After this first large-scale conference, the two local facilitators took charge of developing the methodology for the second conference. The international consultant and the other members of the planning commission helped to improve the design. The same process was applied for the second conference; the major difference was that the international consultant did not participate as a third-party observer. The governing board felt a lot more confident about the method after the first conference and decided that the local facilitators were ready to run the show by themselves.

Student Workshop

In response to the first large-scale conference, the ITESO Students' Association, on their own initiative, held a student workshop on October 29th. They asked for help in designing their meeting along the lines of the large-scale conferences. More than one hundred students, many of whom came and went, analyzed the strategic proposals and recommended adding Student Development and Cam-

pus Life to the three-year strategy. This new proposal was submitted to the university rector.

Revisions of the Proposed Strategic Plan by the Governing Board

The governing board, the rector's council, and the planning commission met on November 10th, using small group methodologies, to work on the changes and additions requested by participants in both the large-scale conference and the student workshop. A new draft of the strategic proposals was made for presentation to the participants in the second large-scale conference. Major changes were made mainly in the fields of research programs, community intervention and development, market differentiation, and institutional management. The strategic proposals on academic programs development, and personnel development and training were considered complete. After much discussion in which differences about this issue were evident, it was decided not to add a new strategic line addressing student development and campus life, since main ideas had been incorporated in other proposals. A task force was appointed to explain this decision to the students.

Second Large Group Conference

On December 9, 2003, the second large-scale conference was held, with the participation of four hundred members of the university community. Although this conference had the same aims as the first conference and some similar activities, the major focus was on implementing the strategic proposals. Much of the conference was structured with natural work units meeting to address the implementation of the proposed strategic issues. ITESO is organized by academic departments, research centers, service centers, and administrative offices. Each of these units was asked to identify the particular programs and projects that they would undertake in the upcoming three years in order to implement the strategic proposals. The ideas collected were numerous. The departments, offices, and centers were also asked to identify key stakeholders needed for them to be successful in their own programs and projects. Records of all ideas and results were created and sent to participants.

Final Strategic Plan

It was the official duty of the governing board to define the final strategic proposal for the years 2004–2006. In mid-December, the governing board met to examine the new recommendations made in the second large conference. In January 2004, a document was issued by the governing board of ITESO and contained the strategic proposals for the six key areas of the university's immediate future. Each area was addressed with a strategic objective, a set of goals, and a set of guidelines.

Further Formulation of Strategic Plan by Organizational Units

The four major university divisions—academic, community, external affairs, and administration—received the strategic proposals for 2004–2006 and were asked to formulate their own strategically consistent three-year plans. It was recommended that the divisions should design their plans in a participatory manner and, if possible, apply whole systems design principles. A three-month period was given for divisions to complete their planning. Subsequently, the academic departments, centers, and offices of ITESO were asked to plan their three-year strategy following the same principles that applied to the divisions. A three-month period was given for departments to complete their planning. In the summer of 2004, the strategic planning process was completed.

Impact of the Whole Systems Strategic Planning Process at ITESO

Follow-up interviews and a survey were conducted six months after the conclusion of the 2003–2006 strategic plan, with members of the rector's council, the planning commission, and some academic department deans (twelve interviews). In addition, the authors conducted a three-hour seminar in June 2005, with thirty faculty and administrators who critiqued the strategic planning process.

These results were very rich and provided solid evidence with which to characterize perceptions of change (or nonchange) as a result of the strategic planning process. Overall, respondents were very encouraged by the participative nature of the strategic planning process. They felt that involving as many people as possible was a key factor in learning about the competitive challenges ITESO was facing. Some respondents were very satisfied with the content and outcomes of the planning process. Others felt that even though it was quite positive to involve all stakeholders, the plan itself was too broad to be of help in achieving a clear strategic direction. Some others thought that even though the strategic direction was clearly set, the organization units did not have the skills to understand the strategic plan and decide how it would be implemented in their unit.

An additional theme in the interviews was that ITESO needs to continue with these participative approaches in order to learn how to implement strategies in a more effective manner. They felt this was the right methodology, particularly because it was consistent with the search for equity and community participation that are key institutional values at this Jesuit university. But some felt that the intervention was not extensive or deep enough to create the change needed in the university.

By early 2004, ITESO reversed the downward trend in student enrollment, which increased by 8 percent at the undergraduate level and 16 percent in

graduate programs. The academic program review was completed, and new curricula were implemented in all university degree programs. Some university departments and centers are actively looking for ways to achieve a qualitative differentiation. A new language can be heard in the discourse of some university authorities, incorporating concepts such as market differentiation and strategic thinking. It is now clear that the university has not threatened its foundational social orientation as it has become more and more aware of competition, market differentiation, and operational efficiency. Debate is being encouraged on areas such as market and competition analysis, academic program innovation, strategic alliances, internationalization, and to some extent, quality assurance.

The whole systems process undoubtedly laid some foundation for change, especially at the level of university authorities and some department and center heads. We are not saying that the planning process dramatically changed these people's frame of mind but that a new way of thinking about strategic decision making and action taking is being incorporated into the agenda of ITESO.

Before the participative strategic process was carried out, the mood at ITESO could be described as oppressive. One could feel that the external competition was getting more and more aggressive, and ITESO's response capacity was very timid, divided, and full of inner tensions. The participative process showed that ITESO could establish a collective dialogue and reach common ground in order to define strategic directions. However, there is no evidence yet of a noticeable impact on the operational base (teaching classes, service personnel performing their jobs, general interactions with students) beyond personal feelings that this process was more participative than any other in the past. It has created a more favorable mood at the university and relaxed some of the tensions.

Overall, it is fair to say that ITESO has strengthened its well-established competitive position after the participative planning process. One of the strategic issues developed—market differentiation strategy—has been key in helping decide specific university programs and investments over the recent months. There is much to do to fine-tune and align the strategies of departments and centers. There is still confusion about how the strategic plan fits within certain units. We know of some instances where administrators did not carry forward the strategic plan by involving their work group in a participative process. This created a great deal of frustration for those individuals involved in the conferences, because they were expecting a similar level of involvement in their own organizational unit.

There have been some major changes within the university over the last year and a half. New academic programs have been developed, and other programs have been updated in a very quick and efficient manner. There is a sense of urgency in doing new things that differentiate the university from its competition. Many university programs are now focused on deploying ITESO's competitive advantages. These appear to be having an impact on community and market perceptions of the university. The action of several ITESO offices and centers has changed noticeably; an example is the re-engineering of the whole admissions procedure, whereby the processes of student recruiting, admission, career counseling, and financial aid were integrated. Before the planning exercise, these processes were fragmented, and each one followed its own particular logic. Now they are working out of one coordinated office, and this has substantially improved operational efficiency for enrollment.

Other examples include investing in campus infrastructure according to the strategic priorities (especially in engineering and the social sciences), strengthening alliances with sister universities, both nationally and internationally, being more aggressive with advertising and promotional activities, constructing closer relationships with high schools, both within Guadalajara and the western region of Mexico. To what extent these new activities are related to the participative planning cannot directly be assessed; however, we think the process has helped decision makers take action consistent with the university strategic plan.

Learnings and Reflections

The cultural side of our learning has been very important. When our consulting group started its practice in Mexico, we all wondered whether these methods would be effective. Yet with major societal changes ongoing in Mexico, we have always been optimistic about the effective use of systemwide methods. We were not wrong. Mexicans in general have felt rather comfortable participating in large groups and involving themselves in participative processes.

We have learned that culture plays a minor role in the successful implementation of Large Group Methods in Mexico. Cross-cultural research has characterized Mexico's society with values of high power distance, high risk avoidance, high collectivism, and moderately high masculinity. But we have found that these cultural values have not limited the use of Large Group Methods. We believe that the primary intervention focus needs to be on addressing and meeting client needs. If you have the right topics, the right stakeholders, and a committed and motivated group, then the methods work very well in Mexico. Focusing on other issues, such as cultural differences, only creates missed opportunities. The evidence to date suggests that given an appropriate learning environment (like those created by Large Group Methods), people from all cultures can dialogue on issues important to them, plan and establish a common vision of their future, and work within the framework of common ground philosophy. Our experience with over fifty consultations in Mexico firmly supports this conclusion.

However, we do believe that some cultural manifestations within Mexico need to be addressed in planning the use

of Large Group Methods. In this way, we view culture with a small "c." The adaptations are useful in that they help participants feel more comfortable with participation, yet these adaptations are not major determinants of intervention success. For example, Mexicans like to receive tangible products throughout a conference. It is expected that a picture of the whole group will be taken and a copy provided to all participants. We do so. Certificates of participation are also given to everyone and are signed by the facilitators. Formal, bound reports are also desired and provided.

Participant discipline with respect to time is very critical to working with large groups. Mexicans, if given a choice, prefer flexibility around time, and the opportunity to discuss a topic as little or as much as they desire. However, we have not had serious problems with time in our sessions. Likely, this is because we stress how important being on time is and how keeping the tight schedule of activities in conferences is necessary to success. Mexicans comply with these requests readily, and we have no problem with the strict time demands of Large Group Methods. One innovation that has been created in Mexico is the use of a red-yellow-green-light system to visually indicate time for the end of an activity (red), getting groups to hurry when time is about up (yellow), and letting groups work freely without time concerns (green). These visual indicators are very helpful for time management with large groups in Mexico. Another version of this is to have yellow and red cards available at each table to control discussions. An individual receiving a yellow card means that others perceive that he or she is talking too much and should limit comments. A red card indicates that others want the individual to stop talking. Again, these help participants manage their own groups by providing feedback in a playful manner that avoids direct confrontation and the loss of face.

We have wondered whether our interventions might help in creating a more participative culture in Mexican organizations. We have not been able to systematically test whether the use of Large Group Methods results in more participative organizations, or whether more open styles of management exist after the interventions have been completed. It is certainly possible that large-scale participative conferences create "cultural islands" in which dialogue and participation thrive, only to return to a hierarchical status quo upon their completion. Yet even if large-scale participation creates a big bubble that is broken the following "normal" day of work, the experience of working with a group of organizational stakeholders to collaboratively develop and affirm common ground is not forgotten. New ideas and new energy start to point the way to change. Cultural islands leave a legacy for the organization's future. Dialogue and new connections, even without common ground, help people know each other better.

Working in Mexico also involves sensitivity to other issues: shoe-string budgets, the disposition that organizations

take to time, the flexibility needed to adjust methods to fit condensed time frames, and the willingness of participants to engage within what many other cultures would consider very spartan working environments.

Whenever data are collected with Large Group Methods, the group must be tasked with finding the common ground in the data through sense making and data reduction. There were some steps of the conferences where data were not reduced and common understandings were not established. When these data were transferred to the board of governors, they found it very difficult to do anything with them. The power of this form of action research comes from the fact that data collection, reduction or analysis, and interpretation is done by the same group of people. To only do one or two steps of this action research process seriously limits the power of these methods.

Even though participation at ITESO was widely spread and all stakeholders had the chance to provide information via open forums on the Internet, some individuals who wanted to be invited to the large group events were not. It is fair to say that they were discouraged. Planning processes like this must involve forums where anyone who wishes can personally contribute their thoughts and ideas. Maybe this means having an additional day or half-day open forum (like an Open Space), where data are collected in a way that is similar to the large group conferences and reduced and summarized by the attendees. This would have been possible in this instance because the ITESO campus is within reach of the vast majority of stakeholders.

Three more learnings seem important outcomes of our work:

• *Need for full implementation.* In addition, some individuals who participated in the large group conferences expected a similar process within their departments and centers. Some leaders carried forward a participative method to determine how their organizational unit would implement the six strategies developed by the planning process; others did not. Maybe these leaders did not use participative approaches because they did not know how to do so, or maybe they were negative about the whole process. This was a critical step of the large-scale planning process that limited the success of this project. In the future more institutional resources and support should be available at the unit level to aid in the understanding and incorporation of the strategic directions in programs and projects. In addition, the leaders who did use participative approaches in determining how the strategic plan would be deployed within their departments and centers found that there were no forums to let others know of their plans and accomplishments. These feedback forums should also be established in the future.

• *Missed opportunity to involve students.* From our perspective, the board of governors missed an opportunity to involve students more fully in the whole systems change process. Although students were selected as representatives to both large group conferences, they felt compelled to hold their own conference forum to send a stronger message to the strategy process. In an amazing and creative response, they designed, found the resources for, and conducted their own conference. They asked for minimal guidance from the consultants to help design the event according to Large Group Method's principles. Their suggestions to the board of governors were quite compatible with the draft versions of the strategic plan. They simply wanted to add one more strategic issue concerning student development and campus life. The board rejected adding another strategic issue and told the students their concerns were already in the plan.

We, as consultants, were a bit dumbfounded by this response. From our perspective, it seemed that to incorporate the students' desires required little or nothing from the board and would have gone a long way to enhance goodwill between the students and faculty and administration. But in this instance, it appears that the traditional hierarchical roles of administrator and student were adhered to. We argued for the board to consider the effect of their actions, but to no avail.

• *Participation in politics and education.* Our experience with Mexican academic institutions (as well as political organizations) leads us to conclude that these settings differ from other businesses. In academic and political organizations, it is important to be emphatic about what "common ground" means and the implication of this principle for data collection and analysis. Participants need to be warned that the outcomes of the conference will be those issues that are supported as common ground by the entire group. Therefore, much of the data generated will fall short of common ground, and this may include issues that individuals feel passionate about. At ITESO, a participant was very upset by the fact that a suggested change in wording was not incorporated into the final version. In this instance, the "common ground" principle was not fully understood.

Our experience with ITESO's strategic plan has also reinforced our views about the importance of gaining "belief" in the procedures used to develop a strategy, as well as a "commitment" to performing the strategic planning tasks. It is critical to the success of whole systems change for there to be widespread belief in and commitment to the strategic planning process and procedures employed. Again, it is our experience that academics and professional politicians find it difficult to believe in organizing processes and, as such, also have difficulty committing to the many strategic planning tasks. Maybe this is due to the general nature of the professoriate and the inherent political danger in showing too much commitment to a particular approach. We suppose that these observations are not particular to Mexico and apply across cultures and societies. Again, we do not experience these difficulties with business organizations. In the future, we advise speaking directly to

groups and individuals at the beginning stages about the understanding that is required to believe in the Large Group Method approach, as well as the required commitment for success.

Open forums to review and critique Large Group Methods are critical to facilitating organizational learning. ITESO as a community is currently struggling with whether these methods were a one-time event or whether they now will become incorporated as an institutional method of strategic planning. Once these participative methods have been employed, it is difficult for organizational members to go back to old methods of planning that were solely controlled by a few organizational members. ITESO will decide within the next few months whether they continue with the Large Group Method approach to planning for the 2007–2009 period. It is hoped that a number of open forums will be created to discuss this issue.

Conclusion

The Large Group Methods events in Mexico always seem to go well, and the major problems we have experienced (lack of follow-through on conference commitments) are common issues encountered wherever these methods have been used—in North America, Europe, Africa, Asia, and now Latin America. We are convinced, however, that we still need to question how we might intervene more effectively to avoid some of the obstacles of implementation and follow-through. We are aware that these obstacles may differ for each specific industry or organization. It might be of great value to anticipate specific obstacles to implementation at the beginning design phase. Following up may have some cultural determinations, but it is our opinion that follow-through is mainly related to available resources and management skills.

References

Bunker, B. B., & Alban, B. T. (1997). *Large group interventions: Engaging the whole system for rapid change.* San Francisco: Jossey-Bass.

Dannemiller Tyson Associates. (2000). *Whole-Scale Change.* San Francisco: Berrett-Koehler.

Emery, F. (1995). Participative Design: Effective, flexible and successful, now! *Journal for Quality and Participation, 18*(1), 6–9.

Hofstede, G. (1980). *Culture's consequences: International differences in work-related values.* Thousand Oaks, CA: Sage.

Manning, M. R., & DelaCerda, J. (2003). Building organizational change in an emerging economy: Whole systems change using large group interventions in Mexico. In R. W. Woodman & W. A. Pasmore (Eds.), *Research in organizational change and development* (Vol. 14). Kidlington, Oxford, UK: Elsevier Science, pp. 51–97.

Manning, M. R., & Binzagr, G. F. (1996). Methods, values, and assumptions underlying large group interventions intended to change whole systems. *International Journal of Organizational Analysis, 4*(3), 268–284.

Weisbord, M. R., & Janoff, S. (1995). *Future Search.* San Francisco: Berrett-Koehler.

FROM STRATEGIC PLANNING
TO OPEN SPACE IN EAST AFRICA

Theo Groot

The Challenge

The old shoes no longer fit.

As a professional development practitioner employed in central and eastern Africa since 1979, I have been focused on bringing about deliberate change in the communities and organizations with which I work. Nowhere is the environment so unstable, so volatile, and therefore so unpredictable as in this part of the world; wars, genocides, droughts, and floods are all unplanned events that seem to occur in an irregular pattern. My work has become predominantly a matter of damage control, using a "repair approach" (Wheatley, 1999).

For most of my career, I have mainly used strategic planning tools with which problems are identified, causes established, and solutions proposed and implemented. Development work, as I then saw it, was mainly a matter of solving problems. Over the years, I have felt increasingly unhappy with this way of working and the results obtained. The nice five-year plans we elaborated in intense workshops with the people never seemed to work the way we expected. Problem and need identification exercises just seemed to bring people's energy down, as they somehow conveyed the message: "You are really poor, ignorant people; look at all the problems and the little you have done so far to solve them." Participation of the local population was reduced to ten to fifteen representatives sitting in our workshops, more or less confirming what we had already figured out. Moreover, because projects are mapped out over several years, with clearly formulated results that have to be obtained, I felt under enormous pressure to make sure that local organizations performed and reached the formulated results, even if the circumstances were such that it was barely possible to determine, in a detailed way, what was to be achieved within three or five years.

Gradually, it dawned on me that real change was not manageable and would never be the direct result of my deliberate interventions. What kind of work would be effective in a volatile situation?

The Method

I read the book, *The Power of Spirit* by Harrison Owen (2000), which expressed what I intuitively had started to know: change cannot be imposed on organizations or communities but must grow from within at its own pace, constantly scanning the ever-changing environment for opportunities to bring the common vision a step closer. Changing organizations and communities is not a matter of motivation, and Open Space Technology (OST) is not just a motivation booster. The focus of my work should not be on diagnosing but on opening up space for the Spirit to do its transformative work.

In Open Space technology I found a method that could help me.

I read the book several times, as well as his how-to manual (Owen, 1997), and then, with the guidance of a distant mentor, just started. Unfortunately, I had not been able to participate in any Open Space meetings before, so I had to facilitate my first meeting all on my own. Luckily, Owen's user's guide is extremely helpful, and although at times it seems he exaggerates in his detailed descriptions, these are, as he explains, necessary and helpful. I kept this book at hand throughout the first Open Space meeting and referred to it over and again— but secretly, in a hidden corner! Not only did it give me clear instructions on what to do (and particularly what not to do), it felt like having Owen whispering in my ear, reassuring me that everything would be fine. And indeed, it worked. It actually worked every time I opened up space, and people just loved it. Moreover, Open Space is a methodology that local people can easily learn. I was amazed by a local community worker who facilitated a fantastic Open Space meeting after a training workshop of five days.

What Happened

Here are three examples of how Open Space has worked in Africa.

Open Space in Kabale, Uganda

"This is the first time we have really been listened to." This was a remark from an illiterate woman in Kabale, Uganda, who had just participated in a one-day Open Space meeting, together with 104 other women from seventeen different women's groups. The meeting took place in the local language and had a simple, straightforward theme: "What can we do to live a better life here in Kabale district?" Participants gathered around 10 o'clock in the morning in a big hall of a local primary school; the floor had been swept and the benches put in a large oval shape. A few of the children from the neighborhood sneaked in; others hung in the open windows, and some participants breastfed their babies. The circle was empty except for the World Peace Flame[1] that burned in a

hurricane lamp in the middle, next to some papers and pens. The facilitator slowly walked the circle, opening the meeting and explaining the procedures in a visual and, at times, theatrical way.

Then the magic moment arrived: Will they come up with issues to discuss? There was some slight uneasiness, some giggling and pushing, but it did not take long for the first person to stand up, walk to the center of the circle, and announce an issue she would like to have discussed. One of the literate women wrote it on a piece of paper and gave it to her, and she then walked back to her place. In no time, nine issues were raised—all different and relevant. The facilitator indicated the first five women who had put up a topic and asked them to go outside and stand at a reasonable distance from one another. Other participants were asked to go out as well and to join the person whose issue they would like to discuss. In less than one hour and a half from the start, five groups were formed and seated on the grass, under the trees, and engaged in lively discussion. At the end of the discussions, every group wrote down its three main actions on a big sheet of paper and fixed it on the outside wall of the hall. They attracted many readers from other groups; literate participants read them out to those who could not read.

The air was filled with excitement. It was time for lunch. While the meeting was going on, a group of women had prepared a simple meal of posho and beans. People lined up, carrying the plates they had brought from home, and in less than one hour the hungry were fed and gathered around the four remaining women for a new round of talks and exchanges.

When all the discussions had ended, every participant was given five beans with which to vote; the three topics with the most beans were to be worked on first. Voting is a serious matter in Uganda, and people took their time to decide where to place their beans, at times consulting others or just reflecting on their own. The "electoral commission" declared the vote free and fair, and participants joined the group that was to work on the topic of their choice. When they came back to a closing circle, more than one hundred actions they could undertake to make their lives better had been raised, from obtaining a loan for a goat to having a serious discussion with their husband about alcohol abuse. Everyone wanted to express their feelings about the meeting and how wonderful they felt about it. It all ended at 5 P.M. with singing and dancing.

This was the first Open Space meeting I organized with rural people in a very low-tech way, but the meeting went perfectly well and people really owned the process. There was real participation, whereby the women made their own agenda, organized themselves, and came up with possible actions that they were ready to undertake. From this and other similar experiences, I have learned that language is never a problem, although it helps if you talk the process through with your translator beforehand, as the correct wording sometimes requires reflection. In all cases, the translator walked just behind me and translated after every few sentences. It also helps to visualize procedures. I first walk the circle, describing how we will organize. But then I repeat the main procedures by actually doing what they are to do in a fun and playful way. True, the richness of the discussions is not captured in full, since the reports are mainly action lists. But for whom should the reports be captured? The person in control? The women who participated in the discussions definitely understood all the issues, and many things were shared during the meal and at other occasions.

One way to seize more of what is said in the groups is to have a few people around who sit in just to capture the main ideas, gather the interesting quotes, and summarize what has been said. These observation reports are then later written out and can be used by the organizers of the Open Space meetings. For the meeting itself, the rudimentary presentation of actions will do. These are oral cultures in which people do not attach much value to words on paper; what counts is the process—the talking together and the being present. Contrary to Open Space meetings I facilitated with more educated or Western participants, when everyone wanted to have a say, I have found this not to be the case in meetings with rural folks. There is a kind of group identity, whereby people fully participate in what is being said without having this urge to contribute. For rural African people, individual identity and group identity merge; without the group there is no identity for them. According to this way of thinking, the individual and the group cannot be viewed in isolation (de Liefde, 2003). However, the quality of the conversations in the smaller groups often does remain a challenge.

Open Space in Mukono, Uganda

The second example is a totally different Open Space meeting that took place in a conference center in Mukono, Uganda, where some two hundred representatives of local governments stayed together for three days. The theme of the meeting was, "Challenges and opportunities for local governments to create a climate that favors human rights." We started the evening of arrival with a storytelling session, asking participants to narrate their own stories about human rights. In about an hour and a half, we listened to some twenty-four stories. Some really made you shiver. At times, there was total silence, with just a frail woman somewhere in the half-dark, telling a very personal story (this proved to be a good bonding exercise, and I use storytelling a lot now).

This meeting was organized by representatives of the European Commission in Uganda. Although it was clearly explained in the invitation letter that this would not be yet another workshop, most people turned up for a conference, which in Uganda includes all kind of allowances for travel and attendance, bodyguards for the high officials, and

drivers. Five participants were provincial governors. Most of the others were among the top leaders of municipalities. For many of them, the start of the conference was a bit of a shock. There was no minister to open the session and no presentation of all the important people. For the provincial governors, this was unacceptable, and four of them walked out by the end of the first day; the others quickly adjusted, and we had a great Open Space.

In this meeting, three secretaries assisted us; group reports were brought in to the secretaries, typed out, and posted on the wall. The room was large, so we sat in a big double circle. Unfortunately, the sound system refused to work, so it became a real challenge to the voice, but "whatever happens is the only thing that could have." It is a special feeling to walk the space in such a big group with more educated people. There were the inevitable questions, but keeping Owen's advice in mind, I refused to answer them and politely brushed them aside and continued. My experience has been that it is better to avoid the "trainer mode," as it never really helps the group to get into questions and answers. Most times, I invite them to discuss their question later with another participant. When people are busy at the market deciding what groups to go to, I am "just around" and may answer a question here and there. Rarely do those who wanted to raise a question in the big circle come to see me. Either they find the answer or, as is often the case, they just wanted to raise the question for the sake of asking one and being noticed. The more important the person thinks he or she is, the bigger their space-invading tendencies!

Again in this second example, participants put together their agenda and organized themselves in some fifteen groups within less than two hours. In total, fifty-three issues were raised in the opening circle, and forty-seven reports found their way to the bulletin board. The secretaries worked well and at the end of the second day were able to create a full report by midnight. Photocopying went on throughout the night, and participants received their personal copy in the morning of the third day.

This Open Space was high-tech by East African standards. When most participants are educated and used to a modern way of doing things, it is nice to have the written reports for everyone to take home. It does not work to have participants type in their own reports, but secretaries are always available and do a good job at minimum cost. People take pride in their own work and are pleased to take it home straightaway. Typically, you have to wait for a long time before receiving a report of a workshop (my personal record stands at a year and a half!). To reduce photocopying costs, we sometimes produce one or two copies for every stakeholder group present rather than for individuals.

A particular feature of this Open Space was the presence of so many dignitaries—a real challenge to the facilitator. Although we were tough and strict as facilitators, we did not escape the final speech during the closing circle and the

written declaration. On other occasions, I have asked the organizers to invite all the high-status people in person and explain the "game" to them, thus making them conspirators with this very new way of behaving. This often works.

Open Space for NGOs

The last example I want to give is actually the very first Open Space meeting I facilitated. It was requested by a regional NGO (nongovernmental organization). They invited eight stakeholder groups around the theme of "collaboration amongst themselves," because so many would just "do their own thing," without keeping an eye on the wider context. Ninety percent of the eighty participants came from the NGO sector, which gave the meeting a totally different atmosphere from the one with the local government people. It was more relaxed and easygoing, with a high initial commitment. This was also a three-day, high-tech meeting, where secretaries typed the twenty-eight group reports and produced a book of proceedings at the end of the second day.

The meeting rolled out very much as in the books. Because I know the organization well and stay in contact with them, I was able to get some feedback about their reactions to the meeting. Here are a few sample responses to my question: "What did you like about Open Space? What did you learn?"

"What made the difference for me was that without much protocol and a leading figure, people generated many productive ideas."

"Members create their own agenda."

"I was surprised by the high number of issues that were brought out and discussed. I was amazed that you can work effectively with such a big group."

"I learned to be more open and to accept other people's view."

"Every person could make a contribution."

Most of these remarks may sound obvious and self-evident for Westerners, but in an East African context they express real issues. Participants genuinely appreciate that they can discuss topics that matter to them, that they can choose where to go, and that they are allowed to speak their mind and be listened to. The times of the African palaver under a tree have gone long ago in most places. People are used to being talked to and preached at in churches, in schools, and in politics. The Open Space recreates a secure surrounding where people dare to speak up and make their point, perhaps much more than in any other setting.

Because I was able to follow up on this Open Space, I noticed that interesting things happened in the year that followed the opening of the space. One of the actions was on corruption, and currently there is a very strong and active anticorruption coalition in the region. Another result of the Open Space meeting is a regular news bulletin and in-

creased networking across stakeholder groups. Several elements of Open Space found their way into the organizational culture. People now sit in circles when they meet, use a talking stick, and have check-ins and check-outs.

Reflections

OST is a wonderful way of strengthening organizations and communities. The different stories of Open Space meetings that I have described show some of what I learned by running those meetings.

Open Space and African Healing Rites

However, the most important learning that emerged out of all my experiences with Open Space in Africa is its closeness to the Bantu African culture and roots.

Harrison Owen (1997) tells the story of his experiences as a photo journalist in a small village in Liberia, where he participated in a boy's *rite de passage,* and how he was struck by the geometry of the circle and the rhythm of the movement. The essence of the rite was the Spirit at work. This, he says, is where he found two of his basic mechanisms of meetings. Two additional mechanisms (the community bulletin board and the village market place) were added, and OST was born. His reflection made me look for other links with African culture. When I worked in the former Zaire, now the Democratic Republic of the Congo, I became interested in the Jebola healing rite of the Mongo people (Groot, 1989) and linked the two. It strikes me that an Open Space meeting and a Jebola rite have many resemblances. I have come to believe that an Open Space meeting can, indeed, be considered a healing rite in itself; it has all the features of central and east African healing rituals.

The first step in the Jebola is that of diagnosis and preparation. In this stage the sick person is diagnosed by the healer, after which the preparations for the ritual are made. Not every form of ill health, however, can be treated with a Jebola rite, and neither is an Open Space meeting the appropriate thing to do in every situation. When an Open Space is considered, ample time must be given to the exploration and definition of a theme. In these discussions, the facilitator helps the representatives of the organization or community to go beyond the obvious and to see the theme in its broader context, just as the healer helps the patient and her family find the story behind the illness.

A second important matter at this stage deals with what Williams (2001) calls the "givens"—what are the things that need to be done, that cannot be altered. Likewise, the Mongo culture determines the framework for the Jebola ritual.

The first divination, which is the second stage in the Jebola rite, frees the voice of the sick person and allows him or her to speak up. A projective space is created, in which the patient has the opportunity to speak up and feels she has nothing to fear from other group members. In an Open Space meeting, after a short explanation of the method by the facilitator, participants are invited to raise those issues they feel passionate about and for which they want to take responsibility. This often leads to an avalanche of issues; every time we start, issues are brought forward. The seclusion period of the Jebola that follows is the time and space where the transformational process can take place. In an Open Space this is the lapse of time between the raising of the issues and the closing ceremony. During this period, participants meet in small groups to exchange ideas about the issues, share meals together, and feel free to take some time off. During the second divination, which is the fourth stage in the healing rite, the now-healed person is presented to the community and accepted by it. Likewise, the closing ceremony acknowledges the work that has been done and celebrates the successes of the last few days. There is the realization that nothing could have been accomplished without the active participation of all; the participants themselves brought about whatever has been accomplished and are responsible for everything that did not work out. As in the healing rituals, the healing is brought forth in the process (Devisch, 1984, 1993). During the Open Space meeting, participants' passion and responsibility grows.

The last part of reintegration is often the most difficult one. Now is the time to integrate the transformations into daily life. In the case of the Jebola, the healer and the community of "healed patients" play a key role. In the case of Open Space, ample attention should be given to the follow-up actions of the groups and more specifically to the coaching of the convenors of the meeting.

The four transformational processes at work in healing rituals are equally present in an Open Space meeting:

1. *Voices are freed.* The patient in the Jebola is encouraged to speak up in a safe and secure environment all that is worrying and troublesome. She will not be blamed for whatever she says, since it is the Spirit who speaks through her. Likewise in an Open Space meeting, participants are free to raise the issues of their concern and to discuss them freely in the small groups. Every voice is heard. If the convenor of an issue finds him- or herself all alone, the person can still write a report that will have an equal place in the book of proceedings and may even be chosen as one of the "hot issues" of the meeting.

2. *Seclusion is a second process.* Both the Jebola and Open Space provide intermediate time and space that allows participants temporarily to step out of their normal life and share and learn from one another.

3. *Full participation is invited from all.* Nothing will take place without all participants freely engaging in the process—the whole system in the room. In the end, no one can remain untouched and be just an observer.

4. *This is a self-generative process of self-renewal that takes place both at the individual level and at the group*

level. When people become passionate and are ready to take up responsibilities, they change—they become renewed and transformed in the process. Like the healer, the facilitator is the midwife who is neither the one giving birth nor the one who will hold the child, but who, by her presence, allows and facilitates this natural, unavoidable process of birth to take place. People always leave an Open Space meeting enthusiastic and full of energy because they have experienced what it feels like when problems are solved, disagreements overcome, and new ways forward created.

This great similarity between an Open Space meeting and the healing ritual is one of the reasons for the enthusiastic response of most participants here in eastern Africa. For the facilitator, organizational confrontations are to be understood in terms of healing and restoring the flow of life. This is a language people immediately connect with. The focus is no longer on problems and problem solving but on strengthening life-giving forces. In the three cases I have described, as well as in all the other times I facilitated Open Space in Africa, this has been one of the most wonderful things to see happening. Ordinary rural people experience that, for this time they are allowed to speak and will be listened to.

At an Open Space meeting I facilitated in Burundi in September 2004, with 280 participants, most of them local farmers, the organizers were astonished to see how easily people adapted and took ownership. Open Space felt natural to them, even if the traditional village meetings no longer take place the way they used to. In those meetings, the elder or chief would normally just open the meeting and then remain quiet for the rest of it, allowing people to speak and to raise their points. He would just be there, holding the space, and at the end he might give a conclusion, often in the form of a parable.

Conversations and Space Invaders

I have learned that there are challenges with regard to the quality of the conversations in the small break-out groups. As the traditional way of meeting erodes, a new norm where people expect to be "talked at" has taken its place. The political elite, often in place because of material wealth or political connections, have governed so that the voice of the ordinary people no longer counts. Even the local NGO field workers often use an "I-am-telling-you" approach. We cannot expect that these ingrained habits will change overnight. However, I have noticed that many groups start incorporating some elements of the Open Space in their own meetings, such as sitting in circles and using a talking stick. Gradually, this brings about changes. Once a group has done this consciously for a minimum of six times, it becomes a new habit.

This returning to the circle has, in itself, a powerful effect, as the circle is not just another way of arranging seating; it is the heart of the Open Space. Baldwin

(1998) calls the circle the first and future culture that equals honesty, equality, and spiritual integrity. In the Open Space meeting in Burundi mentioned earlier, I introduced the talking stick in the small break-out groups on the second day and noticed a great improvement in the way conversations were held. In Burundi, the village elders are the ones to hold a stick when they talk, and they grant permission to speak to participants. Some Burundian trainees in Open Space facilitation who were present suggested that the use of the talking stick might cause problems because no one but the chief is allowed to hold it. Instead, I did not mention the word *stick* and simply asked them to use the marker pen and explained how to pass it around. But while explaining, I sensed very clearly that participants immediately understood what I was talking about and realized that in this meeting they were all "chief" in their own right.

Another challenge for the facilitator is the presence of space invaders. In my experience, the people in authority need special attention. As I mentioned earlier, the more authority a person thinks he has, the stronger the space-invading tendencies. With a group of farmers the conversation normally goes fine, and everyone who would like to speak dares to do so. As soon as you have authorities around, though, things change. First, they want to be acknowledged and presented. This reinstates their authority in front of all the participants. Second, they have often lost all real interest in the people they are supposed to represent;

every public event is an occasion to push their own agenda. In eastern Africa, we have evolved to a situation where even burials become places for public rallying. That is why leaders often ask questions in the opening forum, dominate discussions in the small groups, and want to come up with pronouncements at the end. They are right to be fearful because liberating the Spirit in an Open Space will, in the long run, become a serious challenge to their positions. Open Space promotes real democracy and empowers people. In practice, I have discovered that it often helps if the organizers invite these people personally and explain the process to them beforehand. It makes them a "conspirator" and shuns them from invading the space. In the Burundian Open Space, where several administrators and director generals from ministries participated, this approach worked very well. In the end, as in the case of the provincial governors, they always have the option to use their two feet and leave.

I have now been using Open Space Technology for some three years, and I am fascinated by its power. For me, it is a new approach to development work that is really participatory, focuses on the future, gives ordinary people voice and hope, and opens our development efforts up to the Spirit.

Note

1. The World Peace Flame (www.world peaceflame.com) was created in July 1999 by the Life Foundation (UK) as a gift to humanity for the new millennium. I use it often in my work as a reminder of the ultimate purpose of what we are doing.

References

Baldwin, C. (1998). *Calling the circle* (2nd ed.). New York: Bantam Books.

De Liefde, W. (2003). *Lekgotla, the art of leadership through dialogue.* Houghton, South Africa: Jacana Media.

Devisch, R. (1984). *Se recréer femme* [To become a woman again]. Berlin: Dietrich Reimer Verlag.

Devisch, R. (1993). *Weaving the threads of life.* Chicago: University of Chicago Press.

Groot, T. (1989). *Jebola, un rite de guérison Mongo.* Unpublished paper.

Owen, H. (1997). *Open Space Technology.* San Francisco: Berrett-Koehler.

Owen, H. (2000). *The power of spirit.* San Francisco: Berrett-Koehler.

Wheatley, M. (1999). *Leadership and the new science.* San Francisco: Berrett-Koehler.

Williams, B. (2001). My story of the Open Space Organisation. Available at www. openspacetechnology.com/articles/ mystory.html.

TRAINING INDONESIAN FACILITATORS TO LEAD COMMUNITY PLANNING FOR WOMEN AND CHILDREN

Kim Martens, Rita Schweitz, and Kenoli Oleari

The Challenge

When we three North Americans considered an assignment in Indonesia to train a group of Indonesian facilitators to facilitate Future Searches in forty Indonesian districts, with the aim of ensuring the survival, development, and protection of children and women, we faced numerous known and unknown challenges. What we knew: we were to start in three weeks; we had no chance to meet the client face-to-face; we would not see the venue until we actually began our work; and only one of us was even somewhat familiar with the language and culture. What we didn't know: a political coup was threatening to erupt blocks from where we would be living and working in Jakarta; no translators were assigned to our project; one key person would get sick, another would have a family emergency, and one would resent us and work to undermine our work.

Background

The request from UNICEF-Indonesia in 2001 was for us to prepare forty local facilitators to conduct Future Searches in local districts (regions) on the survival, development, and protection of children and women. The results would be used in the development of UNICEF's next five-year plan. The resident representative of UNICEF-Indonesia selected Future Search for this effort because of the many positive results he had witnessed after introducing Future Search in Asia in 1994. The plan was for three experienced Future Search facilitators to hold an intensive Training of Trainers for two days for four "master facilitators" and four other hand-picked, experienced facilitators; this training would be followed by a five-day "Managing a Future Search Conference" training for approximately thirty provincial facilitators, in which the master facilitators would play a significant training role. The expected result of this training would be a dozen facilitators ready to run the forty district Future Searches over the next three months.

Finalizing Our Contract

After adjusting to our initial excitement about this exotic and challenging assignment, we began our first task: understanding the assignment and contracting carefully. The first thing we questioned was the difference between "master facilitators" and "hand-picked facilitators."

The master facilitators had helped with a Future Search that had been managed by experienced facilitators from the United States four months earlier. They had then participated in a four-day training in the United States, and two had facilitated a Future Search. What else did they need as training? Why were we being asked to spend an additional two days training the master facilitators? And why we were being asked to train them with hand-picked facilitators who had no previous exposure to Future Search?

After a long discussion with the client about expectations for this project and previous experiences with Future Search in Indonesia, we came up with a plan. Once the Training of Trainers and five-day training were completed, we would add a coaching process for selected master and provincial facilitators—an approach in which we, as consultants, would each accompany a small group of newly trained Indonesian facilitators to a different island to coach them through their first Future Search, which would be run in both Bahasa Indonesia (the national language) and the local languages. UNICEF now had just four weeks to organize these three district Future Searches and almost no time for consultation from us, as our time would be consumed with traveling, planning, training, and coaching.

We were also aware that, despite our careful contracting, there was much going on that we could not fully know via phone or e-mail. We began with only a sketchy image of this complex situation, and much more would soon be revealed.

The Cross-Cultural Context

We three trainer-facilitators were North American—all speaking English. None of us had any experience with Bahasa Indonesia. The master and provincial facilitators primarily spoke Bahasa Indonesia and, in addition, spoke as many as four different languages as their native tongues. Some understood or spoke English, and some only spoke their local language.

Not only were there cultural differences between us and the Indonesians, there were cultural differences among the Indonesians themselves. Although Indonesia has been a nation since 1949, the islands are starkly different from each other, each with its own languages, ethnicities, identities, and customs. All of our work would involve Christians, Muslims, and Hindus working side-by-side. Each of these religions has its own rituals and customs and, in some cases, a history of discord with each other.

The Political Context

We soon discovered that, in addition to normal political tensions, a volatile political situation was brewing in Jakarta just as we were arriving. Then-president Abdurrahman Wahid was about to be impeached by the legislature. There was concern that he would refuse to step down and would call in hundreds of thousands of his loyal supporters to use force to keep him in power. As we began our initial Training of Trainers with the eight master facilitators, the situation worsened; the president suspended the Peoples' Consultative Assembly to avoid the impending impeachment process and remain in office. The thirty provincial facilitators who were to join us the following week were uncertain whether it was safe to travel to our training in Jakarta, less than one mile from the president's palace. There were tanks and soldiers in the streets near our hotel-training site, and there was a constant threat of escalation of the violence.

The United Nations has a security officer and system in each country that monitors and plans for "emergencies" such as these and continually assesses when and who needs to be evacuated as the situation changes. Short-term consultants like us would be at the top of the evacuation list, along with U.N. employees' family members and all other nonessential staff. We had regular updates on the situation with our UNICEF colleagues. At one point, we talked about the possibility of canceling the training or moving it to another city. In the end, it was decided to move forward as planned, and the provincial facilitators all arrived and departed safely.

Method and Adaptations

Future Search was the method of choice for this assignment. Future Search is a large group planning process that produces a shared vision of the desired future, as well as action plans that will be implemented. In a very engaging and participative approach, individuals and communities focus on what they themselves can do, not what can be done for them. Future Search participants acquire a broad view, including historical, current, and future perspectives, from personal, local, and worldwide vantage points. By using tools that help to move the group into creative and collaborative modes of experience, Future Search helps people push past their historically limited perspectives and design a future they want to work for (Schweitz and Martens, 2005). We faithfully followed the Future Search principles and conditions for success, while we adapted some of the activities to work in the local situation, as we describe next.

The Starting Point: Our Principles of Practice

We have found that the principles on which our Large Group Methods are based are excellent guides for our work in any culture. Future Search (Weisbord and Janoff, 2000) succinctly describes four of these core principles:

1. *Have the whole system in the room:* Include people with authority, resources, expertise, information, and need. All perspectives are necessary to understanding the whole.
2. *Think globally and act locally:* Explore the whole before fixing any part.
3. *Find a future focus and common ground:* Working toward a higher,

shared purpose stimulates creativity and collaborative action.
4. *Encourage self-management and responsibility for action:* What we do or don't do now affects how things will turn out in the future.

We focus this next section on the kind of knowledge and skill that is needed and the dilemmas that can occur wherever Large Group Methods are used cross-culturally.

Communicating with Participants and Among Groups

We worked hard to speak slowly and clearly in English so that as many people in the room as possible could grasp our meaning. We made sure that our voices were well modulated. We were careful in our choice of words, trying to keep to short words and sentences. Rather than giving four examples to illustrate a point, we carefully chose only one and made it concise to avoid long and complex translations. We often stopped to ask if people understood. If some indicated that they did not understand, we asked the group to discuss what we had said among themselves, in their own languages. We asked again if people understood. It seldom took more than a few rounds before most people did.

Using Metaphors

We examined all the metaphors we used to be sure certain they were culturally appropriate. In one of the district Future

Searches, we chose to use the metaphor of a curving, hilly road to illustrate the emotional ups-and-downs of the Future Search process rather than the typical Future Search metaphor of the roller coaster. We knew that most of the participants had just traveled such a road to get to the site, but we were not sure that many of them had ever seen or been on a roller coaster. In another session that was attended by many fishermen, we used the metaphor of a boat riding a wave.

Addressing Translation Challenges

In the district Future Searches, participants from the UNICEF head office spoke English, and participants from the different islands spoke as many as four different languages. We addressed this challenge by seating people according to their own languages, where possible. When only a few people spoke one language, we made sure that someone in their group was able and willing to translate between the less-spoken language and the more common one. Although we made accommodations for language, we still met the Future Search design principle of max-mix groups with differing perspectives by meeting all other diversity criteria within the minority language group.

We made the incorrect assumption that UNICEF would provide us with experienced translators. Unfortunately, we had not even considered that we would *not* have them and therefore did not

contract for them. Not only was this an impediment during training and coaching, but it was a problem after-hours, when flip charts and materials needed to be created.

We made the best of this situation by prevailing on two of our Indonesian English-speaking master facilitators to become the lead trainers. They did most of the up-front, direct work, while we sat off-center with an over-the-shoulder translator (another master facilitator), using all our skills to observe nonverbal actions and to understand the dynamics in the room. We used our observations and experience to coach the lead trainers in their unanticipated leadership role. Occasionally, we spoke to the group, with the lead trainer as our translator. We reserved our direct comments for critical moments when we could not wait for a break to communicate our intervention to the lead facilitators.

Every so often, one of our lead trainers would engage the group in a way that left us with no idea of what was happening. Sometimes there were very deep silences; at other times, there was very animated conversation. We had no time for a huddle with the lead trainers. We did our best to trust that they understood the Future Search process well enough and could handle what was happening. At intense moments when the process needed to be put back on track, we again trusted that the lead trainer would do what was necessary or ask for help. When we felt we needed to, we broke in to find out what was going on. In situations like these, good partnering, good preparation, and good choice of partners really pay dividends.

After one intense day of training, our lead trainer informed us that she might have to leave suddenly because of a critically ill family member. Fortunately, she did not have to leave until late in the training. The next evening, our other lead trainer became sick and could not attend the training. At these points, we just hoped for the best and relied on other people to fill in the gaps. Luckily, these gaps were not as large as we had feared.

Professional Translators. Had we not had local facilitators who understood the Future Search process, our next option would have been to work through a professional translator. In this situation, we would have been doing most of the talking, followed by the translator communicating our words. Working with professional translators is challenging because most have no experience in process translation and interactive work—the skills needed for Large Group Methods. Instead, they often specialize in a certain field and do translation for academic-type conferences, where they disseminate information. They pride themselves on their accuracy and precision with words and grammatical structure. They work best when given presentation papers ahead of time, as well as lists of specialized vocabulary. They speak an educated language that may interfere with breaking down barriers and working for inclusion.

When we do work with translators, we share our expectations and educate them about the purpose and desired outcomes of the conference, Large Group Methods, and the meeting design before the large group commences. We build rapport with them, asking them what they need from us and then working to provide them with whatever they require. They need to know that they are part of our team and that we will help make their job as effective as possible. We need to be confident that they know that it is not so much about getting the words exactly right as about setting the tone, communicating the whole picture, and building a common relationship.

Simultaneous Translations. Because one of the things that makes Future Search so transportable is its low dependence on technology, simultaneous translation is our least preferred mode. For this assignment, simultaneous translation was not even considered. It is dependent on having the technology available (both equipment and power supply), the proper space for setting up the translation booth (larger with each language that is included), and sufficient funds to cover this service.

We have found that simultaneous translation is not effective in working with large group, participative processes. It sets up a hierarchy among the languages that are "officially" translated and the other, less common languages in the room. It does not address translation challenges in small groups, where there is a mix of participants, each speaking a different language from the others. And when we are staring at a sea of blank faces, it is almost impossible to check with the translators on what they have said when isolated in their booth. Had we been faced with the necessity to use simultaneous translation, we would have had to engage in the same close work with translators mentioned earlier.

Finding and Working with Local Partners

We did not have the luxury of finding our own local facilitators and translators. Luckily, our lead trainers met most of the criteria that we use when we do have time to find these partners. We choose people according to the following criteria:

- A high capacity for understanding English to make up for our unfortunate inability to understand their language
- An interest in learning about Large Group Methods
- A willingness to try new things that often challenge some of their cultural perspectives
- An ability to pair with us and model equality, despite some strongly ingrained practices around hierarchy
- A commitment to the outcomes and to participants
- Natural or acquired facilitation skills that are compatible with our style of facilitation

We need facilitators and translators that are able to ask probing questions, accept difficult feedback, admit to uncertainty, and work long, hard hours with a

sense of humor. Even under the most stressful circumstances, we always try to maintain our equilibrium and have fun together.

Less-Than-Ideal Conditions. We could not have predicted the challenges that we would face during the two-day Training of Trainers. Not all of the facilitators selected to be part of this could speak English. The difference in exposure and understanding of the Future Search process among facilitators was huge. This affected their willingness to lead the subsequent five-day training (in the end, most opted to be participants in this training). We were facing the challenge of not having translators for both the Training of Trainers and the five-day training.

Ideally, we would have had *at least* a whole day to get to know each other, share expectations and working style, concentrate on the preparation of materials, and map out how we would team up to deliver each of the sessions for the five-day training. As it was, we spent the two days trying to understand how the Future Search fit into UNICEF's planning process and translating from our language to theirs and then back to make sure they were getting key concepts that they would need for the upcoming five-day training and district Future Searches. There was no break between the two trainings.

A Quandary and a Difficult Choice. We knew that the stakes were very different for our master and provincial facilitators than they were for us. This is always true when working for an organization such as UNICEF. A job, a relationship, attendance at training—sometimes even a casual remark we might make—could change a person's life and wealth in significant ways. For many of these facilitators, who were the main income earners for extended families, gaining access to multinational organizations as employees, consultants, and facilitators or making connections that provide opportunities to visit or study in another country would have an impact greater than we might be able to imagine. Thus being selected to help, gaining praise or positive recognition, or even participating in our project was extremely significant. Because of the high rank given to respect in Indonesian culture, even receiving or giving respect (or disrespect) could affect a person's fortune.

One of our biggest challenges in Indonesia involved one of the master facilitators. Within a few hours of beginning our training, it became obvious that she resented our presence. We spent an entire week trying to find a way to include and collaborate with her, but were unsuccessful. Her resentment only seemed to increase, and her disruptions became worse. We made the very difficult decision to have her removed from participating in the upcoming district Future Searches. Knowing how much she had to lose by being removed from the project made our decision difficult. Although this type of disruptive person can be found in any culture, this situation was

more complex because of the cross-cultural issues.

In Asia, saving face is extremely important and can sever relationships permanently. Power relations need to be understood and respected to succeed within the Asian context. One of us had lived and worked in Asia for five years and had a sense of this and what it looked like from a group dynamics perspective. The way that the disruptive person was behaving was extremely overt, and the only time this had been experienced before was when the person came from a position of power. So even though we hoped that we could have this person removed from the project, we were not sure we could. This required working our way through the UNICEF hierarchy, questioning what implications there might be to the organization and some of its key relationships with Indonesian partners if we were to have this person removed from the project. Ultimately, it was the resident representative of UNICEF-Indonesia who made the decision to remove her.

We knew that it was the proper decision because the group dynamics and working relationships were much improved following her departure. And even though we had made the right decision, it had not been easy. That we could not find a way to keep her in the project felt like a real failure.

Written Materials and Logistics

All written materials needed to be in the national language—Bahasa Indonesia. We and our local partners stayed up late every night to prepare instructional flip charts and create a bilingual, detailed agenda in both Bahasa Indonesia and English. This was a good way to get ready for our work together. It gave us a chance to review key concepts and go over presentation tips. We also asked that our partners model for us what they believed participants would do when given the instructions. This was a good way to catch miscommunications.

We prefer using instructional flip charts rather than workbooks. The task of translating and ensuring accuracy in a workbook did not justify the time, energy, and money required. Checking the accuracy of translation is a difficult and tedious process, requiring many different people to read the translation and explain to us what they had read. Instead, we chose to spend our time ensuring common understanding of language and process and building trust with the people who would lead with us the five-day training and later lead the facilitation teams in the district Future Searches. We also believe that workbooks often prohibit last-minute adjustments and reinforce a type of hierarchical division with participants who cannot read or write.

Fortunately, we were supplied with flip charts, easels, markers, and tape. We were surprised, however, when we saw the office staff actually cutting small squares of tape into circles because we had requested "sticky dots." Had we been more careful in our instructions to them, we could have avoided a lot of tedious work, since square pieces of tape would have sufficed.

Sometimes locating flip charts and easels can be a problem, though we have been surprised to find that flip charts and markers can be bought in some out-of-the-way places. We have had sponsors make easels. In one case, we were given permission to drive nails into the mud walls of our building and hang flip charts from them. In another, false walls were constructed for hanging our visuals. People around the world are often more resourceful at finding solutions than we, who hail from countries where one can buy a solution for everything.

Cross-Cultural Adaptations

Because many of our participants were Muslims, we adjusted the scheduling of all our work around the daily Muslim prayer schedule. We scheduled breaks and meals to allow adequate time for prayer and lengthened the work day to make up for prayer time.

We also adjusted our schedule during the five-day training to allow time to watch television, to see if the president would be impeached or would continue to resist the legal process, leading to a revolution. At breaks, most of the participants gathered around one small television to see what was transpiring and to learn about the violence near our hotel. When something critical was occurring, the breaks ran longer, and political conversations dominated the training room.

Rather than try to keep on time and resist this natural reaction to such a significant event, we allowed the political conversations to continue and then adjusted our process accordingly. This was made easier because we were in a retreat situation, all staying together, and Asians are much more flexible about time than North Americans; they can become offended if we design and manage the schedule too tightly.

In the district Future Searches, religious leaders from all three religions (Islam, Hindu, Christian) provided welcoming and closing remarks, led prayers at the opening ceremony and at meals, and were included in all activities. Honoring all of these leaders gave credibility and gravity to the entire process.

Running the District Future Searches

We were soon to learn that the "whole system" had not been invited to the Future Searches (one of the prime Future Search criteria for success) and that many who had been invited had no idea of what was going to happen. The concepts of full participation, a level playing field, and common-ground decision making were very foreign to citizens of this country, which had only been a democracy for a short time, following many difficult years of a dictatorship. We three North Americans had to ensure that the conditions for success were met, even though the changes we proposed would be difficult to implement, which we only learned at the last moment. We insisted that a group of out-of-school youth be included to give a youth perspective different from the stakeholder group of in-school youth. Those who had never attended school or who were compelled to work at a young age had very different viewpoints from those who were fortunate enough to be educated. We also negotiated with military officers to not wear their uniforms to the Future Search, as they might be viewed as intimidating by some participants.

During the district Future Searches, we watched the newly trained facilitators manage the process, coaching them before, during, and after each segment. When there were no translators to tell us what was being said, we based our coaching comments on observing nonverbal behaviors. When one of the facilitators decided to change the process without informing us, there was little we could do but watch and debrief after the fact.

The three district Future Searches produced a lot of energy and excitement, as well as more capable facilitators; they also produced specific action plans that would be considered in the UNICEF planning process. Following the training and coaching, the Indonesian facilitators managed more than thirty-five Future Searches in their country. Although we have had difficulties in maintaining contact with the Indonesian facilitators, we are aware that some of them are still using Future Search in their country and that a few are using Future Search principles in tsunami relief efforts.

Our Learnings

As so often happens in working with clients, the presenting issues change as we help clients analyze their situation. For example, issues relating to our contract emerged as a result of the short time we had in which to do our work.

Contracting

In this international work, our planning and contracting were especially complicated by the short time frame and by the impossibility of face-to-face meetings. E-mails and telephone conferences were our primary mode of communication. Insisting on adequate telephone time with our clients to clarify our contract was critical to preparing for the surprises that lay ahead. We found that this additional effort, even in the face of strong resistance, was invaluable in getting ourselves oriented, modifying our contract so we could be more successful, and establishing important relationships and principles. In spite of this, we still faced many uncertainties.

Conducting Future Search Across Cultures

Marvin Weisbord, one of the creators of Future Search, has speculated that Future Search is transportable across cultures because it relies on activities that are

core to human experience, such as telling each other our stories, talking about where we have come from, reflecting on the challenges we are currently facing, dreaming about the future, and talking about actions we will take. We believe that another contributing factor is that the participants, not the facilitators, provide the content and make all of the decisions. Participant-driven practices are much more culturally mobile than those that are consultant-driven.

Although our experience confirmed that Future Search is transportable, it also taught us the necessity of carefully considering cross-cultural communication issues. Consultants working abroad should, if possible, become familiar with the local language, customs, and basic concepts of cross-cultural communication. However, many consulting situations do not provide the lead time to do this. Often the only available tools are authenticity, honesty, and creativity, with a good dose of humility thrown in. The desire and ability to be open and willing to learn is also a critical component of success.

Modeling Our Core Beliefs

Here are some important lessons that were reconfirmed:

• *Stay neutral.* The more we maintained neutrality in content issues, especially in these cross-cultural situations, the more likely we were to be heard. Being content-neutral facilitators was, in fact, a principle of Future Search that we wanted to model. We did this by asking questions of understanding rather than "fixing" what seemed unworkable. We found that our humanity did more to bring us together than our cultures did to separate us.

• *Slow down.* Despite language difficulties, Future Search and most large group interventions are successful because people are asked to engage in activities—talking, listening, and sharing ideas—that they already know about. We facilitators describe tasks and encourage people to be responsible for and manage their own participation. Going slow is important. Throughout the process we model collaboration among the facilitators and with the participants.

• *Allow more time.* Building additional time into all activities was an absolute necessity in our work. We needed extra time in everything we did: to the workshop that would normally take four days, we added an extra day; when we planned a half-hour debrief, we always used at least an hour; when we expected to need two hours to prepare materials, it took four; when we met with our local partners to review the agenda, we needed more time than we had planned.

• *Stay grounded in our principles.* It was very important that we were well grounded in Future Search and had confidence in the process. There were many challenging times when we could easily have been derailed and succumbed to the temptation to make major design changes or ignore the underlying principles. There were times when we could have avoided principle-based confronta-

tions and kept silent in the name of cultural sensitivity. It would have been much easier to avoid talking with military generals about their uniforms, as well as with planning teams that had worked diligently to prepare for the district Future Searches but had overlooked a significant stakeholder group. But because we understood and believed in the importance of following the principles and process of the Large Group Methods we were using, we were able to openly explore these issues with our Indonesian counterparts and ultimately produce the results for which we had been contracted.

• *Take care of ourselves.* Our work in Indonesia was frequently very stressful. We had too much to do, too little time, many unknowns and surprises, and too little sleep. It was very important to take care of ourselves and find ways to relieve our stress. We joined participants in a sing-along and talent show, went for short walks when we could grab some time, found a few moments for alone time, and meditated and laughed whenever possible. The camaraderie among all of the staff was a significant factor in our ability to thrive through our challenges.

• *Establish quality partnerships.* Our insights are not singular to international work. Being out of our country exacerbates unknowns, challenges, and successes. Establishing quality partnerships—with clients, the facilitation team, and the participants—was our answer to the added challenges of large group work in an international setting. This is not simply conventional wisdom; it takes on particular significance because it is the first and most visible place we demonstrate the principles we bring to our clients.

In the end, our rewards were many. We had the satisfaction of working through challenges and inventing ways to overcome unexpected obstacles. We had the good fortune to meet wonderful, generous people. We experienced different customs and cultures and were warmly appreciated. And we left with the knowledge that we had done our best to help Indonesians ensure the survival, development, and protection of children and women.

References

Schweitz, R., & Martens, K. (2005). *Future Search in school district change: Community, connections, results.* Lanham, MD: Scarecrow Education.

Weisbord, M., & Janoff, S. (2000). *Future Search: An action guide to finding common ground in organizations and communities* (2nd ed.). San Francisco: Berrett-Koehler.

WORLD RELIGIONS ENGAGE CRITICAL GLOBAL ISSUES

Ray Gordezky, Susan Dupre, and Helen Spector

The Challenge

In July 2004, at the Benedictine monastery set atop the pink, jagged mountains in Montserrat, Spain, 350 delegates to the Assembly of the Council for a Parliament of the World's Religions gathered for what would be an experiment in global change. They came from the great diversity of the world's cultures and religions—Sikhs, Muslims, aboriginals, Hindus, Jews, pagans, Buddhists, Jains, Christians, agnostics, and more—young people from many continents, television and newspaper reporters, documentary film makers, activists, leaders of major businesses and NGOs, and citizens from many countries. They came knowing that this meeting would break from conventional proclamations, panel discussions, and theological debates of past Parliaments in order to seriously explore four critical global issues: (1) increasing access to safe and clean water, (2) eliminating the crushing burden of external debt on the poorest nations, (3) supporting refugees worldwide, and (4) overcoming religiously motivated violence. In this exploration, they expected to learn deeply and to be moved to take simple and committed action with their own communities to benefit people suffering the burdens brought by these issues. We came to help them change the world one person at a time.

Background

The Council for a Parliament of the World's Religions (hereafter "The Council") works with religious and spiritual communities, as well as government and nongovernment organizations, to create a more just, peaceful, and sustainable world. The Council expresses its mission through several initiatives, including the Parliament and the Assembly held in conjunction with the Parliament. The Parliament, convened every five years since 1993, draws together thousands of people of faith, spirit, and goodwill to encounter the vast and rich diversity of the world's religious and spiritual traditions.

The Council did not want this meeting to focus on building consensus or joint action, but rather wanted to inspire individuals to make commitments to engage their home communities to respond to these crises. Although the commitments desired were individual, we were to build a "community container" in which connection to self, to others, to faith and values, to the issue, and to their local community could occur. The dilemma was how to create this container for people who are often

at odds with one another, are used to having a platform to express their "worldview," and who, more often than not, come together to make declarations about what *others* can do for the betterment of the world rather than to develop and articulate what they will commit to do as individuals.

The council wanted the Assembly to

- Engage key representatives of all faith and spiritual traditions and powerful institutions in issues of critical importance to people around the world
- Include in each conversation people affected by the issues, youth, and subject matter experts, as well as representatives of various traditions
- Inspire committed action leading to change at the local level
- Introduce participants to a practical, repeatable process that could be easily transported and applied in communities back home—in effect, to offer a way to "snowball" the impact

We decided to develop a process that, at the core, would have participants examine the issues in their own hearts and in the wisdom of their own tradition. Here is the situation we faced:

- We needed translation for many languages; which ones were unknown to us.
- We needed simple processes acceptable to many cultures for people to do their work together.
- The differences between people in the room had, in the past, been a barrier to candid and honest conversation. We needed to create and hold a space where people could be genuine, yet express differences and conflict in a way that was not debilitating.
- A number of people in the room would not be used to talking as an equal in a group that included preeminent leaders, Nobel laureates, global experts associated with the issues, young people, and citizens from around the world.
- Some of the participants, by virtue of their position, would be more comfortable "teaching" others rather than reflecting on questions and speaking from a personally vulnerable place.
- There was a history at the assembly of representatives from disenfranchised groups demanding time to air very real grievances and redress past injustices.
- Some individuals would not be used to making commitments for themselves.

We started with a belief that we could be successful if we could do the following:

- Get people connected across cultures, religious and spiritual traditions, generations, roles, and status.

- Make everyone feel welcomed, part of the community, and able to give voice to whatever they wished to share that was related to the task at hand.
- Put a human face on each issue, that is, focus on the human toll these issues have taken on people's lives through the voices of those affected before examining the issues intellectually.
- Give people time to explore how their own and others' traditions compel them to care about the issues and those they affect.
- Enable people to discover the strategies for social change embedded in the teachings of their own and others' traditions.
- Give people enough time and support to figure out a simple and profound act they could take with their own community to ameliorate the suffering of those affected by an issue.
- Keep at bay "external forces" that could easily detract from the work.

Methodology

To meet these challenges, we developed a methodology that drew on our experiences with interfaith dialogue and well-tested large group meeting processes, primarily from Future Search (Weisbord and Janoff, 1995) and Appreciative Inquiry (Cooperrider and Whitney, 1999) but with some important modifications. First, our outcome was not to find common ground; we were seeking individual commitment leading to collective local action. Second, while we used the Future Search condition for success—"Global context, local action"—we also believed that a scan against internal values and beliefs was equally important and would lead to the outcome we were seeking.

Finally, we hotly debated whether to have the groups manage their own conversations or to use small group facilitators to assist the group's dialogue. Based on feedback from previous Assembly meetings, we decided to use experienced facilitators for all small group conversations.

After many iterations and testing, we designed a question-based methodology. We felt that inquiry would offer the simplicity we desired and be familiar to most people attending the Assembly, as it is fundamental to all faith and spiritual traditions. Questions could be used to invite stories about the human side of the issues and about the strengths and resources in religious and spiritual traditions. In addition, questions would provide an easy-to-use framework that would be less dependent on experienced facilitators, supporting the goal of portability.

The questions were built around three core conversations (see Table 6.2), each conversation building on what went before. They were designed to focus on building relationships between and among people before exploring the reality of the issue and the possibilities inherent in the religious and spiritual traditions. We found, through a series of pre-Parliament meetings convened to test the methodology, that giving a lot of information upfront about the causes and complexity of an issue overwhelmed people with the

enormity of the difficulties, decreased energy, and extinguished hope. Connecting people first—presenting each issue on a human scale through a personal story—and then asking each person to speak about his or her own connection with the issue, built associations based on caring and reduced the sense of powerlessness in the face of the enormity of the issues. This slow unfolding of issues helped to extend each person's understanding of why acting is essential and enabled people to see how even the simplest action, such as praying for refugees in specific camps, could be a profound act.

The pre-Parliament meetings also gave us the opportunity to see how generating hopefulness for the future could be built by offering brief presentations from experts on the complexity of the issues, followed by discussions on the barriers to making progress and stories of success in overcoming barriers to action. The stories of success seeded fresh ideas for action that individuals could take to make a difference.

The Assembly

When registrants entered the meeting hall, they found chairs set in forty-five circles, nine to a circle. As people arrived, they were greeted by facilitators and escorted to their seats—a strategy in hospitality. The room quickly became a living and colorful tapestry: Buddhists dressed in saffron robes; swamis in brightly colored cloth, accompanied by a retinue of white-robed followers; business leaders in suits and ties;

TABLE 6.2. THREE CONVERSATIONS

Conversations	Inquiry Questions
Conversations for Relationship Conversations connected participants with each other and with the human dimensions of the issues. These conversations took place in max-mix groupings of 8 to 10 individuals (mixed faiths, youth, persons affected by the issue, an expert, and leader of guiding institution).	• What is your name? Where are you from? What issue are you working on? What is your interest in your issue? What are your hopes for this meeting? • What is your experience with this issue? (Describe what it looks like and sounds like and how it affects your community.) • What moved you or changed for you as you reflect on what you heard today?
Conversations for Possibilities Participants discovered possibilities generated from faith traditions and values, and from examples of success. These conversations took place in same faith groupings and max-mix groupings.	• What do you see now about this issue's complexity? • What are the resources and strengths (beliefs, ideas, practices) in your faith or spiritual tradition or your core values that encourage and compel you to take action on this issue? • How will you represent the resources of your faith or spiritual tradition or your core values in the next conversation with interfaith groups? • What strengths and resources do your traditions provide to help address this issue? • What did you hear from another faith, spiritual tradition, or values that inspire you? • What barriers stop you from acting on this issue?
Conversations for Action Individual participants committed to act and creatively engage their community for positive change. These conversations took place in their original max-mix groupings.	• What ideas have these examples given you for a first step in overcoming a barrier or in taking action with your community? • What one thing could you see changing in your community that would make a difference for people affected by this issue? • What new ideas do you have about simple and profound acts that you can take to your community? • What is a simple and profound act that you will implement in your community? • What community will you engage? What simple and profound act will you commit to take with your community to make a difference for people affected by this issue? Who in your community will you engage to help? What specific steps will you start with?

Note: The idea for the three conversations was inspired by James Flaherty in *Coaching: Evoking Excellence in Others* (Woburn, MA: Butterworth-Heinemann, 1999).

indigenous people in traditional dress, and young people in jeans and T-shirts. To introduce themselves as a group, they were asked to stand by geography, by faith or tradition, and by the issue they had come to discuss. No one issued statements. No one asked them to review, support, or sign anything. Instead they were invited to listen deeply, speak with respect, and seek new understandings without a need to reach agreement or find common solutions. What follows is a summary of what happened each day and how what happened is connected to our challenges.

Getting People Connected Across Cultures and to the Issues (Day 1)

Participants were seated in small groups composed of people from different religious or spiritual affiliations and cultures. This maximized the mix of culture and religion. We included one young person in each grouping to bring freshness and innocence, as well as an experienced facilitator to encourage full participation in the group. All were asked to introduce themselves: tell their name, where they were from, what issue they were working on, why they had an interest in the issue, and what hopes they had for the meeting. These polite conversations established the beginnings of respectful relationships.

Our challenge at this point was how to get everyone participating, when some people did not speak English, Spanish, or Catalan—the official languages of the Assembly. Translation of instructions from the front of the room occurred in all

three languages. Translation in small groups was more problematic, but a group of "translators in training" from UNESCO and a few of our group facilitators were able to provide translation for those in need. We also found that people in the small groups supported one another as best they could. Although translation and language issues certainly slowed down the conversation, the intense listening and slow pacing seemed to deepen the dialogue.

Putting a Human Face on the Issues (Day 1)

Next, participants heard stories from individuals who had been hurt by the calamities we were exploring. Starting with stories seems so simple and yet is so powerful. For example, two women—a Palestinian and an Israeli—told the Assembly of the violence they had experienced. The Palestinian woman, who works as a cardiac care nurse in a Jerusalem hospital, told how she helps to repair the ailing hearts of ill Israelis during the day, then is taunted by Israeli youth on her way home. The Israeli woman, from an orthodox religious community, told how her son nearly died in a terrorist-led bus attack, and instead of seeking revenge, she committed herself to mobilizing Arab and Israeli women to put an end to violence . . . There was no blame, no hatred; rather there was pain, tears, and a desire that their world of violence become different.

Participants were then asked to turn to one another to share their own experiences with the issue of their choice. The impact of hearing such stories on listeners cannot be overstated. A woman who has worked for a long time in settling refugees talked about how, over the years, she had grown distant from people for whom she was working. For her, hearing one refugee share her story was enough to rekindle the purpose and inspiration of her work.

Exploring What Religious and Spiritual Traditions Offer to Encourage Change (Day 2)

At the start of the second day, issue groupings convened in separate meeting rooms. Each group began with an intense exploration of the issue and what the various faith and spiritual traditions offered as support in responding to that crisis. A brief presentation by an expert in the field, offering participants a deeper understanding of the complexity of the issue, was followed by people of similar faiths gathering together to consider the beliefs, ideas, and practices in their tradition that encourage them to care about the issue. These intrafaith conversations were loud and sometimes heated, as co-religionists debated and questioned the meaning of their own various beliefs and practices. They were often surprised at the variation of stories and interpretation among people of the same faith.

Following the intrafaith dialogue, participants self-organized into interfaith groups, where they shared with one another the rich resources that each tradition makes available to respond to the

issue. We saw people lean forward in focused concentration as they learned, often for the first time, of values and symbols from other traditions that informed prayer and action.

Expressing Barriers and Successes in Preparation for Moving Toward Action (Day 2)

Sometimes people cannot move forward until they have an opportunity to talk about the difficulties they encounter in enacting any change. This was another learning we took away from one of the pre-Parliament meetings in Israel. As we were beginning to move people into sharing stories about what they've observed that works, the group could not keep themselves from expressing the varied and multiple barriers they were confronting as they worked to overcome violence in the Middle East. These barriers were *real,* and it proved cathartic for the group to give voice to them—not solve them, merely put them on the table as real forces to contend with. Many of the barriers that emerged were confounding; these were sticky, unanswerable questions:

> "How do I work with my own community when people there, even my family members, reject the very idea of dialogue with those people?"

> "Do we have the patience to resolve long-standing needs and concerns?"

> "Can we find commonalities between religions (and as people) to take the first step?"

> "What is the truth?"

The barriers were listened to with great respect, thus adding more layers to the dynamics of the issue and a deeper appreciation of the dynamics of change.

There were many moments during the meeting where graphic recording helped participants see and hear their differences and similarities. This was one of those moments. Participants witnessed their barriers taking shape visually in colorful murals created by the recorders. Seeing the barriers made concrete in this way was a validation of their experience.

A collective sigh of relief rose in the room as participants moved on. The question they next addressed was: "What is already working in your community?" First an activist shared one success he had had in addressing a barrier and taking positive action for change. Participants then turned to one another in their small groups to share their own experiences of what has worked in their communities. There was an energy shift in the room. People laughed, clapped their hands, and even chanted. One young woman told how she used her music to engage her school mates and friends in caring about and addressing the burdens of external debt. She finished her sharing with a song.

Giving People Time and Support to Create a Commitment (Day 2)

The time had come to focus people on what they would do once they returned home—a commitment to act on behalf of people in their community suffering the effects of these issues. We wanted people to focus on what *they* would do, not on what they wanted others to do. We began with an invitation for individuals to reflect on what one thing they could see changing in their religious and spiritual community, institution, or their neighborhood that would have a positive impact on their issue. Before sharing their reflections, a panel of youth in each issue group offered their thoughts on the future as an inspiration and springboard for everyone.

This had mixed results, as some ideas were inspiring, some not. But one cannot deny the energy these young people contributed, which served the group well at the end of a long day. For example, in the "water" meeting, a university student said his commitment would be to say a short prayer of thanks every time he drank or used water. He wanted to leave the world a better place, he told the group, but was afraid that the world would come to an end before he had grandchildren. Silence filled the room as people considered his words. A rabbi from Holland waved to the facilitator and asked to talk. Speaking to the young man, the rabbi told how, when he was a child during World War II, his parents had given him to a Christian family, hoping they could save him from the approaching Nazi army. "The world was in a desperate and hopeless state then, but I am alive and have grandchildren. You will have grandchildren, too," he said to the young man. There was a profound shift in the room as people spoke, in a generative way, of what they wished for the world.

Making a Simple and Profound Commitment (half of Day 3)

Imagine ending a day of work listening to the angelic voices of a famous boys' choir performing Gregorian chants in the stunning Montserrat Basilica. This interlude set the stage for people to contemplate what they would draft as their simple and profound act—the takeaway of this auspicious gathering. The next morning, the group convened as a whole again, and participants returned to their small groups of the first day. It had the feel of a reunion, of people returning home after a long journey, and in a way this was true. They could hardly wait to catch one another up with what they had learned. Each individual was asked to draft a commitment by answering these questions:

- What community will you engage?
- What simple and profound act will you commit to take with your community to make a difference for people affected by your issue?
- Who in your community will you engage to help?
- How will you get started?

People then paired up to share what they had written and to get feedback from someone else prior to preparing their "formal and final" commitment card. All commitments were shared in the small groups, and we even attempted a mass simultaneous reading of all the commitments.

By the end of the Assembly and then several other meetings connected with the Parliament—all meetings in which we used the same design—over five hundred commitments to "simple and profound" acts were collected.

The council transcribed the handwritten commitment cards and entered the information into a database that will enable tracking and updating of what happens during the five years between assemblies. Some of the commitments have already had an impact: one participant convened a conference in San Jose, California, and engaged four hundred people in a similar process for building "cultures of peace" in local families, the community, and the world; a team of facilitators formed a nonprofit organization to take teams of executives to areas where help is needed and provide tangible services (they have already built a school for a Masai village in Kenya and plan to dig wells to provide water to a village in Africa or India); those making commitments to improve access to safe water have engaged with their local Rotary groups to connect with that organization's initiative to support a Decade of Clean Water. These and other stories are circulating within the Assembly community and providing encouragement to those who have returned home and are facing the challenge of acting alone to mobilize their own community.

Reflections

The community of 125 volunteer consultants, facilitators, designers, logistics experts, photographers, and graphic
recorders that formed to support this
event remains in active conversation, in
many subsets, unpacking what we
learned this past year.

The following are areas of important
work not addressed in the previous
section: hospitality, the power of youth,
the question of whether to use facilitators or not, the use of graphics, cross-
cultural training and the use of mentors,
and the power of the place where meetings are held.

Hospitality

For most, the trip to Montserrat was long
and arduous, culminating with a trip on
a tram up the mountain to the
monastery. We knew that our first point
of contact with participants would be
fateful in either helping us or hindering
us in creating that container for connection and learning. At key locations
(Barcelona Airport, various train or metro
stations throughout the journey, at the
tram station at the bottom of the mountain) participants found Council staff
available to support and direct their journey. Our logistic aides greeted participants upon arrival at the monastery to
assist with handling luggage, finding
rooms, and getting through registration.
A whole contingent of our volunteers
greeted and supported participants

throughout registration. Hospitality was
intentional and everywhere.

Power of Youth

The Council wanted young people to
have a strong voice in the Assembly. We
imagined that if the youth were present
in some force, our concerns about some
of the group dynamics would be miti-
gated—if—and the big question was *if*—
they were not intimidated by the
situation, the setting, the dignitaries, and
the isolation of being the single "young
person" in a small group. The challenge
then was how to ensure their full participation. Fortune was shining brightly
when we learned that the monastery had
a youth hostel on-site to accommodate
all fifty young people, who came from all
over the world. This provided them a
safe haven to build their confidence and
their community.

To engage them further, we asked
them to come a day early, and we put
them in charge of designing a portion of
the Opening Ceremony, under the tute-
lage of one of the young Council staff.
This gave them a task, put them immediately in an up-front role, connected
them, and allowed their presence to be
felt by all.

Facilitators or No Facilitators

The principle of self-management is a
central tenet for all large group methodologies with which we are familiar. *Self-
management* means group members take
responsibility for how they conduct their

conversations and how they report on their deliberations. Although most of us felt that the principle was critical to uphold, the council was not ready to take that step, based on their experiences at prior Assemblies. We respectfully took their wisdom into account and recruited, trained, and used small group facilitators.

Although these facilitators made significant and lasting contributions to this process, based on what we learned collectively we would not compromise this principle again. We found that the purposefulness and the environment the lead facilitators created established enough of a framework for participants to hold productive conversations. For the Parliament meetings held in Barcelona and subsequent meetings in San Jose, small group facilitators were not used, and the results proved to be equal to those achieved at Montserrat. We are not saying that all conversations would be described as highly successful. We are saying that the benefits of self-management outweigh the bumps in the road that happen in most group conversations.

Use of Graphics

Much of the proceedings were recorded by graphic recorders using markers and pastels to vividly honor and capture the conversations. One of our concerns was that people would use the platform of the Assembly to express all sorts of ideas that were unrelated to the task. A strategy that the graphic facilitators used to honor this potential need and diffuse the

possibility that it would happen in the meeting was to put up a blank mural in a prominent spot, with the simple invitation on the top: "What else would you like to say?" Participants filled it with pronouncements, questions, concerns, symbols and pictures, teachings, and expressions of hope.

Cross-Cultural Training and the Use of Mentor Supports

During the work of designing this methodology, we were not able to gather a truly cross-cultural team because of the constraints on resources, travel, and time. So we tapped the expertise of cross-cultural consultants to help us become aware of our own blind spots regarding the ways people from a variety of cultures prefer to work in groups. This introduction to the concepts of circular time, deference to experts and leaders, indirect speaking, and making statements rather than engaging in inquiry helped us appreciate the challenge in front of us—to create a space for participants to connect with each other and with the issues. Ultimately, it reinforced our commitment to the simplicity and universality of the question-based conversation format.

In addition, we provided a team of mentors drawn from the senior members of our design team, who focused on supporting all the volunteer facilitators so that they could concentrate all their attention on their work with Assembly members. This proved a critical resource for the whole enterprise, as mentors helped facilitators to stay aware of the cultural dynamics and, at the same time, gave support and encouragement to continue responding with the heart, and with authenticity.

Power of Place

In our large group work, we always insist on holding the meetings in places where windows let in natural light. But we underestimated the power of a place itself to exert a potent influence on consciousness. The beauty of the mountains, the expansive view, the history of the monastery, the black Madonna, the voices of the boys' choir, the regularly tolling bells, morning prayers—all of these exerted potent influence on the energy and consciousness among and between participants and all who worked to support the meeting. Montserrat was not just any meeting place; it was a meeting place with a feeling of occasion and destiny.

Questions Remaining

The Montserrat Assembly unfolded over three days in a spiritual setting sheltered from the outside world; the group was luminous and religiously, culturally, and geographically diverse—an intergenerational group of people selected specifically for their potential to gather as a group and develop individual commitments to change their home communities. From the Council's perspective it was a huge success. Participants expressed awe and appreciation; a sense of community was built, and commitments were made. The most significant unanswered question is this: Did this methodology, which we now call Values in Action (VIA), lead to the action that we desired?

This question about what happens after the awe and appreciation is one that has surfaced for us in other large-scale change initiatives when, after a meeting that brings a large group together, participants disperse to parts of the world or county where communication and travel infrastructure may be unreliable at best, and where they become absorbed in their busy lives.

Determining the success of the Assembly only by evaluating the achievements of commitments can blind us to the subtle, enriching changes that occur at the individual and small group levels. We do have anecdotal evidence: participants have sent us notes with their stories about how profoundly they were affected by their experience. Some have been moved to take very visible action in their community; others have worked quietly within themselves to cultivate greater respect in their relationships with others.

One hopeful perspective on this conundrum comes from scientists working in the areas of chaos and complexity who write about *emergence*—the unpredictable and often invisible order that can ripple out and affect many people and organizations. The ripples take time to evolve and patience to see. The ripple effect occurs in cities where over a long time certain neighborhoods become centers for the arts or finance without any central planning. This perspective suggests that the interactions at the Assembly were like seeds planted in the soil. Some seeds will sprout into full bloom in a relatively short time; others take a much longer time to leaf, and still others remain dormant. Thus through chance encounters, communities of interest or commitment can coalesce and initiate unexpected change.

Which brings us back to the question: Did this event lead to the desired change? From the perspective of emergence, it takes time for meaningful patterns to form, for abundant will and modest resources to support and sustain the newly emerging changes. We hope that with the database of people and commitments and with a modest infusion of resources, this meeting and others that follow it will speed the desired changes into our world.

References

Cooperrider, D., & Whitney, D. (1999). *Appreciative Inquiry.* San Francisco: Berrett-Koehler.

Weisbord, M., & Janoff, S. (1995). *Future Search: An action guide to finding common ground in organizations and communities.* San Francisco: Berrett-Koehler.

CHAPTER SEVEN

EMBEDDING NEW PATTERNS OF WORKING

What can we do more deliberately in organizations and communities to generate a new culture, a new way of working together that will sustain positive change? We believe this chapter contains some stimulating and thought-provoking answers to this question. We have referred readers to this chapter in other sections of the book, as it addresses some of the concerns that both practitioners and clients have raised about Large Group Methods.

In the early days of Large Group Methods, there was a sense of euphoria about their power to shift whole systems. Within the events there were dramatic changes—new ways of working, exploring issues, and making decisions. There was a great deal of excitement about the potential outcomes. Many of the early proponents of these methods believed that the energy released during these meetings would propel changes in the larger system.

Scant attention was paid, however, to what happened after the events. People often spoke of the ripple effect that occurs when a stone is tossed into a pond. There was an expectation that the ripples created by the Large Group Methods used at an event would spread and finally reach into the workplace or community. Others emphasized the need to give more time to action planning as a way to sustain change, and they encouraged the use of a series of follow-up activities: holding communication meetings, using tracking mechanisms, and charging teams with the responsibility for implementation.

As experience with these methods grew in the 1990s, people became concerned about sustaining the energy for change after the event. There were often difficulties in implementation. Questions were asked: What difference did the event make? Has the change been implemented? What was the impact? As we talked to people who were participants or sponsors in these events or helped facilitate the meetings, the issue of implementation always arose. There was a sense of disappointment. Even when the follow-up seemed organized and people seemed committed, much of the energy dissipated as people re-entered their demanding workplaces. Changes did get implemented—new strategic plans, curriculum changes, a new organizational structure to improve the work flow— but over the long haul the quality of insight, interaction, and problem solving that had occurred during the kick-off meeting disappeared. We were back to business as usual. We might look back with nostalgia at the meetings, but we began seeing them as special events, perhaps even becoming cynical about such meetings and their utility.

A curious experience happened to us several years ago that changed our thinking. We had done a Future Search for a university business school. After the event we learned that most of the initiatives and changes that were the result of the meeting had been implemented! We were sent clippings from the local newspaper on the changes that had been made. In subsequent discussions with some faculty members, however, we learned about their disappointment that *more* had not happened. Expectations had been raised that were not fulfilled. Even though most of the specific changes had occurred, there was an expectation generated by this event that a new way of working internally and externally would happen at the university, because that is what, in fact, happened within the event. This was a meeting where students, alumni, faculty, administration, and outside stakeholders from the local business community worked collaboratively to address the issues facing the business school.

The focus at the end of most of these events is on implementation of whatever has been agreed upon. Little attention is given to the conditions that produced the outcomes. These meetings give people a very different experience but one that is not accompanied by sufficient reflection on and conceptualization of what made the experience unique—different from what happens in the workplace. How can these events become catalysts for carrying out new initiatives and also carry forward a new way of working that can become part of the culture?

The BBC case, described in Chapter Two, is an example of a process that lasted over many months and contained a series of ongoing involvement meetings, communications, and online participatory processes. The merger of the two teachers' unions in Florida is another example of a series of events that occurred over time to effectively change the environment that would support a merger and create a new way of working together.

There is a correlation between ease of implementation and organization culture. As Jack Welch—former CEO of General Electric—says about Work Out (one of the Large Group Methods), "Work Out was responsible for one of the most profound cultural changes in GE during my life time" (Welch, 2005, p. 57). This shift in GE culture was a new way of working together to address problems. It took time and persistence, however, to gain acceptance for Work Out across the GE organization. The cases reflect some of the factors that created a culture shift within these organizations.

The three cases in this chapter are as follows:

- "Work Out: From Courtship to Marriage at General Electric," by Annmarie Sorrow
- "Embedding the Core Principles at Boeing," by Richard H. Axelrod and Emily M. Axelrod
- "Moving to the Next Level at the Canadian Institute for Health Information," by Larry E. Peterson and Rebecca Peterson

"After the Dance," by Glenda Eoyang and Kristine Quade, is an article that presents a framework for thinking about both implementation and shifts in culture. The article illuminates the cultural changes that occurred in the cases. The authors explore three elements they consider essential for these Large Group Methods to work effectively, both during and after the event.

What to Note in the Cases and Article

The core themes that the cases have in common are (1) the involvement of leadership, (2) the building of capacity, and (3) the gaining of credibility. The first important element in all the cases is the active support of the leadership.

Involvement of Leadership

The leaders involved in the cases described here were less interested in seeing a specific idea get implemented than in shifting how the organization worked, both within itself and with customers and suppliers.

At management seminars at GE's Crotonville Training Center, CEO Jack Welch would encourage his young managers to take risks, to become entrepreneurs, to break though the silos and layers. Time after time the group of managers would respond with reactions like, "We can't do that, the culture doesn't permit it, there are too many sign-offs and authorizations required to get even a simple project going." They would then recite a litany of obstacles.

Legend has it that as Jack Welch returned in his plane to GE headquarters from one of these sessions, the idea for Work Out was born as a way to break through the bureaucracy and find a way to change how people worked together. He would often talk about *boundary-less organizations,* with silos and levels minimized—"busting," as he called it, the bureaucracy. Jack Welch was more a driver for change than a mere supporter. His persistence showed the kind of leadership it takes to embed new patterns (Annemarie Sorrow also documents this trait in the case: "Work Out: From Courtship to Marriage at General Electric").

In the Boeing case, Richard and Emily Axelrod describe a project designed to address the underlying cause of an employee attrition problem in the Engineering division. Employees felt that the jobs they did failed to use their talents effectively. People from all levels of the organization were invited to participate in a series of meetings to address the underlying issues. Boeing had used Large Group Methods extensively for a number of years, including the development of the Boeing 777. Because of their experience and familiarity with these methods, the Engineering division decided that they wanted to use *the engagement principles*—the underlying principles that are central to these methods to bring about change. These principles represented how they wanted to work together in the future. Hank Queen, the vice president of Engineering, gave full support to the project. In other words, his division planned to tackle the changes they needed to make using these engagement principles as guidelines rather than using one particular Large Group Method. They recognized that the *patterns* they had experienced in working this way were needed for their next steps. Using these principles allowed the different engineering groups to go in their own direction, tackling the issues that were important to them but with a common agreement about process. What is exciting about this case is that it was not the method that got embedded. Rather, the consultants gave away their knowledge and skills to help people do their own change work in this new way. The remaining question seems to be whether this way of working together can spread to the larger organization.

In the third case—"Moving to the Next Level at the Canadian Institute for Health Information"—the executives and CEO experienced a different way of working together at an Open Space meeting. They saw the value and benefit of a different type of interaction with each other. The strategy had been developed, but it was dependent for its implementation on the managers. They wanted their managers to have the same type of experience that had helped them. The CEO and the executives supported an Open Space meeting for their managers to bring them together to work on recommendations for implementing the new strategy. The CEO and several of the executives attended the next management event. A joint interactive meeting was then held to merge the strategy and the recommended actions. Executives interacted with the managers on their recommendations. There was a change in the traditional pattern of executive-subordinate interaction, as multileveled interactions occurred around the recommendations.

The authors have included some research by the Hay Group. The data indicate a shift in employee satisfaction, with strong feelings of involvement and recognition. We propose that a shift in culture had also occurred. The impact of this way of working is larger than the substantive results of a new strategy and its implementation. Clearly, it affected how people felt about the culture of the whole organization.

In Chapter Three there is another interesting example of how core principles became embedded in a manufacturing plant and the key role the leadership played. In "Creating a World-Class Manufacturer in Record Time," Richard Lent, James Van Patten, and Tom Phair describe a turnaround of a manufacturing plant that highlights some of the key factors just discussed. The leadership of this plant was after more than the immediate issue at hand; he also wanted to develop new patterns of working.

The Building of Capacity

In each of the cases, the skills to run these meetings or to establish new patterns of interaction became part of the organization's way of doing things. Managers, human resource professionals, and employees at all levels were equipped at GE to run Work Out meetings. The skills were internalized; they were part of the tool kit. This was true in the United States, as well as overseas. The GE case indicates that, over time, the organization became less and less dependent on outside consultants.

At Boeing the same sort of capacity building occurred. Under a section titled "Creating the Delivery System," the authors describe the process of local support teams—twenty such teams in all: "Each team consisted of HR-OD representatives, union leadership, and employees. The role of these teams was to recognize systemic issues that needed to be addressed and to support local efforts." In the section on "Learnings," the authors talk about the need for the consultant to let go: "We had to equip many people to do what we do." Giving skills away—equipping people to do this work—is a very important factor in embedding new patterns.

The Gaining of Credibility

Years ago, Herb Shepard—a well-known organization consultant at the time—would advise clients not to work uphill. Sage advice. Don't take on the most troubled part of the organization. Find a challenge that may be small and doable in a relatively short period of time. Annmarie Sorrow, in her case description of a GE Work Out, describes how broad acceptance was gained across the company by small wins. She uses the analogy of a courtship. The couple had to gain acceptance from the larger family. In both these large organizations—GE and Boeing—some of the persistent, irritating problems that had gone on for years were tackled first. This seems wise. We all want big wins, but sometimes the small wins can make a huge difference and build credibility. Later came much weightier issues involving customers, suppliers, and even regulators; the savings and benefits were high. To get to this point took time and patience. Although the Canadian Institute for Health Information began with only thirteen people interacting differently with each other, the results spilled over to enlarge the involvement process and create more cross-functional and cross-level engagement. At one of our Dallas conferences in a small problem-solving group, a manager from an oil company described a huge project that he wanted to start using these Large Group Methods. We were surprised when one of the participants (an hourly worker from another oil company) said, "Start small where you can have an impact." He then described a problem that had plagued the company for years: the length of time it took to get an oil well drilled in the Gulf of Mexico. The employee had been trained in these methods and recognized the importance of the right stakeholder involvement. He went to his management and said, "When we do our planning, we don't have the right people in the room. We need our contractors and suppliers with us. We need to get their ideas, buy-in, and commitment from the start of the project." His suggestion was acted upon, and the result of his recommendation was a huge reduction in cycle time and cost! Asking this question—"Do we have the right people at this meeting to address this issue?"—is a small but powerful way to change a pattern and can bring extraordinary results.

Changing the Patterns

"After the Dance" suggests that after the music stops, people stop dancing; something very important is lost. How do we keep the music going and sustain the dancing—after the dance is over? In the article at the end of this chapter, Eoyang and Quade present a framework for what is essential for maintaining the dance. We had recognized, in the cases, how this process of embedding the core principles in the organization can be facilitated by the participants themselves.

Eoyang and Quade write from a "human systems dynamics" framework. The ideas in this construct come from complexity theory and the concept of self-organizing systems. They provide an excellent lens with which to explore the issues this section addresses. They suggest that in meetings using Large Group Methods, a new pattern is established. People start to dance. The problem occurs toward the end of the meeting when groups shift focus from the decisions agreed upon to the follow-up action required to move forward. "We forget," the authors claim, "the elements of the meeting that allowed a new way of working together to emerge."

The human dynamics frame consists of three elements: (1) a container, (2) diversity, and (3) engagement. The *container* is the purpose or theme that draws people together. *Diversity* is the richness that diverse stakeholders can provide with their views, perspectives, and experience. A highly participative process that involves people in critical thinking about the important issues creates *engagement*. A new pattern for working emerges that is atypical of the organization's pattern. The authors have taken some specific Large Group Methods and illustrated with several charts how this framework applies to activities before, during, and after the meeting.

After an important and energizing event, people can experience frustration when they return and try to initiate change. Project management methods, responsibility charting, and priority setting are all useful tools, but the climate that allowed the ideas to emerge was produced by a different pattern of working together.

Working Within Organizations on Follow-Up and Implementation

These cases helped us see what we had not seen clearly before: there is a strong correlation between a successful implementation and the state of the organization's culture. The more successful the initial event, the more urgent it is that the long-term task is to create new ways of working within the organization that will both facilitate the implementation and support a new pattern for addressing subsequent issues. Quade and Eoyang suggest the importance of finding opportunities to create new patterns of working in the ongoing life of the organization.

Before a successful meeting ends, there should be an opportunity for all participants to reflect on a question like this: What were the principles and structures that helped make this meeting effective? Recently, at the end of a meeting, we presented the human dynamics framework and asked people to consider their experience during the two-day event. They proceeded to describe the advantage of having a diverse group of stakeholders present, the quality of engagement that allowed for multiple perspectives and experience to emerge, and, finally, the opportunity to coalesce around some core initiative that would influence the future. As a follow-up we asked participants to brainstorm in subgroups about opportunities in the workplace to establish new patterns of engagement. Someone commented, "Every meeting is an opportunity to ask, regardless of level or function, Who do we need in the room to address this issue? How do we engage people to get their best ideas?"

What this means is to bring front and center the core characteristics and principles inherent in these methods so that they can be transferred and applied back to the organization. In "After the Dance" there are excellent ideas for breaking old patterns. At the end of every event using Large Group Methods, all participants should be handed a copy of their suggestions on the transfer of these concepts back to everyday organizational life.

Working in Communities: Follow-Up and Implementation

Many of the Large Group Methods we have written about are increasingly being used in communities around the world, often addressing very controversial issues. These events can produce astounding results, as participants find actionable common ground, but the dilemma of follow-up is a serious one—much more difficult to address than those within an organization. Some of the attendees come as individuals who may care passionately about the issue being discussed. Others come representing organizations that have a high stake in the issues. Still others come as part of a coalition of people who are advocating a certain position. The design of these meetings and the interactions that occur have the potential for changing people's understanding of the key issues. Listening to other perspectives, often for the first time, while exploring the environmental context before problem solving or positioning moves people from "Me and my view" to "What are *we* going to do about this?" From this dialogue a new picture of the future can emerge (see Chapter Four). In a world that is becoming increasingly conflicted, what principles can those who attend the meeting carry back with them to their organizations to help with the work to be done and the vision that needs to be sustained? Within the organizations represented, there is often a need to develop new patterns of internal interactions, but in the larger context, there is a need for a different type of inter-organizational engagement.

In Chapter Three, at the end of Marvin Weisbord and Sandra Janoff's case study on their work with the FAA, the authors include a postscript suggesting that it is not the exercises or various activities within the meeting that made the difference but how the group worked together using the core characteristics and principles inherent in these methods. Large Group Methods brought a diverse group of stakeholders to come to some important agreements for the common good. We suggest helping community groups recognize what has made the difference and bringing this to the forefront. This gives those who attend something to take with them that can be used within their own organizations or in interorganizational engagements, which can have a positive impact on follow-up and implementation.

Conclusion

To summarize our advice for using Large Group Methods: (1) help participants recognize the core principles that have created a new way of working during the meeting, (2) help people explore where and how they can bring these new patterns into their own organizations, and (3) help people develop new patterns for interorganizational engagement. For example, a town in New England decided to hold a Large Group meeting every year. Community agencies and faith-based groups come together to learn about each other's activities for the betterment of the community. They discuss future needs of the community that require action. Attendees sit at mixed tables where they meet members of other community agencies. As relationships develop and information is shared, new patterns of collaboration between groups have emerged.

Reference

Welch, J., with Welch, S. (2005). *Winning*. New York: HarperCollins.

WORK OUT

From Courtship to Marriage at General Electric

Annmarie Sorrow

The Challenge

Imagine that you are the CEO of a powerful global organization with highly talented people whose energy has not been fully tapped. How can you unleash this energy to get people involved in helping you shape the organization beyond what you and your leadership team have done? You want to cut through bureaucracy, reduce cycle times, improve processes, and get closer to the customer. Most of all, you want decisions made at the level where they occur because you understand this: "People closest to the work know, more than anyone, how it could be done better" (Slater, 2000, p. 55).

This was the genesis of Work Out at General Electric in the late eighties, when GE's CEO, Jack Welch, with a few other people, developed the concept. The three-day Work Out process included

- Pre-meeting: a meeting to identify issues on which to work, select team members, and prepare business leaders

- Town meeting: three days to conduct the actual Work Out sessions
- Post-meeting: a meeting to follow up on actions and implementation issues

The power of the three-day process was that employees provided solutions to problems and shared these face-to-face with their managers. Their managers responded on the spot with a decision. In my years of experience as an external consultant conducting these sessions, 95 percent of the decisions resulted in a "yes," with extremely few "no's." This was a revolutionary form of decision making, in contrast to the more common, "Let's think it over or study it more."

How did Work Out come to be part of the fabric of the GE organization and routinely used like the Internet? The journey was an evolving relationship. It began tentatively and then got serious. First there was dating, then a wedding, then marriage, and, finally, settling in.

Getting Started: The First Few Dates

How brilliant, yet how simple, the process of Work Out was. GE and Work Out were destined for a relationship. It was clear that the two had much in common. Work Out could

- Broaden debate throughout the organization and make it okay to speak up and challenge the status quo
- Remove the "boss element" (Welch's phrase) from GE
- Have managers listen more and give up their monopoly on decision making
- Reduce waste and simplify processes

Exploring the relationship further, the next steps were to think about what the implementation would look like, that is, how they could best go forward as a couple and be successful. Here are some guiding principles they followed:

- Drive the process strongly from the top of the organization.
- Employ top-notch external consultants assigned to each business segment to drive and facilitate the Work Out process. This provided a neutral party that could bring rigor to the process and, without vested interest, support more candidness.
- Hold business segment leaders accountable for conducting sessions.

- Put in place champions for the Work Out teams.
- Get some successes early in the process.

The couple was in a state of euphoria—that time in the relationship where everything feels magical. GE and Work Out became engaged and began to meet with the organizational family to discuss their impending marriage. They wanted to share with the organization what Work Out was all about—its goals and the process. Yet as in many proposed changes, there was some family-member resistance and some cynicism. What happened?

Buying In to the Couple: The Wooing of the Organization

As you would expect, there were some rocky points early on in the courtship of this couple. The program was mandated in the beginning, and parts of the organization reacted to this as another "program du jour." There were some skeptics and, in fact, a few business leaders downright dug in their heels. As in any change, there were early adopters and resisters. But digging your heels in was not really an option. This couple made it very clear they were going to marry. If you did not get on board, you would not be part of the organizational family. Embracing Work Out became critical to your career.

Many family members were enthusiastic, and hundreds of sessions began to

be held. In honoring the need to get early successes, many sessions resulted in actions like replacing lights, fixing or moving machines, and improving break areas. What once took months or years to get fixed now was taken care of immediately. Although the dollar payoff may have been slight, the impact of taking care of these things was enormous.

Another powerful tool that was used early on was RAMMP, which looked at Reports, Approvals, Meetings, Measurements, and Policies/Practices that got in the way of being productive. As a result of RAMMP, approval processes that required multiple signatures were often slashed. Thousands of reports were found to be redundant or unnecessary, often resulting in major reductions or eliminations. Many meetings were stopped and the number of people attending the remaining meetings reduced. Even business policies and practices were reviewed to determine whether they still made sense or needed to be revised.

The RAMMP outcomes allowed for many successes; participants saw with their own eyes the disappearance of unnecessary work from the organization. All this was achieved in three days—*done!* One team illustrated the need for reducing the number of reports by taking a picture of a stack that was more than four feet high. After the team's recommendations were adopted, the number of reports was reduced by more than 75 percent.

The simpler issues in the early days of Work Out helped managers feel their way through the behavioral change of having to make decisions on the spot in front of employees and other managers. This new leadership behavior was challenging and at the same time rewarding. One manager said he was literally "sweating" and "squirming" in his chair, as he was put to the test of responding to the team's solutions. After the session, he noted how different it was and yet how impressed he was with the team's solutions: "This Work Out thing might just work!"

The quantitative outcomes were easy to measure, and the qualitative outcomes were even more powerful. The camaraderie and the spirit of working together were enormous. Many of the sessions involved cross-functional teams, and the trust that was built from being together for three days began to break down functional walls.

Early successes and the behavioral changes (sharing of decision making and involving employees in determining solutions) began to foster an evolving buy-in of the process.

So the couple assessed just how things were going in this early phase of trying to "woo" the organizational family. Here's what they decided was helping:

- Being top-down-driven and holding leaders accountable to conduct sessions
- Having outside consultants who were rigorous in using the process and enabling participants to be candid
- Assigning a champion for each team to support them, help break down any obstacles, and follow up with them
- Having decisions made on the spot
- Having follow-up on action implementation (many in a thirty-, sixty-, or ninety-day cycle)
- Achieving early successes, even though some were hygiene factors
- Having no threat of "lay-off" if teams made processes more productive
- Strengthening relationships and trust and allowing organizational boundaries to become more permeable and transparent

Some of the concerns were:

- Some family members did not seem to like Work Out. It was not a top priority in their business.
- Some consultants were not the right fit with the organization and had to be replaced.
- Although quick successes were great, it was necessary to push on to more complex issues.

The couple was satisfied that the buy-in was moving in the right direction and that the marriage would take place. They felt strongly that the principles they embraced helped them get to this point and that keeping up the momentum would be important. The wedding was taking place. The couple had the same goals, principles, and strong family teams to support them.

Making a Life Together: The Marriage

Work Outs were taking place regularly and results, although mixed at times, were overwhelmingly successful. More complex issues were being presented, and bigger dollar savings were being realized while "bureaucracy was being busted." The types of issues being solved were these:

- Reduced design and implementation cycle times
- Reshaped inventories and buying routines
- Streamlined proposal processes
- Improved customer service routines

Conference room walls were plastered with sticky notes identifying critical issues; process maps draped the walls to visually display bottlenecks, and pay-off matrixes were drawn to determine which solutions were the best fit. The process was beginning to be applied more frequently. "Let's have a Work Out to solve this" was being heard in the hallways.

The organization began to see the full power of the Work Out process, from building relationships to increasing productivity. Thousands to millions of dollars were being saved, and huge chunks of time were being freed up. It was working—the great marriage of an organization with talented people and a process to help unleash all that talent to take ownership for solving problems.

Strengthening the Marriage: Taking Work Out to a New Level

The payoffs of this process were tangible, and the marriage partners began to see even more ways to apply it in the organi-

zation. To take it to a new level, they decided to

- Build internal capability to conduct the Work Out sessions
- Involve customers and suppliers

The first step was to train people in facilitation skills and Work Out tools and techniques. Typically, these facilitators came from Operations and HR; they teamed up to conduct the sessions. Involving Operations people across the organization and not leaving it just to HR to facilitate helped keep all functions involved. Positive results mounted. The confidence of the internal facilitators in the process increased. The use of external consultants lessened. There was still a periodic need for them, particularly if a Work Out was extremely complex or politically charged. Then it made sense to have a neutral party facilitate.

The most dramatic and highly visible shift was to involve customers and suppliers in the process. Often customers and suppliers were brought to the table with GE personnel to identify key issues that were getting in the way of the partnership and then work together to come up with actions to address these. There was ownership created between the organization and the customer or supplier to work together to resolve the issues.

One business partnered with a key customer to identify the largest issues that the customer had with their products and services. As a result of multiple Work Outs, the business implemented statistical process control on several key manufacturing processes to improve the product and deliver in a more timely way. This resulted in reduced field complaints due to product failures and optimized delivery of the product to better meet customer demands. In so doing, the businesses realized close to a million-dollar total savings.

In another business relationship, a major customer was so impressed with the Work Out process that they conducted sessions twice a year for over six years. The gathering included suppliers and four Work Out teams wrestling with different issues. They tackled big issues from design changes to availability issues; they introduced Web sites to help each other, cleaned up supplier certification requirements, and designed how they could better work together. The sessions were held across the United States; the leadership team that sponsored them and attended for each team's report outs were senior executives representing suppliers, GE, and customers. Millions of dollars were saved and relationships strengthened. This new level of involvement and partnership in solving issues was a tipping point in the Work Out process.

Yet all marriages have their ups and downs. Some sessions with customers and suppliers were testy and results not as strong as they could have been. The relationships needed more attention, and the issues needed to be discussed in more detail. Occasionally, the composition of the Work Out teams may not have been appropriate. It was critical to have people at the table who were part

of and understood the issues. We also learned not to have teams that were heavily populated with boss and direct report relationships.

Yet overall the marriage was solid. Work Out was accepted and embedded in the organization. It occurred without fanfare or resistance. It became a critical part of the GE toolbox.

The Family Grows

Two initiatives were born, first CAP (Change Acceleration Process) and then Six Sigma. CAP was introduced to help with major cross-functional change efforts. The focus of CAP was to gain acceptance of change by using a process that helped people understand the need for the change, learn how best to communicate it, and identify what was needed organizationally to support this effort. Although initially used for major business changes, it was found to be effective on smaller organizational changes as well.

CAP became a powerful partner with Work Out at its side. Often Work Out came up with the recommendations or solutions, and CAP was the process used to envision how best to gain acceptance for these solutions. In fact, often a coupled Work Out and CAP session would take place. Countless Work Out–CAP sessions were conducted across the company and, again, customers and vendors were included as the program evolved.

Six Sigma, now called Lean Six Sigma, focuses on reducing waste and variation, resulting in peak customer performance. There were key places in the Six Sigma process where the introduction to CAP and Work Out tools could be used. The three were closely tied, widely used, and part of the GE lexicon. The embedding of Work Out was further strengthened by the compatibility of CAP and Six Sigma.

Extending the Family Globally

As the family of the initiatives grew, so did the globalization of the organization. Work Out, along with CAP and Six Sigma, were part of the global orientation for employees. Employees around the world were included in Work Outs as they revisited processes or designed a new organization. Work Out was part of the culture; it was a way of doing business, solving problems, and having teams of people come together to better understand issues and, most important, solve them in their time together. A culture of sharing decision making, receiving input, and accepting ideas for change—or different ways of doing business—just came naturally. It was an often-used tool, no longer a threat, and no longer a program du jour.

Having been used extensively for so many years, the Work Out process has adapted to less than the full three days. People throughout the organization understood the power of solving problems at the level at which they occur. People

took ownership for "let's have a Work Out to get this issue resolved." If you asked a group of people to put their hands up if they had attended a Work Out session, you generally got a 60 to 70 percent show of hands.

Growing Older Together: A Mature Relationship

There were times when GE recognized that the process was not being used as often as it could be and was worried that bureaucracy was creeping back into the organization.

The organization wanted to keep bureaucracy minimized and the workplace productive. Work Out had been around for over ten years when the organization decided to revitalize it.

In September 1999 there was a Work Out Blitz, conducted over a three-month period to ensure that the need for this process was once again highlighted. There was a refresher document designed to help people put rigor back into Work Out during this Blitz.

GE and Work Out had been together for over ten years—a long time. Each partner knew what to expect from each other and, like most long-term couples, could finish each other's sentences. Their relationship had matured, and so had they.

Work Out became adaptable in many situations and had evolved into a shorter time period rather than the full three-day process. A lot of its tools were used in meeting settings to help make them more productive. The process was embedded in the culture.

The Couple Looks Back

At the end of the day, what were the critical game changers that made this marriage last? Possibly these:

- Providing full, unbending support from the top of the organization
- Sticking to the guiding principles
- Having people see and feel the results of the sessions
- Letting participants know that Work Out actions would not result in layoffs
- Involving customers and suppliers
- Building internal capability
- Conducting the Blitz to reinforce the value of Work Out
- Letting the process evolve to maintain and enhance its applicability
- Training people globally, using a standardized curriculum

The End of the Journey?

Work Out is now used more in its adapted form than as the original three-day process. Employees understand the process and tools so well that they can accelerate most of the sessions. It has been and still is a process germane to working in teams and solving issues. It would be hard to believe that this highly flexible and valued process would disappear, particularly as it couples itself with CAP and Six Sigma.

Work Out is ingrained at GE, and although it may take some different shapes, it still drives this premise: "People closest to the work know, more than anyone, how it could be done better."

Reference

Slater, R. (2000). *The GE Way fieldbook: Jack Welch's battle plan for corporate revolution.* New York: McGraw-Hill, p. 55.

EMBEDDING THE CORE PRINCIPLES AT BOEING

Richard H. Axelrod and Emily M. Axelrod

The Challenge

People with graduate engineering degrees don't expect to walk a picket line. But that is what you would have seen in February 2000 when over fourteen thousand Boeing employees went on strike—the largest white-collar strike in U.S. history. Three years later, the same employees who went on strike voted by an over 80 percent margin to renew their contract. Today, new programs, such as the 787 Dreamliner and Multi-Mission Maritime Aircraft, have added six thousand new jobs in Washington state. Production rates for commercial airplanes are increasing, and orders are up. And employee satisfaction is at a ten-year high.

But that is now. In 2000, employees and leaders appeared to be angry, hurt, and confused. Many different emotions surface any time a strike occurs. In addition, when employees feel underutilized and hence undervalued, those feelings are magnified. At Boeing, leaders likely felt betrayed by the employees who went on strike, and employees probably felt let down by Boeing's leadership. Double-digit attrition was threatening this twenty-thousand-person engineering organization. Something had to be done.

In August 2000, we met with Hank Queen, then Boeing Commercial Airplane's director of engineering and soon to be vice president of engineering and product integrity, and Charlie Bofferding, executive director of the Society of Professional Engineering Employees in Aerospace (SPEEA)— the union that represents Boeing's engineers. This meeting launched a change process that ultimately affected the whole engineering organization and resulted in a 40 percent improvement in employee satisfaction, along with other productivity improvements. Here is how we went about achieving these results.

Building a Platform for Change

Our platform for change was constructed in three workshops held from October to December of 2000. The first workshop included Hank, his leadership team, and key union officials—a total of fifteen people. The purpose of the workshop was to get clear on what needed to change and how to go about changing it.

The group believed that the underlying cause of the attrition problem and the strike was what the group called "underutilization"—employees did not feel that the jobs they did utilized their talents effectively. Both the SPEEA and engineering management believed that by addressing the utilization issue, they could heal the wounds from the strike and reverse the attrition that was affecting the engineering organization. It

would be a win-win measure for everyone concerned.

However, when it came to choosing how they would go about changing the organization, the group was less clear. Somewhat unusually, we had proposed a principle-based process instead of a traditional change-management approach. A turning point in the day occurred when Hank announced that he did not care whether the group used engagement principles (in which people from all levels of the organization would be invited to participate in the change process from the very beginning) or a more traditional approach to change (in which a few leaders would make decisions that all employees then would be expected to carry out) (Axelrod, 2000). What he did care about was that the group support whatever change methodology they chose. This change was too important, too critical, to receive halfhearted support.

In the end, the group decided that they would adopt the engagement principles as the basis for their change effort because these principles were consistent with how they wanted to work together in the future.

But change is never that easy. Boeing is a very complex organization, and the leadership team knew that if this effort was to be successful, they needed support from other leaders in the organization. Recognizing they could not go forward alone, they decided to invite these leaders to participate in the process. So a second workshop was held with over fifty key leaders and union officials. At this workshop, the purpose—"to create a work environment where people could be successful"—and the boundaries for the work were established.

Having set the framework for change in these first two workshops, the expanded leadership group decided to continue to widen the circle by involving 250 people from all levels and functions, along with key union officials, to help determine the strategy for moving forward. At this third workshop, an education strategy was developed to launch the change process. Fundamental to this strategy were multilevel, multifunctional large group sessions. People were invited to attend these sessions to learn about (1) how they could participate in creating a work environment where people could be effective, (2) the boundaries for the change process, and (3) the engagement principles that would be employed. These voluntary large group sessions ranged from 50 people to 400 people.

As the process gained momentum, the number of people who showed up surprised us. One time we were expecting 100 people, and over 250 showed up. It was a relief that Boeing had large meeting rooms.

Creating the Delivery System

When our platform for change had been built, the next step was to craft a delivery system that included clear boundaries, a set of engagement principles, and supporting mechanisms. Ken Kirwan, the internal project leader, created the "delivery system" metaphor: rockets have a payload and a delivery system. Our goal was to create a delivery system for change that could be used by groups large and small to achieve their own specific goals. The payload—the change goals—would be developed locally.

Clear Boundaries

In a situation where we would set work units free to establish their own change goals, clear boundaries were essential. Clear boundaries are a hallmark of effective systemic change. Boundaries provide a fence around the change process, and the fence defines the area where the game can be played. If the fence gives people little room to play, they feel constrained, constantly bump into each other, and in the end say, "Why bother?" If the fence gives people too much room, they sometimes lose sight of where they are headed and get lost. The trick is to create boundaries that create a meaningful playing field—one where there is room to play and where people do not get lost.

Purpose was our first boundary condition. It describes the *why* of the change. Purpose is what gets us out of bed in the morning. It answers the question, What do we want to create as a result of our work together? When your purpose is compelling, it draws people into your change effort.

The second boundary was "local control," meaning that work units within the engineering organization had to decide what they would do within their area to create a work environment where everyone could be successful. For example, some organizations take on issues such as how they will welcome and orient new employees to their work unit, while others take on issues such as improving the process by which engineering changes are made to existing products.

The third boundary condition was the engagement principles. These became the norms for the change process: widening the circle of involvement, connecting people to each other, creating communities for action, and embracing a democratic mind-set. In other words, the work units were free to do anything they believed would help create a work environment where people could be successful, as long as they followed the engagement principles as they did their work.

Over the course of the change effort, a fourth boundary was added as a result of the experience of George Yamamura (a retired Boeing manager of software engineers) in improving employee satisfaction and productivity in his own work unit. Leaders were expected to meet with their employees and discuss the following questions (Yamamura, 2005):

- What is your current job satisfaction level?
- What is most important to you about your job?
- What are the biggest issues or greatest barriers to improving your organization?

Engagement Principles

We believe that the most practical tool for change is a useful set of principles. If you have a set of principles to guide you, then when you meet up with unexpected situations, you can create your own solutions. If clear boundaries are the hallmark of effective change, then the engagement principles were the fuel for our delivery system. They provided the energy that made the system go and a normative process for the change effort.

- *Widening the circle of involvement* means getting the right stakeholders, regardless of level, involved in your work from the very beginning. Widening the circle begins when you ask the question, Who else needs to be here? This principle builds ownership while supporting innovation, adaptation, and learning.

- *Connecting people to each other* builds a network of people throughout the organization who understand what needs changing and why. Work flows more smoothly when people understand what needs to be done and develop personal connections with each other.
- *Creating communities for action* builds a group of people who have the will to make things happen. Co-creating the future together builds the necessary ownership and commitment. Creating communities starts when you invite people to participate in the direction-setting process from the very beginning.
- *Embracing a democratic mind-set* begins when you recognize that people support what they have a hand in creating. Energy is created when people are included in decisions about what to change and how to change it and know that their contribution counts.

The engagement principles are interconnected. You benefit when you use any one principle, but you get a synergistic effect when you use all four principles in combination.

Deciding to approach an organization with *a set of* principles rather than a standard change-management approach was a departure for us. The engagement principles were used as the basis for the whole change process rather than the implementation of a specific methodology. Methodology faded into the background, as we became less concerned with standard processes and more concerned with applying the engagement principles.

We found that the engagement principles worked for the following reasons: (1) they were few in number and easy to understand; (2) they had validity because people could see how they had been applying these principles all along. As a result, people felt affirmed by them. And the principles provided easy-to-use labels to describe what was being done.

Supporting Mechanisms

It takes more than clear boundaries and a set of principles to change an organization. That is why supporting mechanisms were included in our delivery system. Strong leadership, measurement, a road map for change, resources, and learning fairs were the critical components that made up our supporting mechanisms.

Strong Leadership. Strong leadership was demonstrated by Hank Queen throughout the process and was anchored in the core belief that if people sit down and talk with each other about what bothers them, they will make decisions that benefit themselves and the company. Hank does not just talk about working together. He engages others, sets challenging goals, establishes clear boundaries, provides people the wherewithal to get the job done, and then gets out of the way. Having a leader like Hank allows people to move forward without having to look over their shoulders, wondering whether or not they will be supported.

Measurement. However, Hank's trust was not blind. He expected not only that the job satisfaction and productivity discussions would occur but that progress would be measurable. Hank backed up that expectation by making employee satisfaction a key component of performance reviews. Managers would now be measured on the level of employee satisfaction within their organization.

Road Map for Change. Effective change has a road map, which identifies the direction you are headed, shows markers, and indicates alternative routes and points of interest along the way. You may choose the most direct route, a scenic route, or a route that gets you to your destination at a leisurely pace. This is different from a set of MapQuest directions, which spell out every turn in a step-by-step process for getting from here to there. A road map leaves it up to those taking a trip to choose the route that works best for them.

Our road map for change may have given the organization the most difficulty because it did not lay out a step-by-step approach to changing the organization. Rather, it provided direction by identifying the work environment of the future, gave people a set of tools (the principles), and asked them to decide locally what needed attention. Although many were frustrated by the lack of MapQuest-type directions, they also told us that, had we provided them, they probably would not have followed them.

Resources. Effective change requires resources. From the outset we realized that a support structure would be needed to provide assistance to leaders throughout the process. The structure we developed consisted of an organizationwide support team and local support teams (twenty such teams in all). Each team consisted of local leadership, HR and OD representatives, union leadership, and employees. The teams ranged in size from ten to fifteen members. The role of the organizationwide support team was to identify systemic issues that needed to be addressed to support local efforts. The purpose of the local support teams was to work with leadership to identify local issues that could be addressed and to figure out how to engage employees in resolving them.

Here are some examples of the issues addressed. The Liaison Engineering Group (an interface group between Engineering and Production) put together a series of four sessions to develop the vision, mission, goals, and competencies for the organization. One hundred people attended each session. The 767 Engineering Group developed a coaching process for all managers, and the chief engineer agreed to be the first person to participate in the process. The Airplane Systems Group conducted a technical conference to clarify the roles and responsibilities of Electrical Engineering Subsystems (an organization within the Airplane Systems Group) during the customer introduction process. And the Airplane Validation Group created a training program for managers on how to better engage employees in their work and how to use their talents more effectively.

The support teams received two types of training. First they were trained in the Conference Model (Axelrod and Axelrod, 1999) process, which provided these groups with a background in Large Group Methods and gave them a library of activities and designs that they could use. While some groups used the full Conference Model to address issues, most ended up using selected activities from the Conference Model as a basis for local workshops or large group events.

The second type of training the support teams received was in how to take a set of client requirements and design their own large group meetings using a design template we call the Meeting Canoe (Axelrod, Axelrod, Beedon, and Jacobs, 2004). This canoe-shaped blueprint helps create meetings with an "engagement edge."

Six elements make up the Meeting Canoe. Start by making people feel welcome; find ways to create connections among people; discover the way things are (build a shared picture of the current situation); elicit people's dreams (build a shared picture of where you want to go); decide who does what to create the future you've agreed upon, and attend to the end (review agreements, celebrate progress, and identify next steps). In designing the activities for each of the meeting elements, people learned to use design concepts such as enabling people to discover what they know naturally, fostering curiosity, and engaging the

whole person. Training in the Conference Model, Meeting Canoe, and design concepts equipped the support teams to successfully build their own large group meetings.

Learning Fairs. Learning fairs were another structure that was developed to support the process. At these half-day gatherings, groups from throughout the organization would come to share what they were doing, successes they were having, and what they were learning along the way. Here team members could visit and discuss problems such as how to get leadership support or how to involve people across a three-shift operation. At the end of a learning fair, teams would meet to discuss what they'd learned and how they could apply their learning to their situation.

Projects Both Large and Small

Over the next five years, the previously described delivery system was used to initiate many projects. Here are a few brief examples:

• The Commercial Airplane engineering organization in Wichita, Kansas, currently known as Spirit AeroSystems, Inc., used the engagement principles to design and conduct a series of large group conferences to help employees understand what was required to work in a global manufacturing system and engage them in identifying what they needed to do differently to compete in such an environment. The theme for these conferences was "co-creating our future together." One conference dealt with what globalization meant to the organization and how it would affect career opportunities and job stability. The other conference dealt with improving the "nonrecurring product definition process," which concerned how one-time changes were made to existing Boeing aircraft. These two conferences helped to develop a shared understanding of the competitive environment in which Boeing finds itself and involved employees in identifying how the Wichita organization could compete in a global environment.

• When Boeing needed to work with the FAA to create the first Federal Aviation Regulations–Part 25 Delegated Compliance Organization in the world, the engagement principles were used to formulate the strategy for bringing together leadership, employees, and union officials from both the FAA and Boeing to develop this new organization. In a Delegated Compliance Organization, validation or verification activities formerly done by the FAA are delegated to an aircraft designer such as Boeing. When this project started, many doubted that it would be completed on schedule because of the complex changes in roles and responsibilities for both Boeing and the FAA. Not only was the project completed on time, but it was completed with the enthusiastic support of people from both organizations. Today, others in the industry have expressed interest in

using the Boeing organization as a model for their own operations.

• Not every use of the engagement principles required a huge change effort. One supervisor used the principles to redesign a work unit. First, he formed a group of employees interested in improving work flow through the department. When the group had identified what needed to be changed, they posted their ideas on easel sheets in the work area and asked their fellow employees to comment. Every day their coworkers put more and more sticky notes on the diagram. The group then reviewed these ideas and incorporated them into the final plan. Within two weeks the ideas for a more efficient operation had been implemented, and the new process was up and running!

Learnings

Our learnings were many. Some resulted from the strategy we employed; others were more personal. Some lessons came easy; others were more difficult. Some reinforced previous learning; others plowed new ground. Taken together, they are based on the experiences of everyone involved.

The Power of Education, a Good Set of Principles, and Few Boundaries

Kurt Lewin, one of the founders of social psychology, used to say there is nothing as useful as a good theory. Unlike many change management efforts, our strategy was not prescriptive. There were no extensive manuals and procedures to follow. Although this frustrated some, we believe it is why the strategy was ultimately successful. We set out to educate people about the purpose of the change, the underlying principles, and the boundaries of the change process. In these sessions, we did not expect people to swallow these ideas whole; rather, we engaged in extensive dialogue about the purpose and the upside and downside of the engagement platform and the boundaries. Our leap of faith was believing that once people understood the purpose and the engagement principles, they would begin to see the possibilities for change in their own organization. What we saw over and over again was that when leaders understood the purpose and the principles, they identified places where they could be applied. Many good ideas that later became positive changes were born in these early education sessions.

The Importance of Local Control

In today's organizations, people are highly resistant to top-down, programmatic change. The dilemma facing us was how to create change throughout the organization that had some consistency and at the same time provided work units with the autonomy to do what made sense from their point of view.

"Local control" meant that work units could do anything they wanted to achieve the purpose, as long as they stayed within the established boundaries and employed the engagement principles in doing so. Local control let leaders and support teams identify what issues to address, given their own understanding of what needed to be done. If they needed to widen the circle to include people from other work units, they were free to do so. Some groups chose to develop new employee orientation programs, while other groups chose to tackle technical issues such as developing a new process. The use of the engagement principles provided a common language and process throughout the organization.

Engagement as a Delivery System

Early on there was some confusion as to the role of the engagement principles in the change process. Were we trying to create an organization based on these principles? Was the purpose to shift the engineering culture to one that would be defined by these principles? Or were the engagement principles the framework for how change would take place?

The "rocket" metaphor made this matter clearer. The business issues that local work units decided to work on became the payload. The engagement principles and supporting mechanism were the delivery system. The task was to build the best delivery system possible that would help local work units deliver their payload.

Teaching People to Work with Principles

Teaching people to work at the principle level was at once easier and more difficult than we first thought. It was easier because the principles we used were straightforward. People immediately grasped what they meant, and many intuitively knew how to apply them. However, for some, applying the principles was more difficult. What they needed were concrete examples. It became important to present examples as ideas to build on rather than the only way a principle could be applied. "It depends on the situation" became our caveat. Adding concrete examples to our discussions about the principles enabled people to develop unique solutions that matched their situation.

Bringing principles front and center changed the way we trained people to use them. Previously, we would have led with our consulting framework—the Conference Model—and used the principles to explain how the Conference Model worked. Now, however, the Conference Model methodology became an example of the principles in action. Thus the Conference Model was used less as a complete methodology to follow and more as a library of activities that people could draw from when they were designing interventions.

Teaching people to work with a set of principles sets them free to create answers without having to call in "experts" for advice. It breaks the cycle of dependency that is often created between consultants and clients. In this new relationship, design ideas can come from anyone. This improved capacity empowers the organization members to operate independently in the face of a constantly changing environment.

Letting Go

It is a cliché to say that leaders have to let go in order for successful change to occur. What about the consultants who work with them? While it is one matter for us to suggest to clients that they need to let go of familiar ways of doing things; it's another matter for us to do it ourselves.

In this consultation, we moved from the roles of trainer and leader of Conference Model interventions to those of teacher and social architect. The size of the system dictated that we could not provide consultants for every intervention, and the complexity of the situation required an approach that could be used in a variety of circumstances by people with a wide variety of skills. Once we came to that realization, pet ways of working had to change. What became apparent was that if this intervention was to be successful, we had to equip many people to do what we normally do. This meant teaching not just HR or OD professionals but also leaders and employees the importance of the principles and then how to create interventions based on these principles.

Just as we were asking leaders to let go of leadership prerogatives, we were learning to let go of our need to control the change process. Together we learned that if people are involved in creating a compelling purpose, are equipped with a few powerful principles, and have a clear set of boundaries to guide them, great things can happen.

References

Axelrod, R. H. (2000). *Terms of engagement: Changing the way we change*

organizations. San Francisco: Berrett-Koehler.

Axelrod, R. H., & Axelrod, E. M. (1999). *The Conference Model.* San Francisco: Berrett–Koehler.

Axelrod, R. H., Axelrod, E. M., Beedon, J., & Jacobs, R. W. (2004). *You don't have to do it alone: How to involve others to get things done.* San Francisco: Berrett-Koehler.

Yamamura, G. (2005). *The tenth inning.* Seattle: Author.

MOVING TO THE NEXT LEVEL AT THE CANADIAN INSTITUTE FOR HEALTH INFORMATION

Larry E. Peterson and Rebecca Peterson

The Challenge

The Canadian Institute for Health Information (CIHI) is highly regarded as a productive organization and a concerned employer. It gathers, analyzes, and reports health data from across the country to inform policy and practice. CIHI is an independent organization servicing governments and other constituencies. In 2004, Mediacorp Canada Inc. listed it in *MacLean's* magazine as one of the top one hundred companies to work for in Canada.

In 2001, CIHI hired the HayGroup to carry out an employee survey and compare their results to the HayNorm for similar North American organizations (HayGroup, 2003). The overall CIHI results were very good. The two hundred CIHI employees, on average, rated themselves 20 percent above the Hay Public Sector Norm. The CIHI *managers*, however, rated themselves slightly below that norm, especially on factors such as communication, performance management, training and development, management style, and employee involvement. The managers did not see CIHI fully living up to their expectations and desires. The CEO responded to the results of the survey by developing working groups to address some of the most contentious issues.

Communication, management style, and training and development issues were seen as priorities for executive attention; task forces were established in each area. In addition, the pension plan was reviewed, and there was some substantial restructuring of the organization. Some branches were given particular attention. As part of these initiatives, the managers received both permission and the resources to hold occasional Managers' Forums.

Even with that good record, the CEO knew that performance had to move to a higher level if CIHI were to address the challenges and opportunities it faced. Other think tanks and forums were developing good health data and analysis, and there were more and better competitors from both the public and private sectors. Although the quality of CIHI work was very good, there was significant room for improvement. Advances in technology and the development of new standards and systems for collecting health care data required new strategies. They needed to improve their data quality and get their analysis out to their clients and stakeholders faster and in a form that better met the stakeholders' needs. They needed to develop more effective partnerships with newer, related initiatives that were now getting sizable government funding. They decided to move to additional locations for their offices and knew that the move would increase communication and integration issues. Although CIHI's profile in Canada was good, it could be greatly strengthened in order to develop more stable funding to support growth.

The organization already had a robust business planning process; an award-winning board, as well as the key elements of a business plan, were already established with board approval. In order to lead the organization to the next level of performance, the CEO decided to hold an executive retreat in the spring of 2003. He wanted to develop clear strategic initiatives to realize what he believed was a shared vision of stable funding and growth by 2005. He had set the date and the participants before inviting the first author (the consultant on the project) to work with him to design and facilitate the event.

Why Open Space?

The primary Large Group Method used in this case was Open Space Technology (OST). The decision to use the Open Space approach was made with the CEO, after discussing other options and after some interviews with members of the executive team because it can shift the culture toward taking individual responsibility as well as real teamwork. It does require the commitment of the sponsor to an open dialogue on the topic at hand.

A critical component to the effective use of OST is good planning that determines the client's intention or goals, the theme or question to be addressed, and any boundaries or givens that set the parameters for action and follow-up. In this case, the initial planning was with the CEO. The rest of the thirteen-person executive team was included through brief telephone interviews.

Initially, the CEO established the following goals for the retreat:

- Agree on the top five to seven strategies the executive must carry out to achieve stable funding and growth by summer 2005.
- Build an executive team, with a closer connection among team members.
- Clarify the implementation planning process in order to inform the board.

The contextual drivers for their business improvements had been well established in CIHI's internal planning processes. The CEO developed his statement of a positive vision, or in his words a "willed future," for CIHI in the face of its current challenges. He developed the theme for the executive retreat: "What do we have to do between now and summer 2005 to get stable funding and growth?" A number of substantial changes were required to create a strong position with the growing competition.

The CEO also articulated the "givens" or the boundaries within which the executive members could develop proposed initiatives. For example, the board had developed a scorecard to measure overall performance, and the current approved business plan set the context for implementation planning. Revisions of the business plan required certain steps. The decision to develop offices in western Canada was also to be taken as a given. These previous decisions set the context for both the discussions and the development of implementation strategies. He, with the consultant, also determined that priority setting and action planning with regard to the ideas developed at the retreat would take place at the end of the retreat, with all involved, on the last day.

Based on this planning, the CEO invited executive team members to attend the retreat and informed them of the purpose, the theme question, and the outcomes sought. He also described the nature of an Open Space meeting, the givens for this retreat, and the fact that implementation planning would be part of the session.

One Event Becomes Two

On the first day, the CEO welcomed the thirteen executives and began the retreat by reminding the group of the key reasons for moving to the next level of performance. The CEO then stated his vision for the next two years. He saw CIHI as an essential part of the information processes of key clients and partners and as the vendor of choice for the services it offers. Its information quality would be at the highest level. He saw both a national and an international reputation for its health perspectives. The executive team reached immediate, real agreement on that vision within the hour allotted for this discussion. The CEO had named the shared vision well.

OST was then used to engage the executives in determining the challenges and opportunities for implementing that vision and the strategies for moving forward. The same approach was used as that used for larger groups. Participants sat in one circle. There was no proposed content agenda but instead a blank wall. The agenda topics emerged from the participants, who each stated the aspects of the vision for which he or she had passion and would take some responsibility. The responsibility included entering a report on the laptop computers provided. Groups self-selected and self-organized their conversations. Group initiators chose a start time and location for their discussion from sticky notes. There were four suggested start times for conversations throughout the day, with four pos-

sible locations in the retreat center for each start time. The norms for the behavior during the day were set by the facilitator with the "Four Principles" and "One Law" of OST, which were originally articulated by Harrison Owen, the discoverer of the approach (Owen, 1997b, pp. 95–100).

Executive team members worked in self-organizing small groups over the course of the day, managing their own time frames and energy using the Open Space principles and law. They documented their discussions and plans on laptops after their sessions. The CEO moved from group to group for part of the time; he also initiated a key discussion group. The consultant did not participate in the conversations. Instead, he was both "present and invisible," staying out of the way so that the executives could plan and discover strategies. That facilitator role also meant monitoring the computers as participants entered their reports.

At the end of the day, the participants expressed genuine pleasure and excitement about their learning, the quality of their time together, and the reports they produced. People listened and built on each other's ideas. Disagreements fostered better solutions, and a strong sense of teamwork emerged.

On the second day, they reviewed the book of group reports that detailed the proposed strategies. Copies had been printed overnight for each participant and made available at breakfast. With the smaller group and much of the action planning already in the Open

Space reports, the consultant guided the priority and planning process. Participants were asked to choose the top five reports for attention by the executive team for the next six months. A simple voting procedure was used. Those reports were then addressed in order of priority to clarify how far the Open Space topic group got in its implementation strategy development, what next steps were required to move it forward, and how much leadership energy would be required to move forward in the next six months. Relationships to existing initiatives or executive responsibilities were identified and support for the Open Space initiative confirmed. Participants demonstrated genuine energy for and a strong commitment to the newly developed plans.

The participants realized that the work and the outcomes of the two-day retreat had created their "executive" implementation strategy. They also realized that they had to engage the whole organization's energy to carry out most of their strategies. As they explored how they would lead the organization, the manager's results in the employee survey became a salient part of the executives' conversation.

The CEO reminded the group that he intended to meet with the managers in two weeks. He had planned a fairly traditional agenda—a conversation with the CEO, including presentations and interaction with the managers. However, the executive team's positive experience with OST led to the decision to propose a change to the planned agenda—to engage the managers in planning as they had been engaged. They also committed to take seriously what the managers would produce and to integrate those ideas with their own plans, sharing emergent leadership roles when appropriate.

At the closing of an Open Space event, each participant in the circle is given the opportunity to comment on their experience. In this case, the circle took place after the action planning. The participants thanked each other for sharing information, being honest, and valuing all of the contributions. They expressed surprise at how far they were able to get in their two-day retreat.

Managers' Retreat

The CEO approached the leadership group for the managers' retreat and proposed that the theme, boundaries, and process developed for the executive event be used in the one-day Managers' Forum. The formal leaders of the management group agreed. In the planning for this event, it also became clear that the focus for the managers' event was to be on what the twenty-three managers perceived as their challenges or opportunities for implementing the vision.

After the leadership of the managers' group called the one-day forum to order, the CEO stated the shared vision of the executive team and asked for questions of clarification. Again the vision struck a real chord with the managers. It was big enough to include their interests and clear enough to provide a sense of direction. The CEO also stated that the managers' strategic initiatives would be linked to those of the executive team but were not limited by those the executive team developed. The CEO asked them to explore their roles and strategies as managers in leading the organization toward the vision.

When the "space was opened," individual managers identified strategic topics for which they had a passion. The approach used with executives was repeated with the managers: the circle of chairs, blank wall and emergent agenda, self-organizing discussions, computer reports, and the "Four Principles" and "One Law."

At the closing circle of the one-day event, with substantive reports in the computers and posted on the wall, many managers stated that they felt more connected to each other and to the strategy of the organization. They had also developed some key strategies and implementation plans to move CIHI forward. They thanked the CEO for engaging them in planning in this way.

That "felt connection" could have been stifled by the executive team if they had chosen not to integrate their results collaboratively with the managers. In adjourning the event, the CEO did a quick linking of the topics with those that had been developed by the executive team and stated what he saw as new insights.

There was not a Day 2 for the Managers' Forum. In the following days, however, the executive team took the managers' initiatives seriously. First, the vice president in charge of strategic planning did some integration of obvious connections between the two sets of reports: strategies and next steps. Then he held a joint meeting to clarify the integration of the plans and reach agreement on how to proceed. The specific follow-up action items were listed from both events and related to the Open Space reports. Then the action responsibilities were clarified, along with target dates.

Surprising Results

The consultant met with the CEO two months later, in mid-August 2003, to reflect on the sessions and the strategic work that had followed. There had been substantial agreement on key issues between the executive and the managers but at different levels of specificity. Executives had a broader view for the most part. The integration of the strategies had led to action. There had already been progress on the key issues identified at both events. The CEO also stated that there had been a "huge impact" on the feeling of involvement of the managers and believed that the planning process we followed, including the Open Space events, was a factor.

The CEO's reflections were based, in part, on his review of the results of the HayGroup 2003 employee survey, which had been conducted in late June 2003. For CIHI as a whole, there were real across-the-board improvements relative to the 2001 results and relative to the HayNorm, and these were a genuine surprise.

In the survey, participants were asked to rate CIHI in relation to seventy-five questions as "very good," "good," "average," "poor," or "very poor." The response to each question is compared to the HayNorm for that employment sector in North America. The analysis indicates both the "percent deviation" from the norm and from the last survey. The "deviation" is the difference from the norm of the percentage of CIHI employees who answered a question as "good" or "very good."

The 236 respondents in 2003 represented 95 percent of the employees. There were 184 respondents in 2001 or 94 percent of the employees at that time. All of the twenty-three managers responded to the 2003 survey, with one of the twenty-three not responding in 2001 (HayGroup, 2003, July, Figures 1 and 2).

The scores for CIHI as a whole did improve, with the largest improvements seen to be in the Training and Development factor, that is, the degree to which training is provided and employees believe they will reach their career objectives at CIHI. The overall data also showed a 9 percent improvement in Recognition, that is, in the appreciation of employee efforts. There was also an 8 percent improvement in Organizational Commitment—perceptions of how well the organization will act on their issues and concerns (HayGroup, 2003, July, Section I).

The CEO was most excited, however, by the size of the changes in the managers' results. According to the Hay-Group lead consultant, the amount of change was unusual. Big gains are not expected when starting with already-good results. Yet there were numerous jumps of 20 percent. Some of the highest areas of improvement for managers were in Employee Involvement, Employee Satisfaction (morale), Communication, and Organizational Commitment (HayGroup, 2003, July, Section I). These issues are the most likely to be influenced by OST events.

The Employee Involvement category is a collection of six questions focused on the degree to which employees feel that they have had input, that their interests and concerns are being taken into account, that their ideas have been adopted, that their skills are put to good use, and that they have authority to pursue their work. In 2001 the managers were below the norm for public organizations in North America in this category. In 2003 the managers' results were 19 points above the Hay Norm and 22 points above 2001, while the CIHI total was only 5.5 points above the 2001 result (HayGroup, 2003, July, Section II, pp. 88–93).

The results in Employee Involvement for managers are even more dramatic, given that one of the six questions had only a 5 percent increase. It identified the feeling of contribution to the success of CIHI; 95 percent of managers already believed that CIHI was "good" (or "very good") in that category in 2001, so shifting to 100 percent was not a large change. All other questions in this category, however, shifted by 19 percent or more. The largest shift was in the question about how well CIHI took into account employee interests or concerns when making important decisions. Although there was not a focus on managers per se in the question, there was an astounding 38 percent improvement putting CIHI managers 25 points above the norm for such organizations in North America. The survey showed a 32 percent improvement in the managers' sense that "I have input into the changes happening at CIHI," putting them 33 percent above the Hay Norm for North American public sector organizations (HayGroup, 2003, July, Section II, pp. 88–93).

One of the questions in the category dealing with Employee Satisfaction or Commitment asks about the overall morale at CIHI. There was a 23 percent improvement in the managers' perception of morale, while there was only a 9 percent improvement for the organization as a whole. The question focused on overall CIHI morale, but the morale of the managers would certainly influence their perceptions on such a question (HayGroup, 2003, July, Section II, p. 103).

Another question in the employee survey focused on the opportunities to communicate with the executive team. Twenty-nine percent more managers saw those opportunities as good or very good in July 2003, in relation to a 19 percent increase for the organization as a whole—an important improvement (HayGroup, 2003, July, Section II, p. 32).

Interpreting the Results

Given the positive survey results and the indications of strong steps toward implementation, the first author conducted some brief interviews with four CIHI executives and four managers. Their perceptions reinforced the view that the OST events made a real contribution.

As one research vice president stated, "No direct cause-effect relationship can be claimed" for the planning process. Implementation planning and cultural change are complex processes. The planning process and Open Space events, however, may have been a "nice way to wrap up the efforts at change," according to another vice president. "Managers came back from the meeting with a very positive message." A third vice president acknowledged that the Open Space events created a different "atmosphere" in the organization and that the integrated follow-up led to real action. "Unlike other strategic thinking processes there was more impact on outcomes." Two managers that were interviewed also saw the Open Space event as having a "huge impact." It "lifted the spirits" of the managers. One saw the process working because it led to priorities that "we all now own." Another manager who helped organize the forum stated that "people really liked the event, and there was lots of good feedback." One vice president believed that the fact that managers had the CEO's attention for a full day was both unusual and appreciated. The CEO also believed that the planning process was a factor and that it had a "huge impact on the feeling of involvement."

Confirming OST Experiences

The OST sessions clarified practical strategy and aided its implementation in the whole organization. They also accelerated or enhanced the managers' positive view of the organization and its culture as indicated in the employee survey. The desire and willingness of the CIHI executive leadership to listen and engage made this possible.

Taking that risk was enhanced by the OST planning process used by the consultant, which clarifies the focus and the boundaries. Clarifying what is to be taken as "given" and what will be done with the results enables the event sponsors to "let go" of specific outcomes and enhance the spirited self-organization of the participants. In this situation, both emergent self-organization and hierarchical planning and accountability effectively took place. The planning in this case was one key component of preparing CIHI to take full advantage of both formal accountability and an emergent strategy.

The two Open Space events accelerated the organization's initiatives. In one of the few theses focused on OST, Richard Norris (2000) did a content analysis of OST stories that were published on the Internet or in various periodicals over a specified time frame. He concluded:

The prime value noted is Open Space Technology's ability to help people move below the surface of their personal or organizational façade by uncovering what is already in existence but unseen . . . allowing value to emerge in its most authentic state.

Harrison Owen (1997a) describes the same phenomena in *Expanding Our Now.* OST seems to enable participants to become more aware of what is possible at a given time in an organization.

Other researchers have found similar effects. Linda Olson's follow-up interviews after an OST event at Hewlett Packard discovered five key themes. Participants identified the "ability to collaborate, freedom to make choices, creativity, shared leadership and the ability to make connections as key elements of their positive experience of Open Space Technology" (Olson, 1996, p. 59). Richard Norris found the same kinds of responses in his survey of the literature. The top occurrences of the value of the OST experience were learning, shared leadership, creativity, self-organization, the assumption of responsibility, and increased awareness (Norris, 2000, p. 41).

Open Space has been used at Hewlett Packard for a variety of types of meetings. The experience there fits with the two sessions at CIHI. "Boundaries that previously separated employees disappeared in the Open Space meeting, as new relationships emerged based on common concerns and interests" (Olson, 1998, p. 14). OST created the conditions for emergent collaboration, at least for the time of the event. The CEO and two senior managers were at the managers' Open Space forum. The managers experienced collaboration with each other and the CEO. This was furthered by the integration of the executive and managers' strategies in the ongoing planning process.

Reflections

OST accelerated the development and implementation of a shared strategy. It also accelerated a shift from normal manager survey results to those that were substantially above the norm. Even with a smaller group, this case demonstrates that Open Space can liberate energy and engage effective strategic thinking and relationship building. The HayGroup studies were a fortunate coincidence that provided some supporting evidence for the changes that the authors have experienced for a number of years.

As with any "event," what happens in preparation and in the follow-up activity can substantially influence the experience and the results. In this case, that learning was reinforced. In the short time frames involved, a strong CEO who prepared well for the event was critical in creating the conditions for emergent planning and energy.

Many CEOs or managers, particularly in midsize organizations, believe they can micromanage the organization and its conversations. Letting the agenda and

conversation emerge from the participants is experienced as a risky proposition. They would prefer a process that appears to be more in control, if not of the sponsor then in "control" of the facilitator who would guide the discussions at table groups. Many would prefer to deduce the implementation strategy from their vision, rather than let it emerge in relation to the vision. This CEO also had some of these concerns until the executive team was interviewed by telephone and some boundaries were acknowledged. He chose to take the risk and therefore got substantial results. Our continued learning is that if the sponsor or CEO is not willing to take that risk, then OST is not the appropriate approach.

As in this case, it is sometimes easier for a CEO to take that risk with a senior team or smaller group of managers than with the whole organization. After that positive experience, he and the executive team were ready to risk the use of the Open Space approach with the managers.

The time frames and circumstances of the managers' event were not ideal. The time frame was too short to fully involve the managers in preparation for the event. However, the decision to involve the managers in the planning process with OST and to integrate the two sets of emergent strategies into the implementation plan made it possible to achieve substantial results.

As a result, more managers believed they had input into the changes happening at CIHI and could take responsibility for some of those changes. Managers chose the work groups where they wanted to make a contribution and had the freedom to leave whenever they wanted. The topics or strategies developed by the executive did not prescribe what the managers saw as important. The synergy between the two groups emerged. Thus managers felt and exercised real freedom to make substantive input into the planning process.

As in this case, participants in an Open Space event often experience a "felt sense of connection" to each other—a sense of emergent or deepened community. There are often statements by some participants that they now have a much better understanding of the organization as a whole. They feel more integrated, connected, and positive about their colleagues and the organization. This occurred at CIHI, even though there were two events rather than one, as we usually prefer. This is likely because they were held close together in time, and a few executives attended the managers' event along with the CEO.

There were ongoing signs of collaborative implementation after the two events. The first author also facilitated two shorter working group sessions with the CEO's involvement that partly emerged from the directions established in the Open Space workshops. In those sessions, participants identified strategic criteria for successful population health research initiatives and deepened relationships with a partner organization. In addition, OST was used for a successful Canadawide consultation on obesity policy development where CIHI was one of the sponsors.

References

HayGroup. (2003, July). *CIHI 2003 employee survey: Total CIHI results: Job group & branch.* Toronto, Ontario: Canadian Institute for Health Information.

Norris, R. (2000). *A grounded theory study on the value associated with using Open Space Technology.* Unpublished master's thesis, Webster University, Merritt Island, FL. (Available at http://www.open spaceworld.org/tmnfiles/OSTResearch 2000.htm)

Olson, L. (1998, Winter). The dilemmas of introducing Open Space Technology: A new perspective for organizing and perceiving change. *The Journal of the Bay Area OD Network, 17*(4), 11–14.

Olson, L. (1996). *Open Space Technology and self-organization: A case study.* Master's thesis, School of Business and Management, Pepperdine University, Pasadena, California.

Owen, H. (1997a). *Expanding our now.* San Francisco: Berrett-Koehler.

Owen, H. (1997b). *Open Space Technology: A user's guide* (2nd ed.). San Francisco: Berrett-Koehler.

AFTER THE DANCE

Glenda H. Eoyang and Kristine Quade

The Challenge

The event was a raging success. The exhausted design team sits in a circle in the center of the empty room in order to capture the learning and impressions. Each tells a story of the experience as it was happening over the course of the project: selling the idea, putting the design team together, designing the event, managing logistics, and then holding the event itself. Stories emerge about the transforming conversations heard and about the changes occurring throughout the event. They are as thrilled as they are exhausted. They realize the long-term work has just begun. This event caused a shift in the patterns of organizational interaction, and the new patterns need to be supported and reinforced.

We would like to acknowledge our colleagues from the Human Systems Dynamics Institute who participated in this study and continue to inform our emerging learning, including Royce Holladay, Catherine Perme, and Katherine Barton. We also appreciate the helpful comments from experts in each of the four methods, including Harrison Owen, Robert Jacobs, and Linda Houden.

After confronting this challenge many times, our experience with multiple types of Large Group Methods and the emerging theories of human systems dynamics (HSD) has opened our understanding about what needs to be done "after the dance." We have studied the ways that complexity influences the operations of Open Space (Owen, 1997, 2004), Future Search, Appreciative Inquiry (Cooperrider and Whitney, 1999; Watkins and Mohr, 2001), and Whole-Scale Change (Dannemiller, James, and Tolchinsky, 1999; Dannemiller Tyson Associates, 2000). And we have a clearer understanding of what is essential to maintain the changes that follow.

Three fundamental conditions are required for self-organizing systems that interact repeatedly and in complicated ways to generate unpredictable, patterned outcomes. We will describe those elements in the form of the CDE Model (Olson and Eoyang, 2001), followed by application to four large-scale methods. We will then demonstrate how the pattern set during the event can be amplified or dampened by pattern-setting activities that sustain the effects of change after the dance.

Setting the Pattern

When we facilitate large-scale events, we are always amazed by the ways in which a diverse group of people come together and form meaningful relationships, shared understandings, and aligned commitments to action. We know that it happens consistently, but until recently we could not explain *why* it happens.

The CDE Model

We have found that using a simple model to design, facilitate, and follow up large-scale events has resulted in a shift in how our clients experience the results of their change process. Specifically, the CDE Model represents the three variables that influence a self-organizing process that shapes the emerging patterns, the speed with which they form, and the sequence of their development through time (Townsend, 2002).

The three factors in the CDE Model are the *container* (C), *significant differences* (D), and *transforming exchanges* (E). These three variables are intricately connected. If one of them changes, the others shift to adapt, and the emergent pattern changes as well. The complex interactions of these factors are easy to see when you consider how the size of a room (C), diversity of participants (D), and mode of interaction (E) affect the patterns that emerge over the course of an engagement. Changing any one of the variables may have a profound (and unpredictable) effect on the others and on participants' experiences. All three of these variables affect patterns that emerge during large-scale events and how those patterns might be sustained after the event concludes.

C: Container. The container (C) holds the separate individuals together long enough for a pattern to emerge. Many different elements might function as containers for a single group. The container can be *psychological* (for example, a visionary leader or fear of the unknown), *physical* (for example, a meeting room or national boundary), or *social* (for example, identity groupings or shared experiences). If there is not a sufficient container, a group wanders around, and energy and information are dissipated before they can coalesce into a new and more productive pattern. Containers are critical in effective large group interventions—the place, convening questions, and the time frame are among the constraints that can hold the system together until something interesting happens.

Each Large Group Method depends on different elements to bring participants together. In Open Space, for example, individual passion serves as the primary container. In the course of the event, the circle and the convening questions form other containers that shape interactions and emerging patterns. Future Search dynamics are contained by the relatively small number of persons who are carefully selected to represent stakeholder groups of the larger system. That is why so much of the design time must be committed to deciding who needs to be in the room. If appropriate containers are not established to focus and concentrate efforts following a large-scale event, it will be difficult to sustain the patterns of learning and action that emerge.

D: Differences. Within the container, if everyone is the same, nothing novel will be generated, so significant differences (D) are the second critical condition for self-organizing in human systems. Differences provide the impetus for change and establish the shapes of emerging patterns. Of course, any group of individuals will be different in an infinite number of identifiable ways: formal or informal power within the organization, work location, job role, longevity, or experience levels. Some of these differences may be irrelevant to a task at hand, so they can be ignored. Others, such as power or level of expertise, may be critical to patterns of the future, so they receive focus in the design and execution of an event. Participants' experiences, perceptions, and values are all differences that prove to be significant in almost every large-scale event.

In the Whole-Scale Change method, the design team focuses on critical differences that influence the issues to be addressed, then they use these distinctions to plan for how these issues will emerge and also for a "maximum mixture of the whole" ("max-mix") to ensure that diverse views are represented at each table and within the room. The principle is that each person has knowledge of a slice of the issue. As they meet together, each person, over time, will experience a shift in perspective and a new understanding of the greater issues of the whole.

Appreciative Inquiry, as its name implies, focuses on differences that are positive and encouraging rather than problem-based, so the patterns that emerge can be filled with energy and opportunity. All Large Group Methods help participants identify and understand significant differences that can inform new insights and actions. Unless conditions are established to maintain these constructive differences beyond the event, it will be difficult to sustain the changes.

E: Exchanges. Unless connections are built across significant differences within the container, no change will occur. Transforming exchange (E)—the third condition for self-organizing—provides the connections that allow for change at the individual, team, and whole system levels.

In Open Space, each person is free to determine his or her own exchanges. Although people are expected to speak, listen, and reflect, they also participate in the concurrent dynamic of freedom to leave a group and join another at any time. The exchanges are driven by individual needs. In Appreciative Inquiry, the exchange includes a process of telling

stories about a key incident. The stories help individuals transcend their own emotional connections and connect with a larger story that is being developed. The stories can reflect either times of great challenge and how the challenge was met or times of wonderful success and how that success is similar to that currently within reach of the group or organization. In Future Search and Whole-Scale Change, the exchanges are about learning enough about the system (either from experts or other participants) so that wise decisions can be made and actions can be taken. Though the methods of engagement are different among Large Group Methods, each provides powerful ways for participants and stakeholder groups to engage with each other. And, unless the exchanges continue after the event, the patterns of change are not likely to persist.

Large Group Methods and Human Systems Dynamics

We have come to understand the dynamics of large group events through the study of complexity science and chaos theory and their application to the behavior of human systems. A body of theory is evolving called human systems dynamics (HSD) that connects the nonlinear sciences with the social sciences and provides insights into the self-organizing behaviors of human systems (Eoyang, 2002, 2003).

HSD provides ways to think about self-organizing patterns in large-scale methods and allows us to focus on how individuals change and learn at the same time an entire group is moving to new levels of understanding and action. Acknowledging that human beings are complex and their actions often cannot be predicted or controlled, HSD provides ways to understand and influence the process of self-organizing as it shapes patterns for individuals and groups. Summary analyses of four common Large Group Methods (Open Space, Whole Systems Change, Appreciative Inquiry, and Future Search) are presented in Tables 7.1 through 7.4. (More detailed analyses are available on the Web site at http://www.hsdinstitute.org/dept_press_publications.asp.)

CDE Model and Sustaining the Change

In our experience, practitioners of all Large Group Methods struggle with maintaining the patterns that are generated during the event. The CDE Model helps us consider what conditions need to be set during and following an event to lock in the emerging patterns and continue the learning and change:

- The *containers* that set the conditions for the event must be reinforced to focus the attention and energy of the group and to perpetuate the new way of working.
- The *differences* that were discovered or reinforced during the event must continue to receive attention after the event concludes.

- *Exchange* is a condition that is common to all Large Group Methods, and it may be the most difficult to sustain following the event.

The special conditions that are set during the event help groups discover new patterns of interaction. However, when the event concludes, the boundaries of the convening container are dissolved and the pressure of historical conditions pushes for return. Because patterns are constantly forming and reforming in self-organizing systems, the best way to maintain new patterns is to establish conditions that encourage their continuing formation.

We have found that patterns form around key issues that repeat themselves after an event. The chart shown in Table 7.5 contains examples of what to watch for in pattern development after an event around the issues of relationships, communication, action, focus (or strategic alignment), beliefs, leadership, learning, involvement, and decision making.

Specific Applications

Although there are many examples of the use of the CDE Model during large groups, we have chosen three examples to demonstrate how patterns after the event developed and helped to sustain the changes.

Container. The focus of one organization's experience with Whole-Scale Change was to move out of their tight silos (C), suspicion between levels of management (D), and finger pointing (E) that manifested in a pattern of a risk-averse culture.

The desire was to open the container so there could be a culture of achievement orientation. The first step was to experience achievement in a large group, and the challenge became how to reinforce the new pattern. One way was to establish the strength and identity of a new pattern, based on the new cultural norms created during the event. To reach this goal, the organization conducted a minisurvey about one norm each week. As employees logged onto their computers each Monday, they would answer team, department, and organization assessment questions about the norm of the week. Before employees could get into the system, they had to respond to the survey. All answers were collected by noon on Monday and were reviewed by the leadership team during their Monday afternoon meeting. Great work was publicly acknowledged, and patterns of risk aversion were watched for and handled appropriately.

Differences. A contentious, multi-stakeholder system of forest management led to the 7th American Forest Congress. The event required one full year of planning, including Round Table meetings in each state to discover the diverse needs and views. At the four-day Congress in Washington, D.C., each of the four hundred tables was carefully designed to bring in as much diverse ideology as possible. Special scholarships were established to ensure that all parts of the system were included: students, professors, environmentalists, tree harvesters, lumber companies, government, and labor groups. The high tension at each table was managed by having the first table discussion focus on the question, What will it take for me to stay fully present at this table? The commitments made during this initial session proved to override "special interest" movements that were attempted during the Congress. This initial breakthrough relationship among different stakeholders has been kept alive in diversely supported and ongoing state Round Tables. As the states continue to hold their involvement meetings, they ensure that there is a mixture of stakeholders and that there is ample time for interchange about the different views. The result has been a broad-based support for new legislation and changes in land management curriculum throughout the country.

Exchanges. Customer service was the orientation of one organization's improvement effort. During their event, employees and customers discovered a common meaning and a joy in sharing what a good banking experience felt like. A transition team was appointed, with one member from each of the forty bank branches to meet monthly to share stories of success. Those stories were then repeated back to the banks, and the successes multiplied. One favorite story was about early staff meetings prior to

TABLE 7.1. CDE MODEL AND OPEN SPACE

Dynamics of Open Space: Amplify and absorb new energy and ideas that disrupt old patterns and allow new ones to form. Differentiation is the primary condition that drives change during the event.

Phase	Container	Differences	Exchanges
Before	• Personal passion and responsibility draw participation. • Participant numbers are not limited.	• Diversity of participants is key. • Inviting question captures key differences.	• Invitation is issued with question and logistics. • Design Team is finding "right" question.
During	• Circle • Marketplace • Small circles for specific topics	• Place, time, and topics for small circles • Dampening of all differences except passion and responsibility in the circle and the event	• Individual freedom (law of two feet, bumble bees, and butterfly) • Posting of notes from small groups • Evening news
Emerging Patterns	• Boundaries around ideas become permeable. • Entry and exit into topic areas is based on passion and engagement; leads to commitment. • Self-organizing groups begin to form with ease.	• Slowing down of conversation enables those with different views to be heard. • Noise of the system generated by conflict shifts to learning through intense listening.	• Honest sharing of viewpoints begins. • Strong connections around passion form. • Personal choice and freedom to engage is present.

TABLE 7.2. CDE MODEL AND WHOLE SYSTEMS CHANGE

Dynamics of Whole Systems Change: Shared patterns (alignment) form by establishing clear boundaries and focusing on predefined significant differences. Exchange is the primary condition that drives change during the event.

Phase	Container	Differences	Exchanges
Before	• Leader takes significant role to bound scope and authority prior to Design Team meetings. • Agenda shapes how the event will address key issues. • Participant numbers are limited by size of facility.	• Leadership Team alignment crucial prior to event—any difference among members will be magnified during the event! • Critical mass in number and diversity identified as those needed to sustain change.	• Design Team interaction reflects patterns of the whole—clue to what will happen and how. • Complete logistical information (who, what, when, where) reduces anxiety.
During	• Table members share responsibility by rotating leadership, facilitation, and recording equally. • Table discussions are recorded anonymously and capture all thoughts. • Patterns for action emerge during whole room report-outs.	• Voices of customer and stakeholder included. • Differences between individual dissatisfaction and organizational vision surface. • Dotting of priorities helps to converge on most important differences to be addressed.	• Ongoing reporting from table to whole room ensures system continues learning. • Individual domination of table is discouraged; time for introverts to be heard is provided. • Each exchange of data is designed to move the group from individual dissatisfaction to a greater vision for the whole.
Emerging Patterns	• Activity across boundaries is opened for cross-functional action teams to emerge. • Blaming and judgment diminishes. • System sees self more realistically because there is a greater knowledge of the whole.	• Data from the outside through voice of the customer, stakeholder, or environment are recognized as strong influencers of current reality. • Individuals are able to influence the whole through various methods.	• Respect for the work of others increases due to greater understanding of form and function. • Patience increases. • Desire to improve the whole becomes evident through continued involvement efforts.

TABLE 7.3. CDE MODEL AND APPRECIATIVE INQUIRY

Dynamics of Appreciative Inquiry: Shared commitment is generated through establishing passion-filled exchanges that focus on shared perspectives embedded within stories that reflect assets and opportunities. Exchange is the primary condition that drives change during the event.

Phase	Container	Differences	Exchanges
Before	• Establish an interview protocol centered on issues provoking the system toward change. • Pre-event data are collected through paired interviews. • Participant numbers are not limited.	• Strengths and assets are differences that make a difference. • Smaller groups work to discover and refine common themes.	• Listening (as opposed to discussion of) to the storyteller fosters feeling of being honored and recognized as successful. • Talking and listening to stories slows the system down and opens the door to deeper engagement.
During	• Dream emerges as the container for the work.	• Individual stories reveal different experiences. • Focus is on shared patterns rather than differences.	• Sharing of stories creates an emotional connection to how something was accomplished, what strengths were used for success. • Voting process develops what is significant and has energy.
Emerging Patterns	• Storytelling becomes a container for multiple experiences and connection based on similar emotions.	• Rich visual and emotional connection occurs when sharing the best of an experience.	• Focus on the positive expands the energy of the system.

TABLE 7.4. CDE MODEL AND FUTURE SEARCH

Dynamics of Future Search: Diverse groups come together to establish a picture of a shared future. Shared container is the primary condition that drives change during the event.

Phase	Container	Differences	Exchanges
Before	• Design Team decides who needs to attend (more than what the agenda should be). • Participants limited to 35–90, which includes stakeholder groups.	• Event focuses on ensuring the different stakeholder voices are heard. • Stakeholder differences are encouraged and accented.	• Design Team discusses who should be invited and design of the event.
During	• Specific agenda and activities set. • Convergence built in with search for common ground. • Activities focus on relationship between individual and whole group.	• Conflict is acknowledged but not worked. • There are no experts or speakers.	• There are lots of small and large group "discussion" (as opposed to reporting out). • Diverse activities provide multiple ways to engage.
Emerging Patterns	• Creativity around discovery of past, present, and future leads to excitement to repeat the process.	• Respect for the experiences of multiple stakeholders increases.	• Thoughtful conversations at the system level focus on the whole rather than individual needs or parts of the system.

TABLE 7.5. SUSTAINING THE CHANGE

Pattern		Strategies
Relationships	C	• Include discussions on what is working or not working with relationships in meeting agendas. • Continue to loosen the container so relationship boundaries are permeable.
	D	• Continually connect across groups to ensure magnifying the differences that will make a difference. • Convene sessions where groups are mixed to broaden exposure to differences. • Watch for "groupthink" that indicates different views are being minimized or discounted.
	E	• Ensure that staff meetings match the pattern of conversations created during the event. • Create socials and celebrations to acknowledge the progress. • Consciously repeat the relationship connection and conversation from the event to after-event meetings.
Communication	C	• Use unusual or unexpected message approaches to keep awareness high. • Focus on understanding the event as a small-scale version of the whole system. • Be aware of jargon and technical language that separates groups.
	D	• Occasionally send out a "radical" message to wake up the system. • Ask questions about differences as they emerge. Find respectful ways to make differences explicit. • Explore and amplify "noise" that is generated through the change. Does it help or hinder the process?
	E	• Look at patterns of problem-solving meetings and shift pattern to reflect the new way of interacting.

TABLE 7.5. SUSTAINING THE CHANGE, *continued*

Pattern		Strategies
		• Repeat messages in many different contexts and to many different audiences. Compare and contrast how each message is received. • Look for repeating messages that cover broad spans to determine how messages "land." • Contradict past communications methods: if tightly held, break the rules and open in creative ways; if loose, apply more consistency of time or message style.
Action	C	• Hold topic-centered brown-bag meetings. • Keep boundaries for projects clear and distinct (what is deliverable and by when). • Ensure cross-functional teams have decision-making power.
	D	• Include resistors on project teams and hold them accountable for outcomes. • Acknowledge that employee skills and interests are varied, but the overall goal is common. • Define and track stretch goals.
	E	• Report progress regularly to reinforce the pattern of working in connection with the intention of the whole. • When stress gets high, pick one thing to focus on and celebrate progress. • Provide emotional rewards for hard work and keep the critics at bay. Victories nourish faith in the changes.
Focus	C	• Couple Mission and Vision and address in all public meetings to ensure alignment. • Continually sift through new ideas for components that will impact rather than derail the focus. • Orient new group members to avoid distraction.

TABLE 7.5. SUSTAINING THE CHANGE, *continued*

Pattern		Strategies
	D	• Invest in Stakeholder or Voice of the Customer review meetings for input on progress. • Watch for homogeneous conclusions—support vigorous debate and dissension prior to decisions. • Define and focus on "significant differences" for a given project or initiative.
	E	• Use systems and meetings to check understanding of connection to the part (individuals), the whole (teams), and the greater whole (divisions or organizations). • Provide a central point of virtual contact to make exchanges public and reliable.
Beliefs	C	• Consider how intrapersonal dynamics affect decision making and action. • Test perceptions of how beliefs are being lived on a regular basis. • Use small groups to identify patterns of behaviors that are emerging and feed observations back to the system. • Help system move beyond the boundaries of personal views to see holistic perspectives.
	D	• Ask the design team to consider how their beliefs change in the course of the project. • Provide space for the emergence and adaptation of beliefs, when the old ones are not working. • Distinguish between individual and group beliefs. • Explore distinction between lived and spoken beliefs.
	E	• Ask reflective questions so participants access their own assumptions and beliefs. • Hold regular discussions on beliefs and how they are being interpreted and lived. • Establish rituals that repeat on a regular basis. • Ensure that the voice of the "quiet" has space to get heard.

TABLE 7.5. SUSTAINING THE CHANGE, *continued*

Pattern		Strategies
Leadership	C	• Establish a process for emergent leaders to join the conversation. • Develop a broad perspective of observation over time, as well as short review cycles. • Conduct self-evaluations among leadership teams and share progress toward modeling the change.
	D	• Review assumptions about heroes and villains and align with current reality. • Individuals with stronger expertise invited to meetings to add rigor (versus opinion) to the shared information. • Pay attention to how power and authority are used after the event and encourage leaders to reduce power dynamics and meet others on equal ground, as they did during the event.
	E	• Facilitate interchanges with and among leader groups. • Encourage leaders to talk to groups outside their reporting structures to demonstrate alignment of message. • Help develop a leadership voice with consistent and reliable messages.
Learning	C	• Practice reflection to pause the system and assess the course. • Regularly use tools learned during the event that include listening for understanding, brainstorming, multidot voting, and shared leadership to ensure continued learning throughout the system. • Establish communities of practice.
	D	• Review processes for voices of difference influencing planning and learning. • Continue pattern identification and use this reflection tool as a feedback mechanism to the system.

TABLE 7.5. SUSTAINING THE CHANGE, *continued*

Pattern		Strategies
		• Determine which differences can be magnified or dampened by identifying what is significant, what needs to be kept as an anchor, and what needs additional time for learning from the "opposing advocate."
	E	• Hold teach-and-learn sessions at the end of each project, publish lessons learned, and invite review. • Keep records of decisions and actions to encourage learning from phase to phase. • Use different modalities (play, pictures, message boards, e-mail) in order to increase the understanding of what is happening.
Involvement	C	• Check for who is doing what and whether it is value-added to the focus and action. • View project teams as containers for clear purpose, task, membership, resources, and accountability. • Clarify roles and responsibilities and check for understanding.
	D	• Rotate membership on teams to ensure fresh evolution of patterns. • Allow for self-organizing teams of mutual interest, giving them responsibility and accountability for results. • Provide multiple levels for involvement.
	E	• Celebrate progress often and in creative, public ways to reinforce the emerging, positive patterns. • Stories from the event become mythical and create patterns of courage, trust, hope. • Ask for feedback and respond immediately. • Make documents public on shared Web site.
Decision making	C	• Review decision-making model with larger groups to ensure transparency.

TABLE 7.5. SUSTAINING THE CHANGE, *continued*

Pattern		Strategies
Decision making		• Establish a set of simple rules to guide decision making for continuing work.
		• Use consistent decision-making process.
	D	• Check assumptions for how decisions are made and how conflict is resolved.
		• Explore differences in opinion to reach better decisions.
		• Consider disagreement to be a resource for understanding.
	E	• Continue transparency in decision making and ensure that challenges are aired.
		• Articulate questions and issues clearly.
		• Collect and analyze data to determine what is really driving decisions.
		• When documenting and publishing decisions, ensure understanding of decision within context of entire change effort.

the bank opening on Friday morning. Knowing that it was payday and the customer traffic would be high, the staff would stand in the center of the lobby and talk about what needed to be done and how to effectively deal with the volume of the day. A song from the event "We Will Win" would play in the background, and the staff would often move to the emotion of the song. After a while, customers wanted to know what was going on and what the song was. So the staff set up an outside speaker for the song to play prior to the bank opening on Friday's. Customers said they "loved waiting in line" on that morning because it was so much fun.

What We Have Learned

Acknowledging the self-organizing nature of human systems has profoundly affected our understanding of the complexities of large-scale events, how they are self-organizing, and the impact on individual and organizational changes they encourage. The principles of HSD have transformed the ways we market, design, facilitate, and follow up large-scale events. Some of our key learnings are as follows:

• The pattern of the organization is disturbed when we enter the system. From the first conversation, we are influencing pattern formation. If we want to support patterns that will be sustainable, we have to be conscious from the beginning of how we are affecting the naturally occurring containers, differences, and exchanges.

• Complex systems are sensitive to small changes. Anything we do or say may shift the paths of self-organizing and the resulting patterns. We have to be consistent in our thought, action, and speech to avoid disrupting the system in unnecessary or unproductive ways.

• We recognize that the system will change itself, and we are merely there to help adjust the conditions. It will not take much to accomplish change, but our gentle pushing needs to focus on the conditions (container, differences, and exchanges) that will shape emerging patterns in the future.

• A simple, elegant solution that is implemented is much more effective than a complicated one that does not see the light of day. We try to plan the simplest follow-up activities and to support clients as they implement the activities completely and consistently.

• The dynamics of the group will sometimes establish productive patterns in spite of our intentions and efforts. Sometimes the most powerful and long-

lasting changes are not ones we anticipated or designed.

• On a personal level, patience is critical because patterns need to emerge in the timing and rhythm of their own development. If we feel inclined to jump in and change the conditions, dampen the differences so they are less intimidating, or stop an energetic change, we need to *stop and breathe deeply.*

• Most of all, we have learned that the learning never ends. Each event, each moment in an event, and all those that follow provide endless opportunities to expand our understanding and improve our action. We debrief our work and monitor the impact of the follow-up efforts based on the CDE Model. It helps us to stay focused on the simple, effective measures and encourages the system to learn how to influence its own destiny in a more conscious manner.

References

Cooperrider, D., & Whitney, D. (1999). *Appreciative Inquiry.* San Francisco: Berrett-Koehler.

Dannemiller, K., James, S., & Tolchinsky, P. (1999). *Whole-Scale Change.* San Francisco: Berrett-Koehler.

Dannemiller Tyson Associates. (2000). *Whole-Scale Change toolkit.* San Francisco: Berrett-Koehler.

Eoyang, G. (2002). *Conditions for self-organizing in human systems.* An unpublished doctoral dissertation of the Union Institute and University, Cincinnati, Ohio.

Eoyang, G. (Ed.). (2003). *Voices from the field: An introduction to human systems dynamics.* Circle Pines, MN: Human Systems Dynamics Institute Press.

Olson, E., & Eoyang, G. (2001). *Facilitating organization change: Lessons from complexity science.* San Francisco: Jossey-Bass/Pfeiffer.

Owen, H. (1997). *Open Space Technology: A user's guide* (2nd ed.). San Francisco: Berrett-Koehler.

Owen, H. (2004). *Practice of peace.* Circle Pines, MN: Human Systems Dynamics Institute Press.

Townsend, M. (2002). Lessons from the field: Applying complex adaptive systems theory to organization change. *OD Practitioner, 34*(3), 10–14.

Watkins, J. M., & Mohr, B. J. (2001). *Appreciative Inquiry: Change at the speed of imagination.* San Francisco: Jossey-Bass/Pfeiffer.

PART THREE

RESOURCES FOR LARGE GROUP METHODS

CHAPTER EIGHT

RESOURCES FOR LARGE GROUP METHODS

By definition, Large Group Methods are not static. They evolve and transform, as do groups themselves or as does any system in nature. In this section we provide our readers with some additional resources. Some readers may be familiar with the topics covered in the section that follows:

- "Tools for Effective Transitions Using Large Group Processes," by Thomas N. Gilmore and Deborah Bing
- "Graphic Facilitation and Large Group Methods," by Carlotta Tyler, Lynne Valek, and Regina Rowland
- "Using Interactive Meeting Technologies," by Lenny Lind, Karl Danskin, and Todd Erickson

These authors add new insights and concepts to the practices they describe. They enlarge our thinking about possible applications.

"The Reading List," which is also part of this section, provides guidance on next steps to readers interested in a greater knowledge of Large Group Methods. The list is made up of the articles and books that have informed the thinking of our authors and is organized under three headings:

1. "Overview of Books and Articles on Large Group Methods" contains books and articles that give an overview of most of the methods. The books describe the different methods and include charts that compare the methods on several dimensions.

2. "How-To Books and Articles on Large Group Methods" are pieces written on a particular method by the developer of that method. Each author gives a complete description of his or her method.

3. "Thought-Provoking Books and Articles" is where we have added books and articles that we feel are stimulating and worthwhile. We hope the reading list will serve as guidance to plan more effective large group change meetings.

What to Note in These Resources

We present ideas about several quite different kinds of resources: design advice and activities, using graphics or interactive technologies, and what to read if you want to know more.

• "Tools for Effective Transitions Using Large Group Processes": Thomas N. Gilmore and Deborah Bing describe three transition stages for the Large Group Method: Pre-Event, The Event, Effective Follow-Through. The authors offer suggestions for the enhancement of group performance at each phase. Bing and Gilmore believe that pre-event efforts need to be strongly geared to fully engage the stakeholder in the issues to be discussed; in general, they believe that the importance of pre-event work is often underestimated. Gilmore and Bing also have a series of suggestions for the actual meetings—suggestions for achieving good interactions and the sharing of multiple perspectives. They suggest a variety of configurations for grouping people, as well as designs for providing for divergence of views and methods for creating convergence of views and opinions—an important element in most Large Group Methods. Gilmore and Bing have excellent suggestions for managing the transition back to the workplace that includes effective follow-through on initiatives. Implementing change after the meeting is seen as a continuous process, with the event as the catalyst.

• "Graphic Facilitation and Large Group Methods": Most facilitators are familiar with the use of graphic art during a meeting; this article adds some new dimensions to the method. Carlotta Tyler, Lynne Valek, and Regina Rowland were graphic facilitators, or cross-cultural consultants, at the Parliament of World Religions in Barcelona, Spain (see Chapter Six). The authors give examples of different graphic methods that were used to address cross-cultural issues during the conference. The use of graphics, however, can help in many situations, not just complex cross-cultural meetings. Graphics help people see situations in the context of other issues and provide words and pictures to integrate and illustrate complex information. Graphics can depict the history of an organization, a project, or a place. Pictures can stimulate thinking in the way mere words on a chart cannot. One of the unique contributions of this ancient method was to facilitate greater cross-cultural communication. When people were too shy to speak or it would have been countercultural for them to speak (often because they were women), they would come and tell their story to the graphic facilitator. The artist would record their experience on a large sheet of paper, as they described their encounter with violence, water shortages, or one of the global issues. This was a powerful method for getting many voices into the room. Participants felt thrilled to have their stories heard and seen.

• "Using Interactive Meeting Technologies": Several of the cases in this book rely on interactive technologies: "Back from the Brink at American Airlines" (Chapter Three); "Innovation at the BBC: Engaging an Entire Organization" and "Whole System Engagement Through Collaborative Technology at World Vision" (Chapter Two); "Taking Democracy to a Regional Scale in Hamilton County" and "Building Coalitions to Create a Community Planning Tool in Israel" (Chapter Five).

In this last instance, after the Open Space conference, the planning survey instrument was put on the Web for feedback and suggestions. As the authors of the article on technology point out, there are many ways to use these methods. For example, a meeting with laptops and keypads yields the ability to project themes and agreements on a screen. Another possibility is to use an intranet or e-mail as vehicles for geographically dispersed participants to provide feedback at the actual meeting, make choices, and add ideas. Although there is a value in face-to-face conversations, where the technology simply acts as scribe to the groups, people also appreciate the opportunity to give comments and feedback online and receive continuous information and updates on the topic. People like to have an opportunity to share their views. We think that interactive methods will be one of the most important drivers of the continuous evolution of Large Group Methods. Their effectiveness echoes a phrase used by Marshall McLuhan: "The Media is the Message!" In the case of Large Group Methods, communications that are inherently interactive foster an interactive environment; the ability to work with geographic dispersion and the entire organization is amazing.

TOOLS FOR EFFECTIVE TRANSITIONS USING LARGE GROUP PROCESSES

Thomas N. Gilmore and Deborah Bing

Large group events can be significant in the life cycle of an issue or in the development of an organization or a community of interest (Bunker and Alban, 1992). They are particularly powerful as antidotes to the busy-ness that is causing more of routine organizational life to become "mindless" (Langer, 1989). The pace of change and the omnipresent technologies of paging, voice mail, e-mail, and wireless make it harder than ever to find reflective time to focus on what is really important, to see the familiar through new lenses, and to play with new ideas.

The very forces that cause such events to be more necessary can also serve to encapsulate their impact. A "process high" as the event is finishing successfully gives way to the crush of business as usual. In a few weeks, people look back nostalgically at a "lost weekend" rather than link the thinking that took place to the ongoing organizational challenges.

This is particularly true for the leadership group that sponsored the event. The table shown here characterizes typical levels of engagement of those with active event roles and regular participants in an event cycle.

This makes the "technology" of the event—tools and processes—paramount. Processes that engage participants in real thinking about important issues before, during, and after the event can combat the inevitable forces that

	Pre-Event	*Event*		*Longer Term*
Steering group and staff in active event roles	Manic, dropping other stuff to get it done	Active, engaged	Dead zone, switch to other work to get relief and make up for undone work	Resume ongoing level of engage-ment, wonder why others are not pitching in more
Participants	Skeptical, curious, not very active	Active, engaged, becoming believers	Looking for ways to be more engaged, waiting to see if they are serious and will follow through	If disappointed in follow-up, then reduce availability

pull people's attention away. One risk is that the technology and tools neces-sary to make a large group event effective can dominate the substantive issues and the particular culture and context in which they arise. Procrustes, in an-cient Greece, would trap travelers only to offer them hospitality in a bed that would require that they be stretched or cut to fit the bed. Large group events that focus too much on the technology of the event and not enough on the substantive issues risk creating procrustean beds: critical issues must be cut or stretched to serve the design of the event. The challenge is to keep the focus on the substantive and relational work, not on the techniques. The host of a large group event must provide good enough containment and space for the participants to use their differences and similarities creatively in discussions about the substantive issues that are the focus of the work.

Paradoxically, the focus of this chapter is on tools and processes, especially ones that involve helping with salient transitions that meaningfully engage the issues underlying the event—from before the event, from individual thinking to group work, from groups to plenary, and, most critically, from the event to the wider community of interest. Our aim is to enrich the vocabulary for working in large groups. Thoughtful design can match techniques and processes to the culture of the communities and organizations they are working with and, in doing so, provide a powerful way to engage participants in the thinking and development of critical issues for that community or organization.

This chapter organizes tools and techniques into three stages or transitions surrounding a large group event, each with its own core task:

- Pre-Event: Engage key stakeholders in the substantive issues and the "work" of the event.
- The Event: Engage a microcosm of the community in the thinking, challenging, and doing of real work on key substantive issues.
- Effective Follow-Through: Mobilize the larger community to push forward on plans and ideas crafted at the event.

Beginning Large Group Work: Methods to Engage Stakeholders Before Events Begin

Elsewhere in this volume are cases that describe the essential preparatory work for effective large group events. This section focuses on a few design techniques to increase the engagement of multiple stakeholders in the planning of the event.

Creating a Steering Committee

The creation of a steering group (responsible for planning the event) that contains many of the key boundaries that will be in the large group is an opportunity for working as a microcosm group (Alderfer, 1977), where relationships are both interpersonal and intergroup. This helps the team deepen the work that might take place across important boundaries such as center and periphery, union and management, professional and support, stakeholders and company. The steering group should be "good enough" to create shared authority to convene and charge the work.

Designing the Pre-Work for Participants

There are a variety of ways of capturing people's attention and getting them thinking prior to the start of a large group event, but as so much of the power of large group experiences has to do with seeing through new frames and feeling new energy from connecting across differences, we think advance work should be light and encourage inquiry and divergent thinking.

We have found the simplest and often most powerful pre-work is to invite people to become more mindful (Langer, 1989) of critical harbingers of change in areas that are relevant to the focus of the large group event. You might ask questions such as, "What has startled or surprised or unsettled you lately about X?" Or you might invite people to notice emergent shifts or examples that illustrate some tension. The journalist Tom Friedman is particularly good at noticing the vignette that captures some emergent phenomenon such as globalization. If the pre-work is only thinking, people are less vulnerable to feeling shame from not having done the work. Those who have done it can stimulate the group's thinking, and others can be swept along into taking up their member role in the large group. A variant of this is to invite people to interview someone, especially if they can do it as part of their ongoing life rather than as an added task. This sets the stage for illustrating how much more is available for our learning in the cracks of our current lives rather than as part some extra new activity.

Using Existing Forums to Preview the Event's Themes

Using existing forums where the members of the participant community already show up is one way to begin the thinking work before the event itself. So many existing forums and meetings have become dead events, with participants attending to protect their interests or keep informed rather than to think together in fresh ways. By capturing time on existing agendas, both before and after large events, one can energize without adding to overload.

At a large economic summit in a northeast city, the planning committee used standing advisory group meetings to brief the mayor's key advisers on the topics that would be taken up at the event. This gave them the opportunity to voice their concerns about the "politics" of the event: how controversial issues would be framed, key stakeholders that needed to be invited for the results to have credibility, and issues that were missing and needed to be added to the mix. By the time the event happened, many constituents had already begun the discussions that would be necessary for real progress to be made on the key issues.

The Event

The work of the event is to engage participants in the thinking and doing of the work. Over the arc of an event, groups often cycle through four phases:

1. Joining: getting people to arrive, to care about the issue, to find their voice, to feel heard
2. Diverging: embracing diversity, brainstorming, thinking outside the box, generating options
3. Converging: searching for "yes-able" packages, finding common ground, coming to hard choices, managing the process of losing, deciding
4. Signing up: testing people's commitments to the choices made

The challenge a designer faces is to avoid the common "Greyhound effect" of these events, where participants can show up and leave the driving to someone else, and instead engage participants in a variety of ways. The following section lays out multiple tools and techniques for structuring participation in ways that pull participants actively into the work and the discussion. Next, we briefly review basic group configurations for each stage of the event, as well as some of the configurations' features.

Configurations for "Joining"

Individual work, such as reflecting silently, journaling, jotting down ideas, voting with red dots, and so on, can be enormously powerful in large group contexts. We know that being in a large group (Turquet, 1975) can lead to decreased risk taking, decreased ability to usefully discriminate, and fear of standing out or being original. In order to reframe this usual reluctance, individuals can identify with parts of what others have said or express ideas via alliances with others instead of honestly stating one's own views.

In a multiday strategy session for a large Catholic health care system, after groups had posted images and key words of possible vision statements, the 125 participants were invited to walk around in silence to take in the alternatives and, as they felt drawn to a particular embodiment, to stand quietly next to that station. It recalled Maya Lin's comment about her intent in creating the Vietnam Veterans Memorial: "I create places in which to think, without trying to dictate what to think."

It was moving to feel the seriousness of each individual's decision. Obviously, they could see how others were clustering, but it was a significant contrast with processes used later in the same workshop, with red dots on critical issues, when the process felt much more overtly political, when there were humorous comments of "vote early and often" and about vote buying. This is a small example of tailoring tools to the cultures of the groups using them. This Catholic system often uses silence in meaningful ways as part of their discernment in reaching decisions that we were able to incorporate into this event.

Pairs. Pairs are particularly powerful in helping people come to know their own mind in conversation with a colleague in a shared domain. As E. M. Forster ([1910]2003) has said, "How do I know what I think, until I hear what I say?" Having people interview one another with assigned questions can be powerful ways of getting everyone simultaneously active, either in an explicit, sympathetic, probing, listening mode, or in answering.

Threes. The triad is powerful in that one member can be asked to take up the "observer-in-the-balcony role," as a pair consults with one another. Threes are ways of sharpening arguments by exploring similarities and differences. Given the frequency with which large group processes take up polarized issues, threes can be a vehicle for exploring "both-and" thinking (Collins and Poras, 1994; Johnson, 1992).

Configurations for Diverging

Harnessing the diversity of views assembled in a large group requires the use of containing structures and processes. The following are a set of techniques for diverging that are designed to maximize individual input while remaining inclusive of the breadth of discussion across multiple topics and views.

Cross-Issue Groups. Often when groups have been working in parallel on different issues, a quick intergroup can be a powerful way to give each group a chance to consult and be consulted on their progress. This can be done in pairs, such that each member has to represent the thinking so far and focus on an area for advice rather than rely on a leader. If the two groups are homogenous, such as physicians and nurses or headquarters and field, then each can be invited to give role messages to the others: what they want more of, less of, and the same. Asking them to also think of what the other might want from them creates some energy from the anxiety of how in touch are they with the other's thinking.

Small, Random Heterogeneous Groups ("Max-Mix"). These groups are often used at the beginning of events as a microcosm of the total membership, which can often serve as a home table that participants return to periodically throughout the work. In these configurations, people are often there as individuals and as members of the different identity groups that make up the membership.

Parallel Homogenous Groups. These groups are particularly useful for political caucusing. When working on challenging issues with many different stakeholder interests in play, participants from a particular identity or interest group (for example, nurses, physicians, administrators, trustees) may find themselves advancing new strategies in heterogeneous groups and find themselves getting anxious about the degree of support from their back-home group. Giving groups the chance to caucus can release considerable energy, as they have the space to check in with one another and recharge (both in terms of energy and substantive focus) one another.

> In a health care system large group event with trustees, hospital administrators, and medical school leaders, during the planned parallel working sessions in mixed groups on different issues such as managed care strategy, cost cutting, and the governance processes, we sensed increasing anxiety in each of the stakeholder groups about whether new ideas being created would be accepted by different constituent groups. We gave the three stakeholder groups the chance to caucus for thirty minutes. In addition to their checking in with one another, we invited each group to think about an area or two where they felt most misunderstood, or to surface two or three

stereotypes that they feel others have of them, or to identify what they would like from others. When they each returned to their substantive issue group, there was significantly greater progress. This is a way of capturing what always happens informally in the halls and channeling that energy in the working processes of the large group event.

Configurations for Converging

Having encouraged the breadth of thinking through diverging processes, the challenge is to focus in on a more manageable set of critical ideas, but do so in ways that are transparent and engaging. The following are several process strategies for pulling the thinking of divergent work back into the large group.

Facilitated, Interactive Panels. A powerful mode of pulling small group work into the full group can be through the use of a facilitated, interactive, and often provocative panel made up of stakeholders who represent difficult boundaries in an organization come together for a public discussion; this models for others that tough discussions about important issues are required to move the work forward.

> In a five-hundred-person event with an urban child-welfare agency and its many community partners, the Commissioner had a panel discussion with an advocate who had brought multiple high-stakes lawsuits against him over the past years. The panel focused on what change would be necessary in the coming years to ensure the safety and well-being of children in the system. The relationship between the litigator and the agency had been quite contentious and shut off at times, which made the public discussion between the two unprecedented. Participants were invited to listen and then discuss the panel at their tables. At each table were difficult boundaries: foster parents and birth parents, front line workers and agency heads, private agencies and the public staff. The message was: If the lead litigator for over eighteen years and the Commissioner can playfully explore together the desired future for New York's children, we can overcome our differences.

This format with active facilitation avoids the series of miniparallel presentations as the moderator pulls others into having a conversation, highlighting the seams and connections. After eavesdropping on the panel, participants can be invited to talk among themselves for a few minutes to surface comments or questions. The moderator can pull a few of these and have the panel respond, again at the pattern level rather than one question at a time, which often leads to a sense of fragmentation rather than connection.

Large Group Discussions. At different moments in a large group event, the full community can be invited to converse. If the group is under a hundred and the acoustics are good, this can work. If these conversations are facilitated, it can be powerful to use quick straw polling to get a sense of the group on any given issue. Inviting members to pose various questions to get a quick read on the group's views enacts their self-management.

Linking Speakers with the Full Group. Speakers in large group settings contradict the ideology of distributed intelligence and can create an "audience-versus-engaged-participants" scenario. Yet brief, well-crafted presentations can vitalize a large group event if well linked to the work. A powerful approach to link a presentation to the next stage can be to pull from each participant some thinking that uses the resource of the presentation in a next step.

> In a recent large group process of a medical school's leadership team, a member of the community briefly framed the challenges in each of the major mission areas: research, education, and clinical care. Each participant, after the brief presentation, was charged by the Dean to jot down on separate Post-its responses to the following question: "What would be 2–3 actions that we could take in the coming months that would signal to ourselves and the larger community that we were making significant progress on the issues framed by the presenter?" These post-its were collected immediately and given to the colleague who was facilitating the next phase of the work, with three smaller groups working in parallel on developing a recommended strategy.
>
> As the small groups began, they faced a wall of the post-its that mixed their own ideas with the ideas of colleagues who were now in different rooms, so they had to integrate the thinking across those in their small group, as well as those not present. Finally, post-its enabled rapid and easily revised categorization by the small group, making transparent

different members' theories of how ideas might cluster to create broad strategies.

Signing Up: Managing the Transition Back to Work

One of the dilemmas of large group processes is that they are often counterstructural to encourage thinking across levels and functions and both inside and outside the sponsoring organization or group. The thinking can remain too loosely attached to the authority necessary to carry the work forward after the event. Next, we briefly described tools that help link thinking to roles.

Charging Memoranda. Large group processes often use an in-box to convey instructions to groups (Dannemiller Tyson Associates, 2000). An important addition to this method is great clarity about who is the authorizing source—executive, steering group, standing committee, work-life committee—for this particular piece of work. Often it will be the steering group. But it can also be an existing group, external to the event, with a particular link to that issue beyond the event's time boundaries. For example, if the large group event is about strategy but has, as a follow-up, the search for a new leader in that domain, the memorandum could come from the search committee with a request to focus on key challenges and attributes to guide the search. In parallel groups, different groups can have different memoranda, from different sources of authority. For example, at the transition out of the event, they could come from different organizations that have temporarily aligned for the event but now have to each take up their part of the ongoing work.

An effective memorandum has the following elements:

- The authorizing group
- The charge, a task, a set of questions
- The relevant background and context, often some additional data
- A timetable
- Desired output
- Suggested process

A well-crafted charging memorandum can be a "substitute for leadership (and facilitation)," creating a self-managing work group with the task as the source of coherence. It obviates the need for a chaotic dependency on creating "instructions" from the front of the room. Clear links to authorized bodies that will carry the thinking forward dampens participant cynicism that the energy will be left behind.

Fishbowl Meeting. A powerful ending would be to have the executive team or steering group meet in a "fishbowl"—that is, they would sit in a small group in the middle or front of the room, viewable by all other participants, who then would observe while the inner group has a public conversation—to reflect on what they have heard and what they see as the next steps. This allows the participants to audit their responsiveness.

One-Minute Essay.[1] Rather than evaluate the meetings via the usual like-dislike scales that locate the responsibility disproportionately on the leaders versus the members, use the one-minute essay: Each participant is asked at the end to take a minute to write about one or two important ideas from the session and jot down any unaddressed issues. These can be summarized and sent back.

The benefits of the one-minute essay are:

1. It requires more active listening from participants.
2. It helps to identify for the presenters what people are understanding and where they have questions.
3. It helps to document for participants that they are indeed learning.

Fast Follow-Up Meeting. It is powerful to schedule the convening group for a half-day right after a big event—just when people feel most tired and drained but also filled with real intelligence and feeling about the successes and failures of the recent event. The task is to learn from experience, extract lessons, and chart a future course.

Effective Follow-Through on Large Group Events

Next are strategies to capitalize on the hoped-for momentum and to avoid the dead zone that so often occurs after such an event. The more all of the follow-up strategies have been discussed and committed to before the event happens, the greater the success and impact. The steering group needs to frame the finish line for the initiative beyond the event connected to the ongoing real work of the organization, not a conference report. By reviewing the ideas presented next and developing the post-event strategy *before* the event, the steering committee can sustain the momentum.

• *Identify already-scheduled meetings both inside and outside the organization after the event and infiltrate relevant follow-up from the large group event on to those agendas.* By framing those who are attending from each organization as delegates, one creates an expectation that they will carry learnings back to their units. As preparation, they can be charged with bringing the views of their staff to the event. Listing the regular and special meetings that will take place in the days and weeks after the large group event, one can find venues to engage actively with the issues of concern. These should not just be perfunctory reports that can increase the sense of being excluded. Rather, those who attended should actively engage those who did not, selecting particular issues of interest to the group. Stressing the future opportunities for others to contribute to the issue can also help. Successful large group events often are a crucible for new relationships among stakeholders such as suppliers and a manufacturer or service providers and clients. Creating new opportunities for ongoing interaction by adding representatives to an existing group can help pull learnings from the conference into other venues and keep the working alliances alive.

• *Identify key stakeholders who were unable to attend and arrange to brief them immediately.* When someone makes an effort to brief an individual on an important event that he or she was unable to attend, people feel much more involved in the ongoing work and ready to join in the implementation of the key changes. It also deepens working relationships between the attendees and individuals being briefed.

• *Use e-mail to connect to staff who were unable to attend and thank them for keeping the work going during the event.* Recipients of such an e-mail feel that they were at least kept in mind during the event, if not actually present at the event. The e-mail can also actively pull them in on a relevant issue. Letting people know what resources might be available on a Web site if they were interested (for example, issue briefing materials, data sets) enacts that attendees were carrying their interests into the large group event.

• *Think about re-use of the event briefing materials and working notes to sweep in people who were unable to attend.* A huge amount of staff work goes into a large group event both before and during the session, resulting in position papers, relevant articles, data sets, presentation notes, focus group themes, lecture notes, and to-do lists. These are frequently overly "bound" in a workbook and do not get broken apart and distributed in pieces that are relevant to the on-going real work of the organization or convening community of interest. For each of the major elements of the event, think actively about constituencies that would find that material of value. Find ways to get it to them in an engaging, rather than a dumping, fashion.

• *When having meetings, think about sweeping in new participants to keep alive some of the collaborative conversations begun at a large group event.* One of the common values of such events is the presence of interesting outsiders: customers, suppliers, government officials. Rather than having these connections occur only in these large events, it can be powerful to pull in particular stakeholders at regular meetings in ways that are linked to the issue at hand. For example, at a major child-welfare conference many foster parents, birth parents, and youth were present. By engaging them on a more ongoing basis, the sponsoring organization has been able to enact one of its key themes of partnership.

• *Circulate ideas from the large group event or sections of the plans and invite comments from both attendees and others on specific issues. Acknowledge people who take the time to respond.* Cialdini (1993) has identified reciprocity as a key source of influence. When one person does something for another, it creates a relationship. In addition, when someone needs something from someone else, it deepens the connection. Many times 98 percent of the effort goes into producing reports from an event and only 2 percent into framing the transmittal. Imagine the difference in getting a report with a boilerplate transmittal versus a personal note, asking for "your feedback on a particular section." In the latter case, the recipient feels "on the hook" and needed.

• *When composing implementation or planning teams, explicitly draw from people who stood out at the event to harness their energy.* These events can be informal assessment centers where people have a stream of opportunities to interact in different ways than hierarchy or traditional roles allow. Those who are given formal roles of facilitating, note taking, or presenting should get feedback so that they can learn from their active involvement. The steering group should notice and follow up with people who stood out as particularly thoughtful or committed during various conversations. Obviously, the more interactive the designs are, the greater the chances for active practice and learning about participants' skills and interests.

• *Make a point of following up with new contacts from the event to keep conversations going and to create links that can be used in the future to advance issues that were addressed.* When one follows up on new contacts, they become part of an individual's network. If one does not follow up, the contacts fade quickly. If the steering group meets immediately after the event, the many informal conversations are fresh. They can list people to contact about particular interests. As mentioned earlier, some of the outsiders can be pulled into advisory boards or even targeted as potential employees.

• *Use routine newsletters to put in some intriguing information about the event or the follow-up.* Any organization or community of practice has many regular vehicles for communication. By planning in advance of the event, one can often have a sequence of follow-up stories through the organization's routine vehicles.

Large events are costly in out-of-pocket dollars but even more so in terms of the scarce resources of time and attention (Davenport and Beck, 2001). The value of those investments can be greatly enhanced by paying attention to the follow-through issues before, during, and after the event. The payoff is significant take-up of the ideas and new relationships formed in these sessions.

Note

1. The original concept for the "one-minute paper" comes from R. J. Light (1990) and was adapted for the CFAR tool (CFAR, 1999).

References

Alderfer, C. P. (1977). Improving organizational communication through long-term intergroup intervention. *Journal of Applied Behavioral Sciences, 2*(13), 193–210.

Bunker, B., & Alban, B. (Eds.). (1992). Editor's introduction: The large group intervention—A new social innovation? *Journal of Applied Behavioral Sciences* [Special issue], *28,* 473–479.

CFAR. (1999). "One-minute essay: meetings work: A guide to participative systems (from Building a meeting cycle section of Meetings workbook)." Philadelphia.

Cialdini, R. B. (1993). *Influence: The psychology of persuasion.* New York: Quill/William Morrow.

Collins, J. C., & Poras, J. I. (1994). *Built to last: Successful habits of visionary companies.* New York: HarperCollins.

Dannemiller Tyson Associates. (2000). *Whole-Scale Change: Unleashing the magic in organizations.* San Francisco: Berrett-Koehler.

Davenport, T. H., & Beck, J. C. (2001). *The attention economy: Understanding the new currency of business.* Boston: Harvard Business School Press.

Forster, E. M. ([1910]2003). *Howard's end.* New York: Barnes & Noble Classics.

Johnson, B. (1992). *Polarity management: Identifying and managing unsolvable problems.* Amherst, MA: HRD Press.

Langer, E. J. (1989). *Mindfulness.* Reading, MA: Addison-Wesley.

Light, R. J. (1990). The Harvard assessment seminars: First report, 1990. Boston: Harvard University, pp. 36–38.

Turquet, P. (1975). Threats to identity in the large group. In L. Kreeger (Ed.), *The large group: Dynamics and therapy.* London: Constable, pp. 87–144.

GRAPHIC FACILITATION AND LARGE GROUP METHODS

Carlotta Tyler, Lynne Valek, and Regina Rowland

From July 2nd to July 13th in 2004, more than 100 self-subsidized volunteers from different countries and cultures assembled in Spain to facilitate a Large Group Initiative sponsored by the Council for the Parliament of the World's Religions and designed to begin a dialogue that would enhance understanding across cultures, languages, geography, and faith traditions (see Chapter Six, fourth case). Among them, ten graphic professionals—six women and four men—came together to do graphic facilitation in Montserrat, Spain at an Assembly of 400 invited religious and spiritual leaders, expert resources, youth and individuals affected by four global issues under consideration, as well as representatives of relevant guiding institutions.

This case is reprinted from *The Journal of Applied Behavioral Science* (March 2005). Used by permission.

We would like to acknowledge the graphic facilitators and contributors: Amy Keill, graphics team leader; Timothy Corey; Greg Gollaher; David Hasbury; Nusa Maal, and the Graphic Facilitators: Don Braisby and Briagh Hoskins. We would also like to acknowledge the steering committee and process designers who worked with the Council for the Parliament of the World's Religions, the volunteers, and the participants of the Assembly held from June 5–7, 2004, in Montserrat, Spain, the Parliament of the World's Religions held from June 8–13, 2004, in Barcelona, Spain, and Helen Spector, CPWR Board Member.

In Barcelona, Spain, they were joined by participants who self-selected from among the 8,600 multi-faith community organizers, social activists and members of the public who attended the fourth Parliament of the World's Religions with a theme of "Pathways to Peace: the Wisdom of Listening, the Power of Communication." Participants came from over seventy nations, representing more than fifty-five religions and spiritual affiliations, spanned ages from teen to grandparent and spoke in more than thirty-five languages.

The purpose of these events was to encourage individuals to engage their communities of faith and conscience in simple, yet profound acts that could ameliorate the impact of four issues: increasing access to safe water, eliminating the international debt burden on developing countries, supporting refugees worldwide, and overcoming religiously motivated violence. The application of large-scale methodology in service to enhancing dialogue and constructive action among a global cross-section of leaders and activists represents a significant milestone in the applied behavioral sciences. Further, the application of graphics built bridges of communication and understanding between individuals and groups in a multi-lingual, multi-ethnic and multi-faith context in ways that expanded the implications of large-scale interventions.

Setting the Context: A Process Overview

Although this was the fourth in a series of Parliaments spanning one hundred and eleven years, it was the first time large-scale change methodology was used. A design team spent a year developing a replicable model to guide a diverse audience through a process conceived as a conversation-based experience. Framed by a progression of questions, each succeeding question aimed at deepening participants' understanding and connection to one another and to the issue the participant selected for exploration. The design was field tested and refined in Israel and Kenya four months before the Assembly in Spain. In Montserrat volunteer facilitators led the two-day program with a reiteration the next week at the Parliament in Barcelona.

Graphic recording played a key role in the implementation of this simple, yet elegant design. Early on the first day of the program a smooth transition was created by using the graphic to shift the discussion from small, same faith groups to a whole group dialogue engaging the full spectrum of faith traditions in the room. The graphic recordings captured the call outs resulting from a discussion of intrafaith resources which participants then applied to seek resolution of the issue. The resulting compendium of the strengths of that faith was recorded on a wall graphic. This stimulated a spirited discussion to answer the question: "If these are the strengths at hand, what stands in the way of resolving this issue?" A discussion of the barriers, by now, engaged everyone present in an energetic exchange. The colored markers and chalk of the graphic facilitators flew across the paper on the wall, as they captured emerging images arising from the discussion, in the moment, and under the watchful eyes of the audience. Participants could see the shape of their ideas progress across the wall as the day went on and their understanding of the issue and one another grew. By the second day, increasing numbers of participants were engaging with the images on the wall, adding to them, correcting them, using them to illustrate a point to a colleague. For example, a group of Sikh bankers were seen using a graphic to explain their loan structure. Graphic facilitation proved to be an essential component that provided a readily accessible, participatory, dynamic and evolving record of these conversations.

Defining Graphics

There are many terms in general use to describe what the graphic professional does when visually representing a group's process. Some call themselves "visual cartographers," others "graphic consultants," still others "graphic recorders." For the purpose of this article, the individuals who created the graphics will be called "graphic facilitators," and what they created—or the spaces they provided for others to utilize graphically—will be called "graphic recordings."

The act of graphic recording at the Assembly and Parliament was improvisational. Beginning each day with a blank sheet of paper, 5 feet high by 12, 15, or 20 feet long, and without an investment in the final outcome, the graphic facilitators captured, in large visual images, the substance of what was emerging from group discussions, as well as the essential dynamics in the interaction of participants as they engaged with one another about important and difficult topics.

The nature of graphic facilitation is interpretive. Whether recording "call outs" from the group process or giving shape and form to people's experiences and aspirations, the graphic facilitator listens for the story in the conversations, translating verbal and non-verbal inputs into visual forms that serve to synthesize and integrate individual and group thinking, to focus and direct group process.

The art of graphic facilitation involves deep listening on multiple sensory levels. When performed at the level of complexity of this intervention, the graphic facilitator needs to combine a system lens with acute observational skills that take into account both verbal and nonverbal data. S/he needs skills that combine cultural sensitivity with knowledge of group dynamics and the ability to translate stories into visual metaphors, in the moment, and capture subtly nuanced conversations as compelling images. All of the graphic professionals who were attracted to this project had training and experience in the applied behavioral sciences, organization development and/or group facilitation.

The Use of Graphics in Large Group Interventions

The challenge of facilitating the graphic recording of a broad-scope, fast-paced event such as this was to remain flexible in adapting the graphic form to the needs of the lead facilitator and/or the group, while remaining alert to the tenor, as well as the topic, of the group. Each graphic facilitator was unique in the execution of their graphic recording; however, all used some form of the following seven types of recording at one time or another. Of these seven distinctive types, the graphic facilitator performed six. The participants initiated the contribution to the seventh. The types of graphic recording were Fast Catch: a word/image-capture, Deep Listening: a story/metaphor-capture, Graphic Journalism, Holistic Reflection, Signage, Historical Graphic, and "In Your Voice" participant-initiated graphics in two forms, monitored and unmonitored.

1. *Fast Catch: Word/Image Graphic Recording* used text and pictures to capture information in the moment by recording, as closely as possible, the exact words being used by the participant (for example, having the group participants identify and "call out" the strengths of their faith tradition). This method sometimes employed templates, a predetermined layout which anticipated the positioning of important elements indicated by the design or the topic, such as a path peopled with figures meandering bottom, left to top, right across the paper to indicate the refugee's journey. A flow chart technique was also

frequently used, including arrows, boxes, and circles to organize and relate topics and to indicate the progression of the discussion. While templates and flow charts enable graphic facilitators to pre-plan, if used exclusively word/image-capture can miss the emerging nature of the discussion and the dynamic activity in the room.

2. *Deep Listening: Story/Metaphor Graphic Recording* occurred when the graphic facilitator listened on multiple sensory levels for the story emerging from individuals and translating that, in the moment, to a visual that captured the essential metaphor. The graphic facilitator generally used a blank sheet approach, without a preconceived idea about the form or content of the incoming data, recording the graphic representation of the story as it unfolded in real-time in the room. Most graphic facilitators encouraged group participation in the production of the graphic recording by asking participants to come up and draw their own stories, add words/meaning in their own languages to existing graphics, and give additional stories and designs to the graphic facilitator to draw. In one session, Mahatma Gandhi's granddaughter translated the English text into Hindi. This interpretive form of graphic recording is a way of organizing and presenting information in a non-linear way which encourages story telling, whole system, big picture thinking and stimulates participation and ownership of the outcomes. In the Assembly and the Parliament, this technique allowed for the inclusion of subtle process issues and topics that may not have surfaced in the small or large group context, such as the silencing of minority sub-groups or individuals.

3. *Graphic Journalism* uses a news reporter's approach to gather more data to inform the image-making process when a concept or story is either too complex for immediate graphic recording or not understood due to language translation. This method was used when representatives of the Mayan culture told of their people's resistance to the assignment of international debt through an interpreter. The emotional affect of the speakers did not fit the unemotional language and demeanor of the translator. In an effort to discover if something important was being lost in translation, a graphic facilitator spent time with the contingent, eliciting more information about their experience and point of view. She synthesized their grievances against past colonial exploitation and resistance to the present international debt structure into four succinct graphics, which were then added to the day's record. "Ah, that is exactly right," commented the Mayan group's translator. The small group facilitators often assisted in this process by bringing to the graphic facilitators' attention a significant

issue or story not being heard outside of the small group. In this instance, Graphic Journalism enabled a metaphoric style of expression to surmount the barriers of a more formalistic language, while retaining the strong spirit at the core of their issue.

4. *Holistic Reflection* uses an expansive lens to capture the essence of what is emerging from the whole system. One graphic facilitator was designated to use this form at the Assembly and Parliament, working in a central space adjacent to the group meeting rooms. She circulated among the large and small groups over multiple days, observing, listening, and receiving input from facilitators and participants. Reflecting on the input on multiple sensory levels, the graphic facilitator wove the strands of information and impressions with art and intuition. The resultant graphic expressed the dynamic flow of a highly diverse system in process. By periodically taking the pulse of the system, she opened to the deeper rhythms and layers emerging from individuals and the collective, becoming like a sieve through which the whole experience flowed, unimpeded by the details, capturing the spirit and emotional energy in pictorial images. The Holistic Reflective lens raises the awareness of participants to the systemic nature of their process and illustrates the larger perspective, the underlying connections, the harmony and congruence flowing beneath what appear to be surface differences.

5. *Signage,* requested by lead facilitators and logistics coordinators, met a wide range of immediate and emerging needs, from simple directional signs to complex instructions for participants. Many of the requests, especially at the start of the day, required rapid delivery. The objective at a culturally complex intervention such as this was to communicate essential information clearly, to assist non-native English speakers, to help set the tone of the session using color and imagery, and to illustrate instructions for how to do things (for example, guidelines for conversation). Consequently, many signs were translated into multiple languages. Spanish and Catalan frequently accompanied English text. Participants often offered to add translations in their own language.

6. *Historical Graphic Recording.* Since this was an ongoing initiative that took place in multiple locations over many months, it was important to establish and maintain a sense of continuity between the iterations. Graphic recordings helped to fulfill that purpose. The pictorial results produced during preceding sessions were hung outside the community meeting room before the first session to indicate the flow of the process they were to enter and to acknowledge the contributions of those who had participated in earlier sessions.

Participants reported that they felt the sense of connection to a larger whole and returned to that space to review the process as it flowed over time. The use of historical graphics with a newly convened group also serves to model graphic recording for those unfamiliar with the technique; it acts to stimulate creative thinking and to establish a rich, visual environment.

7. *"In Your Voice": Participant Voice Capture.* There were two types of spaces added by the graphic facilitation team during the Montserrat Assembly. They were intended to create approachable spaces in which individuals could express themselves in their own way without having to go through group filters. The first was a response to participants who came up to the graphic facilitators during the breaks with the request to "Please put this up there for me" or "Would you add my people's voice?" In each of the four issue group meeting rooms, a large sheet of paper, variously titled "In Your Voice" or "Add Your Voice," was put on the wall. People who used these relatively anonymous spaces found a place for the voice they could not use in the group. This was especially true for people whose cultures discourage their use of voice. Subtle cultural and faith differences found expression in this space. Every effort was made to confirm that participant input in a language unknown to the facilitators was culturally appropriate.

The second was the establishment of a public "Graffiti Wall" in common areas, apart from the large and small group meeting rooms. This created an even more anonymous space for creativity, humor, and individual expression. After announcing that a graffiti wall was available, the space was immediately and enthusiastically used by participants to display, by word and image, the wide spectrum of ideas and concerns, hopes and sayings, phrases in their own language, and images that had special meaning in their culture and/or faith. After a few days The Graffiti Wall was a vibrant, chaotic, and fun place for strangers to meet and share informally across culture and language. The first space was monitored to ensure accurate spelling, translation, and cultural sensitivity; the second was not.

Cultural Considerations

The challenge of creating visual images in this globe-spanning event was to avoid cultural insensitivity. Edward Hall (1976) knew that "there is not one aspect of human life that is not touched and altered by culture." There were few cultural aspects that were not represented in this intervention, including national group, gender, class, ethnicity, religious and spiritual affiliation, generation, language group, and organizational position. This potential for acting with cultural insensitivity was significant since the majority of the volunteer facilitators were from North America and Northern Europe. For that reason, the graphic facilitators made a point of requesting that participants bring to their attention any culture-specific perspectives, images, and symbols that were incorrect or missing. Participants enthusiastically complied with this request, establishing a self-corrective feedback loop useful for the entire facilitation team. For example, when a participant shared a story about the one pail of water an African family in her village had to use for a week, the graphic facilitator drew a pail with blue water in it. The participant asked that the water be changed to green, to reflect the color and characteristics of water where she lived. In another instance, a Sufi participant requested that the graphic facilitator "stay right there" while he returned to his hotel to don his Sufi turban and robes so that someone of his faith could be depicted "up there" on the graphic "with all the others." Participants also interacted with the graphic recordings by making suggestions like "Draw how water cycles through life" or "Add more rain drops" to depict their cultural experience and understanding. In those moments, the act of graphic recording transformed the walls into a vibrant community space.

Translators and participants were valuable in assisting graphic facilitators by translating English phrases into Spanish, Catalan, and their native language. Since one function of culture is to create a selective screen—to determine what gets attention and what is ignored (Hall, 1966)—the graphic recordings served to create a "meta-culture" by focusing the attention of participants toward some things and away from others. After each graphic recording was finished at the end of the day, it was hung in the room and/or moved into the hallways, filling the environment with stimulating visual signposts indicating the flow of the design and the continuity of the process over time.

The language used on the graphics was augmented by images that added a quality—in some cases an emotional content expressed by participants— to the word itself (for example, a nation burdened by international debt was characterized as a small person struggling to carry a large money bag labeled with the word *debt*). Participants watched the graphic recordings with interest, often correcting, suggesting, and refining the graphic recorders' cultural context and meaning. The visuals drew an audience and created a magical space for community.

Cultural sensitivity was heightened by the use of symbols in the graphics. In one large group graphic, facilitators went to considerable lengths to find participants who could add accurate traditional symbols from faiths whose symbols were unfamiliar to them.

Kolb (1984) defines four phases of learning: concrete experience (learning by feeling and by relating to people), reflective observation (learning by watching and reflecting), abstract conceptualization (learning by thinking and logical analysis and through subject experts), and active experimentation (learning by doing). The graphic facilitation at the Council for a Parliament of the World's Religions Assembly and later at the Parliament provided opportunities for the full spectrum of Kolb's learning styles. Concrete experiences were provided by the testimony of experts and individuals from communities impacted by one of the global issues. Reflective observation was extended for those who wanted to ponder ideas longer than a conversation might last, since completed panels were placed conveniently in common spaces where participants had free access. Abstract conceptualization was provided by the diagrammatic mapping of ideas expressed in the room onto the graphic, creating and forming relationships between elements. Active experimentation was also provided for all those who accepted the invitation to add their input to the graphics. Graphic recording at the Assembly and at the Parliament of the World's Religions events utilized all four of Kolb's learning styles.

Implications for Large-Scale, Multicultural Interventions

As the platform for large-scale change interventions expands globally to embrace a diversity of language, culture, and forms of expression, such as those encountered in the Assembly and the Parliament of the World's Religions, graphic representation becomes ever more important. In this process, graphic facilitators captured conversations in a rich and dynamic manner, honoring cognitive, affective, and behavioral domains. The following describes how graphics added significant value to this large-scale intervention.

• *Graphics engage participants.* Marvin Weisbord (1987) said, "People will support what they help to create." Individuals and sub-groups become engaged when they see their words, their expressions, their stories visually represented on the graphic. During breaks in the sessions, people came up to the graphic facilitators to refine the graphic images relating to their group input or to translate quotes into their native language. Groups could take more ownership of the process when they saw their conversation represented in the graphic recordings.

Graphic facilitation engages people through multiple senses. Participants become emotionally involved through the visuals, first, through the experience of seeing their own words and thoughts reflected in the graphic recording; second, if they were non-English speaking, through the language translation process, which—in many groups—was a collaborative effort; third, through observing the movements of the graphic facilitators in the creation of the graphic recording, and fourth, through direct participation by adding their own words, stories, songs, and images on participant voice-capture graphic recordings.

• *Graphics focus and ground the energy of the group.* Graphics were effective to shift the focus of the group from individual reflection, to small group dialogue, to large group sharing. Graphics serve to amplify the energetic field of large system work. The energetic field is the often unconscious, emotional affect that ebbs and flows throughout large system gatherings. This effect and its potential to advance or impede the primary task of the group were noticed by Le Bon (1896) and Bion (1961).

The use of graphics influences the energy resonating in small and large groups. By focusing attention on the patterns and flow of the large-scale intervention, the graphic record grounds the group's energy in a visual, tactile way. It was noticed that interest was piqued and the level of interpersonal energy in the room rose as the graphic recordings neared completion at the end of each day.

• *Graphics provide a space where participants feel heard.* Graphic recordings provide a form of communication that adds to spoken language and allows people to feel validated. When the graphic facilitator practices "deep listening" for the metaphors expressed in the stories, for the words not spoken, for the undiscussables, s/he honors the group and its individual contributors.

• *Graphics bridge cultures.* The dialogue format was intended to encourage collaborative and mutually respectful ways of talking and working together, acknowledging cultural differences without requiring participants to lose their cultural identity. The breadth of the cultural diversity of attendees and the preponderance of North American volunteer facilitators required cultural consideration. The graphic group discussed ways to ensure cultural sensitivity.

The graphics provided a feedback loop that allowed participants to communicate discrepancies, which was especially effective in integrating culture-specific language and symbols. Culture gaps were avoided in instances where participants left their own words, stories, songs, and images on participant voice-capture graphic recordings and on graffiti walls.

• *Graphics surface unheard voices.* The "dilemma of voice," noted by Bunker and Alban (1997), can be a significant issue in the dynamics of small and large groups. The inability to be heard in a group can be a structural problem of group size, power relationships, and the amount of available time. Each of these problems were, predictably, present. However, there were two notable dynamics that occurred at both events that reflected cultural rather than structural barriers.

Female participants sought out the female graphic facilitators at the breaks or at the beginning or end of the day to have them add images and stories to the graphic recordings that they had not shared in their groups. This happened so frequently that the female graphic facilitators started to notice a pattern and suggested the addition of participant voice spaces. In Your Voice and The Graffiti Wall, coupled with the availability and willingness of female graphic recorders to privately add images and stories to the graphic evolving recordings, provided an opportunity for women whose cultural traditions discourage them from speaking their views in public and women who are personally reticent to speak out.

• *Graphics provide a summative and integrative function.* Graphics provide a summative and integrative function in the data rich environment of the large group setting. An important use of graphic recording is to have the graphic facilitator review the graphic at the end of the day with participants. This process was found to invite quiet reflection and encourage integration of the day's discussion. Although this review was not always integrated due to time constraints and design changes, most of the graphic facilitators agree that this review is essential for an effective use of graphics.

Graphic facilitation aided in the success and sustainability of the 2004 Assemblies and Parliament multicultural, inter-faith dialogues. The primary outcome in the design of the process was to have participants commit to a "simple and profound act" that could impact one of the four global issue areas. Necessary strategies for arriving at a commitment include future-pacing, linear thinking, and detail-oriented problem solving, which are not inherent to various cultures with a holistic and present-oriented frame of reference. Therefore, developing specific commitment statements may have been awkward and/or difficult for many participants. Encouraging further participation, graphic recordings displayed commitments and modeled the process.

• *Graphics provide continuity and enhance sustainability.* After the events, participants have access to a visual record via the website, (http://cpwrglobal.net), to relive and share their experiences, additionally providing a community record of these events. Even those who were not physically part of the Montserrat Assembly or Parliament in Barcelona can enter into conversations and continued dialogue through the website.

Graphic recording provides a vehicle for continuity and serves the greater vision of the organization. The graphics previously developed are a part of the permanent record, assist in the on-going CPWR process, and are available for subsequent Assemblies and Parliaments to use as a starting point in a progression of visual representations.

Lessons Learned

• *Include graphic recording in planning and design phases.* Including the graphic facilitators' expertise and insights was important, especially regarding the use of graphics to shift attention and energy from individual to small group to large group process or from reflection, to dialogue, to action.

It was also helpful when the lead facilitators of the issue group met in advance with the graphic facilitator to discuss the development and placement of pre-charts or visuals. Often the set-up of the room was as intensive as the live graphic recording, and it was important that graphic facilitators had sufficient time to prepare.

• *Bond early to build team strength.* In an intervention of this scope, pace, and complexity, where change is a constant, flexibility and adaptability are essential attributes. The effort required in the implementation of a large system change initiative calls for a high degree of collaboration between and among planners, facilitators, logisticians, translators, and other volunteers. Appreciating one another without hierarchies of status is important for building the trust and respect needed to collaborate on these complex interventions. Eating together, rooming together, playing together, laughing together—all simple acts—which are the glue that holds the large group initiative together when the scope expands and the pace picks up.

It is essential that all parts of the graphic facilitation team spend time before and during the event to process issues, coordinate actions, and get comfortable with one another. Attention to process strengthened the graphic facilitators as a task group, since the group had not come together as a whole before meeting at Montserrat the first evening of the event.

Based on the lessons learned by graphic facilitators in the field test, some basic operating norms were suggested:

- Remain flexible and responsive in the face of last minute changes and to the lead facilitators' styles.
- Have all requests for graphic deliverables routed through the team leader.
- Have regular meetings throughout the event to discuss issues surfacing in the system, among the lead team, or among members of the graphics group and, whenever possible, to eat meals together.

Conclusion

The nature of graphic recording is ancient, preceding written records, as the cave drawings at Lascaux attest. However, the use of graphic recording to assist transformative, large system change processes is relatively new to many organization design and development professionals. When used creatively and integrated fully, graphic recording and graphic facilitators provide powerful support for the large-scale, whole system change process.

References

Bion, W. R. (1961). *Experiences in groups.* New York: Basic Books.

Bunker, B., & Alban, B. (1997). *Large group interventions: Engaging the whole system for rapid change.* San Francisco: Jossey-Bass.

Hall, E. (1966). *The hidden dimension.* New York: Doubleday.

Hall, E. (1976). *Beyond culture.* New York: Doubleday.

Kolb, D. A. (1984). *Experiential learning.* Upper Saddle River, NJ: Prentice Hall.

Le Bon, G. (1896). *The crowd: A study of the popular mind.* London: T. Fisher Unwin.

Weisbord, M. R. (1987). *Productive workplaces: Organizing and managing for dignity, meaning, and community.* San Francisco: Jossey-Bass.

Using Interactive Meeting Technologies

Overcoming the Challenges of Time, Commitment, and Geographic Dispersion

Lenny Lind, Karl Danskin, and Todd Erickson

In all meetings, all communication—in organizational life in general, and even in nature—you will find feedback cycles. They are organic and fundamental to life. This is the way we humans come to understand things—through give and take, discussion, and deliberation. Interactive meeting technology simply accelerates those cycles and, in doing so, redefines the possible outcomes of meetings.

Technology-enabled processes fundamentally change the experience of participants in large group meetings. In small groups of ten to twenty, most participants can address the group and feel that their voice has been heard and taken into account; a small group offers the experience of full participation. But now, even when *large* groups meet, technology-enabled processes allow participants to have a remarkably similar experience—that of sharing their thoughts with the whole group, seeing what the rest of the group is thinking, and all of it done without adding time to the meeting. This has enormous value for participants and meeting leaders alike. How such participation is enabled is the focus of this article.

First, any discussion about "interactive meeting technologies" is only worthwhile if 10 percent of the discussion is spent on technology and 90 percent on the interactivity—the people part, the design, the feedback cycles.

How any technology is actually used makes all the difference. Using interactive meeting technology well involves room layout design, agenda design, facilitation preparation, decisions about which software tools are used, when they are used, what questions are asked, how responses are themed, how themes are addressed, and more.

The Tools

The use of technology in meetings has evolved dramatically over the past forty years—from flip charts and overhead projectors to PowerPoint presentations and laptop PC groupware systems, from supporting groups of twenty to fifty to groups of two thousand to five thousand, from one-way communication (mostly top-down) to interactive, all-to-all communication (see Table 8.1).

For a meeting designer, the challenge is to choose technologies that will support participants in achieving the desired meeting objectives. And while flip charts and PowerPoint presentations still have their place, we are focusing here on interactive technology that allows for conducting real-time, all-to-all communication processes in situations where engagement is valued. The experienced meeting designer can then have the full range of meeting technology options at his or her disposal.

All-to-all processes enable and encourage the voice of most participants in large meetings who normally do not have a say in the proceedings. There are two types of interactive meeting technologies that support all-to-all processes available today: (1) keypad polling systems and (2) laptop PC groupware systems. The latter allows for fast text feedback, as well as polling in large meetings of fifty to five thousand participants. The largest to date—"Listening to the City"—in New York in July 2002 included five thousand people, seated at tables of ten; both technologies were used for maximum time-effectiveness.

Keypad polling systems have been used for over thirty years. Each participant uses what looks like a common VCR remote control to give their numbered response to a question posed on the big video screen in the room. Within minutes, all can see the group's collective scores on the same large screen. It is done quickly and is useful for gathering demographic information or narrowing a well-understood list of choices. The impact on a large group can be significant if the process before and after the poll is designed well. But the

TABLE 8.1. TECHNOLOGY FOR MEETINGS

Technology for Meetings		
Technology	**Process**	**Communication**
Flip chart	Presentation	One-way (one-to-small group)
Overhead or slide projector	Presentation	One-way (one-to-medium group)
PowerPoint and video projector	Presentation	One-way (one-to-large group)
Video- or teleconference	Presentation and Q&A and call-outs	Two-way (small, remote groups connected)
Keypad polling system	Polling everyone on pre-set questions	All-to-all (polls only)
Laptop PC groupware system	Gathering and distributing ideas from and to whole group; polling everyone on pre-set questions	All-to-all (dialogue; any-sized group)

system cannot project participants' voices into the room, only their preferences. Participants have no sense of dialogue with the rest of the group and no sense of building the options, only choosing among the options given.

Laptop PC groupware systems have been used for twenty years. In large groups, two or three participants (sometimes more) can discuss issues or questions presented to the whole group and then share a laptop computer to input their thoughts and ideas. This input, often filtered through a theming process, is immediately available to the group, so that everyone knows what other people's thoughts and ideas are. Groupware systems also offer several options for polling. Groupware systems are useful for generating and refining choices, as well as prioritizing those choices as input for decision makers. The following image (Figure 8.1) shows the layout of a meeting of the top 350 managers and executives of a 35,000-person global company.

Interactive technology is used most often when a meeting's outcomes are deemed critical, when agenda time is short, and when engaging the hearts and minds of participants will make all the difference. Using this technology to enable full participation becomes cost-effective whenever the group size is larger than would allow for open discussion, or roughly over thirty to forty participants.

The Challenges

As leaders of today consider motivating their large organizations, they are driven by three challenges as they reach for the highest effectiveness in their meetings. We will look at these challenges in detail, as they are also embedded in the difficult situations described throughout this book.

Overcoming the Challenge of Time

Large group meetings are necessarily brief, usually one or two days. A single, truly inclusive feedback cycle can easily take a whole day. But technology-enabled interactive processes make it possible to greatly *accelerate* fully inclusive

FIGURE 8.1. INTERACTIVE MEETING TECHNOLOGY

feedback cycles. This acceleration allows designers to build agendas based on multiple feedback cycles and thus pave the way for groups to achieve alignment quickly. The acceleration of the feedback cycle is dependent on both technical and process infrastructure. The technical infrastructure—the groupware system—allows everyone to "say" what's on their mind. The process infrastructure makes it possible for all participants and leaders to "hear" what's been said and to work with it live. This combined infrastructure allows for both speed and inclusivity.

Since 1992, CoVision has supported hundreds of facilitators in thousands of meetings using the Council groupware system; as a result, the following best practice has evolved. It shows how to create maximum effect from a speech using PowerPoint slides, which is the most common activity at large meetings. We have come to call it the "fast-feedback cycle" (see Figure 8.2).

The parts of the feedback cycle are as follows: (1) the speaker presents key points, (2) the group responds, (3) the Theme Team distills, and (4) the speaker responds to the group.

Step 1. The speaker presents: The speaker (or panel) presents information that is known to be important for the group, but the presentation is shortened to 50 percent of the time allotted. The speaker is asked to "hit hard" the points

FIGURE 8.2. COVISION'S FAST-FEEDBACK CYCLE

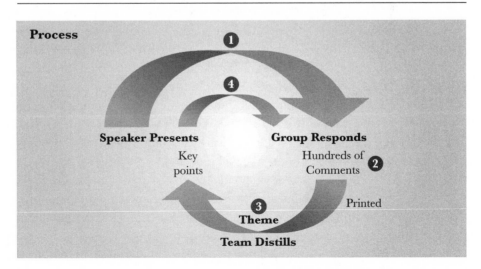

that he or she is committed to getting across. The speaker concludes with, "and now it is your turn to respond."

Step 2: The group responds: The speaker then asks the participants to spend a few minutes in their small groups discussing a question like, What do you need to know more about in order to achieve the targets we have set? As good responses emerge in discussion, participants key them into the laptop PC shared by each small group.

Step 3: The Theme Team distills: During the same five to ten minutes, while participants are buzzing and capturing responses, a special table group called the Theme Team, located off to the side of the main group, reads all the responses and works hard and fast to distill the big messages. The speaker meantime stands near the Theme Team table and listens as the final theme statements are refined.

Step 4: The speaker responds to the group's key points: After a couple of minutes of coaching and focusing with staff, the speaker retakes the stage to complete the presentation, this time responding directly to the expressed needs of the whole group.

The fourth step of the fast-feedback cycle is the payoff for all concerned. Participants hear the speaker's now-focused effort at communicating essential information requested by the group. In doing so, the speaker comes away with a clear sense of what the organization needs from him or her. And management comes to know more about the organization and how to lead it. But not so obviously, everyone in the room, from top to bottom, becomes aware of "where we stand as an organization on these issues," as well as "where I stand relative to the organization." This is new information for most participants in large meetings. And further, it translates into increased attention and participation, as the next speaker—and cycle—begins.

It is important to understand that the underlying technical and process infrastructure allows this interactive meeting technology to work. During different parts of the fast-feedback cycle, different aspects of that infrastructure come into the foreground. We will look at a few examples.

At Step 2—the group responds—the acceleration of the feedback cycle is supported by the technical infrastructure. The networked laptops allow everyone in the room simultaneous access to a channel for expressing their thoughts and reactions. There are tools for brainstorming, discussing, selecting, organizing, prioritizing, and polling. In addition, the groupware system allows for "leveling the playing field" when using the option of keeping participants' input anonymous.

Anonymity is one of the key components of the infrastructure, and it often raises a debate among design team members over whether it adds or detracts from a meeting. We have seen many executives forcefully describe how they expect their team members to make their positions known and not "hide under the cover of anonymity." To understand the true value of anonymity in fast-feedback cycles, one must reply with the question, By when? Consider that a senior manager in a meeting of a hundred other senior managers and peers, who is holding both concerns and insights about a controversial issue, surely will *not* be standing up and voicing them too soon. Most likely those concerns and insights will not be heard at all, unless possibly among a few trusted associates on a coffee break. Conversely, that same person's concerns and insights will be "voiced" anonymously through an interactive groupware system early in a large meeting. What a surprise for that person, and for senior leaders, if those concerns and insights happen to be echoed throughout the group. In that case, anonymity serves to get critical issues onto the table quickly, where they can be dealt with constructively by all. It is an even greater surprise to that same person when he or she is standing and speaking similar concerns out loud to the large group a day later and after the interactive process has been shown to be safe, effective, and highly constructive. This is the essence of the fast-feedback cycle: *it is the fastest time to understanding and commitment.*

In Step 3—the Theme Team distills—the process infrastructure plays the key enabling role. In order for the fast-feedback cycle to deliver maximum results, you must first have a high-functioning Theme Team. Its role is critical, and it is the social invention that makes "interactive meeting technology" work at all. The Theme Team is responsible for getting everyone's voice heard collectively in the room. The team is usually composed of three to five persons, each selected for their quick thinking, knowledge of the organization, reputation for fairness, and ability to work under pressure collaboratively. The work is not for the fainthearted, but neither are these sorts of people difficult to find in any organization. Normally, we orient and train Theme Team members on conference calls, well before the meeting. We discuss the purpose of the meeting, the processes we will use, the task of theming, how the software works, when it will be used in the agenda, how the screens look and feel, and, most important, how they feel about their role. We also ask whether they have any questions or concerns. During the meeting, they are introduced, coached, and thanked publicly when their service is done. It is a very satisfying role to play in important meetings. It is also a fine role for key teammates who otherwise may not be invited to attend.

Over time, we have experimented with a variety of theming options, including using teams as large as twenty (for a group of five thousand) and as small as two. Normally, we advise three to four members. Occasionally, the facilitator or an executive decides to theme "live" in front of the group, asking that the participants' responses be projected onto the big video screen and then reading and sharing their first-impression themes. At other times it is more valuable if the participants themselves do the theming, in which case they are asked to stop sending new responses, to click on the "Read" link on their screens, to spend five to ten minutes reading everyone's responses, and to jot down themes in their small groups. Then the facilitator asks tables, one at a time, to call out a theme, which is captured live onto the big video screen. In this way, everyone in the meeting will become thoroughly familiar with all of the input. In each case, the theming step allows the speaker (or other leaders) to respond directly to the group's core questions and needs. If you count success in a large meeting in terms of achieving a certain level of understanding on the important issues being discussed, and if you consider that it always takes significant and precious time to reach that level of understanding, then you could say that this fast-feedback cycle approach is the quickest route to that high level of understanding.

During Step 4—the speaker responds to the group's key points—again, it is the process infrastructure that plays the enabling role. It is important to recognize the critical importance of coaching presenters and executives as they navigate this new and unfamiliar fast-feedback process the first few times. Although most will proclaim they are all for hearing from their subordinates, it is also true that most naturally shy away from this seemingly risky position, which some have described as "drinking from a fire hose." Therefore, it is a critical component of interactive meeting technology that consultants encourage executives beforehand and live during the meeting when they face each new unfamiliar situation, reminding them, for example, of the stages of building alignment, how groups move through the stages, where the group is right now, how the Theme Team will support them, what can be said at this moment to affect deeper understanding, and what is fair to say and what is "out of bounds," or what can be discussed but in a different forum or in the near future. In most all cases, executives (and facilitators, too) who are new to this process understand their enhanced role clearly within the first day. You can think of the groupware facilitators as providing "training wheels" on the first ride of the bicycle, keeping everything upright. It is worthy to note that interactive technology providers have failed in the past fifteen years because they underestimated the importance of these human dimensions of their service, focusing primarily on the technology.

And last but not least, the technical infrastructure provides a written record of all the responses, captured verbatim. This is often a valuable resource for managers and others responsible for follow-up throughout the organization.

Overcoming the Challenge of Commitment

In most cases, the meetings of large organizations are held when there are very large communication objectives. Examples are "getting everyone on the same page," or "getting buy-in," or announcing a new strategy and launching its implementation, or the deceptively simple, "alignment." Yet while large meetings are undertaken to *solve* communication challenges, they often *create* their own set of challenges: How do you keep people's attention through many presentations? How do you know whether they understand what is presented? What about hidden resistance, which could lead to failure? Is there any? Or the toughest: How do we get people *committed* to this new direction? Commitment is a state of readiness, personally and collectively, to fully implement the shared, understood goals of the organization. This takes time.

Many large meetings are designed as if guided by the "myth of immaculate reception," in other words, that everyone will hear exactly what was intended to be communicated, that each participant will understand it without questions or concerns, that each will take it as their own, and that each will go forth and implement to the best of their abilities. In these meetings, commitment is often mentioned as one of the meeting goals, but then no time in the agenda is planned for actually achieving it. The myth lives on in presentation after presentation as a *hope* for commitment. This, coupled with severe time constraints, describes the "real-world" challenge of large meetings and of gaining anything approaching commitment in them. This is also where interactive meeting technology plays its most significant role.

In order to achieve real understanding, alignment, or commitment, participants need time to listen, question, digest, kick around, push back, and hear others' opinions. Participants need to bounce their thinking and ideas off the group. They need to know what the group is thinking and how the group is responding. This feedback from the group and the leadership to every individual is what enables the group to arrive at shared understanding and a real readiness to act.

Over thousands of meetings that CoVision has supported, we have seen distinct stages that a group must move through in order to arrive at true, collective commitment to a shared plan of action (see Figure 8.3). Each stage stands on those preceding it and represents not only increased understanding but also increased trust within the group. Each stage is achieved through the completion of additional feedback cycles, each building on the last, each bringing individual participants through the stages, maybe at different rates but steadily toward real alignment.

As a large organizational meeting begins, participants are commonly either ambivalent or expectant, but rarely more. As presentations begin, participants become "aware" of the big issues. If there are Q&A sessions or break-out meetings, participants can get their questions and concerns addressed, and they will achieve personal "understanding" rather quickly. But what about understanding in the whole group? Is there an emerging consensus? Are there some areas of push-back? In order to move to the next stage—mutual understanding—table groups must be invited to report about their discussions, summary statements must be built, polls possibly taken, and questions must be addressed by senior members. Without technology support, it is possible to achieve mutual understanding, but it requires significant time *that is rarely allowed for in today's jam-packed agendas.* Only with technology and all-to-all communication processes

FIGURE 8.3. COVISION'S FAST-FEEDBACK CYCLE

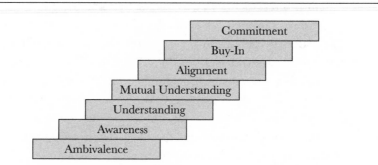

can you realistically achieve mutual understanding and beyond, within normal time frames.

When a participant reaches an understanding of where he or she stands vis-à-vis the whole group, real alignment begins to happen. As issues and the whole group's positions come into focus, individuals can make their own decisions about "buying in" to the organization's directions and goals. Only then can a broad commitment to those goals become real. So people must go through a communication process—a very interactive one—in order to actually commit to organizational goals.

The all-to-all communication process is a means of closing the feedback loop between the group members, with each other and with the leadership, and consists of cycles that are repeated as often as possible. As each cycle repeats, a large group *will move toward alignment*. We have found that there is a cumulative effect from multiple feedback cycles. Participants learn quickly their ability to affect the outcomes of the meeting through their feedback, so they listen better and respond more constructively as the cycles repeat.

You might wonder at this point, are any of the outcomes described measurable? Unfortunately, little empirical research has been done over the years. Like most of the organizations we support, the current focus is always on the upcoming project while integrating learnings from the last one. We have found, however, one measurement within meetings that is quite effective for leaders and participants alike: the "confidence check"—a two-step groupware process. The first question is asked in a Likert Scale format on a scale of 1 to 5, low to high, "What is your level of confidence that we will succeed with the *xyz* initiative, as just discussed?" That question is followed on the same screen with a text-response question, "If your score was 4 or below, what would have to change in order for you to raise your score?" This process takes five to ten minutes, even in meetings of hundreds, and can reveal more than hours of "normal" meeting time without technology support. Some clients use it at the beginning of a meeting, or segment of a meeting, and again at the end to measure increased understanding, alignment, or commitment.

Although scores of meetings could be held up as examples in which these challenges of commitment and time have been addressed well, a series of Sprint meetings in the late 1990s is most instructive. The first of the four meetings included the top three hundred senior executives and was focused on the challenge of creating "One Sprint"—correcting an increasing problem of organizational "stovepipes." Reprising Sprint's advertising of that time, you could have heard a pin drop at the beginning of the two-day meeting, when the CEO asked for verbal responses via microphones to some of his questions. A day later, after many cycles of feedback, executives were lining up at the floor microphones to make passionate statements. On the morning of Day 1, after the CEO had observed one cycle, he asked us to install two monitors on the floor in front of the stage and for us to scroll incoming comments—live—on those screens. Then he and his COO got into a tag-team, real-time dialogue with the three hundred participants. While one spoke and responded to the big messages from the group, the other read ahead and looked for his next response. Leaders and participants alike tested the process during the first couple of cycles and then began to use it full-force. An extraordinary amount of trust was built quickly, the executives were seen in a new light, the content and understanding achieved was dramatic, and both the purpose and the theme of the meeting—"Catalyst"—were fulfilled. Following this success, three more regional Catalyst meetings were held within weeks for the directors.

Overcoming the Challenge of Geographic Dispersion: Extending the Feedback Cycle Through Time and Space

Increasingly, organizations are composed of employees spread across many buildings, across the country, and around the globe. These people are often traveling, visiting clients, or having meetings; they are *not* in their offices. For managers who are trying to lead and facilitate the success of groups of far-flung team members, the challenge is growing. Periodic meetings to achieve focus and alignment of efforts become more important, yet not all can attend. And for those who do, the time is often crunched. All manner of technologies, from phone and fax to Blackberries, e-mail, and audio-video conferences, are utilized between meetings, but without a cohesive process design, people can become overwhelmed with communication demands. It is more difficult each day to keep dispersed groups focused and aligned.

Overcoming the challenge of dispersion requires consciously building on the related challenges of commitment and time, as just discussed, and designing for continued acceleration of feedback cycles while participants are apart. These designs must address the question, What kind of cohesive process design, coupled with interactive technology, will most efficiently maintain and increase organizational alignment and commitment? Since we are all humans and long-time members of tribes, we believe there will always be reasons and deeper needs for meeting face-to-face periodically. But once we know each other, it is not necessary to meet *as often*. The question becomes, How do we stay in touch most effectively when we are apart? Or in other words, How do we maintain the feedback cycles while we are apart?

If you consider that important meetings are not *ends* in themselves but rather are *means* to some end, then you can think about the "before-during-after" aspects of a meeting, and how it is all a process designed to achieve agreed-upon goals. We have already addressed how to maximize the effectiveness of a meeting with fast-feedback cycles; now we are addressing the periods before and after the meeting (see Figure 8.4).

Before an important meeting, online processes can be designed that orient participants to the key issues and get their thinking started before they arrive. We call this an "on-ramp process." The time demand must be small, the purpose clear, and the instructions simple; it is best if the request for input comes from a senior leader. With this input, segments of the meeting can begin with statements about the whole group's starting positions and where leaders would like to move them during the meeting. In addition, follow-through processes can be designed before the meeting and then demonstrated and started up near the end. These online processes may run for months afterward, through a series of progress checks, until the next large meeting. We call these "after-burner processes." They consist of a series of conference calls that are fueled by online input tasks. The key is to introduce the processes during the meeting and do everything possible to gain buy-in from all participants that

FIGURE 8.4. AN EXTENDED VIEW OF "MEETING"

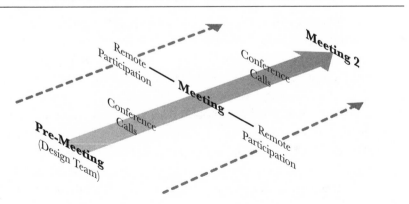

each will participate in the processes afterwards. It is vital that leaders frame the urgent reasons for this ongoing participation, and, incidentally, they must participate themselves in order to keep up the overall energy.

Striking new formats for meetings are now possible through the use of interactive technologies and the Internet. A fascinating example of this is a meeting we designed with the American Camping Association. The year prior, we had supported their annual meeting in which a new vision for their work was presented, discussed, and adopted with great excitement. While designing the next annual meeting, a question was posed whether we could include representatives of scores of other sister organizations in the fast feedback cycles, somehow, from their remote locations. So we designed a process that used the groupware system in the main meeting room, as we have described here, and then connected the room to the Internet, linking with over one hundred sites around the country. All sites had an audio feed from the main meeting room via telephone, and each could upload their responses via the Internet to the same questions as participants in the meeting were answering. The Theme Team, which included six members, could then develop themes from ACA members in the room and somewhat different themes from associates in the field. For a modest cost, the ACA was able to achieve a truly national conversation that generated solutions, as well as cohesion, among all participants and sponsors.

Conclusion

After many years of experimentation and practice, interactive meeting technology has evolved to the point of enabling all-to-all communication in large and very large meetings. The technology came early and easily; the human adaptation came much more slowly, but the successful processes are now well understood. Now people can be active participants in large meetings, not just passive audiences. Leaders can lead visibly, responsively, sometimes dramatically. Meeting designers can now choose this approach with confidence when the outcomes depend on mutual understanding and alignment or when the time is too short or the issues too contentious. This technology-enhanced, fast-feedback approach can be integrated flexibly with many of the Large Group Methods mentioned in this book, for example, Whole-Scale, 21st Century Town Halls, The World Café, Future Search, and so on. And it works well, even in situations other than those described, when leaders and presenters have something to communicate and are driving for understanding. For example, meetings for strategic planning, regional planning, creating joint futures, sharing best practices, multistakeholder engagement, and even conflict resolution, can all benefit significantly by processes and technology that encourage full participation.

Where there are ample feedback cycles, there is understanding and alignment and, if necessary, commitment.

THE READING LIST

If you are unfamiliar with the various methods, we suggest you start with the "Overview of Books and Articles on Large Group Methods." That will give you some guidance on the methods in the "How-To Books and Articles on Large Group Methods" section that you may want to explore in depth. The "Thought-Provoking Books and Articles" are ones that you may want to pursue when you have time; we jokingly called this the "Summer Reading List." When you have time, you can look over this list and see what sparks your interest. Some of the books on this list have nothing directly to do with Large Group Methods but can help inform your thinking and practice. Enjoy!

Overview of Books and Articles on Large Group Methods

Bunker, B. B., & Alban, B. T. (Eds.). (1992). Large group interventions [Special issue]. *Journal of Applied Behavioral Science, 28*(4).

Bunker B. B., & Alban B. T. (1997). *Large group interventions: Engaging the whole system for rapid change.* San Francisco: Jossey-Bass.

Bunker, B. B., & Alban, B. T. (Eds.). (2005). Large group interventions [Special issue]. *Journal of Applied Behavioral Science, 41*(1).

Holman, P., & Devane, T. (1999). *The change handbook: Group methods for shaping the future.* San Francisco: Berrett-Koehler.

How-To Books and Articles on Large Group Methods

Axelrod, E. M., & Axelrod, R. H. (2000). *The Conference Model.* San Francisco: Berrett-Koehler.

Axelrod, R. H. (2000). *Terms of engagement.* San Francisco: Berrett-Koehler.

Axelrod, R. H., Axelrod, E. M., Beedon, J., & Jacobs, R. W. (2004). *You don't have to do it alone: How to involve others to get things done.* San Francisco: Berrett-Koehler.

Brown, J., & Isaacs, D. (2005). *The World Café: Shaping our futures through conversations that matter.* San Francisco: Berrett-Koehler.

Cooperrider, D. L., Whitney, D., & Starvos, J. M. (Eds.). (2003). *Appreciative Inquiry handbook: The first in a series of AI workbooks for leaders of change.* Bedford Heights, OH: Lakeshore Communications.

Dannemiller Tyson Associates. (2000). *Whole-Scale Change: Unleashing the magic in organizations.* San Francisco: Berrett-Koehler.

Dannemiller Tyson Associates. (2000). *Whole-Scale Change tool kit.* San Francisco: Berrett-Koehler.

Emery, M., & Purser, R. (1996). *The Search Conference.* San Francisco: Jossey-Bass.

Hirano, H. (1990). *5 pillars of the visual workplace: The sourcebook for 5S implementation.* Portland, OR: Productivity Press.

Jacobs, R. (1994). *Real Time Strategic Change.* San Francisco: Berrett-Koehler.

Klein, A. (2005). *SimuReal: A large group method for organization change*: Columbia, MD: Klein Consulting (alan@klein.net).

Ludema, J. D., Whitney, D., Mohr, B. J., & Griffin, T. J. (2003). *The Appreciative Inquiry summit: A practitioner's guide for leading large-group change.* San Francisco: Berrett-Koehler.

Owen, H. (1997). *Open Space Technology: A user's guide* (2nd ed.). San Francisco: Berrett-Koehler.

Slater, R. (1999). *The GE Way field book.* New York: McGraw-Hill.

Spencer, L. J. (1989). *Winning through participation.* Dubuque, IA: Kendall/Hunt.

Watkins, J. M., & Mohr, B. J. (2001). *Appreciative Inquiry: Change at the speed of imagination.* San Francisco: Jossey-Bass/Pfeiffer.

Weisbord, M., & Janoff, S. (2000). *Future Search: An action guide to finding common ground in organizations and communities* (2nd ed.). San Francisco: Berrett-Koehler.

Thought-Provoking Books and Articles

Adams, J. D. (2003). Successful change: Paying attention to the intangibles. *OD Practitioner.* Winter, *35*(4).

Bennett, J., & Bennett, M. (2003). *Becoming a skillful intercultural facilitator.* Forest Grove, OR: Summer Institute for Intercultural Communication.

Bradford, D. L., & Burke, W. W. (Eds.). (2005). *Reinventing organization development: Addressing the crisis, achieving the potential.* San Francisco: Pfeiffer/Wiley.

Burke, W. W. (2002). *Organization change: Theory and practice.* Thousand Oaks, CA: Sage.

Collins, J. C., & Poras, J. I. (1994). *Built to last: Successful habits of visionary companies.* New York: HarperCollins.

Frost, P. (2003). *Toxic emotions at work.* Boston: Harvard Business School Press.

Gladwell, M. (2000). *The tipping point.* Boston: Little, Brown.

Pascale R., Millemann M., & Gioja, L. (2000). *Surfing the edge of chaos: The laws of nature and the new laws of business.* Westminster, MD: Random House.

Hargrove, R. (1998). *Mastering the art of creative collaboration.* New York: McGraw-Hill.

Hofsted, G. (1997). *Cultures and organizations: Software of the mind.* New York: McGraw-Hill.

Johnson, B. (1992). *Polarity management: Identifying and managing unsolvable problems.* Amherst, MA: HRD Press.

Kasl, E., & Elias, D. (2000). *Creating new habits of mind in small groups.* San Francisco: Jossey-Bass.

Lipman-Blumen, J. (2005). *The allure of toxic leaders.* New York: Oxford University Press.

Mirvis, P., Ayas, K., & Roth, G. *To the desert and back.* San Francisco: Jossey-Bass.

Ogilvy, J. (2002). *Creating better futures.* New York: Oxford University Press.

Olson, E., & Eoyang, G. (2001). *Facilitating organization change: Lessons from complexity science.* San Francisco: Jossey-Bass/Pfeiffer.

Ringland, G. (1998). *Scenario planning: Managing for the future.* New York: Wiley.

Rothwell, W. J., & Sullivan, R. L. (Eds.). (2005). *Practicing organization development.* San Francisco: Pfeiffer/Wiley.

Schoemaker, P. (2002). *Profiting from uncertainty.* New York: The Free Press.

Schein, E. (1999). *Process consultation revisited: Building the helping relationship.* Series on organization development. Reading, PA: Addison-Wesley.

Steil, G. (1998). *The magic is in the principles: Consulting today.* New York: Ardsley-on-Hudson.

Townsend, M. (2002). Lessons from the field: Applying complex adaptive systems theory to organization change. *OD Practitioner, 34*(3), 10–14.

van der Heijden, K. (1996). *Scenarios: The art of strategic conversation.* New York: Wiley.

THE AUTHORS

Billie T. Alban is president of Alban and Williams, Ltd., Consultants to Organizations. She was vice president and general manager of Transpetroleo Corporation in South America. Since 1980, she has won distinction as a national and international management consultant. Some of her activities include strategic planning and organizational redesign. She has worked with joint ventures and helped in the development of international management teams. In recent years, her practice has been focused on working with organizations and communities on large-scale change efforts, using highly participative methods, which increase the ownership by participants of the new direction and strategies.

Some of her clients include ITT, General Electric, Kraft Foods, Bankers Trust, Johnson and Johnson, NASA, Mount Sinai Hospital, National Health Service (United Kingdom), The Kings Fund, Exxon/Mobil Corporation, British Airways, Cathay Pacific Airways, Pfizer Pharmaceuticals, Equitable Life, Hewlett-Packard, and INTEL. In addition Billie has consulted for nonprofit and government organizations. Some of these clients include the Federation of Protestant Welfare Agencies in New York City, the Episcopal Diocese of Washington, D.C., the United Way, the Department of Social Welfare in New Zealand, and the IRS.

On several occasions Billie has served on the staff of the Tavistock Institute in England. She has been the dean for Presidents and Executives Workshops for the National Training Laboratories. She is a core faculty member for Executive

Development Programs for Columbia University, Pepperdine University, and others. She has been on the Board of Advisors of the Yale Divinity School.

Billie wrote her first book on organization development in Spanish with Miguel Bernal: *Desarrollo Personal y Organizacional*, NTL Institute. With Barbara Bunker she edited two special editions of the *Journal of Applied Behavioral Science* on Large Group Interventions. Her book with Barbara Bunker, *Large Group Interventions* (Jossey-Bass, 1997), led to a series of workshops that she and Barbara offered for professionals interested in using these methods in their organizations and communities.

Billie lives in Connecticut and enjoys working in her community. Recently she organized a Community Conversation on Education for a town in Connecticut, a conference on youth for the city of Danbury, and a conference on aging for the city of Greenwich. She also enjoys international travel and is deeply interested in international relations. Several years ago she cofacilitated an international ecumenical group in Barcelona, Spain, on the issue of third world debt. In all the above instances she applied the Large Group Methods described in this book. She believes in the importance of gathering people to sit down and "reason together" about an issue of common concern. (www.odpartners.com)

Barbara Benedict Bunker is a social and organizational psychologist and Professor of Psychology Emeritus at the University at Buffalo (UB). At UB she was head of the Social Psychology Doctoral Program and director of graduate studies. Although officially retired, she continues to teach cross-cultural psychology and small group processes. She is also chair of the UB Council of International Studies and Programs and is actively involved in the internationalization of the campus and the many relationships UB has with other academic institutions around the world.

Bunker's first career was in student activities. She was on the staff of the Woman's College and Director of Religious Life at Duke University for eight years. Participation in the Civil Rights Movement as well as developing leadership training for students introduced her to the new field of small group research and practice. This led to a shift in career direction and a decision to pursue a Ph.D. in social psychology (1970) at Columbia University, Teachers College with Morton Deutsch.

New York in the 1960s was a gathering place for professionals using Applied Behavioral Science to assist organizations to become more effective. Matthew Miles, Ronald Lippitt, and Goodwin Watson worked at Teachers College on some of the earliest organization development (OD) projects in school systems. Richard Beckhard and Herb Shepard, early independent OD consultants from the New York area, participated in meetings to talk about the experimental work that was going on. The authors of this book met at one of these meetings and the two have been good professional colleagues and friends since then.

Barbara Bunker has sought in her thinking and writing to bridge theoretical research and practice. She is the author of numerous articles on topics such as organizational change, trust in work relationships, commuting couples, women's competitive styles, and large group interventions. Her books include *Social Intervention* (1971, with H. Hornstein and others), *Mutual Criticism* (1975, with M. Levine), *Conflict, Cooperation, and Justice* (1995, with J. Z. Rubin), *Large Group Interventions* (1997, with Billie Alban).

She is an internationally known organizational consultant to a variety of clients. She has taught in executive development programs at Columbia, Pepperdine, and Harvard Universities. She has been a director and chair of the board of directors for the NTL Institute of Washington, D.C. In 1984 and 1991, she held Fulbright Lectureships in Japan, first at Keio University and later at Kobe University. In 2005, she received the Lifetime Achievement Award from the Organization Development Network.

Currently, Bunker divides her time between her Buffalo home and office and the family natural beef farm that her husband manages in the hill country about an hour south of Buffalo. (www.odpartners.com)

The Contributors

John D. Adams is professor and chair of the organizational systems doctoral program at Saybrook Graduate School and Research Center, San Francisco, California. He also provides seminars, consultation, and coaching internationally in wellness and resilience, successful change implementation, and sustainability program development. He is the founder and principal of Eartheart Enterprises in San Francisco.

Nancy Aronson is a partner in Arsht/Aronson, Radnor, Pennsylvania. In her work, she brings practical, collaborative methods to organizations and communities facing complex issues. She codeveloped the System Coherence Framework for Change Leadership and is a contributing author to *Future Search in School District Change: Community, Connection and Results* (Scarecrow Education, 2005).

Tova Averbuch, founder of Ogain, is an organization development (OD) consultant and a large group process designer and facilitator working with businesses and communities. Having brought Open Space Technology to Israel, she is a pioneer in applying whole system interventions to business and political life in Israel and worldwide initiatives.

Richard H. Axelrod and *Emily M. Axelrod* pioneered the use of Large Group Methods to redesign organizations. Richard authored *Terms of Engagement: Changing the Way We Change Organizations* (Berrett-Koehler, 2000). Richard and Emily coauthored *You Don't Have to Do It Alone: How to Involve Others to Get Things Done* (Berrett-Koehler, 2004).

Rosemarie Barbeau is a northern-California-based OD consultant who helps clients develop strategy, implement key initiatives, and build successful partnerships. She contributed to *The Flawless Consulting Fieldbook and Companion: A Guide to Understanding Your Expertise* (Jossey-Bass/Pfeiffer, 2001) and *Organization Development Classics: The Practice and Theory of Change—the Best of the OD Practitioner* (Jossey-Bass, 1997).

Julie Beedon is one of the leading authorities on Large Group Methods in the United Kingdom and is the CEO of VISTA Consulting Team, Ltd. She coauthored *You Don't Have to Do It Alone* (Berrett-Koehler, 2004), and *Meetings by Design* (Vista Consulting Team Limited, 2002, www.vista.uk.com).

Deborah Bing is a principal at the Center for Applied Research, a consulting firm in Philadelphia and Boston. She is an expert in negotiation and mediation and helps organizations successfully implement large-scale change while building buy-in with multiple stakeholders. Her clients include owner-led businesses, foundations, and hospital systems.

Albert B. Blixt is a partner and senior consultant at Dannemiller Tyson Associates. He is a developer and practitioner of the Whole-Scale approach to systems change. He is the coauthor of three books: *Navigating in a Sea of Change* (Society of Competitive Intelligence Professionals, 1996), *Whole-Scale Change: Unleashing the Magic in Organizations,* and *The Whole-Scale Toolkit* (both Berrett-Koehler, 2000).

Steven Brigham is COO for AmericaSpeaks, a nonprofit that conducts large-scale citizen engagement projects on public policy and planning issues. Steve recently led projects for the Clinton Global Initiative, the National Health Service in the United Kingdom, and the mayor of Washington, D.C.

Jack Carbone worked in the Florida Education Association (FEA) in various capacities for twenty-five years, most recently as the director of organization development. The recent focus of his work has been the merger integration presented in the case in this book.

Mee-Yan Cheung-Judge has run Quality & Equality since 1987. The company is a U.K.-based OD consultancy firm in Oxford. She works to build and enhance OD capacity in Europe. Her special interest is facilitating large-scale, big-system change.

Sophia Christie is CEO of Eastern and North Birmingham Primary Care Trusts, ensuring health services for 500,000 people in England, with a combined turnover of almost £billion a year. She holds degrees in English and the sociology of contemporary culture and has a long-standing interest in ensuring participation and responsiveness for staff, patients, and partners in the organizations she leads.

Ann L. Clancy, president of Clancy Consultants, Inc., is an OD consultant, professional facilitator, and researcher in qualitative studies. For over twenty years, she has partnered with a wide range of clients, including nonprofits, government agencies, and corporations. She has specialized in designing public meetings with diverse groups and has facilitated a citizens' advisory council for an oil refinery since 1990.

Karl Danskin is large group meeting consultant at CoVision, Inc. He pioneered the processes for accelerating feedback cycles in large groups. His work has been characterized by the integration of technological infrastructure with nontechnological processes toward the realization of "giving everyone in the room a 'voice' and the possibility to 'hear' everyone else."

José DelaCerda is vice president for external relations at ITESO Jesuit University in Mexico. His experience includes top positions in public management and business consulting, and extensive application of Large Group Methods in Latin American organizations. He has written several books and articles on Mexican management.

Susan Dupre uses large group principles to create new designs that make it possible for diverse groups to work together, determine what they want to do, and plan how to do it. Susan likes working in different cultural contexts where she collaborates with other consultants. She lives near Sacramento, California.

Glenda H. Eoyang is the founding executive director of the Human Systems Dynamics (HSD) Institute. She facilitates the development of theory and practice in HSD, as she writes, speaks, and consults internationally.

Todd Erickson is a senior consultant and region manager for CoVision, Inc. He has vast experience in utilizing various collaborative technologies to aid in strategic planning and organization-alignment initiatives enabling organizations to tap into the creative and critical thinking of large numbers of stakeholders in short time frames.

Ronald Fry is associate professor of organizational behavior at Case Western Reserve University, where he directs the master's program in positive organization development and change. Fry is a co-creator of Appreciative Inquiry. His recent work includes large system AI Summits with the U.S. Navy, World Vision, and Roadway Express.

Beth Ganslen, a leader with over twenty-four years of experience at American Airlines, has held positions in line management, human resources, training, and organization development. Beth's current OD practice encompasses work in employee involvement, change management, process improvement, organization design, performance management, leadership development, and executive coaching.

Michele Gibbons-Carr is an independent consultant and president of Phoenix Consultants in Wellesley, Massachusetts. She specializes in large group strategic planning methods that focus on creating shared vision and planning for alternative future scenarios, qualitative organizational assessments, change that is data-driven, team facilitation, and individual coaching.

Thomas N. Gilmore is vice president of the Center for Applied Research (CFAR) and an adjunct associate professor at the Wharton School. He has written extensively, often with clients, on issues of leadership, large group engagement processes, reorganizations, downsizing, and team building. He is a founding member of ISPSO (International Society for the Psychoanalytic Study of Organizations).

Ray Gordezky works with people to transform difficult situations into more positive and realistic possibilities for change. He co-creates and facilitates collaborative future planning processes for organizations and communities around the world. Ray is interested in the capabilities and attributes leaders require to initiate and sustain societal learning. He lives near Toronto, Canada.

Theo Groot, trained in agricultural extension and cultural anthropology, has been a development practitioner in Africa since 1979. He recently started an independent practice using whole system methodologies and solution-focused approaches. Groot is also an organic small-holder and lives near the Ugandan capital, Kampala.

Sylvia L. James, partner in Dannemiller Tyson Associates, pioneered Whole-Scale Change in aerospace in the early 1980s. Today she works globally with complex systems to facilitate healthy change in strategy, merger integration, culture change, and organizational design. She is coauthor of books and articles and presents at conferences and workshops around the world.

Sandra Janoff is codirector of Future Search Network—an international non-profit dedicated to community service, colleagueship, and learning. She has trained more than three thousand people worldwide in the practice of Future Search.

Soren Kaplan is cofounder of iCohere and OvationNet—a joint venture with Appreciative Inquiry founder, David Cooperrider. Former manager of Hewlett-Packard's internal strategy group and a recognized speaker and author, Soren assists organizations in expanding the impact of strategy, organizational change, and professional development through collaborative technology.

Richard Lent is an independent consultant and cofounder of Brownfield & Lent. He partners with clients to help them work, learn, and change together to achieve better outcomes. He does this by supporting organizations in completing rapid cycles of change in action and review of results.

Lenny Lind, president of CoVision, pioneered the use of networked laptop computers for advanced facilitation of large groups, both in meetings and online. Since 1992, CoVision has supported three thousand meetings and hundreds of facilitators. Lind codesigned the WebCouncil TM online collaboration software and coauthored the best-selling *Facilitator's Guide to Participatory Decision-Making* (New Society, 1996).

Michael R. Manning is professor of management in the College of Business, New Mexico State University, and is a consulting faculty with the Fielding Graduate University, Santa Barbara, California. He conducts executive seminars and consultations internationally. His research and publications focus on various topics related to the management of change, whole systems change using Large Group Methods, and organizational stress.

Kim Martens is an independent consultant whose work focuses mainly on participatory planning, issue-based stakeholder meetings, and children's rights. She has over twenty years of North American and international experience working in cross-cultural settings and with conflicted groups. She is fluent in English and French.

Marie T. McCormick specializes in helping systems, organizations, teams, and individuals tap into their underlying "knowing" to deal with mission-critical issues and possibilities. Her experience includes managerial and consulting experience, having worked in industry for over a dozen years. She has done extensive work in health care, education, nonprofit, and service sectors.

James McNeil is a senior organizational change consultant assisting leaders in introducing and implementing "world class" strategies and systems. He's the principal of STRATEM Associates, coauthor of *Whole-Scale Change: Unleashing the Magic in Organizations* and *Whole-Scale Change ToolKit* (Berrett-Koehler, 2000). He wrote "Creating and Maintaining Successful Strategic Alliances," in *ODN Journal*, 2003.

Kenoli Oleari is a consultant and international expert in public participation and community building. As cofounder and codirector of the Neighborhood Assemblies Network, he has pioneered the innovative use of large group, whole systems methodologies in community building and direct-democracy applications around the world.

Larry E. Peterson is an independent consultant and the principal of Larry Peterson and Associates in Transformation. He is a founder of Open Space Institute of Canada, has facilitated over 250 Open Space events, and is known worldwide for his work in training and publishing with an integral perspective.

Rebecca Peterson is an associate professor in the faculty of environmental studies at York University in Toronto, Canada. She has taught and conducted research in environmental psychology, feminist perspectives, health and environments, and facilitation.

Tom Phair is director of operations at Emerson & Cuming, a Business Unit of National Starch and Chemical Company. He led the transformation of E&C's culture from a large batch-and-queue to a lean operation, producing huge gains in productivity, safety, quality, cost, and morale.

Edward H. Powley is a visiting assistant professor at Case Western Reserve University, where he received a doctorate in organizational behavior. He received a master's degree in organizational management from the George Washington University. His research interests include organizational change, resilience, crisis, and interpersonal connections. Powley previously worked for the World Bank and the Corporate Executive Board.

Kristine Quade, an independent consultant, combines her background as an attorney with a master's degree in organizational development with her twenty years of practical experience. Her consulting work centers on senior management teams and whole systems work in over twenty countries. Recognized as senior practitioner by colleagues, Kristine is an innovator, leader, and author.

Regina Rowland is currently developing visual language systems for the multicultural context. In addition to teaching, she consults as intercultural communication practitioner for corporate, nonprofit, and educational settings. She is also coauthor of a series of articles on the genre of graphic facilitation.

Rita Schweitz, an independent facilitator and consultant, specializes in planning and facilitating productive meetings and conferences that produce desired results. With over twenty years of national and international experience, Rita has assisted nonprofit organizations, foundations, education systems, communities, environmental organizations, and governments to find common ground and move forward.

Annmarie Sorrow is a management consultant with a focus on facilitation, leadership, and teams working with multifunctional and global businesses. She has conducted Work Out in GE, the military, utilities, health care, and the food industry. Prior to this, she worked for GE for over seventeen years in human resources.

Helen Spector consults with organizations to help them improve their effectiveness. She works with colleagues adapting large group processes to support organizations and communities who seek meaningful change. Helen is vice-chair of the board of the Council for a Parliament of the World's Religions and teaches organizational psychology. She lives in Portland, Oregon.

Gilbert Steil Jr. has made Large Group Methods the heart of his consulting practice since 1990. He enjoys teaming with others, both in the United States and internationally. He has a passion for designing new large group interventions and teaching group dynamics.

Carlotta Tyler advises organizational decision makers on ways to strengthen work cultures for change and coaches leaders at all levels to implement the plans. Graphics are one way she helps change agents track their process. Her work is informed by a multicultural lens that she has developed over three decades of experience on four continents.

Lynne Valek is an assistant professor of organizational leadership at Chapman University College, Orange, California, and an adjunct faculty at Alliant International

University in California. In addition, she does independent organizational and trial consulting.

James Van Patten is president of Trinity Performance Systems in Boston, working primarily with Fortune 100 companies to develop significant development and performance systems. Jim's specialty is combining the technical components of lean manufacturing and Six Sigma with the OD practices of group dynamics and large systems change. His integrated approach delivers rapid, measurable improvements and productive, satisfying, and safe workplaces.

Marvin Weisbord is codirector of Future Search Network—an international nonprofit dedicated to community service, colleagueship, and learning. He has trained more than three thousand people worldwide in the practice of Future Search.

INDEX